D1479590

Urban America

POLICIES
AND
PROBLEMS

**Timely Reports to Keep
Journalists, Scholars and the Public
Abreast of Developing Issues, Events and Trends**

August 1978

**CONGRESSIONAL QUARTERLY
1414 22ND STREET, N.W., WASHINGTON, D.C. 20037**

Congressional Quarterly Inc.

Congressional Quarterly Inc., an editorial research service and publishing company, serves clients in the fields of news, education, business and government. It combines specific coverage of Congress, government and politics by Congressional Quarterly with the more general subject range of an affiliated service, Editorial Research Reports.

Congressional Quarterly was founded in 1945 by Henrietta and Nelson Poynter. Its basic periodical publication was and still is the CQ *Weekly Report,* mailed to clients every Saturday. A cumulative index is published quarterly.

The CQ *Almanac,* a compendium of legislation for one session of Congress, is published every spring. *Congress and the Nation* is published every four years as a record of government for one presidential term.

Congressional Quarterly also publishes paperback books on public affairs. These include the twice-yearly *Guide to Current American Government* and such recent titles as *U.S. Defense Policy: Weapons, Strategy and Commitments; Electing Congress;* and *Taxes, Jobs and Inflation.*

CQ Direct Research is a consulting service which performs contract research and maintains a reference library and query desk for the convenience of clients.

Editorial Research Reports covers subjects beyond the specialized scope of Congressional Quarterly. It publishes reference material on foreign affairs, business, education, cultural affairs, national security, science and other topics of news interest. Service to clients includes a 6,000-word report four times a month bound and indexed semiannually. Editorial Research Reports publishes paperback books in its fields of coverage. Founded in 1923, the service merged with Congressional Quarterly in 1956.

Editor: Robert A. Diamond.
Contributors: Irwin B. Arieff, Elizabeth Bowman, Christopher R. Conte, Suzanne de Lesseps, Harrison H. Donnelly, Martin Donsky, Edna Frazier, Kathryn Waters Gest, Barry M. Hager, Brigette Rouson, William V. Thomas, Margaret Thompson.
Editorial Coordinator: Barbara L. Risk.
Indexer: Diane Huffman.
Art Director: Richard Pottern.
Production Manager: I. D. Fuller. **Assistant Production Manager:** Maceo Mayo.
Book Department Editor: Patricia Ann O'Connor.

Library of Congress Cataloging in Publication Data

Congressional Quarterly, inc.
Urban America, policies and problems.

Bibliography: p.
Includes index.
1. Cities and towns — United States. 2. United States — Social policy. 3. Urban Economics.
4. Community development, Urban — United States.
I. Title.
HT123.C633 1978   309.2′62′0973   78-13734
ISBN 0-87187-138-6

Table of Contents

Editor's Note

Urban America: Policies and Problems surveys the major urban issues confronting federal, state and local governments. It is being published at a time when President Carter's comprehensive urban policy proposals, announced in March 1978, are being considered by Congress. Part I, "Urban Policy: An Overview," examines the enduring urban crisis, how urban policy has been developed by the Carter administration, what Carter has proposed and congressional action on his proposals.

Part II, "Urban Employment and Economic Policies," discusses a broad range of federal programs designed to reduce urban unemployment including public service and public works jobs and countercyclical aid to cities. Also examined are New York City's financial crisis, a symbol of the nation's urban plight, and the problem of property taxes — the growing taxpayer opposition to the traditional system of financing many important urban services. Part III, "Community and Human Development," focuses on policies designed to improve the quality of urban life — welfare, education, housing and mass transit programs.

The appendix contains important background material in a summary of major urban legislation for the period 1973-77. There is also a selected bibliography.

Introduction

"The deterioration of urban life in the United States is one of the most complex and deeply rooted problems of our age," President Carter declared March 27, 1978, as he unveiled his comprehensive package of urban policy proposals.

Stating that "everyone in this land has a personal stake in the health of our urban places," Carter called for a "new partnership" of federal, state and local governments; private industry; and neighborhood and volunteer groups to work to conserve urban communities.

The president's wide-ranging urban package included employment, economic development, fiscal assistance, and community and human development programs. Among these were a national bank to foster economic development through grants, loans and interest rate subsidies; a labor-intensive public works program stressing renovation and maintenance; tax incentives to hire young, poor workers and to promote investment in "distressed" areas; supplementary fiscal assistance for "distressed" cities and towns; and state incentive grants to develop state-level urban revitalization programs.

Carter's policy also called for the review of existing programs to make them more urban-oriented by eliminating or changing regulations viewed as "anti-urban." In addition, the policy called for analyzing major new federal programs to determine their impact on urban areas.

Carter had been under pressure since early in his administration to come up with a national urban policy. He formulated his policy proposals against a backdrop of more than a decade of sharply contrasting policies and dramatic changes in housing and urban affairs.

The "Great Society" Programs

Although federal government housing programs date from the Depression and the New Deal, and urban renewal efforts from the 1950s, a specific government concern with the problems of the cities is primarily associated with the Johnson administration. In his "Great Society" speech, delivered in May 1964 at commencement exercises at the University of Michigan, President Johnson said: "It is harder and harder to live the good life in American cities today. The catalog of ills is long: there is decay in the centers and despoiling of the suburbs.... It will be the task of your generation to make the American city a place where future generations come, not only to live but to live the good life."

In response to President Johnson's call for action, Congress enacted four major housing bills during the years 1965-68. The bills constituted the most far-reaching achievements in housing and urban development in decades. In 1965, two of the bills became law. One of them authorized rent supplements to help poor persons who could not afford decent housing on their own incomes. The second bill established a Department of Housing and Urban Development (HUD) to give Cabinet-level status to the government's housing activities and to bring increased importance to federal efforts to solve urban problems. Congress enacted in 1966 legislation establishing a model cities program to pump federal funds into needy cities. A landmark housing bill, enacted in 1968, was designed to promote home ownership for the poor by providing federal subsidies to lower the interest cost of a home purchaser's mortgage.

Enactment of the Johnson administration's urban programs coincided with and was overshadowed by a rising tide of civil disorders in the nation's major urban centers. Cities in most parts of the country experienced racial incidents of some type and many of the larger cities with substantial black populations were severely damaged in major riots. A report released in March 1968 by the National Advisory Commission on Civil Disorders counted 164 "civil disorders" in the first nine months of 1967. Later in April 1968, the assassination of civil rights leader Dr. Martin Luther King Jr. was followed by rioting and looting in many cities including New York; Washington, D.C.; Birmingham, Ala.; and Memphis, Tenn.

With this period of racial violence came a growing disenchantment with the programs of the "Great Society," paving the way for a period of retrenchment of government programs to aid the cities.

Nixon and Ford

In 1968 candidate Richard M. Nixon campaigned against the urban programs initiated by President Johnson. In his acceptance speech to the Republican National Convention he charged that Johnson's "Great Society" program had "reaped a harvest of frustration, violence and failure across the land." He promised that his administration would not launch new and costly social programs. Returning to these themes in his Inaugural Address in January 1969, he maintained that "We are approaching the limits of what government alone can do." The general thrust of his domestic policies was to cut back many of the social programs developed in the 1960s.

In the only major housing act enacted during the Nixon-Ford term (1973-76), Congress in August 1974 approved an administration proposal to replace the federal housing subsidy program, which Nixon had suspended in 1973, with a new program of rental assistance. Also included in the 1974 act was an administration proposal to consolidate nearly a dozen categorical urban aid programs created in the 1950s and 1960s into a single block grant program for community development. The new program offered funding to suburban areas and smaller communities under a fund distribution formula which hurt some of the larger cities that were the beneficiaries of the aid programs written in the 1960s.

Carter and the Cities

Many observers, comparing the status of the cities today with that prevailing a decade ago, agree with President Carter's bleak assessment of the conditions in urban America. In their view, the major problems that existed then — unemployment and inadequate housing — still persist.

As of August 1978, most of Carter's urban proposals were bogged down in Congress. It was too early to say whether the proposals would be enacted during Carter's presidency. And it was impossible to determine whether the policies would respond to the enduring problems of urban America.

Urban Policy: An Overview

Urban Problems of 1960s Unsolved in 1970s

In contrast to the urban strife of the sixties, quiet summers have prevailed in most American cities in this decade. Though scars of past destruction are still in evidence, some localities have shown hopeful signs of progress. Once dilapidated neighborhoods in densely populated urban centers of the Northeast and Midwest are being refurbished, while new financial incentives and lowering crime rates have begun to attract businesses and needed tax dollars back to the cities.

But the disturbing fact, according to black spokesmen, is that most big cities are no better off now than they were 10 years ago. Many urban experts agree, contending that the same social and economic problems that contributed to civil unrest in the 1960s remain largely unsolved. Improved community services, better income and housing opportunities continue to be unrealized goals for most of the urban poor.

The Carter administration, after being accused of neglecting the cities, now seems committed to adopting a national urban strategy that concentrates on employment and incentives for new economic activities. Most municipal officials, however, contend that America's cities cannot survive without massive financial assistance. Every major difficulty cities face today, said a spokesman for the United States Conference of Mayors, "boils down to money — too much is leaving and not enough is coming back."

This lack of money can be traced primarily to the large migration of the white middle class from the city to the suburbs. The migration began in a big way immediately after World War II and accelerated during the civil disorders of the 1960s. With the gradual departure of businesses, jobs grew scarce, property values fell and welfare payments multiplied. To make up for lost revenues and diminishing tax receipts, some cities began to use their capital budgets to cover normal operating expenses; others borrowed heavily to meet expenses. Demands by municipal employees for higher wages and added pension benefits led to more borrowing and bigger budgets and deficits. In a seven-year period from 1970 to 1977, New York City's budget rose from $6.7-billion to $13.5-billion; Detroit's more than doubled, climbing from $583-million to $1.2-billion.

"The financial crisis of New York City has made the fiscal condition of all state and local governments newsworthy," Emil M. Sunley Jr. of the Brookings Institution has commented. But he goes on to say that while New York is fighting to stave off bankruptcy, Houston is enjoying a budget surplus. The same is true of Fort Worth and several other growing cities of the Southwest. *(New York aid chapter, p. 45)*

There are other rays of optimism on America's otherwise gloomy urban landscape. At a meeting of the U.S. Conference of Mayors, held in June, 1977, at Phoenix, Ariz., the black mayor of one of this country's most troubled cities — Kenneth Gibson of Newark, N.J. — said the urban prospect is looking "a lot better than it was." In a similar vein, Detroit Mayor Coleman Young said: "Two years ago we were on our knees. Now we're standing up." Young's op-

timism was based in part on Detroit's new Renaissance Center, a $337-million hotel-office-shopping complex, which it is hoped will stabilize the city's decaying downtown business district. Some urbanologists, however, are skeptical about the long-term effect of big, self-contained city projects like the Renaissance Center. Glittering downtown areas, they say, may only mask the true state of affairs in urban America.

Carter's Response to Charges of Neglect

Amid criticism by the National Urban League and the Congressional Black Caucus that the Carter administration was not providing promised relief for the nation's poor and its cities, the president in the spring of 1977 created a Cabinet-level task force to formulate a comprehensive urban policy. The task force, headed by Patricia R. Harris, a black woman who is secretary of housing and urban development, announced its intention to stress economic redevelopment for troubled cities rather than broad social programs. Harris said the emphasis would be on stimulating private investment in cities.

However, the creation of the task force did not still the criticism. Vernon E. Jordan, executive director of the Urban League, angrily denounced the Carter administration for what he regarded as its failure to "launch a massive attack on the problems of black people and the cities where they live." Carter was reminded that much of his election strength was in urban, and especially black, areas. But new initiatives suggest the president has made the welfare of the cities a major domestic concern. In October, 1977, Carter signed into law the Housing and Community Development Act authorizing $12.5-billion to be spent over the next three years. Aimed at benefiting the older large cities with diminishing populations, the new legislation makes available funds to stimulate private enterprise to locate in urban areas. In addition, it increases money for rent subsidies and lowers down-payment requirements under the Federal Housing Administration.

Not included in the act or among the Carter administration's immediate objectives were social programs in health and education. These represent concerns that were being handled separately, according to Stuart E. Eizenstat, assistant to the president for domestic affairs and policy. The choice was made to restrict the formulation of urban policy to "programs that affect cities as cities, that will make them more livable, encourage their growth, stabilize their tax bases, make them better providers of services," he said in a September 1977 interview with *The New York Times.*

Key Proposals for Assistance to the Cities

The cornerstone of the administration's unfolding strategy was the promotion of private investment in cities. One proposal encouraged the establishment of incentive grants to give extra money to cities that enlist help from the private sector in reviving distressed neighborhoods. Related

"In the history of urban settlement I do not suppose there has ever been a phenomenon such as the destruction of the South Bronx over the past decade. Never. Nowhere on earth."

Sen. Daniel Patrick Moynihan, D-N.Y.

"There are some devastated areas where American citizens live that are a disgrace to our great country. There is no immediate solution that can be offered. I have visited the South Bronx, which is enough to shake our confidence in the structure that we have evolved."

President Carter

to this were proposals to discourage middle-income families from moving to the suburbs by underwriting reduced-interest mortgages on home purchases in central cities.

Such subsidies would not only permit lending institutions to offer cut-rate financing but they would free additional money for new loans. The administration in November 1977, announced regulations designed to end "redlining," the refusal of some lenders to give mortgage loans in certain inner-city areas. The new rules empowered the Federal Home Loan Bank Board, which regulates the nation's savings and loan institutions, to develop standards to be used in processing loans to insure fairness in home financing practices.

The most ambitious of the proposed aid programs is an urban bank, or "urbank," that would provide low-interest financing to businesses that relocate or remain in cities. The idea of an urban bank has drawn support throughout the administration, but there is likely to be a good deal of congressional debate over funding and whether it should make direct loans to city governments unable to secure them elsewhere.

The administration's policy was expressed by a member of the White House Office of Domestic Affairs and Policy to a *Wall Street Journal* reporter: "We presume in this administration that government simply doesn't have the resources to create long-term employment.... So, to reverse the tide, we must find ways to make the private sector change its locational preferences. With the right kind of incentives — insurance, lower interest loans and other things we're working on — we are convinced we can induce the private sector to make business decisions it wouldn't make without these incentives."

Urban planners suggest that the creation of permanent jobs must fall to private industry. They say sustainable, long-term urban recovery cannot be based on short-term federal "make work" projects. Nor, they add, can the government continue to encourage programs such as federally aided highway construction that have tended in the past to foster suburban sprawl.

It is being said that the federal government cannot afford to waste large sums of money in a futile effort to make cities attractive for economic activities that can no longer thrive there. "It's not enough to build up the private sector and hope that benefits are going to trickle down and accrue to those at the bottom," said Rep. Parren J. Mitchell, D-Md., leader of the Congressional Black Caucus in an appearance on NBC-TV's "Meet the Press." "Any urban revitalization plan is doomed to fail unless it is accompanied by an overall comprehensive economic policy." Such a policy, according to Mitchell, should contain new inducements for business and industry to use existing urban resources, a wholesale revision of federal and local tax systems, and a full employment plan.

Meeting in Washington in October 1977, the 162-member U.S. Conference of Black Mayors appealed to the president and Congress for more federal funds to assist in the development of community improvement cooperatives, aid to small towns, and job training for the unemployed. They spoke of the need for an elaborate "Marshall Plan" for cities patterned on America's program of aid to war-torn Europe in the late 1940s.

Changing American Metropolis

It is said that America developed an anti-urban bias in its rural beginnings and retained that bias long after it became a nation of city dwellers. Lewis Mumford and other urbanologists profess to see the roots of today's urban ills in this national trait.

When the first census was taken in 1790, a mere 5 per cent of the 3,929,214 people lived in cities; there were only 24 towns with populations of 2,500 or more. A strong anti-urban bias was already ingrained in the national character. In an age when technological progress was giving rise to the first industrial centers in Europe, the American social and economic outlook was decidedly agrarian. Most politicians and citizens were at one in their distrust of cities, which Thomas Jefferson believed were not conducive to the exercise of virtue. Jefferson's warning notwithstanding, American cities steadily increased in population. The lure of urban life is reflected in the following Census Bureau figures showing the country's five most populous cities in 1820 and again 50 years later when the population center of the United States had shifted westward.

1820		1870	
New York	152,000	New York	1,478,000
Philadelphia	65,000	Philadelphia	674,000
Baltimore	63,000	St. Louis	311,000
Boston	43,000	Chicago	299,000
New Orleans	27,000	Baltimore	267,000

First as seaports, then as trading and manufacturing centers, cities in America grew in response to economic needs. "Villages expanded into towns; towns became metropolises," Mumford wrote in *The City in History*

(1961): "In every quarter, the older principles of...rural culture were replaced by industrial power and pecuniary success, sometimes disguised as democracy."

> Between 1820 and 1900 [Mumford continued], the destruction and disorder within...cities was like that of a battlefield. . . . Industrialism, the main creative force of the nineteenth century, produced the most degraded urban environment the world had yet seen. . . . Men built in haste, and had hardly time to repent of their mistakes before they tore down their original structures and built again, just as heedlessly. The newcomers, babies or immigrants, could not wait for new quarters: they crowded into whatever was offered. It was a period of vast urban improvisation: makeshift hastily piled upon makeshift.

Expansion of Cities; Emergence of Suburbs

By the late 19th century, most large American cities had become socially and economically stratified. The affluent lived in their posh neighborhoods, comfortably isolated from the poor in their ethnic ghettos, while the middle classes tended to move to the less-expensive outlying areas. As populations spread, many central cities simply annexed those areas to which the middle class had gravitated. New York, for example, added more than 250 square miles in 1891 and in 1914 Boston doubled its area. Some states established automatic annexation procedures. By 1920, however, political opposition to the absorption of fringe areas mounted and large cities, especially in the congested Northeast, found themselves unable to keep pace, through annexation or consolidation, with suburban migration.

During the 1920s, general prosperity and the increasing number of automobiles gave new impetus to the growth of the suburbs. In that decade, the suburban populations around the 17 largest U.S. cities rose by nearly 40 per cent, while the rate of growth for most cities fell sharply. But until the 1940s, the central city remained the focal point of business and industry; the surrounding suburbs were primarily commuter villages.

Following World War II, suburbia began to take on the character of a retreat from the city, its congestion and its poor. Highways, built largely with federal money, carried exurbanites to enclaves far beyond city limits. The suburbs filled with families moving outward from urban cores and inward from rural regions. From the early 1950s on, the suburbanization of America was the country's dominant growth pattern.

In the East and Midwest, the residential shift was particularly dramatic. The five boroughs (Manhattan, Brooklyn, Queens, the Bronx and Staten Island) of New York accounted for 68 per cent of the metropolitan area's population in 1910 but only 39 per cent in 1970. Cincinnati's share dropped in that time from 63 to 33 per cent, Cleveland's from 85 to 36 per cent, and Detroit's from 77 to 36 per cent. Business and the jobs followed the people to the suburbs. In the 1960s, New York City lost 9.7 per cent of its jobs, while its suburbs gained 24.9 per cent. For Los Angeles the figures were 10.8 and 16.2 per cent, and for Chicago 13.9 and 64.4 per cent, according to figures cited by Robert C. Weaver, Secretary, Housing and Urban Development (1966-68), in *Civil Rights Digest,* spring 1977.

Urban Renewal's Goal of Slum Clearance

The downward spiral that gripped most central cities in the wake of the exodus to suburbia prompted the federal government to undertake the rebuilding of slum areas by feeding large subsidies of public money into the normal operations of the private market. The first federal urban renewal effort was authorized by the Housing Act of 1949. The act called for the public acquisition of land by negotiation or condemnation and its resale to private contractors for redevelopment. The program's two main objectives were to:

> 1. Eliminate substandard housing through slum clearance and the reconstruction of blighted areas.
> 2. Stimulate housing construction and community development sufficient to remedy the postwar housing shortage.

Despite the availability of $500-million in federal urban renewal funds, by 1954 only $74-million had been spent. That same year, Congress passed the Omnibus Housing Act, requiring cities applying for federal housing assistance to submit a comprehensive plan for the elimination and prevention of slums. The 1954 bill also expanded the definition of urban renewal to include the redevelopment of commercial as well as residential property.

From its beginning in 1949 through its high point during the Johnson administration, urban renewal was the subject of intense debate. In *The City and the Frontier* (1965), Charles Abrams wrote that the program "has spurred civil and cultural improvements." Critics, however, have always found fault with the basic philosophy of the plan and its practical effect on those who are displaced by redevelopment. "The federal renewal programs allow those in control...to change one kind of neighborhood into another kind by destroying the old buildings and replacing them with new ones," wrote Martin Anderson in *The Federal Bulldozer: A Critical Analysis of Urban Renewal, 1949-1962* (1964). "Naturally, the new ones they choose for the cleared land...are those they feel are desirable, from their viewpoint of what the public good is. . . . The people who are most seriously affected by the program come from low-income, minority groups that for various reasons do not or cannot attempt to correct the injustices to which they are subjected."

Beginning in 1964 with the passage of the Economic Opportunity Act, the government's war on poverty called for more neighborhood participation in federally assisted projects. One of the most ambitious undertakings in urban restoration during the Johnson years was the Demonstration (later named Model) Cities and Metropolitan Development Act of 1966. The aim was to rebuild entire urban areas by tying together a wide array of existing federal and local programs for a coordinated attack on inner-city blight. Although it was praised for encouraging citizen participation and local initiative, Model Cities was beset with a number of failures. In public housing, the most notable of these was the destruction and abandonment of the 55-building Pruitt-Igoe apartment complex in St. Louis, which was constructed with federal support in the 1950s and eventually torn down in 1972 after years of crime and vandalism led to the abandonment of most of the units. Citing improper management and budget cutbacks, the Nixon administration brought the Model Cities program to an official end in August 1975.

Signs of Middle Class Return to the Cities

While high-rise public housing has been denounced as a failure, the restoration of old homes in the inner city by affluent young homebuyers is regarded as one of today's success stories. The trend toward renovation is attributed

Population Changes in Metropolitan America

During the first half of this decade the central cities lost population while the suburbs continued to gain. But the suburban gain was less than in the 1960s, as is shown in the following Census Bureau figures:

	1976 Population Estimates (millions)	Change From 1970 Census	1970 Change From 1960
U.S. total	210.3	5.3%	13.3%
Metropolitan	142.5	4.0	16.6
Inside central cities	60.7	—3.4	5.3
Outside central cities	81.8	10.3	28.2
Non-metropolitan	67.7	8.2	6.5

While the black population of central cities continued to rise, and the white population declined, the percentage increase of blacks in the suburbs was three times greater than in the central cities, as is shown below in 1976 population figures and percentage changes (in parentheses) since 1970:

	Whites (millions)	Blacks (millions)
Metropolitan	121.4 (2.1)	21.2 (16.9)
Inside central cities	45.2 (—7.6)	15.5 (11.1)
Outside central cities	76.2 (8.8)	5.7 (36.3)
Non-metropolitan	61.2 (8.7)	6.5 (1.5)

There also has been a geographical shift in population. In 1950, only one of the nation's 10 largest cities (Los Angeles) was located outside the Midwest or Northeast. By 1975, five cities in the Southwest were among the top 10.

1950		1975	
New York	7,896,957	New York	7,481,613
Chicago	3,620,962	Chicago	3,099,391
Philadelphia	2,071,605	Los Angeles	2,727,399
Los Angeles	1,970,338	Philadelphia	1,815,808
Detroit	1,849,568	Houston	1,357,397
Baltimore	949,708	Detroit	1,335,085
Cleveland	914,808	Baltimore	851,698
St. Louis	856,796	Dallas	812,797
Washington	802,178	San Diego	773,996
Boston	801,441	San Antonio	773,248

largely to economics — it has become cheaper to buy an old house and repair it than build or buy a new one. The buyer typically is unmarried or a young couple without children who prefer city living but want a house of their own.

While some of these homebuyers have returned from suburbia, the poor quality of inner city schools is still a barrier to many middle class families. James Young, the deputy mayor of Boston, said in an interview published in the November-December 1977 issue of *The Center*

Magazine: "The quality of education in the central cities is perhaps the single most important factor when people choose where to live. Middle class people with children find that the urban school systems do not meet their requirements."

Many municipalities are encouraging migration into urban neighborhoods by making available low-cost city-owned houses to non-commercial buyers who agree to refurbish them and live in them for a specified period. In Wilmington, Del., under a special "urban homesteading" program, such houses have been sold for as little as a dollar. A similar project in New York City resulted in the rehabilitation of several abandoned tenement buildings by community improvement groups, who invested toil rather than money in restoring deserted real estate. The idea seems to have caught on in a number of other eastern cities and towns and is being closely studied by housing officials nationwide.

In such neighborhoods as Boston's South End, Washington's Adams-Morgan, Philadelphia's Queen Village, Seattle's Capitol Hill and Baltimore's Fells Point, restoration is well under way. But the redevelopment of some urban districts has not been without its problems, especially the displacement of the poor, who are often forced to move as rents and taxes in renovated areas rise along with property values.

Although cities welcome affluent returnees, settlement has been generally confined to a few areas. So far, local governments have been slow to generate plans to curtail speculation or distribute investment evenly in center cities to protect poor residents from being victimized by redevelopment. The outcome of the new movement into cities, if its present pace increases, could be a heavier migration of inner-city minorities and the poor to nearby suburbs and towns. Urban blacks, once confined almost wholly to the inner city, have been moving into the suburbs in growing numbers in this decade. According to Census Bureau population estimates in April 1976, some 5.7 million of the 21.2 million blacks in metropolitan areas were living outside the central cities, an increase of 36.3 per cent since 1970. *(Box, this page)*

In the early 1970s, in an effort to minimize the pressures of overcrowding and ease the strain on city services, a number of communities placed restrictions on growth. This was usually done through zoning laws or the refusal to hook up any additional housing units to water or sewer lines. Some cities have set population growth quotas. Boulder, Colo., for example, in 1977 set a quota of 2 per cent yearly growth. In a similar action, Prince George's County, Md., which borders Washington, D.C., imposed a limit on the construction of low-income housing.

Legal action has arisen over a number of these attempts to slow or stop local growth, and the plaintiffs have sometimes forced the communities to lift or modify their no-growth or slow-growth plans. However, in 1972 the U.S. Court of Appeals in New York affirmed a lower federal court decision upholding the right of towns and cities to limit growth by halting the construction of sewers and roads. By declining to hear the case on appeal, the Supreme Court sustained the ruling.

Options for Shaping Urban Policy

To demonstrate his commitment to cities, President Carter on Oct. 5, 1977, toured New York's South Bronx. The

South Bronx, with its burned-out tenements and prevalent crime, has become a symbol of the woes besetting many American cities. Once a proud multi-ethnic, middle-class community, it is now a ruined landscape where violence and fear are a way of life for a population that is 56 per cent black and Puerto Rican, most of whom are poor and unskilled. In 1960, whites accounted for 76 per cent of the population.

Some urbanologists believe the fact that the South Bronx is made up mainly of large apartment projects owned by absentee landlords contributed to its rapid decline in the mid-1960s when Puerto Ricans and blacks began to move there in great numbers. Recently, New York City officials estimated that in 1974 the absentee owners of thousands of rundown housing units in the area were delinquent in paying the city nearly $35-million in taxes, while in that same year South Bronx residents received "a significant portion" of the city's $1.7-billion welfare outlay.

Among the causes cited for the collapse of many inner-city neighborhoods are welfare recipients who do not pay their rent. The practice starts a chain reaction of decline that often proves fatal to a community. Landlords retaliate by refusing to make repairs or pay city taxes. The city's revenue base shrinks and, for lack of revenue, essential services are reduced. A bill to permit local welfare agencies to pay the landlords directly was defeated by the Senate in 1977 after passing in the House by a wide margin. Backers of the bill who vowed to reintroduce it, say property owners would be less likely to abandon their buildings if they were assured rental payments. Foes of the bill said it was coercive and offered no guarantee that landlords would pay their taxes or improve their property.

The administration did not take a public stand on the legislation. But HUD Secretary Patricia R. Harris in an interview said that she and other Cabinet members had "some real problems with a bill that placed rent above health needs and groceries." Harris acknowledged, however, that the abandonment of central city housing has reached the crisis stage in some areas.

In a speech to the U.S. Conference of Black Mayors on Oct. 28, 1977, Harris said that in January 1977 nearly 50,000 units of public housing were vacant, costing the government millions of dollars in lost revenue. The administration, she said, is pledged "to revitalizing deserted neighborhoods." It extended the rehabilitation loan program and increased urban homesteading funds from $5-million to $15-million. HUD also freed mortgage interest subsidy grants that were frozen by President Nixon in 1973. "We are now targeting more funds more carefully to the urban poor," Harris said. "Seventy-five per cent of the block grant money received by any locality now must directly benefit low and moderate income people." The HUD block grant program distributes money in lump sums to cities for community development. Previously such funds were given out under individual development programs. Harris added that "substantive monitoring" would make sure that national objectives were being carried out by local governments getting federal funds.

Possibility of Tax Incentives to Create Jobs

The out-migration of residents and the economic decline typical of decaying inner cities have been met in the past with federal investment and public jobs programs. President Carter has shown an inclination to combat the urban "housing crisis" by increasing direct government sup-

port. But there are signs the administration may take a different approach in its effort to revive the anemic economies of poverty-stricken urban areas.

Carter's urban policy included tax incentives to induce businesses and industries to invest in cities where unemployment is highest. Tax reductions and increased depreciation allowances have been used successfully during wartime to boost war-related industries, and administration officials seem certain that the same technique can be used to pump money back into cities.

The present investment tax credit is 10 per cent — businesses may deduct 10 per cent of their capital investment from their federal income taxes. To raise it to 15 or 20 percent in areas of high unemployment would increase the volume of additional investment at no extra cost to the Treasury, according to James L. Sundquist of the Brookings Institution. "The object of the tax differential would be to provide enough subsidy to an investing firm that takes jobs to the workers to offset the gains it would otherwise realize by locating on the suburban fringe," Sundquist wrote in an October 1977 article in *The Washington Post*. Of all the industrialized countries, the United States alone has no established program to steer employment to depressed regions where it is needed, Sundquist said.

The Urban Growth and New Community Development Act of 1970 committed the federal government to come up with a national policy to counteract economic distress in cities. However, President Carter is the first president to propose taking action mandated by the legislation. One feature of his urban policy is to change the federal government's emphasis from giving direct cash grants to localities with excessive unemployment to the creation of special financial benefits to influence businesses to shift jobs to metropolitan centers.

How far the White House should involve itself in local economic matters could become the main domestic policy issue of the 1980s. The Carter administration's program calls for greater participation by private enterprise in the welfare of cities. But many economists believe that federal agencies will have to play a leading role in encouraging local and state governments as well as private industry to change their present spending and investment priorities.

Changing Appraisal of Rapid Mass Transit

The growing need to move large numbers of people in and around urban areas economically and with the least disruption of the environment sparked considerable interest in subway construction in the 1960s. Although the cost of building subways was high, many federal and local officials viewed them as essential for relieving traffic congestion and revitalizing downtown businesses. In a swell of enthusiasm, Congress appropriated funds to help several cities plan or to begin building rapid transit lines. San Francisco and neighboring communities started laying track on their 71½-mile route in 1963; ground was broken for metropolitan Washington's 102-mile rail network in 1969. *(Mass Transit chapter, p. 75)*

After nearly a $700-million cost overrun, San Francisco's Bay Area Rapid Transit (BART) system began operation in 1972 but almost immediately came under criticism for failing to live up to its promise. Studies have shown it has done far less than expected to remedy the area's traffic problems. Plagued by cost increases from its inception, Washington's subway project, called Metro, will cost more than twice as much as originally predicted.

Federal Revenue Sharing

Since 1972 billions of dollars in federally collected revenues have been passed on to 39,000 state and local governments with relatively few strings attached. These shared revenues in 1976 alone amounted to $6.4-billion. The Office of Revenue Sharing in the U.S. Treasury said it does not know how much goes to the cities.

A study by Richard P. Nathan and Charles F. Adams of the Brookings Institution provides some insight as to how 29 cities and some other jurisdictions spend the revenues they receive. The findings were published in June 1977 in *Revenue Sharing: The Second Round.* Nathan and Adams reported that while smaller cities used about three-fourths of their funds for spending programs (usually building projects), cities over 100,000 population used one-half or more to hold back tax increases or avoid borrowing.

When construction began in 1969, the price tag was put at $2.5-billion. With 25 miles of the proposed 100-mile system finished, officials have said the final bill will be close to $6.7-billion, although there is only enough money on hand at present to build 60 miles.

In the face of mounting construction costs and increasing doubts that subways are the answer to urban transportation woes, Seattle and St. Louis dropped plans to build rapid transit systems; in 1976, Los Angeles voters rejected a proposal to build an $8-billion project similar to BART. Washington, Atlanta and Baltimore are going ahead with construction of new rapid rail transit systems and Miami, as of August 1978, had completed the design work and engineering for its subway and was preparing to break ground. (Buffalo has plans for construction of a light rail transit system.)

The Department of Transportation has supplied 80 per cent of the capital costs of local transit systems since 1973. But it has begun to reappraise its support program and to cut back funding in some cases for systems it judges to be inefficient or too expensive. The administration has given notice that elaborate undertakings, like BART and Washington's Metro, will find "little encouragement" in the future. The March 29, 1977, *Wall Street Journal* reported that President Carter had told Secretary of Transportation Brock Adams in a memo: "I suspect that many rapid transit systems are grossly over-designed." Building new subways could be avoided in most urban areas, Carter said, if the administration pushed cities to develop off-street parking, one-way streets and special commuter lanes.

The Department of Transportation proposed an increase of $500-million in mass transit funding for fiscal year 1979. For the first time, under the new DOT plan, money would be allocated to cities according to their size for bus purchases and for the repair of existing street rail transit systems. Some local governments that once regarded the subway as "the city's salvation" have begun to look to less expensive forms of mass transportation, including modernized buses and streetcars.

Revenue Sharing Between City and Suburbs

The theory that urban ills inevitably radiate out to the suburbs has prompted some state and federal officials to seek regional solutions to the deterioration of the nation's cities.

State governments, with their enormous power over taxes, land use, highway building, and the administration of federal allocations, may, in fact, prove to be the salvation of ailing urban areas. In the past, federal and state policies often have worked at cross-purposes with the result that cities have frequently lost out on needed financial help.

Michigan, under Republican Gov. William G. Milliken, has installed what some observers are calling a model revenue sharing program. In 1976, the state made payments of almost $30-million for services Detroit regularly provides its suburbs. In addition, the state has enacted a 12-year tax benefit to encourage factory improvement and new industrial construction in Detroit. Despite opposition from some legislators representing rural districts, Milliken plans to expand the state assistance program to other large cities in Michigan.

In order to stem rural opposition to urban relief legislation, Massachusetts has developed a strategy to aid both cities and small towns, which often suffer the common ills of unemployment, property blight and poor housing. Gov. Michael Dukakis charged that states have "paved the way for the job drain" out of cities by providing interstate highways and interchanges for suburban industrial parks. Both small towns and populous cities desperately need state and federal help to survive, Dukakis said.

A national city-town policy similar to the one Massachusetts has adopted could have a powerful appeal, according to Neal R. Peirce, who writes a nationally distributed column on city problems. "It would be pro-growth—stipulating only that growth should occur in or beside established centers," Peirce said. "It would be anti-sprawl — and thus conservationalist. It would save energy, and thus dovetail perfectly with Carter's overall policy. And it might be more acceptable to suburbanites, whose communities are now reeling with the explosive growth of recent years, than politicians think."

No matter what federal program guidelines are finally chosen, intense controversy is likely at every step. For while there is a great concern about the future of cities, there is no consensus on what specific measures should be taken to ensure their survival. What is certain is that left unattended urban problems will surely grow worse, threatening not only the billions of dollars already committed to cities but more important the well-being of millions of people who have invested lifetimes there.

∎

Urban Policy Package Floundering on Hill

Announcing his long-awaited urban policy March 27, 1978, President Carter sent Congress a message proposing a new series of job, tax incentive, grant, loan and public works efforts and a fundamental redirection of existing federal programs in order to reverse what he described as the "deterioration of urban life" in the United States.

The administration plan — produced by a special task force that labored for 12 months to shape a program to the president's liking — was designed to rehabilitate cities that already have suffered significant economic and physical decay, and to prevent other cities in better health from experiencing the same social and economic problems in the years ahead. *(Urban policy formulation, p. 19)*

There was no "centerpiece" to the program; the task force report to the president declared that "no simplistic centerpiece policy will achieve our urban commitments. Instead a comprehensive policy approach is necessary."

As a result, the administration plan contained what one observer described as a "smorgasbord" of programs ranging from a National Development Bank to stimulate corporate investment in "distressed" areas, to tax breaks for businesses that hire hard-core unemployed or locate plants in inner-cities, to modest amounts of money for urban parks, social service programs, housing rehabilitation and urban arts.

Moreover, some elements of the plan appeared geared toward fighting poverty and unemployment regardless of the setting. Administration officials agreed that the concept of "distressed" areas applies in some cases to both urban and rural areas.

"Urban problems are found everywhere," said Patricia Roberts Harris, secretary of the Department of Housing and Urban Development (HUD).

Carter, who outlined the policy to a gathering of state and local officials at the White House, said he was "convinced that it is in the national interest not only to save our cities and urban communities, but also to strengthen them and make them more attractive places in which to live and work."

The president said the federal government had the "clear duty" to lead the urban revitalization effort. But, reflecting the "New Partnership" theme of his policy, Carter said that state and local governments, neighborhood and volunteer groups, and the private sector also had crucial roles to play. The urban program contains various incentives — mostly money — to stimulate involvement by each of those groups.

Little Congressional Action

As of mid-August 1978, there was little action in Congress on Carter's urban proposals, and there was serious doubt as to the chances of enacting major portions of the program in the remaining two months of the 95th Congress, scheduled to adjourn in October. *(Major urban policy proposals, p. 14; box score of congressional action on proposals, p. 16)*

As a result, urban activists are growing increasingly pessimistic about the prospects for passage of key measures worth several billion dollars to state and local governments.

"I imagine what we are going to get is $15 million here and $10 million there and so forth," said M. Carl Holman, president of the National Urban Coalition.

By mid-August 1978 only the smaller pieces in the urban program — loans for housing rehabilitation, grants for neighborhood fix-up programs, inner-city health clinics, social service projects, crime prevention programs, urban mass transit programs and urban parks — had won support from Congress.

A crowded legislative agenda, delays in drafting the bills, disagreements over critical aspects of the legislation, increased wariness of more federal spending in the wake of Proposition 13, and what appeared to some congressional observers as an uneven lobbying effort by the White House combined to make passage questionable for the major spending bills in the urban programs.

Administration officials insisted that by the time Congress adjourned most of the major spending bills would be enacted. They targeted three as having the "highest priority." Those are the "soft," or "labor-intensive" public works programs, supplementary fiscal assistance to local governments, and incentive grants to states to prod them into developing their own urban revitalization programs.

White House officials said a concerted effort would be made to push those bills through Congress in 1978. Some administration officials conceded that failure to get those measures enacted would have considerable political impact on the president.

The fiscal assistance measure, for example, would parcel out $2 billion during fiscal 1979-80 to thousands of local governments, with some financially strapped cities like New York receiving substantial sums. "There is an awful lot of pressure to get this bill through," said one White House official. "There are a lot of local governments out there that [already] have the money in their budgets." *(Chapter on fiscal assistance and countercyclical aid, p. 39)*

But to win approval of the measures, the White House could be forced to accept some fundamental changes in its urban proposals. For example, the administration viewed a third round of local public works projects as inflationary, but it might have to back off from that view in order to win approval for its "soft" public works proposal.

Spending

The president proposed only limited increases in federal spending for the new programs in the urban package. Although the administration asked Congress for an increase in budget authority for fiscal 1979 of $4.419 billion, it plans to increase actual spending by only $742 million. In fiscal 1980, the administration will seek an increase in budget authority of $6.087 billion, with new spending of $2.933 billion. And in fiscal 1981, the administration will seek an increase in budget authority of $5.642 billion, with spending of $2.874 billion.

In addition, tax breaks for businesses, if approved by Congress, will cost the federal government about $1.7 billion in revenues in fiscal 1979, another $1.7 billion in fiscal 1980 and $1.5 billion in fiscal 1981.

Finally, the administration proposed loan guarantees totaling $2.2 billion in fiscal 1979, $3.8 billion in fiscal 1980 and $5 billion in fiscal 1981.

Limited Increases. The limited increases in spending proposed by the administration reflect at least three factors. Administration officials said the start-up time required for many of the new programs limits the amount of money that actually can be spent in 1979. Secondly, congressional budget leaders, who were consulted by administration officials during the preparation of the policy, have predicted that Congress would not approve much more than $2 billion in additional urban spending for fiscal 1979.

Thirdly, and most important, Carter and other administration officials have emphasized repeatedly that the federal government already is pumping substantial sums of money to local governments. Estimates cited by officials placed that figure at $30 billion annually.

Indicative of that view, Carter maintained in his message to Congress that while some new spending by the federal government was required to fill "gaps," the long-term answer to saving urban areas rests with marshaling the existing resources of the federal bureaucracy to make various programs more sensitive to urban needs.

"For those who live in our urban areas, the gravest flaw in past federal policy was not that we failed to spend money. It was that too many of the programs were ineffective and too many that did work had their benefits canceled out by other federal and state activities," the president declared in his message.

Redirection

To translate that view into specific policies, the administration's urban task force, formally known as the Urban and Regional Policy Group, recommended more than 160 changes in 38 existing programs to make them more urban-oriented by eliminating or changing regulations viewed as anti-urban. Some changes required legislation, although many others would be done administratively.

Administration officials maintained that the review of existing programs was an essential part of the policy. "If we did little else than that it would have been worth going through the exercise," said Stuart Eizenstat, the president's chief domestic adviser and a major architect of the urban program.

For example, the Environmental Protection Agency (EPA) would alter guidelines for water and sewer grants to discourage large projects in developing areas, which have in the past contributed to urban sprawl. Instead, according to the administration, the focus would be on revitalization of existing facilities in cities.

Carter also said his administration intended to triple the level of the Ford administration purchases from minority-owned businesses, which generally are located in inner cities, and require, for the first time, that all government agencies submit goals and timetables for increasing those purchases.

Although the task force cited dozens of instances where federal programs were not working, it did not recommend the elimination of any single one. Instead, the task force proposed various improvements, most of which were not spelled out in detail, to make the programs "more effective."

Also, the urban policy calls for major new federal programs to be subjected to an "urban impact analysis" to determine the potential ramifications of the program on urban areas. The analysis would be conducted by the agency running the particular program and would be reviewed by the Office of Management and Budget (OMB) and the White House domestic staff.

Targeting

One theme does underlie much of what the administration proposed: the concept of "targeting" programs to areas with the greatest need. Repeatedly, in documents outlining the urban policy and in public statements, the administration emphasized targeting as essential if the urban policy is to have any impact.

Eizenstat and Harris in briefings for reporters took pains to note that the urban policy was based, as Harris put it, on the "targeting of need, rather than of cities."

For example, many "Sun Belt" cities of the South and West were experiencing tremendous population and economic growth, and thus can not be described as "distressed" cities. Yet these same cities — Houston and Dallas were cited by Harris as two notable examples — suffer from what she called "pockets of poverty." By targeting jobs programs to areas of high unemployment, Harris said, those cities will be eligible to share in some of the money from the urban package.

Yet, although Harris declared that "distress is not simply a Snow Belt phenomenon," most administration officials agreed that cities in the Northeast and Midwest, the Snow Belt, would probably receive the bulk of federal funds. But, they said, that was because those cities had the most acute urban problems.

Brookings Analysis. In a preliminary analysis of the president's urban plan, Brookings Institution urban specialists cited the "heavy thematic emphasis" on targeting as a major plus. But the Brookings analysis also noted a lack of specific details on the critical components of parceling out federal money: formulas and eligibility requirements. Administration officials acknowledged the lack of specific formulas; one White House official said methods of distributing the money had been drawn up but no final decisions had been made.

Some urban experts, like Brookings' Richard P. Nathan, believed the greater emphasis on targeting the better, especially given the modest amounts of new spending proposed by Carter. Otherwise, Nathan said in an interview, the funds would be spread too thin to have any substantive impact.

Nathan, like others, was anxious to see the specific formulas for distributing the money. "The name of the game in urban policy is formulas," he said.

Initial Reaction

President Carter's urban policy triggered some sharp responses from Capitol Hill, with part of the criticism reflecting regional rivalries in Congress between the

"Snow Belt" states of the Northeast and Midwest and the "Sun Belt" states of the South and West.

Especially strong criticism came from Sen. William Proxmire, D-Wis., who as chairman of the Senate Banking, Housing and Urban Affairs Committee could play a key role in debate on the president's program.

Proxmire lauded Carter for trying to make existing federal programs work better, but he vehemently opposed any new federal spending for urban areas. Signaling the prospect of lengthy debate, Proxmire declared, "With respect to the specific funds he [Carter] asks for, we should ask some searching questions."

Tax Credit Controversy

Criticism also surfaced during an April 3 hearing on the urban program held by the state and local government task force of the House Budget Committee. The committee chairman, Robert Giaimo, D-Conn., and the head of the task force, Elizabeth Holtzman, D-N.Y., questioned the worth of a special tax credit Carter proposed for companies that invest in "distressed areas."

The president's urban program called for an expansion of the investment tax credit to 15 percent for companies that build or renovate plants in "distressed areas." Existing law allows companies to claim a 10 percent credit on the purchase of machinery and equipment. In his January 1978 tax message to Congress, Carter proposed extending the credit to cover construction of new plants and renovation of existing ones as a means of further stimulating economic growth.

The credit would cover industrial expansion regardless of location. In hopes of "targeting" economic development to distressed areas, the president's urban message suggested adding a 5 percent differential to the credit, thus making it possible for a company to receive a total credit of 15 percent if it invested in a "distressed area."

But Giaimo, reiterating an argument made by other northern members of Congress, predicted that the 10 percent investment credit would hasten industrial relocation from inner cities, especially in the North, to other areas, particularly the South, where labor, energy and other costs are generally cheaper. Further, Giaimo doubted whether the 5 percent differential would be enough to counteract the potential impact of the 10 percent credit.

Coalition Views. The Snow Belt's formal organization in the House, the Northeast-Midwest Economic Advancement Coalition, made a similar argument in its response to the urban program. Although the coalition praised much of the policy, it said: "The president's proposed [10 percent] investment tax credit would provide a $1.4 billion investment incentive to private business. In contrast, the targeted investment tax credit proposed by the president [in the urban package] is limited to only $200 million per year; these proposals are very much at odds."

HUD Response. Patricia Roberts Harris, secretary of the Department of Housing and Urban Development (HUD), defended the tax credit proposal. In testimony before the task force April 3, Harris acknowledged that budget restraints resulted in the $200 million ceiling, but she argued that the 5 percent differential would have "some significance" in stimulating economic development in "distressed areas." However, under questioning, she conceded, "I cannot give you any data."

Privately, though, the HUD hierarchy had serious reservations about the 10 percent investment credit proposal. An internal memorandum analyzing Carter's 1978 tax program in terms of its impact on urban areas said the 10 percent credit "may accelerate job movement from central cities to suburbs and from declining regions to growing ones."

HUD officials said they hope the 5 percent differential would offset some potentially "anti-urban" effects of the investment credit. Robert C. Embry Jr., assistant secretary for community planning and development, said the $200 million available in tax credits was enough to attract some $4 billion in capital investment. "That is significant," Embry said. "This proposal [the 5 percent differential] was a compromise," he added.

Calls for Higher Spending

Outside Congress, reaction in many instances reflected the amount of money and program control offered to different governmental units and interest groups affected by the urban proposal.

Mayors and governors praised their involvement in the program, although some called for higher spending. The National Association of Neighborhoods, whose members would be eligible for grants, warmly praised the program. But the National Association of Counties complained that it was excluded from any substantive involvement in the program.

The call for more money was nearly a universal theme from urban spokesmen.

"There's only $150 million for the whole country," said New York Mayor Edward I. Koch, referring to the housing component in the Carter plan. "It's not enough for the state," he added.

Carter program aims to reverse the "deterioration of urban life" in the United States.

Vernon E. Jordan, president of the National Urban League, was perhaps the most critical of the urban package. Jordan termed the program "disheartening" and a "missed opportunity." He urged changing the program into a "Marshall Plan" for the cities.

The criticism did not entirely focus on spending levels. Some urban experts questioned the "Christmas tree" approach taken by the administration for parceling out money to a multitude of federal agencies, some of which were cited by the urban and regional task force as having little success with current programs aimed at improving urban life.

The Brookings analysis inquired: "Can the federal bureaucracy make these kinds of refined and fine-tuned urban policy changes?"

Major Urban Policy Proposals

A summary of the major proposals in President Carter's urban program, and their status in Congress as of mid-August 1978 is as follows:

- National Development Bank, S 3233, HR 13230—Economic development tool, providing mix of grants and loans and interest rate subsidies. Pending in House and Senate Banking Committees. No action expected in 1978. Hearings likely later in 1978.
- Labor-Intensive Public Works, S 3186, HR 12993 — $3 billion, three-year program of "labor-intensive," "soft" public works stressing renovation and maintenance. Pending in public works committees in House and Senate.
- Employment and Investment Tax Credits — Financial incentives to hire young, poor workers, and invest in "distressed" areas. Proposals were not included in the tax bill approved by the House Aug. 10.
- Supplementary Fiscal Assistance, S 2975, HR 12293 — $2 billion aid for fiscal 1979-80 for "distressed" cities and towns to replace existing countercyclical revenue sharing to states and cities. Rejected by House Intergovernmental Relations Subcommittee. Senate Finance Committee approved extension of countercyclical aid through fiscal 1980 and authorized $650 million to "distressed" cities and towns. *(Countercyclical aid, p. 39)*
- State incentive grants, S 3209, HR 12893 — $200 million for fiscal 1979, and $200 million for fiscal 1980, for grants to states to develop state-level urban revitalization programs. Pending in House Banking Subcommittee on Housing and Community Development, hearings scheduled. Joint jurisdiction in Senate Intergovernmental Relations and Housing subcommittees; Senate Banking Committee action postponed until 1979.

Development Bank

The National Development Bank designed to spur private economic development in "distressed" areas was not likely to be voted on in 1978.

Administration officials, once confident that the proposal could be enacted, hoped that the House and Senate Banking Committees would schedule hearings.

"We'd be naive to think we could get it through this year," said one White House official involved in monitoring the progress of the urban package on Capitol Hill.

The idea of a development bank has been discussed in Congress for about a decade — at least six different proposals have been introduced in the current session of Congress.

"It's the kind of idea that is still novel enough that you have to build a large consensus to move it. It requires a long educational process," said a staff member of the House Banking Committee.

As proposed by the Carter administration, the development bank (S 3233, HR 13230) would provide $8 billion in loan guarantees, $3.8 billion in interest rate subsidies, and $1.65 billion in grants during a three-year period to help local development authorities attract private businesses to both urban and rural slums.

The bank is intended to provide long-term financing to new or existing industries that want to expand or move into "distressed" areas but are unable to obtain normal bank financing.

The administration shaped the bank proposal so it could be used to spur private investment in both urban and rural areas since many rural areas suffer from some of the same problems as urban areas — declining populations, lack of growth of jobs, and stagnating tax bases. The broad appeal of the bank was also designed to marshal support from rural congressmen, many of whom have been reluctant to support urban measures.

Explaining how the bank would work during a speech to the U.S. Conference of Mayors, Vice President Mondale emphasized the inclusion of both large and small cities and urban and rural areas.

"The bank can serve the economic need of all areas of our country. The bank can serve a big city like Atlanta or a rural Georgia county like Hancock. It could serve New York City and it could serve a pocket of poverty in a city like Houston," Mondale said.

But there was some doubt in Congress that the bank would do what its sponsors say. Others question whether a new program is really needed. These critics suggest that the urban development action grant program run by the Department of Housing and Urban Development (HUD) is performing the same function, providing public funds to stimulate private spending. *(Urban development action grant program, p. 69)*

The question of who will run the bank has also generated debate. HUD and the Department of Commerce conducted what was described as a bitter bureaucratic battle for control of the bank when the administration was developing the urban program last fall and winter.

As resolved by the White House, though, control was divided among HUD, Commerce and Treasury, with the secretaries of all three agencies serving as a board of directors for the bank. Some critics think the administrative arrangement is far from the best way to run a bank, let alone any other federal program.

Sen. William Proxmire, D-Wis., chairman of the Senate Banking Committee, and Rep. William S. Moorhead, D-Pa., chairman of the House Banking Subcommittee on Economic Stabilization, have said they will hold hearings on the bank proposal, but none has yet been scheduled.

Public Works

Congress appeared certain to rewrite the $3 billion public works section of the administration's urban program. As a result, Carter may be forced to choose between endorsing a measure he views as inflationary, or vetoing a program considered politically popular both in Congress and in city halls across the country.

The administration proposal (S 3186, HR 12993) calls for spending $3 billion — $1 billion each in fiscal 1979,

1980 and 1981 — for so-called "soft" public works projects like renovation and maintenance of public parks, government offices and schools. The program would be "labor-intensive," that is, between 50 and 80 percent of the cost of each project would be spent for labor. Further, about half of the 50,000 jobs the administration said would be created through the program are to be earmarked for low-income, unskilled, unemployed persons.

The "labor-intensive" focus, and the emphasis on hiring unskilled, low-income workers, represents a basic change from the local public works program enacted by Congress in 1976 and expanded in 1977. That program, which has pumped $6 billion in federal monies into the economy, was "capital-intensive," focusing on major construction of new projects, and did not require the use of large numbers of unskilled, long-term unemployed workers. *(Public works program, p. 41)*

The administration proposal has generated support, with some modification, from the National Urban Coalition, the Sierra Club, the U.S. Conference of Mayors and the National Association of Counties.

But the construction industry vehemently attacked key sections of the program, and urged instead that Congress spend more money for major construction projects.

Armed with pages of facts and figures, the Associated Builders and Contractors (ABC) argued during hearings that the most labor-intensive projects rarely exceed 40 percent of the costs, well below the requirements set by the administration. Further, the ABC objected to another requirement mandating high wages for unskilled workers.

One contractor, heatedly opposing the bill during testimony before the House Public Works Subcommittee on Economic Development, characterized the "real purpose" of the bill as a "publicly financed attempt to reduce unemployment in the short-term through temporary make-work projects with absurd cost-benefit ratios."

Using a charge frequently leveled against public works projects favored by the construction industry, the contractor declared that the administration's proposal was "pork barrel legislation that is completely out of step with the times and the sentiments of the American taxpayer."

Some members of the House subcommittee also questioned whether the administration's program would work.

"The subcommittee is overwhelmingly in favor of another round of local public works," said Rep. Robert A. Roe, D-N.J., chairman of the subcommittee.

The existing program has proved easy to administer. Moreover, since building projects are plain to see, members of Congress view the program as a way to demonstrate their political effectiveness.

"They also get a lot of ribbon-cuttings to go to," said one congressional aide.

"Only strong presidential leadership can eliminate the . . . inconsistencies . . . and overcome the traditional turf conflicts that stand in the way of a successful national urban policy."

—Gov. Michael S. Dukakis

Roe, Rep. Harold T. Johnson, D-Calif., chairman of the House Public Works Committee, and Sen. Quentin N. Burdick, D-N.D., chairman of the Senate public works subcommittee handling the measure in the Senate, met with President Carter to discuss the prospects for the measure in Congress.

The House Economic Development Subcommittee drafted its own public works bill (HR 11610) after the negotiations with the Carter administration apparently failed to produce a measure acceptable to both sides.

The subcommittee met Aug. 15 to mark up the bill. Instead of $1 billion sought by the administration for fiscal 1979, the subcommittee approved spending $3 billion, with $2 billion of that to be used to provide a third round of "capital-intensive" local public works projects.

Roe emphasized that the subcommittee proposal was open to further debate, and predicted that changes would be made during markup by the full Public Works Committee. The committee was expected to mark up the bill shortly after it returned from the Labor Day recess.

Burdick's subcommittee concluded several days of testimony in July 1978, but subcommittee sources said the members were not certain how to proceed.

"The members are very cautious. They would on the whole prefer the money to go for more construction, but they are concerned about the inflationary impact," said one source.

The initial local public works program was proposed as an anti-recession tool to combat a lagging economy and unemployment. Some senators believe those conditions no longer exist, and are skeptical of any kind of public works funding.

State Incentive Grants

To prod state governments into developing their own urban revitalization programs, the administration proposed an incentive grant program of $200 million (S 3209, HR 12893).

Few disagree with the reasoning behind the decision to seek greater state involvement in fighting urban decay. Patricia Roberts Harris, secretary of the Department of Housing and Urban Development, outlined the reasoning during recent Senate testimony:

"State law shapes and defines local government by establishing its boundaries, powers and revenues and by providing assistance and mandating responsibilities which affect its services to a great degree," she said. "With a capacity to tax far greater than that of localities, a geographic scope that empowers them to treat area-wide problems and a growing trend toward increased assumption of responsi-

"States are in an excellent position to play a leading role in the revitalization of urban America."

—HUD Secretary Patricia Roberts Harris

Boxscore of Congressional Action on . . .

The "new initiatives" in the Carter administration's urban program fall into four general categories: employment and economic development; fiscal assistance; community and human development; and "coordination, streamlining and reorientation of federal, state and local activities."

Here are the proposals and congressional action on them through mid-August 1978:

Employment, Economic Development

● A three-year, $3 billion program of labor-intensive "soft" public works to rehabilitate and renovate public facilities. Contractors bidding for these projects would have to accept half of their workers from the ranks of the hard-core unemployed hired for public service jobs under the Comprehensive Employment and Training Act (CETA). About 180,000 jobs would be created by this proposal. *(CETA, p. 29)*

Action. House and Senate subcommittees held hearings. Marked up by House subcommittee.

● Employment tax credits for employers who hire CETA workers between the ages of 18 and 24. Employers would receive a tax credit of $2,000 the first year and $1,000 the second per youth. The estimated revenue loss would be $1.5 billion annually.

Action. Omitted by House Ways and Means Committee in markup of the tax cut bill.

● A National Development Bank, to be run on an inter-agency basis by a board composed of the secretaries of the Departments of Housing and Urban Development (HUD), Commerce and Treasury. The bank would guarantee loans totaling $11 billion during the next three years to businesses locating in distressed areas, both rural and urban.

The loan guarantees would be linked to a program under which companies could get grants of up to 15 percent (or a maximum of $3 million) of their capital costs for fixed assets of a project. The grants would come from HUD and the Commerce Department's Economic Development Administration (EDA). Along with the grants, companies could obtain the loan guarantees (a maximum of $15 million per project) to cover 75 percent of the remaining capital costs. The usual interest rate would be slightly above Treasury rates (currently about 7.5 percent) although the bank in special circumstances could subsidize the interest rate, lowering it to 2.5 percent.

The grants and loan guarantees would be conditional on obtaining the balance of the financing from the private sector. EDA, through its Title IX economic adjustment assistance program, and HUD, through its urban development action grant program, would each get $275 million per year in increased funding for the grants to be used with the loan guarantees.

Action. Awaiting scheduling of hearings by House and Senate Banking Committees. No action expected in 1978.

● A special tax credit for companies investing in "distressed areas." Under existing law, companies can obtain a 10 percent tax break on the purchase of machinery and equipment. Carter's tax proposal calls for expanding that investment tax credit to cover new construction and rehabilitation of existing plants. The urban policy proposal calls for an additional 5 percent tax break, on top of the 10 percent, for investment in distressed areas. The program would be run on an experimental basis and would be limited to $200 million in tax credits per year.

Action. Omitted by House Ways and Means from tax cut bill, which was passed by the House Aug. 10.

Fiscal Assistance

● A new financial aid program to replace "counter-cyclical" revenue sharing program, which was scheduled to expire Sept. 30, 1978. The current program channels $1 billion a year to state and local governments if the national unemployment rate passes 6 percent. The new program would eliminate the state share and distribute $2 billion over two years (fiscal 1979-80) to cities with high unemployment rates ("distressed cities"). Because states would lose money under the proposal, governors and state legislators opposed the plan.

bility, states are in an excellent position to play a leading role in the revitalization of urban America."

There was uncertainty in Congress, however, over whether the program proposed by the administration would push states into taking a leading role in urban revitalization. Some members questioned whether HUD should be the agency to run the program, and just how the administration program would work.

"The idea sounds nice, but the fundamental question is nobody knows what the program would do," said an aide to the Senate Intergovernmental Relations Subcommittee, which shares jurisdiction over the bill with the Senate Housing Subcommittee.

Some critics questioned whether financial incentives would have any impact. First, the $200 million would be parceled out, according to HUD, to between 10 and 15 states. According to some critics, that would limit the amount of money available and reduce whatever financial impact there might be.

Other critics questioned whether another federal grant program was going to make any difference. "The question is how do you change the political forces that control a state? How do you bring about changes in attitude?" asked one official who has closely examined the administration's proposal.

Some questioned whether HUD should be the agency to run the program. These critics argued that the White House itself should oversee the program, in order to demonstrate to both the states and to the various federal bureaucracies that the federal government was intent on marshaling all its resources on behalf of urban revitalization.

"If the objectives of this bill are to be achieved, it is clear to me that HUD cannot do the job alone," said Gov. Michael S. Dukakis of Massachusetts, a leading advocate of a greater role for state governments in fighting urban decay.

Testifying before the Intergovernmental Relations Subcommittee in June, Dukakis argued that HUD failed in

...Carter Administration's Urban Proposals

Action. Rejected by House Intergovernmental and Human Resources Subcommittee. Senate Finance Committee approved extension of countercyclical aid and authorized $650 million per year for 1979-80 to "distressed" cities.

● A change in the fiscal relief portion of the administration's welfare reform proposal to allow immediate financial aid to states. As initially drafted, the fiscal relief under the welfare reform measure would not become available until 1981.

Action. Special House subcommittee approved welfare reform proposals. Senate hearings begun in Finance and Human Resources Committees. House Speaker Thomas P. O'Neill Jr., D-Mass., announced June 22 that it was too late in the session to get welfare reform through the 95th Congress. *(Welfare, p. 83)*

Community, Human Development

● An increase of $150 million above the $125 million the administration has proposed to spend in fiscal 1979 for the Section 312 housing rehabilitation program in HUD. The program provides low-interest loans, at 3 percent interest, for rehabilitation of housing.

Action. Senate-passed HUD fiscal 1979 authorization bill authorized $370 million. The House-passed bill authorized $245 million. House-and-Senate-passed HUD appropriation bills contained $245 million appropriations. An additional $30 million would be available for fiscal 1979 from unspent fiscal 1978 funds.

● $50 million for inner-city health clinics.

Action. Approved in Senate and House health authorization bills.

● $150 million for special social services grants under the Social Security Act for meals for the elderly and day care.

Action. The House passed a bill authorizing $400 million for social services grants. No Senate action.

● $40 million for an urban volunteer corps, to be run by ACTION, to create a pool of professionals such as lawyers, architects, planners and others with specialized skills available to help neighborhood renewal programs.

Some of the money would also be used for small grants for items like tools, supplies, materials and "administrative support" to carry out voluntary projects.

Action. Senate-passed bill authorized $25 million. House committee bill authorized $40 million.

● $15 million for a neighborhood self-help fund for neighborhood and volunteer organizations for specific housing and revitalization projects. To ease criticism from mayors, who opposed direct aid to neighborhood groups, the administration proposed that grants for each project be approved by mayors.

Action. Senate-passed bill approved $15 million authorization. House bill pending in committee.

● $200 million for mass transit, to be used to build new transit facilities and pedestrian transit malls, and to support joint public-private development around transportation stations.

Action. The Senate committee bill would authorize $200 million for such projects. The House committee bill would earmark $50 million for intermodal terminals and joint development projects. *(Mass transit chapter, p. 75)*

● $20 million for a "livable cities" arts program to be run by HUD with participation by the National Endowment for the Arts.

Action. Senate-passed HUD fiscal 1979 authorization bill included $5 million for livable cities. No House action on the program.

Federal, State, Local Activities

● $200 million in incentive grants to states to encourage urban planning and redirection of state programs toward urban areas. Initially, the administration contemplated penalizing states that did not cooperate by withholding revenue sharing funds, but it backed off in the face of vigorous opposition from governors.

Action. Senate hearings held by Intergovernmental Relations and Housing Subcommittees; Banking Committee postponed action until 1979. House Banking Subcommittee hearings held in August.

---

the past to deliver on its mandate to help America's cities because other federal agencies and corresponding state agencies, were busy neutralizing and negating its efforts.

"Only strong presidential leadership can eliminate the interdepartmental inconsistencies in policies and programs and overcome the traditional turf conflicts that stand in the way of a successful national urban policy," he said.

But HUD has resisted any effort to be removed as the lead agency on the bill. Secretary Harris emphasized that during her testimony before the same subcommittee.

"The administration believes that this program can best be administered by HUD," she declared. But she did not explain why the administration felt that way. Instead, she said the legislation "recognizes the need for interagency coordination," and said the HUD secretary would consult with other federal agencies concerned with the purposes of the bill in reviewing grant applications.

Some sources noted that the state incentive program is the only major spending program in the urban package giv-

en to HUD to run. "If they lose this all they are going to have is peanuts to throw around," said one congressional aide.

Two Senate subcommittees — intergovernmental relations and housing — have held hearings on S 3209, but neither has begun markups. The administration reportedly signaled a willingness to draft a "compromise" bill in order to meet concerns expressed by some senators, including Edmund S. Muskie, D-Maine, chairman of the intergovernmental relations subcommittee. But nothing concrete emerged by early August 1978.

The House Banking Subcommittee on Housing and Community Development had, however, scheduled hearings for Aug. 8, 9 and 10, 1978.

Fiscal Assistance

The proposed Supplementary Fiscal Assistance Act (S 2975, HR 12293) was the subject of hearings in both the

House and Senate in mid-May.

The administration proposal called for spending $1.04 billion in fiscal 1979 and $1 billion in fiscal 1980, with the money going to cities and towns suffering from long-term economic problems. The administration bill would replace the existing Anti-Recession Fiscal Assistance program, which would expire Sept. 30, 1978.

Although the administration said it wanted to target aid to cities with the most pressing financial needs, the new proposal would increase the number of cities and towns that would receive financial aid. That provoked substantial opposition in Congress, with critics complaining that dozens of wealthy suburban communities would qualify for aid under the Carter proposal.

The Department of the Treasury, which is handling the bill, has said it was willing to amend the legislation to insure that wealthy suburbs do not qualify for aid.

State governments have also lobbied to receive a share of the money. Under the existing anti-recession aid program, also known as countercyclical revenue sharing, state governments receive one-third of the monies.

The administration, arguing that state governments have improved their economic health since the 1974-75 recession, when the program was first conceived, proposed eliminating the state share.

"We still believe that, given the budget constraints of the program, the most effective use of the money can be made by giving it solely to local governments," said a Treasury aide who was handling the bill.

The House Intergovernmental Relations Subcommittee voted Aug. 2 to postpone indefinitely consideration of HR 12293. The Senate Finance Committee Aug. 10 approved a compromise plan (HR 2852) that would continue anti-recession aid to states and cities through fiscal 1980.

(Details in chapter on countercyclical aid and fiscal assistance, p. 39)

Tax Proposals

The administration also proposed tax credits for employers who hire young workers referred under the Comprehensive Education and Training Act (CETA) program, and investment tax credits for private companies that locate or expand in "distressed" areas. The tax credits would total $1.7 billion for fiscal 1979 *(Chapter on CETA, p. 29)*

Some "Snow Belt" legislators from Northeast and Midwest states disputed the potential impact of the investment credit by arguing that it would be undercut by another proposal included in the administration's tax package. The administration had proposed expanding a 10 percent investment credit for industrial expansion, regardless of location, to include the rehabilitation of structures. (The existing investment credit included just plant machinery and equipment.) On top of that, the administration proposed another 5 percent credit, making a total possible credit of 15 percent for industries that invest in a "distressed" area.

Snow Belt congressmen contended that the initial 10 percent investment credit would hasten industrial relocation from inner cities, especially in the older cities in the North and Midwest, to the Sun Belt states of the South and West. They argued that the 5 percent differential for "distressed" areas would make little difference

The House Ways and Means Committee was expected to consider Carter's proposals for tax credits for hiring CETA workers and investment tax credits for locating or expanding in "distressed" areas. However, neither proposal was included in the tax bill approved by the committee July 27 and by the full House Aug. 10.

How Carter Urban Policy Was Developed

To create its new urban policy, the Carter administration went through an elaborate, turbulent process that in some ways may have been as important as the policy it produced.

The policy's yearlong gestation was marred by well-publicized bureaucratic turf fights, false starts and delays, charges of poor staff work, and a deadline crush that left Carter with only hours in which to make billion-dollar decisions on the shape of this major program.

Despite those flaws, the process was one the administration touted as uniquely successful — primarily because of the massive involvement of virtually the entire range of government agencies and the probing examination of existing federal programs affecting cities.

While the urban policy development shows Carter's commitment to better management, it also points up the difficulties he has in guiding the federal government in a clear direction.

'Open' Process

While administration aides resisted making the explicit comparison, the process was vastly different from the one used in developing the Carter energy program in 1977. It was clear that criticism of the behind-closed-doors approach to the energy problem had its effect. Aides repeatedly emphasized how "open" the urban policy process had been.

Just before the president rendered his final decision, Bert Carp, top aide to Stuart Eizenstat, the president's assistant for domestic affairs and policy, discussed the process in an interview. He emphasized that not everyone who had been consulted would agree with the administration's positions. But Carp argued they should feel that they had been heard out and had been informed of administration thinking.

For example, he said, "I don't expect to satisfy the mayors, but I hope they will view this as an encouraging and unprecedented response.... There's a difference between losing an argument and being 'sandbagged.' Nobody is going to feel that they've been sandbagged by this policy."

In briefings to the press just after the president had signed off on the policy in March, Patricia Roberts Harris, secretary of housing and urban development, itemized the "strengths of the policy process."

She too praised the broad consultation with non-federal groups, but she laid particular stress on the extensive involvement of federal agencies that manage programs with an urban impact.

Harris and Eizenstat asserted that the involvement of the federal agencies was unprecedented. "We turned the government upside down to find everything we could that impacted negatively on urban areas and to do something about it," Eizenstat said. Harris stated, "There has never been an analysis of existing federal programs to see how they impact urban areas."

The result was twofold.

● They had generated some 160 administrative changes, most of which required no legislation, which would make the federal programs more beneficial to cities.

● The agencies had become committed to the president's proposals, both administrative and legislative, through their extensive inclusion in the process.

Carp suggested that "other administrations have created new agencies to administer new programs in part because they couldn't get the old, ignored bureaucrats to do it." He added that the Carter process was intended to avoid the "consistent difficulties presidents have had getting programs enacted or administered."

To help in getting the legislative portions enacted, it was necessary to consult with key members of Congress, which Carter aides claimed was done. One Eizenstat assistant stated, "I don't think there was ever a time when a member of Congress called and wanted a briefing or answers to questions on the urban policy when Stu didn't himself go up to the Hill to talk with the member."

That aide estimated that 20 to 30 meetings between Eizenstat and members of Congress took place in the final two months of developing the urban policy.

The claims of extensive consultation with Congress were partly corroborated from Capitol Hill. Henry S. Reuss, D-Wis., chairman of the House Banking, Finance and Urban Affairs Committee, agreed that he had been "heavily consulted.... I don't feel under-consulted in any way."

Reuss added that he felt some of his suggestions had taken root in the Carter policy, but he and other key members noted they had not been shown the actual set of options laid before the president. Hence they were not committed to support the administration on the specifics finally endorsed by Carter.

Bill Cable, top White House liaison with the House, cautioned that "consultation is understanding where your differences are. Some people jump from consultation to consensus awfully quickly. It doesn't always mean that."

HUD Secretary Harris briefs President Carter

Texts of 2 Intergovernmental Relations Memos

Following is the text of the memo President Carter sent to the heads of the executive departments and agencies Feb. 25, 1977:

Throughout the campaign and transition period, I made a firm commitment to state and local officials that they would be involved in the development of my Administration's policy and budget priorities and programs. I pledged that such consultation would occur at the earliest possible stages in order to make it significant and fruitful.

That kind of state and local involvement is critical to the ultimate success of this Administration because:

- State and local sectors constitute the delivery mechanisms for *most* of the actual services the federal government provides;
- State and local concerns, as well as their expertise, should be considered as programs are being developed in order to ensure the practicality and effectiveness of the programs;
- Such early participation by state and local officials in our planning process will help ensure broad-based support for the proposals that are eventually developed;
- It will ensure that priorities developed at the federal level will work

in conjunction with, and not at cross purposes to, priorities at the state and local level.

In order to assure that these objectives are met, please include in any major policy, budget or reorganization proposal which has significant state and local impact, a brief description of how you fulfilled this commitment on my behalf. It is not necessary to hold large and time-consuming public hearings, or to establish large task forces to accomplish this goal. Selecting state and local officials expert in a particular issue and asking for their assistance in developing a program will often serve our purpose.

The most important part of this consultative process is that it be genuine and timely.

Following is the text of the memo Carter sent March 21, 1977, to the Secretaries of Treasury; Commerce; Labor; Health, Education and Welfare; Housing and Urban Development; and Transportation:

During my campaign, I pledged an urban and regional policy based on mutual trust, mutual respect and mutual commitment between state and local governments on the one hand and the

federal government on the other. Although we do not have as yet a national urban and regional policy, the first step toward achieving that goal must be coordination among federal departments and agencies.

I would like you to form a working policy group on urban and regional development. The purpose of the group will be to conduct a comprehensive review of all federal programs which impact on urban and regional areas; to seek perspectives of state and local officials concerning the role of the federal government in urban and regional development; and to submit appropriate administrative and legislative recommendations.

Under Executive Order 11297, Pat Harris has the responsibility to convene such a group and will do so shortly. I want to emphasize that development of an urban and regional policy should be a joint project with full participation by each of your departments, as well as from other federal agencies where appropriate. This is a high priority for my Administration, and I have asked Jack Watson and Stu Eizenstat to facilitate and support your collective efforts in every way possible.

I look forward to receiving a preliminary report on your progress and findings by early summer.

Cable added that his role is to present the congressional position to the administration, but the president ultimately must exercise his option to forge his own policy.

Negative Views

The administration's own upbeat assessment of the policy development process was not shared by all. The lengthy effort received recurrent criticism, including some from members of Congress from urban areas.

Sen. Daniel Patrick Moynihan, D-N.Y., complained just after Carter's Jan. 19 State of the Union Address that the administration's longstanding failure to devise an urban policy was unacceptable. "How would people who felt strongly about foreign policy feel if the administration kept promising to produce one soon and never did?" he queried.

Some members also suggested privately that the consultation had been primarily a matter of the administration telling members of Congress what they were considering. A few complained that there was little interest shown in hearing ideas from the Hill.

For example, a meeting between Eizenstat and members of the Northeast-Midwest Coalition, led by Michael J. Harrington, D-Mass., was characterized by some Hill participants as a near-monologue by Eizenstat, with little input from representatives.

Urban Policy Group

The long deadline-missing process of crafting an urban policy began with a March 1977 Carter memo informing Cabinet officers that HUD Secretary Harris was to head an

interdepartmental task force, the Urban and Regional Policy Group. *(Text of memo, this page)*

But the pace of that group's progress was bogged down at least in part by predictable fighting among agencies over who would gain administrative and budget clout from the emerging proposals.

The infighting between HUD and the Department of Commerce was particularly intense, but other agencies also were involved. The HUD-Commerce competition was acute since both departments administer programs that assist economic development in urban areas, a major component of the urban policy that evolved.

Reorganization

Moreover, the "turfing" and the delay appeared to be unintendedly exacerbated by the administration's reorganization efforts.

Carter assigned overall reorganization authority to the Office of Management and Budget (OMB) and that agency parceled out the work to project teams that were studying specific issue areas. One team began in June 1977 to study reorganization of the government's "community and economic development" programs.

The likelihood that the president's reorganization team would ultimately recommend some consolidation of existing and new urban programs — particularly in the economic development area — initially heightened the tendency of the departments to fight for ascendancy in the development of urban policies.

One idea partly attributed to the reorganization unit was the creation of the Interagency Coordinating Council, a step that also echoed the suggestion of Joseph A. Califano Jr., secretary of health, education and welfare (HEW), that the administration designate a White House advocate for urban concerns. Another was the significant retargeting of Environmental Protection Agency sewer construction grants.

Urban Bank

The most visible object of the vying between HUD and Commerce was the placement of the proposed urban development bank. Both departments wanted control over it, and one White House official said the two were even lobbying members of Congress to have them pressure the White House to resolve the question in their favor.

In the end, Carter chose to finesse the dispute by providing for tripartite control over the proposed National Development Bank by Treasury, HUD and Commerce. (Treasury was credited with originally proposing the bank, but typically does not administer such programs.)

A reorganization official noted that resolution of the bank issue showed the need for ultimate organizational changes in the urban area. He predicted that such a reorganization would be endorsed by the president by early 1979. In his March 27 announcement of the urban policy, Carter explicitly noted that "over the long run, reorganization of the economic and community development programs may be necessary."

Draft Criticized

Given the obstacles confronted by the urban policy group, it was October before any tangible results were seen, and then the product was a draft statement that was heavily criticized as being largely a hash of urban problems without adequate ideas about policy or solutions.

In November a second, more expansive draft was somewhat better received. But the persistent criticism was that the urban group had not honed down its general policy suggestions to specific program proposals.

Budget Impact

Meanwhile, still another administration effort was going forward that inevitably affected the urban policy initiative: the first full-blown budget preparation for the Carter administration.

By December, the OMB drafters of the fiscal 1979 budget and Eizenstat's domestic policy staffers felt the need to give Carter some specific program choices regarding urban policy. Otherwise, his decisions in that area could not be reflected in the budget he was to present to Congress in mid-January 1978.

Drawing on the general proposals advanced by the urban policy group, the OMB and White House staff prepared a hefty budget briefing book on urban initiatives for Carter. The book contained line items for Carter to sign off on, deciding whether to fund them.

Carter Displeased

At an ill-fated December meeting between Carter and those aides, Carter rejected that approach.

According to a number of aides who were present, Carter simply indicated that he wanted first to decide what his urban policy was — then he would proceed to check off on actual programs. Thus, costs for the urban policy were not included in his January budget.

Carter's reaction to that December meeting spawned rumors and press stories that plagued the urban policy persistently thereafter. Press reports indicated that Carter was displeased with Harris and her staff's work and that he had rejected the suggestions of his urban group.

HUD, White House and OMB officials all denied that version of events. HUD aides pointed out that Harris was not even at the meeting and was not consulted in developing the presentation to Carter. Other aides concurred that Carter had not agreed or disagreed with the urban policy group's suggestions — he had only indicated that he wanted an overall policy before making those decisions.

Nonetheless, there was concern on Carter's staff about his displeasure. Some aides were not entirely joking when they discussed whether a certain wrinkle that appeared on the presidential forehead meant he was upset.

Carter's reaction appeared to galvanize the urban policy effort for the first time. Eizenstat and his staff became more heavily involved, and he and Harris worked together to draft a brief Jan. 11 memo to Carter setting forth suggested urban goals and objectives.

Program Analysis

Those were essentially accepted by Carter. He responded in a Jan. 25 note, emphasizing the need to provide a role for the private sector and for volunteer groups. Most importantly, he said he wanted to see more about how existing federal programs squared with the newly clarified administration urban objectives.

Thus from late January to mid-March a "base program" analysis was conducted. Some 30 agencies were sent memos setting out the objectives and asking for an assessment of how existing programs could be strengthened or altered — or eliminated — to advance the urban goals. This was the core of the consultation with federal agencies about existing programs of which the administration was proud.

Those agencies also were sent tandem memos asking how suggested new program initiatives — many of which had originated with those agencies through the urban policy group — also stacked up against the administration objectives.

The flurry of agency responses, meetings and additional volleys of memos kept a considerable number of top bureaucrats of the executive branch busy for weeks. Eizenstat and Carp spent an estimated 30 to 40 percent of their time on urban policy development. Agencies throughout the government likewise were committing large chunks of the time of top officials to the process. Saturday interagency meetings at the White House supplemented already full weeks of activity.

Budget Deadlines

By March, the pace was quite forced, since after nearly a year of slow progress the administration had awakened to the then impending congressional budget deadlines.

Their apparent haste to produce an urban policy before Carter left March 28 on his South America-Africa trip ironically subjected them to criticism for rushing too hard to paste something together. But the reason was that Congress was about to begin considering the first fiscal 1979 budget resolution, which had to clear by May 15.

Carp, who previously worked on the Senate Budget Committee, said that the budget deadlines imposed by Congress in 1974 were understandable, but "they are for the convenience of the legislative branch and not the executive."

Failure to announce the proposals before the end of March could have further imperiled any chance of gaining congressional acceptance in time for the proposals to take effect in fiscal 1979.

On March 15, Carter was briefed for the first time by Harris and the urban policy group on the results of their work. Utilizing two sets of bulky charts, Harris presented to the president the problems and the proposed general solutions to the urban malaise.

But specific programs still were not discussed in any depth. Carter reportedly even joked that he had promised Califano and Secretary of Commerce Juanita M. Kreps not to make any programmatic decisions at that meeting, since they were not going to be there to defend their interests.

Late on March 21, the urban policy group forwarded to the White House a final draft of recommendations. Eizenstat attached a cover memo and the 200 pages of documents went to Carter early on March 22 under the names of Harris, Eizenstat and OMB Director James T. McIntyre Jr. The package gave Carter some 70 options for specific programs to endorse or reject.

Final 48 Hours

Unfortunately for Carter, the delays in the process had backed him into a tight time squeeze. He had little more than 48 hours to make the multiple, billion-dollar decisions about the shape of his urban policy.

White House aides insisted that his prior exposure to the issues and the work of the urban group enabled him to make the decisions rapidly, but his only apparent prior involvement with the process had been the December and March 15 meetings, a handful of memos exchanged in between, and his private communications with Eizenstat.

Even in those final 48 hours, Carter was not free to focus strictly on the proposals before him. He was then deeply immersed in the visit of Israeli Prime Minister Menachem Begin and the Middle East crisis. He also received British Prime Minister James Callaghan and took time off to go to a world premiere ballet in those sparse hours.

Accounts differ as to just what Carter did when he turned to the urban policy on March 24. Some reports claimed that the president initially rejected substantial portions of the group's recommendations, cutting the amount to be allocated to urban programs by billions of dollars, and restoring the cuts only after last-minute persuasion from Eizenstat, Vice President Mondale and political adviser Hamilton Jordan.

White House aides denied that Carter had cut the allocations, asserting that the president instead, in the normal course of making his decisions, had wanted more justification and explanation of some programs before granting his approval. Once he got that in the brief March 24 parleys, he agreed to several additional initiatives.

But by either account, the president in hours decided up and down on programs totaling billions of dollars and significantly altering the shape of his urban policy.

Armed with those final decisions, Harris, Eizenstat and their aides hustled to grind out the press briefings and formal announcement statements that would present the policy to the world.

Again, the time crunch forced the administration to announce its policy on the awkward day of Easter Monday when members of Congress invited to the announcement were typically far from Washington. Cable and other administration officials conceded the regrettable aspect of the timing, but said little could be done at the end to prevent it. ∎

Urban Employment and
Economic Policies

CQ

Unemployment: It's Not What It Used to Be

Unemployment just isn't what it used to be.

Once the most compelling economic statistic, the unemployment rate had taken a back seat to inflation in the minds of policymakers and the public by mid-1978.

While congressional supporters of the Humphrey-Hawkins full employment bill (S 50), named for its sponsors, the late Sen. Hubert H. Humphrey, D-Minn., and Rep. Augustus F. Hawkins, D-Calif., struggled to enact its national goal of a reduction of unemployment to 4 percent of the work force by 1983, a slow but fundamental change in the meaning of the unemployment rate for society seemed to be taking place.

Moreover, inflation had become the overriding issue in 1978. "The political climate has shifted, so we're swimming upstream," said one supporter of S 50.

Unemployment fell sharply in June 1978, to 5.7 percent from 6.1 percent in May. But in July, it climbed up to 6.2 percent, more than erasing its encouraging June drop.

Changing social habits and government policies, population shifts and human nature have combined, however, to make unemployment politically less important than it once was. Unemployment statistics may themselves undergo major changes as well. A national commission was looking at new definitions of employment and unemployment that could substantially alter national and local jobless rates.

Who Are the Unemployed?

The Labor Department estimated that in June 1978, 5,754,000 persons looked for work but could not find any. Together with the 94,819,000 persons who had worked at least an hour during the month, the total work force was 100,573,000.

The 5.8 million unemployed thus accounted for 5.7 percent of the work force — 1.4 percentage points below the level of June 1977. But because 3 million more people entered the work force during the year, the economy had to provide over 4 million more jobs in order to improve the unemployment rate by 1.4 percent.

The ratio of employment to the total non-institutional population over age 16, sometimes cited as an alternative to existing methods for measuring the employment situation, reached an all-time high of 58.9 percent — 1.5 percentage points higher than in June 1977.

Differing Rates

As examination of the June figures made clear, the unemployment rate, which was a national average, concealed vast differences among subgroups of the population.

The unemployment rate for blacks and other minorities was 11.9 percent in mid-1978, more than double the 4.9 percent level for all whites. Adult black males experienced a 7.8 percent unemployment rate; 11.3 percent of adult black women were out of work.

Women had a harder time finding work than men did. The adult female unemployment rate was 6.1 percent, compared with 3.9 percent for men.

Teenagers faced the worst unemployment problems of all. The unemployment rate for those aged 16-19 was 14.2 percent, as against a 4.8 percent rate for everyone 20 and over. The 14.2 percent rate did, however, represent a substantial improvement from the situation in May 1978, when 16.5 percent of youths were jobless.

Much of the teenage unemployment decline could be attributed to above-average success in providing temporary summer jobs. Almost all of the drop was concentrated among white teenagers, who went from 13.8 percent unemployment in May to 11.6 percent in June.

Comparing the extremes among population groups, the unemployment rate for minority teenagers, 37.1 percent, was more than 10 times as high as the 3.4 percent rate for adult white men.

Workers in low-paying and unskilled jobs generally had the worst unemployment problems. Managers (1.8 percent) and professionals (2.4 percent) experienced very low rates. But factory workers (7.9 percent) and non-farm laborers (9.9 percent) faced severe difficulties finding work. Construction workers were 9.3 percent unemployed.

Almost half (46.4 percent) of the unemployed were out of work for less than five weeks — in part representing the inevitable "frictional" unemployment caused when people look for new jobs in even the healthiest of economies. People who suffered through more than 15 weeks of joblessness made up 21 percent of all unemployed. The average period of unemployment was 12 weeks.

The largest single cause for being unemployed was from losing a previous job. Workers who had been laid off accounted for 10.5 percent of the unemployed, while 30.1

"The discomfort of being unemployed — that's clearly less than it was before."

—Assistant Secretary of Labor
Arnold H. Packer

---

percent lost their jobs for other reasons. People who quit their last jobs were 14.7 percent of the unemployed. The rest of the jobless were coming back into the labor market after being out for a while (30.6 percent) and looking for a job for the first time (14.1 percent).

Hardship Measure

One factor in the decline in the central importance of the unemployment rate is that unemployment just doesn't hurt as much as it used to. Whatever the real human pain of being out of work, unemployment's broad impact on society has been lessened by changing social habits and government policies.

In the past, noted Sar A. Levitan, chairman of the National Commission on Employment and Unemployment Statistics, "unemployment was more or less equivalent to economic deprivation." Although some people could get help from relatives or charity, Levitan said, "basically people either worked or starved."

For one thing, most families depended on the support of one wage earner. "The man was the breadwinner," Levitan said, and if he was thrown out of work, the family's income was often immediately reduced to zero.

But by the mid-1970s, owing to a variety of changes in social norms, almost three-fifths of families benefit from the earnings of more than one worker. "There are many more families where both parents are working," observed Arnold H. Packer, assistant secretary of labor for research. Obviously a second income provides a buffer against economic catastrophe caused by loss of work.

Less Discomfort

Social programs enacted since the New Deal provided an even more important protection against the consequences of unemployment. "The discomfort of being unemployed — that's clearly less than it was before," said Packer.

Unemployment insurance offers help to the short-term jobless; welfare and other forms of public assistance aid the long-term unemployed. Together with food stamps, these programs provide much greater benefits than were avail-

---

Some economists think that the increasing numbers of women and young people in the labor force have brought about an unavoidable increase in the unemployment rate.

---

able even in the early 1960s. Social Security payments go to the aged and disabled, who otherwise might be forced to seek work.

These changes have had an important effect on the motivations and expectations of those looking for work. As the "cost" of being unemployed — the difference between the amount of public assistance available and the wages of a potential job — has gone down, so too has the incentive to find work as quickly as possible. Where in the past a breadwinner with a family to feed would likely jump at the first job that came along, now he or she has a chance to hold on for a while in the hope of finding the best paying or most satisfying employment.

Demographic Changes

Changes in the age and sex composition of the work force also can have a substantial effect on the unemployment rate and its validity as an overall indicator of economic well-being. Some economists think that the increasing numbers of women and young people in the labor force have brought about an unavoidable increase in the unemployment rate, regardless of particular economic conditions.

Women have greatly increased their participation in the world of work. Since 1950 the percentage of women

over age 16 who have looked or are looking for jobs has gone from 33.9 percent to 46.8 percent in 1976. The sharpest increases have been among young women. The percentage of women aged 20-24 who are in the labor force, for example, rose from 46.1 percent in 1950 to 65.0 percent in 1976, with the greatest part of the increase coming during the period 1965-70.

The explosive growth in the number of young people caused by the "baby boom" of the 1950s has also skewed the composition of the work force. The number of persons aged 16-19 who were part of the work force grew from 4.5 million in 1950 to 9.4 million in 1976 — a far greater proportionate increase than found in the total population.

These social and demographic changes have sharply reduced the former predominance of adult males in the work force. In 1950 males over age 24 accounted for 59.0 percent of the total civilian work force. But by 1975 their share of the labor market had fallen to 46.9 percent. Women went from 29.6 percent of the work force in 1950 to 40.0 percent in 1975, while young men increased from 11.5 percent to 13.1 percent during the same period.

Problem Groups

These changes are important because, in the real world, women and young people seem to have higher "natural" rates of unemployment. If these groups have inherently greater employment problems, their increasing participation in the work force makes achievement of a full employment goal set during a time when adult males dominated the work force all that much harder to achieve.

Although the birth rate has fallen to relatively low levels in recent years, young women still tend to have more unstable employment patterns because of their role in child bearing and rearing. The overwhelming majority of women not in the labor force cite their responsibilities in the home as the reason for not seeking work.

Women returning to the job market after time devoted to the family face difficult employment problems. Isabel V. Sawhill, director of the National Commission for Manpower Policy, said there "is clear evidence that in the case of women there are a large portion of new entrants in the pool of the unemployed." In 1976 40 percent of unemployed women over age 20 were re-entrants or new entrants into the labor force, compared with only 19.5 percent of unemployed men.

Being young and new to work, young people generally have more unstable job histories than their more settled elders. "Young people come in and out of the job market more frequently," said Packer. Many are in school, looking only for part-time or summer jobs. Others, taking advantage of the natural freedom and curiosity of youth, try out different jobs. "You would expect that teenagers would experiment with jobs," said Levitan. Young people also are often the targets of layoffs, since their skills are fewer and their job seniority minimal.

Impact of Changes

Economists are divided as to the exact impact of demographic changes on the unemployment rate. Levitan, while conceding that "we ought to expect in 1978 a higher unemployment rate than we had in the 1950s," downplayed the overall impact of the demographic shifts. But Michael L. Wachter, an economics professor at the University of Pennsylvania, has estimated that the changes in the composition of the work force have increased the "non-

Selected Unemployment Rates

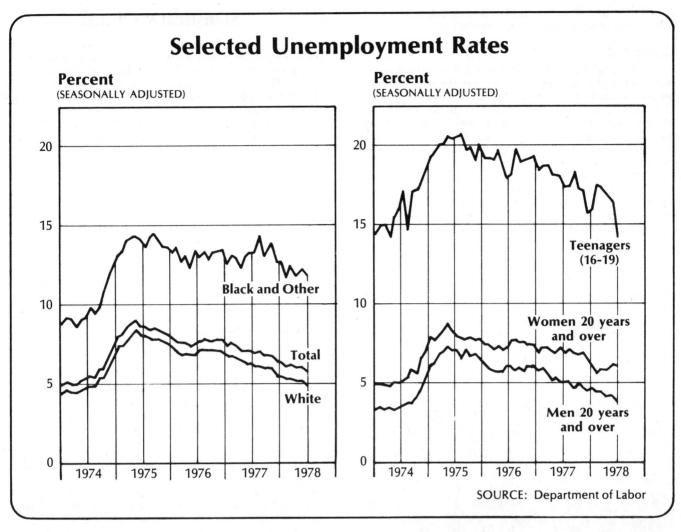

SOURCE: Department of Labor

inflationary" full employment rate from 4 percent in 1957 to 5.5 percent in 1975.

One bright spot in the picture is the low birth rates experienced during the 1960s and 1970s. Once the baby boom children begin to work themselves into the mature labor force, policy makers will be faced with a much smaller group of young people starting to look for jobs every year. According to one projection, the percentage of young males in the work force could decline from 13.1 percent in 1975 to 9.4 percent in 1990.

Another argument is that, in addition to having inherently higher unemployment rates, women and youths frequently, but not always, have less urgent needs for jobs than adult males. Supporters of this idea point out that the impact on society of the joblessness of a married woman seeking to escape the boredom of home-making, or of a teenager looking for part-time work after school, is clearly not as great as that of a family breadwinner or single person.

But supporters of the Humphrey-Hawkins bill and other government jobs programs angrily reject the notion that the employment needs of women and youth are somehow less real than others. They point out that in addition to the 38 percent of women who work to support themselves, many of the working wives are married to low-income men, and seek to work out of dire economic need.

"I'm continually impressed with the number of women who have to work from necessity," said Rudy Oswald, research director of the AFL-CIO. John Carr of the Full Employment Action Council said that "the vast majority of these women are not trying to escape boredom," but to make their families' ends meet.

Full employment proponents also argue that jobs for young people yield other desirable social benefits besides just providing an income. By working, young people stay out of trouble and learn good work habits — the daily discipline of getting up and going to work that is essential for holding a steady job in later life. "The prospect of a generation of young people brought up in idleness, dependency and without skills or work habits ought to jar some of the commentators out of their complacency," said Murray H. Finley, president of the Amalgamated Clothing and Textile Workers Union.

Public Perception

The changing character of unemployment also has affected the public perception of the importance of the problem. As joblessness has become concentrated among smaller groups of the population, its central relevance to the lives of most people has declined. The escalating concern over inflation, which affects everybody, has tended to overshadow the problem of unemployment, which affects only a relatively small portion of the population.

Gallup Poll

In May 1978 the Gallup Poll found that three times as many Americans thought inflation was the nation's most serious problem as worried most about unemployment. Over half, 54 percent, cited inflation as the No. 1 problem, while 18 percent pointed to unemployment. The 18 percent naming unemployment represented a substantial drop from the 24 percent who gave unemployment as the most pressing problem in October 1977.

Concentration of unemployment among minorities and young people, and in certain communities, has helped to lower the profile of unemployment in the public consciousness. Packer observed that "if it's somebody else that is unemployed, then it's less of a problem." Oswald recalled the old adage that "you have a recession when your neighbor is unemployed; you have a depression when you are unemployed."

But when the unemployed person is a black teenager from the central city, the problem is less immediate to a middle-class suburbanite.

Another factor in the decline in public perception of unemployment is that the problem has been getting better than it was a few years ago. From a high of 9.2 percent in May 1975, the unemployment rate fell by more than a third in three years.

The unemployment rate for teenagers in June was almost three times as high as the rate for everyone aged 20 and over. The unemployment rate for minority teenagers was more than 10 times as high as the rate for adult white men.

Statistical Methods

In addition to disputes over the proper interpretation of unemployment statistics, there is considerable controversy over the validity of the techniques used to collect them. The National Commission on Unemployment Statistics has been considering major revisions in how to count the unemployed.

Unemployment statistics are collected as a survey of 55,000 households, taken monthly by the Bureau of Labor Statistics (BLS). Because of regular changes in the work force every year, the raw figures are seasonally adjusted. Persons who have worked at least an hour a week are counted as employed; those who are out of work and looking for a job are unemployed; everyone else is considered not in the work force.

Since they are a random survey, unemployment figures can differ significantly from the actual number of unemployed. Changes in the seasonal adjustments can produce an apparent change in unemployment where none really exists. But the biggest problems facing the commission lie in deciding who to count as unemployed.

Discouraged Workers

The exclusion of "discouraged workers," for example, is a frequent subject of criticism of unemployment statistics. Under BLS rules, a jobless person who hasn't looked for work recently is considered not in the labor force, and thus not unemployed, regardless of how much he or she may need a job. Discouraged workers are those who think their chances of finding a job are so poor that they've given up even trying.

Critics argue that, by not counting discouraged workers, the statistics leave out precisely those with the worst problems — thus artificially lowering the true unemployment rate. The BLS estimated that there were 842,000 discouraged workers in the second quarter of 1978. Inclusion of this group would raise the unemployment rate to about 6.7 percent in the second quarter.

Part-Time Workers

Then there are the part-time workers. BLS considers anyone who works at all to be employed. Similarly, anyone looking for part-time work is counted as unemployed.

But the situations and needs of part-time workers are different from full-timers. A worker with a 10-hours-a-week job could be near starvation, but still be counted as employed by the BLS. On the other hand, the presence of thousands of university students looking to earn a little extra pocket money through part-time work can artificially drive up the unemployment rates in some areas.

Military Personnel

Another group which the commission would have to decide whether to count is the military. Members of the armed forces have not been considered part of the labor force. But, since abolition of the draft, the armed forces now compete for workers, through pay and benefits, along with other sectors of society. Thus it is arguable that the 2.1 million military personnel should be counted as employed — a change that would lower unemployment rates, especially in areas with large military bases. ∎

CETA: A Success or Federal Subsidy?

In 1978, many members of Congress were worrying that a program originally intended to help the hard-core unemployed had become something very different — a new form of federal revenue sharing.

That issue lay at the heart of legislation that would reauthorize the 1973 Comprehensive Employment and Training Act (CETA). The Carter administration requested a four-year extension of the act, which otherwise would expire Sept. 30, 1978.

CETA programs provide on-the-job and classroom training to the unskilled, operate Job Corps and summer job programs for disadvantaged youths, and put the unemployed to work in public service jobs.

Under the public service employment system, state and local governments get federal money to hire the unemployed to perform new services to the community. First created as a small-scale effort directed towards the severely disadvantaged, it was expanded during the 1974-75 recession to fight unemployment on a broad basis.

The problem is that many cities and counties are not using the money to hire additional workers. Instead they are paying for old jobs previously funded by local taxes. Known as "substitution," this tactic improves local fiscal standing, but gives little help to the millions of unemployed.

Moreover, many governments apparently are becoming "hooked" on CETA money. Some cities have a quarter or more of their employees on the CETA payroll; the ratio is even higher for many county governments. This suggests that in practice CETA has become a disguised form of federal subsidy for local government operations.

Some studies of public service employment have estimated that CETA money pays for four old jobs for every new one created. At that rate the cost of true job creation rises to astronomical levels.

Supporters of the program have been encouraged by a Brookings Institution study which found the levels of substitution to be much lower than previously estimated. These results were based in part on the idea that communities with fiscal problems would have had to lay off workers in essential positions without CETA help. If CETA was paying for a job that would not otherwise have been available, the argument goes, then the effect was the same as the creation of a new job.

Critics also charge that CETA has failed to serve the right people with the right kind of help. Set up to assist persons whose employment future was hurt by educational deprivation and racial and sexual discrimination, its participants are mostly white, male and educated. Meant to help people in the long run get permanent, unsubsidized jobs, it places only a fraction of its participants in regular positions.

In addition, the program has been buffeted by repeated charges of misuse of funds. Since its workers are hired outside of normal government hiring procedures, CETA is a tempting plum for local politicians who want to expand their patronage powers. In some areas investigators have found that political associates and relatives of politicians have been hired for programs meant for the needy. In other areas CETA workers have been found to be doing work for political parties or officeholders.

Administration Proposals

President Carter Feb. 22, 1978, sent to Congress his proposal for an extension and revision of the CETA system. He emphasized that the plan was aimed at the "structural" employment of minorities and youth, and that its goal was to "make sure that more of our people share in the benefits of growth."

Stressing the need to help those "who have difficulty finding work even when overall economic prospects are good," the president noted that in 1977, "even while unemployment was falling to 4 percent among white males above the age of 20, it was rising — from 35 to 38 percent — among black teenagers."

The Carter administration reauthorization bill (S 2570, HR 11086) would extend CETA through Sept. 30, 1982. It would maintain public service employment at roughly 1978 levels (725,000 jobs) through fiscal 1979. After that the number of jobs would vary with the unemployment rate. Local areas with high unemployment would get 100,000 jobs regardless of the national unemployment rate. When the national rate exceeded 4.75 percent, another 100,000 jobs would be authorized, with the total rising by 100,000 for every .5 percent increase in unemployment.

To keep local government from substituting CETA workers for traditional positions, the bill would limit the time that workers could stay in public service jobs to 18 months. Salaries for participants would be held below $10,000 a year.

In response to criticisms that CETA has not served those for whom it was intended, the bill would limit eligibility to those whose income was below 70 percent of the Bureau of Labor Statistics lower living standard — a limit of about $7,000 for an urban family of four.

To increase the movement of workers from CETA programs to the private sector, the bill would establish a new program designed to increase linkage with business.

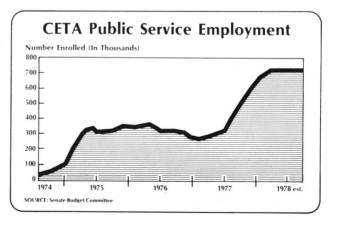

CETA Public Service Employment

Number Enrolled (In Thousands)

SOURCE: Senate Budget Committee

CETA at the Grass Roots

Howard County, Md., a growing county between Washington and Baltimore with urban, suburban and rural characteristics, offers an example of how CETA programs look when put into practice.

Part of a consortium of counties in and around Baltimore, Howard County has 120 public service employees working in government and community organizations. The county, with a population of about 120,000, received $848,000 in public service employment funds in fiscal 1978.

A large majority of public service participants are enrolled in Title VI programs. Positions range from laborers to para-administrators. Public service employees work for the county government, for example, as correctional guards, clerical workers, recreation aides, road-crew laborers and community workers. The average wage among all public service employees in the county is $4.16 an hour.

Among the community groups with CETA workers are a retarded citizens organization, the Community Action Agency, the YMCA, the Lung Association, and local colleges. About two dozen young people enrolled in experimental youth employment and training programs work in private companies and receive educational and vocational counseling.

Howard County has so far escaped charges of substituting CETA workers for regular employees. But, according to county official David White, a tight budgetary rein is needed to make sure agencies don't surreptitiously try to substitute. "Even if you don't plan to do that [substitute], the tendency among some agencies is pretty strong," he said.

Local industry training councils would be set up to plan more on-the-job training and other strategies, particularly those aimed at unemployed youth.

The bill also would begin to lay the groundwork for the administration welfare reform plan. It would fund 50,000 jobs to demonstrate the feasibility of guaranteeing jobs to heads of households in place of welfare.

Background

CETA developed out of the vast array of job and training programs spawned by Democratic "Great Society" legislation in the 1960s. It featured both centralization of the programs, concentrating overall supervision in the Labor Department, and decentralization, giving control of implementation of the programs to local governments.

Federal efforts to fight unemployment through job training began in 1962 with passage of the Manpower Development and Training Act (MDTA). Originally intended to provide retraining to workers who lost their jobs to automation, it was soon modified when it became clear that young workers with no training at all needed help much more than workers with outmoded skills.

The continuation of high minority unemployment rates during the boom periods of the 1960s led to further emphasis on training for groups with special employment problems. The Economic Opportunity Act of 1964 established the Job Corps, which provided training to disadvantaged youth in

residential centers, and the Neighborhood Youth Corps, which helped high school dropouts and poor youths needing part-time or summer jobs to stay in school.

Another program sponsored by the Johnson administration, Job Opportunities in the Business Sector (JOBS), worked through the National Alliance of Businessmen to encourage employers to hire the disadvantaged. Funds were provided to help employers bear the additional training costs of hiring unskilled workers.

Studies of these and other employment programs showed that they had a substantial effect on participants' subsequent economic performance, though their effect on overall unemployment was limited. Participants in institutional and on-the-job programs increased their earnings on the average between $1,000 and $2,000 a year. The JOBS program was successful beyond initial expectations, with many employers forgoing available government assistance for hiring.

But the programs were difficult to administer, scattered as they were through various government offices. Agencies were forced to make separate contracts with thousands of training centers, making oversight difficult.

Nixon Approach

The Nixon administration preferred a different approach. In concert with his plans for revenue sharing, President Nixon proposed that manpower funds be given directly to local governments to run their own programs.

Until enactment of CETA in 1973, Nixon and Congress engaged in a running battle over another aspect of manpower policy, public service jobs. Since the mid-1960s congressional liberals had pushed for public service jobs to put the unemployed to work. In 1970 Nixon vetoed a manpower bill providing $2.5 billion for public service employment, saying "WPA-type jobs are not the answer." But in 1971 he did consent to the Emergency Employment Act, authorizing $2.25 billion for public service jobs.

Passage of CETA in 1973 was a compromise between Nixon, who wanted to turn administration of manpower programs over to localities, and the Democratic majority in Congress, which wanted public service jobs.

Title I of the act consolidated most of the various manpower programs into a single system of block grants to local governments. Funds were provided by formula to city, country or state "prime sponsors."

Public Service Jobs

Title II established a limited program of public service jobs. It addressed problems of "structural" unemployment by providing jobs for those with long-term employment difficulties. Only persons unemployed for more than a month were allowed to participate. Assistance was provided by formula to areas with unemployment of more than 6.5 percent.

As the recession deepened in the mid-1970s, congressional leaders saw in CETA a vehicle for fighting increasing unemployment. In 1974 Congress added a new Title VI to CETA, authorizing $2.5 billion for public service jobs, allocated on the basis of unemployment rates. But in contrast to the structural emphasis of Title II, Title VI was a "countercyclical" measure attacking unemployment caused by recession.

In 1976 Congress extended and expanded the Title VI public service employment program. In addition to increasing the numbers of positions available, the extension bill contained provisions designed to limit substitution and focus programs on the poor. It required that new positions

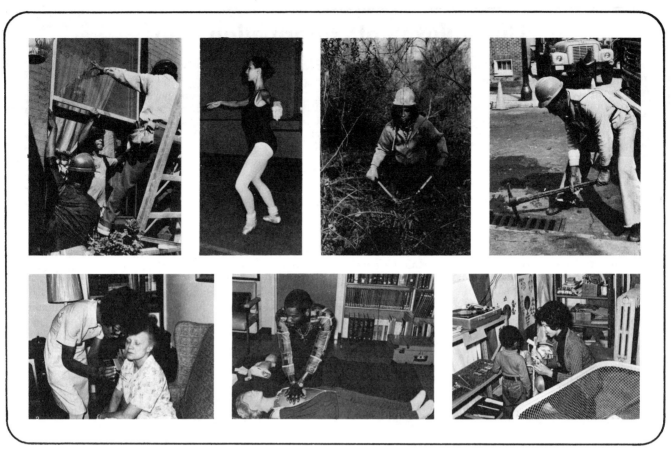

The Faces of CETA: Public Service Employees in the Baltimore Metropolitan Area

be used in community projects that could be finished within a year, and be limited to persons unemployed for more than 15 weeks who had low incomes.

In 1977 a new CETA Title VIII, designed to aid disadvantaged youth, was added. Title VIII established a Young Adult Conservation Corps and funded various experimental projects.

Also in 1977, Congress passed a simple one-year extension of CETA, authorizing the program through the end of fiscal 1978. The Carter administration requested a short-term extension in order to gain time to thoroughly study the program and propose substantive changes, as it did in 1978.

CETA in 1978

The backbone of the CETA system in 1978 were some 450 "prime sponsors" who administer employment and training programs in their areas. Cities and counties with populations over 100,000, or groups of smaller units, can qualify as prime sponsors. State governments handle the areas not covered by local prime sponsors.

Under Title I of CETA, prime sponsors in fiscal 1977 provided job training to 1,415,000 persons. Programs include classroom training, on-the-job experience, and some public service employment. Prime sponsors may contract with community groups to operate services. *(Box, p. 34)*

Public service employment under Titles II and VI reached early in 1978 the goal of 725,000 jobs set by the Carter economic stimulus plan; the total was 753,000 by the first week of March. Jobs funded range from police and firefighting positions to park workers and arts instructors.

As originally conceived, Title II was to provide structural public service employment — for those with long-term employment problems, while Title VI was to concentrate on those out of work because of an economic downturn. But in practice the distinction between the two programs has been blurred. Shifting eligibility requirements and prime sponsor reluctance to divide up their employment programs into separate parts has made the distinction difficult to enforce.

"Prime sponsors have not heavily weighted the distinction," according to Jon Weintraub, associate director of the National Association of Counties. Statistics show that the two titles serve substantially similar target groups.

One distinction that is applied divides public service jobs into sustainment and project positions. The 1976 CETA expansion required that new Title VI funds go first to sustain the level of public service jobs already in operation. The remaining funds were to be used in projects, defined as related undertakings which could be completed within one year and would not otherwise have been started.

Impact on Cities

Whatever the type of jobs, public service funds have become a vital factor in county and municipal finance. In Buffalo, N.Y., for example, CETA workers accounted for 32.8 percent of the city government work force, while in Hartford, Conn., they made up 25.8 percent in 1978.

Unemployment: Information Gap

One problem with designing an employment and training program is that no one knows how much unemployment there really is.

Unemployment statistics are sensitive to subtle changes in techniques unrelated to real economic conditions. For example, a drop in the unemployment rate in the last months of 1977 was caused in part by a change in the way seasonal employment changes were computed in the unemployment rate formula. "A material shift in the national perception of whether unemployment is going up or down can be effected solely by a changing in methodology," said Sar A. Levitan, chairman of the National Commission on Unemployment Statistics, a study group established by Congress in 1976.

Even more difficult to determine accurately are local area statistics, which are vitally important because they decide where employment and training funds will go under CETA. In January 1978 the Bureau of Labor Statistics (BLS) began using new techniques to measure local unemployment, with a potentially sizable impact on the distribution of federal dollars.

Previous BLS procedures set local rates at a ratio, derived from the 1970 census, of larger area unemployment rates. In 11 large cities figures were computed on the basis of data from Current Population Surveys.

Under the new system local unemployment statistics will be based mainly on unemployment compensation claim data, with allowances for new entrants into the job market. The big cities argue that unemployment compensation data will significantly underrate their joblessness, since cities are more likely to have large numbers of workers outside the unemployment insurance system.

The growth of the unreported labor market in the cities illustrates the need of those computing labor data to take into account changes in social patterns. Most important, according to Eli Ginzberg, chairman of the National Commission for Manpower Policy, is the tremendous increase in the number of working women. "The BLS has been constantly underestimating the number of women who are seeking to enter the labor market — they don't recognize that there's a revolution going on."

Other changes in labor patterns complicate the situation for statisticians even more — "there's a lot of funny things going on out there in relation to employment," Ginzberg said. For example, young people are not always following the traditional pattern of entering the labor force soon after getting out of school. Men are leaving the work force earlier; Ginzberg estimated that one-quarter of men who are 55 years old have already stopped working or looking for work.

Finally, the growth of the unreported or illicit economy, especially in the cities, leaves the government ignorant of how many people are really supporting themselves. "There are very few people who don't work a little," Ginzberg said. One study of New York City estimated that a quarter of a million people supported themselves in "fringe," illicit ways. Another study estimated that the illegal and unreported sector represented 7 percent of the national economy, leaving large numbers of people outside the calculations of employment experts.

Those statistics are disturbing to regular government employees. Municipal workers feel threatened by CETA workers, according to Nanine Meiklejohn of the American Federation of State, County and Municipal Employees, because they are hired outside of normal procedures designed to protect permanent workers. Regular workers dislike the creation of special job titles for CETA workers, who are paid less than regular workers, and fear in general that the program will result in a "gradual replacement of workers and a lowering of labor standards," she said.

Substitution

In addition to providing jobs for those out of work, public service employment offers to local governments the possibility of a substantial reduction in labor costs. If the federal government is willing to pay CETA workers to do jobs that the local government would otherwise have had to pay for, then the city or county will be able to use the savings to provide other services or cut taxes.

The CETA funds can either create new jobs, or pay for old ones. But the line between created and substituted jobs is very difficult to draw. The existence of fiscal problems in many local governments blurs the distinction. For governments that for budgetary reasons have had to lay off permanent, essential workers such as police and firefighters may be reluctant to use CETA funds to pay for dance instructors.

One type of job creation, then, occurs when a local government uses CETA funds to fill a position that would have been vacant because of lack of local money. These jobs are considered created jobs because they would not have been available without CETA. Other types of job creation occur when a government begins new programs, or expands old ones, or undertakes a special project that can be completed within a year.

An obvious case of substitution occurs when a government lays off employees and then rehires them, after the minimum period of unemployment, back to their old jobs with CETA funds. Solvent governments that allow the permanent work force to decline through attrition, while hiring CETA workers to fill vacancies, are also substituting. Another type of substitution occurs when governments use CETA workers to perform tasks traditionally contracted out.

Although CETA prohibits substitution, most observers agree that some substitution is taking place. But estimates of its exact extent vary tremendously.

The first studies of substitution showed very high rates, particularly in the Public Employment Program of 1971. Estimates of substitution ranged from 39 to 90 percent. A 1977 Congressional Budget Office study found that substitution reached 100 percent after two years.

Another study, however, argued that these estimates are questionable because of the inherent limitations of the "econometric" methodology on which they are based. An analysis of past substitution studies, written by Michael Borus and Daniel Hamermesh for the National Commission for Manpower Policy, found that estimates of the same situation could be vastly different depending on the statistical assumptions on which they were based. "We can't be sure of what really is going on," observed one congressional analyst.

Brookings Study

Another study for the Manpower Commission, conducted by the Brookings Institution, used an entirely different method and came to strikingly different results. Instead of working from a mathematical model, Brookings researchers contacted a network of academics in selected areas around the country. These analysts examined public service programs in their own areas. They interviewed officials, looked at data on employment and the fiscal state of the area governments, and made independent estimates on the extent of substitution.

The Brookings study found that substitution accounted for 20 percent of all public service positions. Sustainment positions were found to be 21 percent substituted, while the newer project approach had a rate of 8 percent. Contrary to past assumptions, the study found that substitution positions did not go only to experienced workers; minority and disadvantaged participation rates were about the same as in other public service jobs.

One reason that the substitution rate was low was that the researchers found a high level (31 percent) of program maintenance, in which CETA funds were used to continue positions that otherwise would have been discontinued for fiscal reasons. Thus the low rate of substitution rested in part on the individual perceptions of researchers that the prime sponsors were in difficult financial situations. Taken together the results show that jobs formerly paid for by local government accounted for about half of all public service jobs.

'Red Herring'?

Whatever its exact extent, substitution raises serious questions as to the efficacy of public service employment. Sen. Gaylord Nelson, D-Wis., chairman of the Human Resources Employment Subcommittee, said that substitution even at the lowest estimates still involves "a very substantial amount in dollar terms." Sen. John H. Chafee, R-R.I., raised the common complaint that "CETA has become in effect a revenue sharing for the communities — even in the school systems CETA is carrying a tremendous load."

Critics of the program argue that the existence of substantial substitution raises the cost of new job creation to unacceptable levels. For example, at an 80 percent substitution rate the government would have to pay for five jobs in order to create one new one. Rep. Bill Frenzel, R-Minn., ruefully observed that this would mean that each new job would cost more than the salaries of members of Congress.

But others contend that substitution is infrequent and probably not so bad after all. Greg Wurzburg, executive director of the National Council on Employment Policy, called substitution "a red herring — a non-issue," peripheral to the real problems of municipal finance. Weintraub questioned "whether substitution is that dirty a word," because the eligibility requirement for CETA workers has had "very positive effects on affirmative action needs" of local governments. Substitution also can have local stimulative effects if CETA funds permit governments to cut taxes.

Outlays for CETA Programs

(by fiscal year, in millions)

	1974	1975	1976	1977	1978* (estimated)
Title I (training programs)	$1,136.6	$1,648.8	$1,697.5	$1,756.2	$1,891.4
Title II (public service employment)	—	519.2	544.1	496.0	970.4
Title III (special programs including summer employment)	495.1	262.2	724.4	837.1	1,572.1
Title IV (Job Corps)	164.1	170.4	180.6	201.6	274.0
Title VI (public service employment)	—	319.2	1,872.3	2,340.4	4,765.0

* Includes a requested supplemental appropriation for increased minimum wage costs.

SOURCE: Labor Department, Employment and Training Administration

Ernest Green, head of the Labor Department's Employment and Training Administration, testified Feb. 23, 1978, that the administration had already stepped up its monitoring of substitution violations, leading to the recovery of $1.4 million from prime sponsor violators. To supplement this the administration bill provides for limits on salaries and lengths of time worked. Public service employee salaries would be held below $10,000, with the recommended average wage set at $7,800. Prime sponsors would be prohibited from supplementing salaries by more than 10 percent of all public service funds received. Participants could stay in the program only up to 18 months.

Green argued that the effect of the limits would be to make "[CETA] jobs inappropriate for permanent substitution." But critics predicted that the measures would hurt participants without checking the practice. A spokesman for the Conference of Mayors said that the proposals were "totally inappropriate. The net effect impacts on workers — they're the ones that pay the price." A $10,000 limit could pose problems in some high-priced cities, where even entry-level workers often get more.

Targeting

A frequent criticism of CETA programs is that they fail to target on those who need assistance most — the economically disadvantaged and long-term unemployed. "We're not coping with the hard core," observed Sen. Thomas F. Eagleton, D-Mo. Instead of being made up mostly of the disadvantaged, argued Rep. Barber B. Conable Jr., R-N.Y., "the characteristics of CETA workers show that they are the most skilled of the unemployed."

The figures on CETA participation tend to back up Conable. Workers in public service programs are largely white, male and high school graduates. Only 15 percent come from welfare families. Critics contend that the figures show a persistent tendency by prime sponsors to "cream" the labor market — skim off the most skilled of the unemployed.

The struggle over the means for distributing CETA funds arises from the huge difference between the scope of the programs and the number of people conceivably eligible.

Role of Community Groups

Local governments are not the only entities that carry out CETA programs. Community-based organizations (CBOs) also play an important role in delivering employment and training services to the un-employed.

Prime sponsors can contract with CBOs to run job training centers. Or they can provide public service employees directly to the organizations to help run beneficial services for the community such as storefront health clinics.

There are two types of CBOs. Four national organizations — Opportunities Industrialization Centers (OIC), the National Urban League, SER-Jobs for Progress and Mainstream — are specifically named in CETA legislation. Then there are hundreds of locally based neighborhood groups, many of which sprang up in response to CETA.

CBOs have the advantage of having closer ties with poor and minority client groups than local governments. Dick Johnson of the Department of Labor said that "CBOs do a better job of getting down to the people." They also offer increased possibilities for transition for their public service employees, since they typically have higher turnover of regular staff than local governments. But many prime sponsors resent what they feel is pressure from Washington to use CBOs regardless of local conditions.

The national CBOs enjoy solid support on Capitol Hill. Johnson, a former Senate committee aide, said that "there's a great deal of feeling in Congress that the CBOs have been very effective in providing services."

Under Department of Labor regulations, CBOs are supposed to receive 35 percent of job slots under the economic stimulus program of Title VI. But the most recent evidence indicates that CBOs have been getting about a quarter of the jobs, according to an Employment and Training Administration official.

Eli Ginzberg, chairman of the National Commission for Manpower Policy, estimated that as many as 22 million people could be eligible for CETA assistance — a "colossal discrepancy" with the number that could be served. "We're holding this program out to 22 million people," observed Sen. Donald W. Riegle Jr., D-Mich., "but we can only reach a minor fraction of those in need."

CETA assistance can basically be distributed in three ways — to individuals who meet income and unemployment standards, to areas on the basis of unemployment and economic hardship rates, or to special groups that Congress is especially interested in helping.

Focus on Individuals

Current individual eligibility standards are confusing and contradictory, making program coordination by prime sponsors difficult. Applicants for Title II jobs, which were originally intended for the economically disadvantaged, have no income limit — they have only to have been unemployed for 30 days. But the largest part of Title VI, meant to help those laid off by temporary changes in the economy, is now limited to persons unemployed for more than 15 weeks, with a family income below 70 percent of the lower living standard — the poor. Other programs have different criteria. This proliferation of eligibility standards, argue prime sponsors, creates administrative headaches and makes it difficult to transfer participants to appropriate programs.

The administration bill would limit participation to the economically disadvantaged — defined as those below 70 percent of the lower living standard — who had been unemployed for five or more weeks.

Prime sponsors argue that the emphasis on tightened eligibility standards reflects a suspicion that, given the chance, prime sponsors will ignore the needs of the poor — a charge they feel is not borne out by the facts. Too tight standards will also exacerbate social tensions and "stigmatize" CETA workers, Wurzburg said. Opening CETA jobs only to the poorest would amount to creating "a separate kind of job for a separate kind of people," he said, further causing "too much isolation from the mainstream of the labor market."

Focus on Areas

Another way to distribute funds is to areas on the basis of local unemployment or poverty rates. Under existing law, Title I training funds are distributed to prime sponsors according to the following formula: 50 percent on the basis of the previous year's allotment, 37.5 percent on unemployment rates, and 12.5 percent on the number of poor families. Title II funds are allotted only to areas that had unemployment rates of 6.5 percent for more than three months. Half of the Title VI funds available to prime sponsors are allotted on the basis of unemployment rates in all areas; one quarter is reserved for areas with more than 6.5 percent unemployment; the remainder is distributed on the basis of the number of unemployed in areas with over 4.5 percent unemployment.

The administration bill did not propose to change the allocation formulas. Administration representatives said that the uncertain nature of the recent changes in methods for determining local area unemployment rates made alteration of formulas problematic. But they left open the possibility of new formulas once the impact of the methodological changes could be evaluated.

Representatives of areas hard hit by unemployment argue that changes in allocation formulas are needed to give extra help to the areas that face the greatest problems. Sen. Jacob K. Javits, R-N.Y., who had introduced legislation to change the formulas, said that changes were essential to help older cities facing chronic unemployment caused by an exodus of jobs to the "sunbelt" regions. His legislation would give greater weight in the formulas to the relative severity of unemployment and poverty, diverting more funds to areas with the worst structural employment problems. Supporters of giving more weight to poverty in allocating training funds say that the change would concentrate assistance in areas with long-term problems, rather than on areas with cyclical unemployment, where workers might not need more training.

Focus on Groups

Finally, special consideration can be given to selected groups within the eligible population. In 1978, Labor Department regulations required prime sponsors to give special consideration to veterans, welfare recipients, former manpower trainees and teachers.

But many prime sponsors dislike the imposition of special consideration. One city representative pointed out that there were hundreds of different population sub-groups that could be selected, in disregard to local conditions. "Prime sponsors don't want to be dictated to," he said. Joan Wills, director of employment programs for the National Governors' Conference, disputed the idea that special quotas help the groups that seek them. "They're such a sham for the people who need the services the most," she said, since "there's just not enough to go around" for every group that could push for special consideration.

Transition

Critics of CETA worry that the employment and training programs are failing to meet the stated ultimate goal — preparing people to take unsubsidized, permanent jobs. If participants fail to make the transition to regular jobs, it is questionable how much benefit they have obtained from a temporary, stopgap solution to their long-term problems.

Green conceded that "the current CETA program is not yet successful enough in moving workers from unsubsidized employment to the private sector." Labor Department statistics show that 39 percent of participants in Title I training programs transfer to unsubsidized jobs; 17.7 percent of Title II and 34.0 percent of Title VI public service employees make the transition. Labor Department regulations set a goal, but not a requirement, of 50 percent annual transition.

Problems

One problem with achieving high rates of transition is that it sometimes works in opposition to other desirable goals of the program. One Brookings analyst said that "it appears to me that attempts to maximize the transition rates are frequently in conflict with other goals of the program, such as minimizing displacement and reaching social targeting objectives." An urban spokesman observed that "the more placement standards you have the more creaming you get," since prime sponsors trying to meet high transition goals were likely to "recruit the folks that are more apt to find jobs."

Other reasons for the low transition rates were general economic conditions and the way the program was operated. CETA was just getting off the ground when the 1974-75 recession struck. Employers who were forced to lay off old employees were not likely to go to prime sponsors seeking new people to hire. "Anytime you have an employers' market," asked Wills, "why shouldn't the employer take the better qualified?" Furthermore, critics contend, public service jobs provide very little training to make participants more employable.

Prime sponsors and others say that many of the transition problems stem from the confusing and irritating bureaucratic aspects of the program. Private employers participating in programs must fulfill substantial record-keeping requirements — "there are too many administrative headaches and too much red tape" for the private sector to want to get involved, Wurzburg said.

Public Sector Jobs

Prime sponsors have been most successful in transferring CETA participants to permanent jobs in the public sector. This makes some people worry that training and public service programs will end up preparing workers only for the limited public sector. Chafee said that "the problem I have is that these CETA jobs are the ones that have a very

Oversight vs. Local Control

Running throughout the CETA debate is the tension between the need to give prime sponsors enough independence to run programs suited to local conditions, and the fear that they will abuse the privilege. Prime sponsor independence was a fundamental precept of the original CETA legislation. But repeated charges of corruption and misuse of funds in local programs have jeopardized that independence.

A frequent criticism has been that public service jobs are awarded on the basis of political influence or nepotism. In Chicago, jobs were reportedly handed out on the basis of recommendations from political officials. In the District of Columbia, city council members were using CETA funds to hire friends and political associates, according to newspaper reports. In Buffalo, N.Y., participants were allegedly required to do work for the local Democratic Party.

The Employment and Training Administration (ETA) in 1978 stepped up efforts to halt violations. Labor Secretary F. Ray Marshall established a special task force to track down allegations of misuse. Chicago was ordered to return nearly $1 million in CETA funds because of political favoritism and substitution. In February 1978, the ETA for the first time revoked a prime sponsorship, in East St. Louis, Ill., for violations.

Administrative Problems

Prime sponsors contend that the real problem with ETA oversight is a rigid application of national rules to local conditions. "ETA continues to apply broad-brush solutions to individual problems," said one county official. "Rather than dealing with an individual problem, they write a national regulation that decreases the flexibility of program implementation."

Hundreds of decentralized programs are more difficult to monitor than a single program run directly from Washington. The ETA has been hard-pressed to keep up with the expanding number of programs.

Prime sponsors complain that they are deluged with hundreds of ETA directives every year. "You could fill a room with the regional directives," remembered one former local program director. They also say that weekly reporting requirements impose burdensome paperwork.

The administration has cited reduction of paperwork as a major goal of its new bill. The measure would consolidate administrative functions in one title, reducing duplicative reporting requirements. Nonessential data would be cut back.

limited private sector outside requirement." He cited the example of a fireman hired under CETA — "after 18 months, that person's marketability is very limited" in the private sector.

1978 Legislative Action

House and Senate subcommittees April 26, 1978, approved bills extending the CETA programs for four years, through fiscal 1982. The bills were revised versions of the legislation requested by the administration. On May 10, the full House Education and Labor Committee approved a bill (HR 12452) aimed at quieting criticism of the program. In extending the job program for four years, the committee added a number of provisions designed to stop what critics have called a widespread pattern of corruption and misuse of funds. The Senate Human Resources Committee reported a companion CETA extension bill (S 2570 — S Rept 95-891) May 15.

Meanwhile, the Labor Department stepped up its efforts to use its existing authority to uncover fraud in CETA programs. Labor Secretary Marshall April 13, 1978, announced creation of a permanent special investigations office, charged with correcting abuses in CETA and other department programs. The office, which had been in existence on a temporary basis, began looking into problems in 11 local jobs programs.

House Floor Action

After losing a series of key votes on the House floor Aug. 9, sponsors of the CETA legislation postponed further action on the bill until September. Debate on the CETA authorization extension revealed such strongly critical sentiment among House members that leaders decided to hold off on final action, lest the legislation be crippled or totally defeated.

House Speaker Thomas P. O'Neill Jr., D-Mass., was apparently determined to complete action on the bill Aug. 9, keeping members in session until 10 p.m. But the House just scratched the surface of the many expected amendments, without considering the crucial public service employment titles.

The late-night session drew a heated reaction from Ronald V. Dellums, D-Calif., who charged that House members were "making a mockery of the legislative process." "We are tearing this legislation apart," he said, "...but many of us do not understand what is going on."

Two crucial amendments adopted by the House Aug. 9 lowered the ceiling on wages that could be paid to CETA workers and slashed authorized funding for public service employment.

The cutbacks came despite the strenuous efforts of a CETA task force of House members and intensive lobbying by unions and local government officials, many of whom are heavily dependent on the program. Lobbyists warned that the cutbacks would render the program virtually unworkable, particularly in the expensive urban areas that face the most severe unemployment problems.

The atmosphere surrounding the bill was so negative that even members who had supported CETA in the past argued that some reductions were necessary to satisfy popular complaints, and to avoid even more stringent congressional restrictions in the future.

Continuing publicity over fraud and abuse in CETA put heavy pressure on members to support some cuts. Robert J. Cornell, D-Wis., observed in an interview that many members felt that "the way to show you're against abuse is to be against the program."

Even more threatening to CETA was criticism directed to more basic questions of how many public service workers to have, and how much to pay them. Conservatives, who have long argued that the job training aspects of CETA should be emphasized at the expense of public employment, were joined by some liberals who feared that the high wages paid to participants were making the program politically indefensible.

Bill manager Augustus F. Hawkins, D-Calif., said Aug. 10 that the bill had been delayed to allow additional lobbying in support of the program by local officials. He said further action on the bill before the recess would result in "individual members taking their feelings out on CETA and responding to their emotions," by approving gutting amendments.

Wage Limits. An amendment offered by David R. Obey, D-Wis., to impose more stringent limits on wages paid to CETA workers was adopted by a vote of 230-175.

Cosponsored by Budget Committee Chairman Robert N. Giaimo, D-Conn., Ronald A. Sarasin, R-Conn., and others, the Obey amendment limited CETA wages paid by the federal government to $10,000 a year per employee. The committee-approved bill had set the same maximum for most areas, but had allowed wages of up to $12,000 to be paid from CETA funds in high-wage regions.

For the high-wage areas, the Obey amendment did allow local governments to supplement the CETA wages with their own funds, up to a total of an additional 20 percent of wages, or $2,000. The committee bill allowed local governments to add 25 percent of their own money.

In effect, the Obey amendment set a $12,000 limit for high-wage areas and a $10,000 limit for the rest of the country, compared with the $15,000 and $12,500 limits backed by the committee.

The Obey amendment also cut, to $7,000 from $7,800, the required average annual wage of all CETA workers. It allowed the average to be indexed according to the consumer price index.

Obey argued that the amendment was needed to prevent even further cuts in the program by the Appropriations committees. "If the members think we have trouble in passing this bill, I invite them to watch the trouble we are going to have in funding the appropriations down the line," he said, warning that the House Appropriations Committee might approve an amendment to hold all CETA jobs to the minimum wage.

Supporters of the Obey amendment said high wage levels under the program had generated strong public opposition. Obey called CETA "the second most unpopular program in the country after welfare." Robert J. Lagomarsino, R-Calif., said the public "resents the high-paid public payroll jobs that are higher . . . than many jobs in the private sector." "It is much more attractive to be in this program than it is to be in the real world," Sarasin lamented.

Opponents of the Obey amendment predicted that it would make the program very difficult to operate in many areas of the country. That was because CETA workers have to be paid the same amount as regular government employees doing the same job. In some urban areas wages for even the lowest government jobs exceed the required average wage of the Obey amendment. Thus there would be no easy way to reach the $7,000 average. "In the high-cost areas of their country where we have a large number of poor unemployed, we are in fact going to be killing the CETA program," said Ted Weiss, D-N.Y.

Public Service Jobs. The other key change made by the House Aug. 9 was an amendment that reduced funding for public service jobs. The amendment, offered by James M. Jeffords, R-Vt., was approved 221-181.

The Jeffords amendment cut about $1 billion from Title VI jobs programs by placing a $3.2 billion cap on the authorization. If unemployment exceeded 6.5 percent, however, the amendment removed the cap.

In place of the $1 billion public service cut, the Jeffords amendment substituted $500 million in extra funding for youth employment and private sector programs: $350 million for Title IV youth programs, $50 million for the Title VIII Young Adult Conservation Corps and $100 million for the administration's new Title VII private sector program. Jeffords said the amendment would still allow for about the same number of jobs, since "you get almost twice as many total jobs in the youth area for the same number of dollars."

Jeffords told his colleagues that CETA priorities needed to be rearranged to meet the greatest need — unemployed young people. Although young people accounted for 50 percent of all unemployment, he said, they were the targets of only 20 percent of CETA funds.

Hawkins said the amendment would end up cutting 100,000 jobs without supplying their replacements for youth. He said the administration had testified that it already had enough money for youth programs and could not effectively use any more.

The complex issue of the use of CETA funds for payments to local government pension funds gave members a chance to vote against supplementing local budgets with money intended for job creation. After a complicated series of amendments, the House adopted an amendment by John N. Erlenborn, R-Ill., to ban use of CETA money for payments to retirement plans after 1979. The amendment was adopted 254-148.

John Krebs, D-Calif., proposed an amendment to the Erlenborn amendment that was the product of a compromise between bill sponsors, local government officials and public employee unions. Local governments didn't care if CETA funds were used, as long as they didn't have to make the contributions themselves; employee unions didn't worry about who paid, as long as benefits were paid for those likely to draw from the pension funds.

The Krebs amendment eliminated required contributions to retirement programs for CETA workers who were unlikely to benefit from the plans; local government thus would no longer be liable for payments. It allowed federal CETA money to be used if workers were likely to benefit.

But sentiment against use of CETA money for pensions was too strong for the exemption allowed by the Krebs amendment. John M. Ashbrook, R-Ohio, proposed an amendment to the Krebs amendment to strike the exception for those likely to benefit. It was adopted 209-194, after which the Krebs amendment was rejected by voice vote.

The Erlenborn amendment drew a distinction between payments for immediate benefits, such as health insurance and unemployment compensation, and the retirement plans. It exempted pension plans from the requirement that CETA workers get the same benefits as regular workers, thus absolving local governments from the need to make the payments, and prohibited use of federal funds for the payments beginning Jan. 1, 1980. It allowed payments for the immediate benefits.

Before adopting the Erlenborn amendment, the House rejected a Bill Goodling, R-Pa., amendment to give local governments the option of not paying unemployment insurance for CETA workers. The amendment was rejected 197-211.

The closest vote of the evening came on an amendment by Andrew Maguire, D-N.J., to tighten the rules for use of CETA funds to pay outside consultants for legal or "associated" services. The amendment, adopted 200-198, allowed such payments if the work could not have been done by local government employees or the Department of Labor, and the consultant charged a reasonable fee.

Senate Floor Action

The Senate Aug. 25 passed legislation extending a variety of jobs programs established under the Comprehensive Employment and Training Act (CETA) for four years, through fiscal 1982.

The measure (S 2570) was approved by the Senate by a 66-10 vote after adoption of numerous amendments, including one tightening eligibility requirements for public service jobs and another strengthening the Department of Labor's ability to prevent fraud in various CETA programs.

As a result of the amendments, and weeks of behind-the-scenes negotiations by key sponsors, S 2570 was passed with little of the criticism and angry debate that marked House floor consideration three weeks earlier and led sponsors to postpone a final vote on the House version (HR 12452) until after the Labor Day recess.

The chief sponsors of the measure, Gaylord Nelson, D-Wis., chairman of the Senate Human Resources Subcommittee on Employment, and Jacob K. Javits, R-N.Y., the subcommittee's ranking Republican, acknowledged that CETA has had its share of problems since it was established by Congress in 1973.

But both members argued that CETA has had considerable impact on reducing unemployment and training potential workers and said that with new safeguards written into S 2570 fraud and abuse would be sharply reduced.

Citing amendments added to give the Labor Department more power to crack down on widely publicized abuses of the program, Nelson declared, "This legislation will protect the integrity of CETA funds from fiscal mismanagement at the expense of both the public and those it is intended to assist."

Key Provisions. As passed by the Senate, S 2570 extended most of the jobs programs established under CETA for four years, through fiscal 1982. Several youth employment programs established under CETA were reauthorized for two years, through fiscal 1980.

The bill did not contain specific authorization ceilings for CETA programs, since levels of public service employment would vary with the rate of unemployment. Nelson estimated, however, that $11.4 billion would be expended in fiscal 1979, under the following distribution of funds: $3.1 billion for comprehensive employment and training programs; $1.9 billion for youth programs; $6.1 billion for public service jobs, and $326 million for the Job Corps.

Nelson estimated that in fiscal 1978 about $9.9 billion would be spent on CETA programs, including $2.5 billion on comprehensive employment and training, $1.2 billion on youth, $5.9 billion on public service jobs, and $320 million on the Job Corps.

The Senate-passed bill included two "major initiatives" sought by the Carter administration.

One authorized up to $400 million in fiscal 1979 for a program designed to increase private sector employment of low-income persons through on-the-job training. Under the program Private Industry Councils would be established by CETA state and local government "prime sponsors" to secure contract pledges from private employers to hire economically disadvantaged persons.

The second program would provide up to $200 million in fiscal 1979 to test two proposals — employment vouchers and employer incentive bonuses — offered as ways of getting welfare recipients off public assistance.

Fraud and Abuse. During floor debate, the Senate adopted two amendments designed to prevent fraud in CETA programs and provide the Labor Department with enough power to crack down quickly and effectively on violators. Both amendments were adopted with little debate and no opposition.

One amendment, sponsored by Pete V. Domenici, R-N.M., established a monitoring system in the department and extended criminal penalties already in the bill for CETA prime sponsors to contractors and subcontractors. The amendment included a provision establishing a division of monitoring and compliance within the office of the secretary of labor.

The Senate adopted the Domenici amendment by a 91-0 vote after adding a second section to the amendment, proposed by Edward W. Brooke, R-Mass., to establish an office of management assistance to enable the Labor Department to offer management and technical advice to prime sponsors where needed.

The second amendment, sponsored by Richard S. Schweiker, R-Pa., and adopted by voice vote, was designed to protect against abuses in the public service employment program, especially the problem of "substitution" of regular local government employees with CETA workers and other abuses such as kickbacks, political patronage and nepotism.

The Schweiker amendment gave the secretary of labor the power to suspend funding for a public service employment program accused of questionable use of CETA money until the problem was resolved. It also gave the secretary power to require reimbursement of misspent funds from monies other than those provided by CETA. The House, in its version of the reauthorization measure, adopted a similar provision during floor debate Aug. 9.

The Schweiker amendment was in addition to changes included in the bill by the Senate Human Resources Committee aimed at preventing substitution. The committee provisions expressly prohibited the hiring of a CETA participant when any other person is on layoff from the same or a substantially equivalent position, and required that CETA jobs must be in addition to those that would be funded by a state or municipality. The committee bill also placed time limitations on program participation, limitations on wages and supplementation, and restricted eligibility requirements for public service jobs.

Eligibility Requirements. During floor action the Senate also adopted an amendment, offered by Bellmon and endorsed by the sponsors of the bill, to further tighten eligibility requirements for public service jobs and place greater emphasis on providing jobs for welfare recipients.

Bellmon said his amendment would move the CETA program a "considerable way" in the direction pointed to in a major welfare bill (S 2777) that he and several other senators had sponsored in the Senate. *(See p. 91)*

The Bellmon amendment limited eligibility for Title II public service jobs, which are intended for the structurally unemployed, to persons receiving Aid to Families with Dependent Children (AFDC) or Supplemental Security Income (SSI) benefits, and persons unemployed 15 weeks or more whose family incomes do not exceed 70 percent of the Bureau of Labor Statistics lower living standard. As reported by the committee, S 2570 required 12 weeks minimum unemployment and did not make AFDC and SSI recipients automatically eligible for Title II jobs.

The amendment also revised eligibility requirements for Title VI public service jobs, which are intended to relieve countercyclical employment. The amendment required that persons eligible for the jobs would have to be unemployed for at least 10 of the previous 12 weeks and either have family incomes of less than 85 percent of the Bureau of Labor Statistics lower living standard, or be receiving SSI or AFDC benefits. The committee recommended only 45 days of unemployment and did not make AFDC and SSI recipients automatically eligible.

The Bellmon amendment also eliminated a provision that required Congress to appropriate at least $3 billion for public service jobs for the structurally unemployed under Title II of the bill before any money was appropriated for countercyclical jobs under Title VI. Bellmon said the amendment would leave Congress free to decide the levels and mix of structural and countercyclical public jobs and training programs in each year's appropriations process.

Other Amendments. Altogether, the Senate adopted 34 amendments and rejected one. Many of the amendments made technical changes in S 2570 and were designed to clarify provisions already incorporated in the bill by the committee. Several amendments mandated that specific studies of various employment-related issues be conducted, or specified ways for the Labor Department to reduce paperwork associated with the CETA program, or established certain reporting requirements for the Labor Department. ∎

Plan to Increase Aid to Cities Before Congress

President Carter's comprehensive urban aid package, proposed March 27, 1978, included a new financial aid program to assist "distressed" cities with $1.04 billion in fiscal 1979 and $1 billion in fiscal 1980. The new program was designed to replace a "countercyclical" revenue sharing program, enacted in 1976, extended in 1977, and due to expire on Sept. 30, 1978.

The countercyclical aid program channeled about $1 billion annually to *state and local* governments when the national unemployment rate exceeded six percent. The program proposed in 1978 by the Carter administration would eliminate that state and local government share and distribute the money to *cities* with high unemployment rates.

Because the states would lose money under the proposal, governors and state legislators opposed Carter's plan. On Aug. 2, 1978, the House Intergovernmental Relations Subcommittee voted to postpone indefinitely consideration of the proposal.

The Senate Finance Committee, however, adopted a compromise bill Aug. 10 that appeared to have a better chance of congressional approval than the proposal originally submitted by the Carter administration. The compromise would extend the existing countercyclical fiscal assistance program through fiscal 1980. The Senate committee bill authorized $650 million per year for fiscal 1979-80 for cities with high unemployment rates. The action raised the hopes of urban advocates that some form of financial aid to "distressed" cities would clear the 95th Congress.

House Speaker Thomas P. O'Neill Jr., D-Mass., said that supporters of the bill intended to tack it on to a House-passed measure.

In his March 27 message Carter urged replacing the existing Anti-Recession Fiscal Assistance program with a new program aimed at cities and towns suffering from long-term economic problems. The existing program, commonly known as countercyclical revenue sharing, was enacted over two vetoes by President Ford and extended in 1977 as a means of providing short-term financial relief to state and local governments suffering from the effects of the 1974-75 recession.

Changes in Existing Program

The Carter proposal would make several major changes in the current fiscal aid program.

State Exclusion. Under the plan, state governments would no longer receive the one-third share of funds they were receiving under the countercyclical program. In proposing that change, the administration argued that the financial condition of state governments had improved to the point where they no longer needed countercyclical dollars.

Dual Formula. The administration proposed altering the eligibility formula in order to "target" funds to the most "distressed" cities.

The countercyclical program went into action when the national unemployment rate rose above 6 percent. In order to receive money, cities must have unemployment rates above 4.5 percent.

The Carter plan proposed eliminating the 6 percent national "trigger" and leaving the 4.5 percent local unemployment rate as the main eligibility requirement.

In addition, the administration proposed an alternative formula, making it possible for governmental units also to qualify for aid if they had growth rates below the national average during the last five years in two of the following three categories: per capita income, population or employment.

In proposing the alternative formula, the administration argued that unemployment data was not reliable for small towns and rural areas. The second formula, the administration said, was designed to be "sensitive" to "distress" in those areas.

Aid Ceiling. The administration also proposed limiting the amount of money any city could receive under the program. The "cap" would be the amount of money a city received under the existing countercyclical program.

Congressional Action

Members picked apart the Carter proposal during hearings before the Senate Finance Subcommittee on Revenue Sharing May 3 and the House Subcommittee on Intergovernmental Relations May 4, 5 and 9.

Much of the criticism focused on whether the legislation submitted by the administration actually would target financial aid to the most distressed cities.

During questioning, administration witnesses said the number of cities and towns eligible for aid would increase from 16,000 under the countercyclical program to about 26,000 if the new fiscal assistance proposals were approved.

That increase troubled several lawmakers, including Rep. L. H. Fountain, D-N.C., chairman of the House subcommittee, who questioned whether 26,000 cities and towns really were "distressed."

Robert Carswell, deputy treasury secretary and the chief administration witness, said the 10 most financially distressed cities would receive about 24 percent of the money, and the 48 most distressed cities would receive about 33 percent. That distribution pattern, he said, corresponds to the distribution pattern under the current countercyclical program.

According to a study by the Treasury, the 10 most financially pressed cities are, in alphabetical order, Boston, Buffalo, Chicago, Cleveland, Detroit, New Orleans, New York, Newark, Philadelphia and St. Louis.

Formulas Challenged

The two eligibility formulas in the Carter bill also drew substantial criticism. Several members suggested that the minimum local unemployment rate should be raised from 4.5 percent to around 6 percent.

Sen. Edmund S. Muskie, D-Maine, the original sponsor of countercyclical aid legislation, took issue with the alternative eligibility formula proposed by the administration. Testifying before the Senate subcommittee, Muskie said expanding the number of eligible cities would lessen the impact of targeting efforts. Muskie said an analysis by his staff showed that under the Carter proposal many wealthy suburban communities would receive fiscal assistance. "I hope we can resist the ever-present temptation to spread the federal dollars around," Muskie said in opposing the second eligibility formula.

Carswell defended the proposal, arguing that "the diversity of communities is so great that you will never develop a formula without aberrations." He said some 66 wealthy communities would be eligible under the Carter proposal for aid but described that as a "statistical aberration." To mollify critics, Carswell said the administration was willing to amend the bill to prohibit aid to the wealthy communities.

Ceiling Criticized

Some members saw a contradiction between the administration's desire to target aid to the most distressed cities and its decision to establish a ceiling on the amount of aid any city could receive, with the "cap" set at current aid levels in the countercyclical program.

"How are these two things logically consistent?" asked Rep. John W. Wydler, R-N.Y., the ranking Republican on the House subcommittee.

Carswell cited budgetary concerns and a desire by the administration not to increase dependency on the federal government. There are policy decisions, he said, "that lead to results that are not consistent" with the overall policy goals.

After learning that New York City would not get any more money, Sen. Daniel Patrick Moynihan, D-N.Y., declared, "What it comes down to is you're going to get what you got."

House Committee Postponed Action

The House Intergovernmental Relations Subcommittee Aug. 2, 1978, voted 7-6 to postpone indefinitely consideration of HR 12293, the Carter administration's proposed Supplementary Fiscal Assistance Act.

The vote drew angry criticism from supporters of some form of financial help to cities with long-term economic programs.

Carter's proposal, which would distribute millions of dollars to many of the largest cities in the country — cities that have become dependent on current anti-recession funds to fill gaps in their budgets — was in trouble long before the subcommittee met Aug. 2 to mark up the measure.

In May 1978, Fountain, D-N.C., the subcommittee chairman, and several other members, attacked the methods used to decide whether cities were suffering from "distress" and the formula used to parcel out the money. Some members were irked by the fact that some wealthy suburban communities would receive money under the Carter proposal. Moreover, Fountain, a conservative lawmaker with a largely rural constituency, was never sympathetic to urban fiscal aid.

Finally, while the subcommittee did have some members who supported urban aid, it did not have any members whose districts included large cities in deep fiscal trouble.

The motion to postpone consideration of HR 12293 was made by Elliott H. Levitas, D-Ga. Joining Levitas on the 7-6 vote were Fountain; Don Fuqua, D-Fla.; Glenn English, D-Okla.; John E. Cunningham, R-Wash.; Clarence J. Brown, R-Ohio; and Jack Brooks, D-Texas. Voting against the motion were Les Aspin, D-Wis.; Wydler; Frank Horton, R-N.Y.; Henry A. Waxman, D-Calif.; John W. Jenrette Jr., D-S.C.; and Michael T. Blouin, D-Iowa.

Wydler maintained after the voting that the issue wasn't dead. "As far as I'm concerned this matter is not settled," he said, hinting that he might attempt to tack the proposal on to another bill as a floor amendment.

Administration officials also pledged to carry the fight to the Senate, where an identical measure (S 2975) was pending in the Senate Finance Committee. Their strategy, they indicated would be to attach a fiscal aid bill to another measure, retain the provision during conference, and win final support on the House floor.

Senate Committee Action

The Senate Finance Committee, prodded by chairman Russell B. Long, D-La., approved a compromise bill Aug. 10.

The bill would extend the existing anti-recession fiscal assistance program through fiscal 1980 with some key modifications, but it would not pump as much money into "distressed" cities as the Carter proposal would. The total cost of the compromise for fiscal 1979-80 was $350 million less per year than in the Carter plan.

The Finance Committee compromise had greater appeal to members of Congress from the Sun Belt states of the South and West. Their votes could be crucial in getting the measure passed by the Senate and House.

Although the Finance Committee proposal differed from the Carter bill in several important respects, administration spokesmen nonetheless were backing it. "The administration is very pleased with the compromise," said Roger C. Altman, assistant treasury secretary for domestic finance.

The nation's mayors, many of whose cities have become dependent on anti-recession aid, were also pleased.

"We're fully in support of the compromise," declared Detroit Mayor Coleman Young, who led a delegation of mayors in a major lobbying effort two days before the Finance Committee acted.

The Finance Committee compromise (HR 2825) would continue the existing anti-recession fiscal assistance program (commonly known as countercyclical revenue sharing) for two years, through fiscal 1980, retaining the basic premise of the program — to provide cities with short-term financial help to buffer against reduced revenues caused by economic recessions.

The funding would also remain the same. As long as national unemployment was 6 percent or more, money would be parceled out to states and cities that had unemployment above 4.5 percent. The program would provide $125 million per quarter plus an additional $30 million for each tenth of a percentage point unemployment is above 6 percent. The actual amount of aid would be computed on the basis of a state or city's general revenue sharing allocation and the degree of unemployment above 4.5 percent.

The Senate proposal would make one change. Unemployment figures for two quarters, rather than for one, would be used in computing the national unemployment rate. Thus, unemployment would have to fall below 6 percent for two consecutive quarters (6 months) for the aid to

Public Works Jobs Another Part of Stimulus Plan

In addition to revisions in the countercyclical aid program, Carter in 1978 proposed revamping the public works projects program, calling for spending $3 billion — $1 billion each in fiscal 1979, 1980 and 1981 — for so-called "soft" public works projects. The Carter plan represented a major overhaul of the public works jobs programs enacted by Congress in 1976 and extended and expanded in 1977.

The 1976 law was part of a three-pronged stimulative package that channeled $2 billion to state and local governments for public works construction. Also included in the law was the $1.25 billion countercyclical aid measure as well as $700 million in additional funding for wastewater treatment plant construction.

The anti-recession assistance program took shape in 1975 as Congress prepared its own proposals for stimulating the economy out of recession through increased federal spending. Responding to Ford's opposition to any new spending initiatives, House Democratic leaders in March 1975 unveiled a $5-billion proposal for increased spending on state and local public works projects as part of a package of emergency economic legislation fashioned by an ad hoc leadership task force headed by Rep. Jim Wright, D-Texas. The Democratic plan was supported by organized labor and local government officials.

The House approved the $5 billion measure in May 1975. The Senate approved a scaled-down public works measure that was combined with the countercyclical aid program in July. Conferees in December agreed to cut public works funding to $2.5 billion.

1976 Vetoes

Those 1975 deliberations set the stage for crucial 1976 veto battles between President Ford and Congress over the stimulative public works/countercyclical aid package. The president won the first fight, but Congress was successful the second time around.

The House adopted the conference report on Jan. 29, 1976. On Feb. 13, Ford vetoed the measure, calling it "little more than an election year pork barrel." Instead of the 600,000 jobs that Democrats contended the program would create, Ford argued that the legislation would produce at most 250,000 jobs whose costs would be "intolerably high, probably in excess of $25,000." The president also criticized the countercyclical aid program.

The House Feb. 19 voted 319-98 to override the veto — 41 votes more than the required two-thirds majority. Less than three hours later, however, the Senate sustained the veto in a 63-35 roll call that fell three votes short of the required two-thirds.

However, the Senate resurrected the vetoed bill in April, paring the total authorizations down somewhat to a maximum of $5.3 billion for all programs, including $2.5 billion for public works projects. The House passed its version of the bill in May. The conference agreement, reached on June 9, included, in addition to the countercyclical aid program, a $2 billion authorization for public works projects through Sept. 30, 1977, for three types of grants on which on-site labor could begin within 90 days of project approval: 1) direct grants providing full federal

funding for state and local public works projects or the completion of plans for such projects, 2) grants to bring the federal share of financing up to 100 percent for projects already authorized by federal law that had not begun because of lack of required state and local matching funds and 3) grants to cover either the state or local share of projects authorized under state or local law.

Ford vetoed the package on July 6, arguing that "bad policy is bad whether the inflation price tag is $4 billion or $6 billion." The president estimated that the second conference bill would create 160,000 jobs at most, compared to congressional projections of 300,000 to 350,000 jobs.

But this time Congress was prepared to shrug off the president's opposition. The Senate voted to override the veto July 21, 73-24. The House confirmed the override with 39 votes to spare in a 310-96 vote on July 22.

1977 Action

In submitting his stimulus package to Congress in January 1977, President Carter called for, among other things, an additional $2 billion for public works jobs in fiscal 1977. He called for an additional $2 billion for public works jobs in fiscal 1978.

Congress completed action May 3, 1977, on the first component of Carter's economic stimulus package, legislation (HR 11 — PL 95-28) authorizing an additional $4 billion for an emergency public works jobs program.

Final action came when the House approved a compromise version of the bill by a 335-77 vote. The Senate had approved the measure April 29 by a 71-14 vote.

The emergency public works jobs program, provided $2 billion in grants to state and local governments for a variety of quick-starting construction projects. Each $1 billion spent under the program was expected to create between 40,000 and 75,000 jobs, primarily in building and construction trades.

In addition to boosting the authorization for public works jobs, HR 11 significantly revised the existing program, to ensure that funds would reach communities with high rates of unemployment and severe economic problems. Because of a large backlog of projects denied funding in 1976, only applications already on file with the Commerce Department were eligible for a share of the funds made available by HR 11.

Although HR 11 had been passed by the House Feb. 24 and the Senate March 10, conference action on the bill was delayed by a dispute over an unrelated Senate amendment providing $9 billion for sewage treatment plant construction. The House refused to consider interim funding for the water treatment activities unless coupled with substantive revisions in the water pollution program. A Senate-House conference committee ultimately dropped the water pollution amendments, thus freeing the jobs bill.

In addition to increasing to $6 billion, from the existing level of $2 billion, the total authorization for the public works program, the bill allocated 65 percent of funds to states on the basis of absolute numbers of unemployed, while reserving the remaining 35 percent for states with unemployment rates above 6.5 percent.

stop flowing. That change was designed to give the program more stability by preventing the aid spigot from shutting off every time the unemployment rate dropped slightly below 6 percent for one or two months at a time.

The Senate compromise contained a second section designed to keep aid flowing to states and cities with higher unemployment rates once the national rate drops below 6 percent. The second program would keep aid flowing to those states and cities with unemployment rates above 4.5 percent as long as the national rate was between 5 and 6 percent. States would get one-third of the money available under the program, although they could not receive more than they received under the existing program. Initially, $125 million per quarter was to be authorized for the second program. But a change in the formula adopted by the committee would probably increase that amount from $500 million for fiscal 1979 to $650 million for the fiscal year.

The compromise bill is somewhat different from the measure proposed by the Carter administration. For one thing, the administration sought to remove the "national trigger" from the program, allowing cities and towns to continue receiving aid as long as their unemployment rates were above 4.5 percent.

But drafters of the compromise — including Sens. William D. Hathaway and Edmund S. Muskie, both Maine Democrats — wanted to preserve the "countercyclical" nature of the program and thus insisted that a national trigger be retained.

Despite initial opposition by the administration, state governments will also continue to receive money under the Senate compromise. The administration bill removed state governments from the aid program on the grounds that for the most part state governments had budget surpluses and did not need continued aid. The National Governors Association disputed the administration's contention, and lobbied vigorously to remain in the program.

As it turned out, the governors won. One Senate staff aide who did much of the actual drafting said state governments were kept in the program in order to ensure their political support in getting the measure through Congress.

Background: Countercyclical Aid

In July 1976, the Democratic-controlled Congress overrode President Ford's veto of a $3.95 billion public works jobs bill (S 3201—PL 94-369). In February, a Ford veto of a similar bill had been sustained. Included in the bill was $1.25 billion for "countercyclical" grants to help state and local government maintain services.

The bill's supporters, including labor and state and local groups, argued that it would relieve problems almost untouched by general economic improvement. They pointed to strained state and local budgets and persistent high unemployment in the construction industry.

But Ford argued in his July 6 veto message that the bill was an unproductive and inflationary way to create jobs. He maintained that the legislation would have little immediate effect on unemployment problems.

Congress overrode the veto, however, with the help of a substantial number of Republicans, who deserted the president's position. They included Senate Assistant Minority Leader Robert P. Griffin, R-Mich., who cited continuing unemployment problems in his home state. One lobbyist supporting an override suggested that Griffin had been

The Bottom Line

Senate Finance Committee Chairman Russell B. Long, D-La., lectured the administration on the fundamentals of political decision-making during hearings on President Carter's fiscal aid bill.

Under questioning by Long, Deputy Treasury Secretary Robert Carswell said the administration had not yet prepared data showing how much money would go to each state under the bill. Long's reply:

"It seems to me that frankly, Mr. Carswell, that most of these senators will vote for or against a formula by just looking at how their state makes out . . . how much money they do get or do not get. . . . All you have to do is show a senator a sheet of paper, here is how your state makes out under this formula. . . .

"The chairman of the subcommittee would like to know how his state would make out and the chairman of the full committee would like to know how his state would make out, and I would think that you would be prepared to answer those $64,000 questions.

". . .Is that not the bottom line? Look, if I try to explain to my folks back home, it is easy enough to explain why you are voting for it if they get more money. That is easy enough. If your state gets less money, you have more explaining to do."

under heavy pressure from Detroit business and other groups to back the bill.

Provisions of 1976 Act

Following are major provisions of the 1976 act authorizing grants to state and local governments:

● Authorized the Treasury secretary to make grants for five calendar quarters (beginning July 1, 1976) to help state and local governments maintain services, avert layoffs of public service employees and avoid tax increases.

● For each quarter, authorized payments totaling $125-million plus $62.5 million for each .5 percent by which the national unemployment rate for the quarter ending three months earlier exceeded 6 percent; authorized no funds if the national unemployment rate did not exceed 6 percent during the quarter that ended three months earlier or the last month of that quarter.

● Limited the aggregate authorization for the five calendar quarters beginning July 1, 1976, to $1.25-billion.

● Reserved one-third of available funds for grants to state governments and two-thirds for grants to local governments including counties.

● Barred grants to any state or local government unless its own average unemployment rate for the quarter ending three months earlier was at least 4.5 percent and its rate during the last month of that quarter exceeded 4.5 percent.

● Based the amount of a grant to a state on a formula comparing its fiscal 1976 general revenue-sharing funds and its "excess" unemployment rate (the difference between its existing rate and a 4.5 percent rate) to similar data for all states.

● Based the amount of a grant to a local government on an identical formula.

● Required the secretary to set aside one lump sum for grants to local governments within states for which verified unemployment data was not available; allowed the states to allocate these funds under a plan submitted to the secretary.

• Allowed state and local governments to use the grants to maintain customary basic services; barred use of funds for construction or acquisition of materials unless needed to maintain services.

• Required governments to submit statements providing assurances that funds would be used to maintain public employment levels and basic services; required governments to comply with federal labor standards and anti-discrimination requirements in the use of funds.

• Required governments to notify the secretary of any increase or decrease in their taxes, reductions in public employment levels or cuts in services.

• Authorized the secretary, after a hearing, to withhold grants from governments that did not comply substantially with the requirements of the act.

• Required the General Accounting Office to investigate the impact of the grants on state and local government operations and the national economy.

1977 Extension

Congress May 16, 1977, cleared legislation extending and expanding an emergency program of "countercyclical" grants to state and local governments, after the House decisively defeated a move to make major changes in this element of President Carter's economic stimulus package.

The countercyclical aid extension was included in a bill (HR 3477 — PL 95-30) containing the remains of the administration's tax stimulus proposal.

The final version of HR 3477 incorporated provisions of a separate countercyclical aid bill (HR 6810) which the House had passed by a 243-94 vote May 13.

The final version extended the program for an additional year, through fiscal 1978, authorizing a maximum of $2.25-billion for the five quarters beginning July 1, 1977. A supplemental appropriations bill (HR 4876 — PL 95-29), cleared May 5, provided an extra $632.5-million in countercyclical aid for fiscal 1977.

The administration initially requested a five-year extension of the program, through fiscal 1982, with an annual authorization of $2.25-billion. As under the existing program, funds would be "triggered" only when the national unemployment rate exceeded 6 percent. The administration also sought an additional $925-million for the program in fiscal 1977, along with certain changes in the funding formula intended to make the program more sensitive to fluctuations in the unemployment rate.

But the proposal quickly encountered resistance in the House Government Operations Committee, which had attempted to kill the original program in the 94th Congress as well. Though he agreed to introduce the administration's bill, Committee Chairman Jack Brooks, D-Texas, continued to attack the countercyclical aid program as a thinly disguised version of general revenue sharing, which he also opposed. Subcommittee hearings in March produced some evidence of delays and other difficulties with the existing program, further stiffening the opposition.

At the urging of Sen. Edmund S. Muskie, D-Maine, the program's original sponsor in the 94th Congress, the Senate April 29 attached to HR 3477 provisions reauthorizing the countercyclical aid program through fiscal 1978 (Sept. 30, 1978). By this time, the administration had abandoned hope for a longer extension.

In addition to administration backing, the program had strong support from state and local government officials, the AFL-CIO and unions representing public employees.

Provisions of 1977 Act. As signed into law May 23, 1977, the countercyclical aid provisions of HR 3477 (PL 95-30):

• Extended the countercyclical aid program for an additional year, through fiscal 1978.

• Authorized up to $2.25-billion for the program for the five-quarter period beginning July 1, 1977.

• Revised the funding formula, effective July 1, 1977, to authorize $125-million per quarter when the national unemployment rate reached 6 percent, with an additional $30 million per quarter for each .1 percentage point increase in the unemployment rate above 6 percent.

• Made technical improvements in the allocation formula to use the most recent general revenue sharing data and modified the computation of applicable unemployment rates for rural areas and small communities.

• Reserved 1 percent of program funds for Puerto Rico, Guam, the Virgin Islands and American Samoa.

• Applied to the countercyclical aid program the same prohibitions against discrimination required under the general revenue sharing program. ∎

Congress Approves New York Guarantees

The scheduled expiration on June 30, 1978, of a patchwork agreement that saved New York City from bankruptcy in 1975 set off an intense squeeze play in 1978 over the city's financial future. The key issue was whether federal assistance to the city should be continued.

Participants in the drama included the Carter administration, a sharply divided Congress, New York City and state government, the city's municipal employees' unions, banks, and city and state pension funds.

Most New York officials, as well as the banks and pension funds that could supply the money to keep the city solvent, argued that continued federal aid was a prerequisite for any new financial arrangement.

The Carter administration said it was inclined to agree, but Congress, which was split on the issue during the city's 1975 financial crisis, appeared even more hesitant in early 1978. Despite congressional misgivings, however, Congress once again rescued New York from municipal bankruptcy. By an unexpectedly large margin of 247 to 155, the House on June 8 approved legislation to provide the city with federal loan guarantees of up to $2 billion on city bonds. One week later, on June 15, the Senate Banking, Housing and Urban Affairs Committee approved a measure similar to the House bill by a vote of 12 to 3, despite the opposition of the panel's chairman, William Proxmire, D-Wis. On June 29, the full Senate approved the aid measure by a vote of 53-27. The Senate version was less generous than the House-passed bill. The Senate-approved bill would provide $1.5 billion in guarantees.

House-Senate conferees July 13 reached a compromise providing $1.65 billion in federal loan guarantees. The House passed the bill July 25, by a vote of 244-157, the Senate July 27, by a vote of 58-35.

Background

New York City's financial problems first became a national issue in March 1975, when the city suddenly found itself unable to raise money on the municipal bond market. Subsequent investigation showed, however, that the difficulties began long before that.

Ever since 1960, the city's revenues had been inadequate to meet its rising expenditures. It made up the shortfall through borrowing, and also by using a variety of accounting "gimmicks" that masked the true extent of the city's indebtedness until the problem had grown so large that it could no longer be concealed.

In part, the city's financial weakness resulted from problems familiar to many cities. Its tax base had steadily eroded due to the flight of businesses and affluent taxpayers to the suburbs or other parts of the country, and at the same time the portion of its population most dependent on government services — the aged and disadvantaged — had increased.

In addition, the city provided some of the most extensive public services of any American city. While some have argued that those services were unduly extensive, others have suggested that they were reasonable for a jurisdiction the size of New York.

The fiscal problem was exacerbated by the recession of 1974-1975, during which New York's economy-sensitive income and sales taxes dropped substantially even while the demand for welfare and other social services increased. The result was that the city's annual operating deficit climbed higher and higher.

In 1975, the city had borrowing needs totaling $8 billion, but it was unable to sell any bonds because investor confidence in the city had hit a new low. That raised the danger the city would default on its loans.

The 1975 Solution

Over a period of months in 1975, city, state and federal officials quilted a short-term solution to keep the city solvent.

In June 1975, the state legislature established the Municipal Assistance Corp. (MAC), a state agency authorized to borrow funds to continue essential services in the city. The MAC bonds were to be backed by city-related state tax collections and by state aid payments to the city. Part of the law setting up the new agency required that the city balance its budget in three years — with the exception of about $600 million in expenses that were being funded by the city's capital budget.

In September 1975, another state law was passed requiring the city to develop a three-year financial plan and establishing the Emergency Financial Control Board to supervise the city's financial affairs.

Still later, officials put together a special financing package, which culminated in congressional enactment of the New York City Seasonal Financing Act (PL 94-143), under which the federal government agreed to extend up to $2.3 billion a year in short-term loans to the city.

The act, which caused considerable controversy before winning congressional approval, required the secretary of the treasury to determine that the loans could be repaid during the year they were borrowed before extending them. It also required that the city pay interest on the loans one percentage point higher than the interest rate at which the treasury borrowed money for them.

Other parts of the city's financing package included a virtual freeze on wages for municipal workers; a pledge by city employee pension funds to extend $2.5 billion in loans through June 30, 1978, to meet the city's long-term financing needs; an $800 million annual advance in state aid payments to the city in each fiscal year; and a state law ordering a three-year moratorium on repayment of $2.4 billion in short-term city notes and reducing the interest rate on the notes.

The moratorium was declared unconstitutional in late 1976 by the New York State Court of Appeals, forcing MAC to issue additional bonds to raise money to pay off those loans.

Experience Since 1975

By most accounts, the city has made substantial financial improvements since the 1975 crisis. In testimony before the Senate Committee on Banking, Housing and Urban Affairs on Dec. 14, 1977, Treasury Secretary W. Michael Blumenthal praised the city for taking the following actions to correct its fiscal plight:

● Reducing its work force by more than 60,000 jobs, to a new level of 300,000.

● Negotiating the wage freeze for city workers.

● Eliminating the city's operating deficit.

● Converting $4 billion in short-term notes into long-term MAC bonds.

● Requiring for the first time that students attending city colleges pay tuition. The city also increased its mass transit fares.

● Implementing a $16 million management information and expense control system to improve the city's fiscal controls.

Blumenthal reported that the city had borrowed substantial sums under the seasonal loan program, and that it had repaid each loan with interest on time or ahead of schedule. During the city's fiscal 1976 year (July 1, 1975-June 30, 1976) it borrowed $1.26 billion. In fiscal 1977 it borrowed $2.1 billion, and in fiscal 1978 it borrowed $2 billion, the treasury secretary said.

The seasonal loans have produced a profit to the federal treasury of about $30 million.

Blumenthal told the lawmakers that the Treasury Department increased pressure on the city during the 1978 fiscal year to try to find private sources of money rather than rely on the federal loans. That pressure resulted in an attempt by the city in November 1977 to sell between $200 million and $400 million in six-month notes. The effort collapsed, however, when Moody's Investors Service gave the note issue its lowest rating. Moody's agreed that the city was likely to pay off the note issue on time, but it judged the city's financial condition to be "so precarious as not to preclude the possibility of bankruptcy in future years."

The poor rating prompted the issue's underwriters to pull out, leaving New York still shut off from the municipal bond market.

The Situation in 1978

Despite its progress, New York City in 1978 was far from being financially healthy. While the budget is balanced according to state law, considerable sums of expense money were still buried in the capital budget. In addition, the city projected that its revenue shortfall would be $457 million in fiscal 1979, $704 million in fiscal 1980, $903 million in fiscal 1981 and $954 million in fiscal 1982.

Koch's Proposal

On Jan. 20, 1978, 20 days after he took office, newly elected New York City Mayor Edward I. Koch unveiled what he called a "candid and realistic" four-year plan to restore the city to financial health.

The mayor proposed reducing the city's workforce by an additional 20,000 jobs over the four years, and he suggested a series of management improvements and purchase reductions to save $174 million in the coming fiscal year.

He said that would leave a $283 million gap to be filled by state and federal aid.

The key element in Koch's strategy included a proposal to continue the seasonal loan program, at decreasing levels, and to begin a new federal and state loan guarantee program.

He proposed that the city be allowed to borrow up to $1.2 billion under the seasonal loan program in fiscal 1979. The borrowing ceiling would drop to $800 million in fiscal 1980, to $400 million in fiscal 1981 and be phased out entirely thereafter.

Under the loan guarantee program, the federal government would guarantee 90 per cent of the value of long-term bonds up to $2.25 billion. The state of New York would guarantee 10 per cent of the value of the bonds, and it would set aside a $225 million contingency fund to back up its guarantee. Koch said the bonds would be sold to New York city and state pension systems.

Senate Opposition

Even before the new proposal was made, strong opposition to any continuation of federal aid to the city had arisen in the Senate.

In a letter to President Carter on Dec. 23, 1977, Senate Banking Committee Chairman William Proxmire, D-Wis., and the committee's ranking minority member, Edward W. Brooke, R-Mass., came out in opposition to extending aid to the city beyond June 1978.

That message was repeated in even stronger terms in a report unanimously endorsed by Proxmire's committee on Feb. 10 (S Rept 95-635).

The report suggested that the city no longer faced the danger of bankruptcy, and it said that continuing federal aid when the immediate crisis was over might encourage other cities to look for federal aid. That, in turn, would "weaken the incentive for fiscal discipline at the local level and erode the foundations of our federal system."

The committee was even more opposed to federal loan guarantees, arguing that they would "greatly increase the federal government's financial exposure, while severely limiting its ability to safeguard its investment through the types of controls that are presently available."

The committee argued in its report that the economic situation in both the city and the nation had improved since 1975. As a result, the city should be in a better position to take care of itself. Even if it was not, the impact of a city bankruptcy would be more "circumscribed" in 1978, because the municipal bond market had stabilized and other cities were in better shape, the report concluded.

The senators backed their assessment of the city's financial situation in some detail. First, they disputed Mayor Koch's contention that the city needs $5.1 billion in long-term financing over the next four years. They said that $1.6 billion of that sum, while desirable, was not essential to avoid bankruptcy, and thus need not be raised immediately.

The city's long-term financing plan called for about $800 million in new long-term bonds to be sold to replace some costly high-interest short-term bonds. The senators said that could wait.

The city plan also called for $800 million in new bonds to take the place of the annual advance payment the city was receiving from the state. The senators agreed that "bonding out" that sum would be appropriate at some point. But they argued that the advance should be continued in the short-run because it was a guaranteed source of funds for the city. Moreover, they noted that replacing the advance payment would benefit primarily the state of

New York at just the time that the state should be increasing its commitment to the city.

The Senate committee made further recommendations for how the city could raise the remaining $3.5 billion to meet its "basic capital needs" in the next four years.

The city pension systems, the report said, could supply $2.25 billion without increasing their fiscal 1978 commitment by agreeing to reinvestment of $941 million in maturing bonds and investing $1.3 billion — or 35 per cent — of new investable funds.

The pension systems in 1978 had about 35 per cent of their assets in New York City paper — almost all of it invested since the fiscal crisis began in 1975.

The committee suggested that the Municipal Assistance Corp. (MAC) could raise the remaining $1.25 billion to meet the city's long-term capital needs.

The committee further suggested that the city could reduce its needs for $1.8 billion in seasonal financing — money needed for short periods each year prior to collection of taxes and state and federal aid — by $400 million, and that the remaining sum could be acquired from financial institutions, and city and state pension funds since the risk involved in such short-term loans is relatively small.

House Response

House leaders generally were more supportive of the city than the Senate committee was. Banking Committee Chairman Henry S. Reuss, D-Wis., and the chairman of the committee's Economic Stabilization Subcommittee, William S. Moorhead, D-Pa., said that a preliminary investigation by their staff supported the city's request for more aid.

But, conceding the considerable power of Proxmire on the New York City question in the Senate, they said they would not force House members to face the political difficulties of voting on the controversial issue unless there was a good chance the Senate committee would allow a vote in that chamber.

In the meantime, Moorhead began hearings in his subcommittee to build the case that further aid was needed to prevent a city bankruptcy and to avoid disruption of urban bond markets and possibly the economy in general.

House Hearings

Lead-off witnesses at the hearing on Feb. 21, 1978, included Felix G. Rohatyn, chairman of MAC; New York Comptroller Harrison J. Goldin, and Jack Bigel, a municipal union pension consultant.

Rohatyn said the Senate committee plan was "unworkable" because financial institutions and the union pension systems would refuse to buy city bonds without continued federal credit assistance. He said the Senate plan achieved the "appearance of plausibility" by cutting the city's long-term financing requirements by $1.6 billion, but he argued that the city would be unable to re-enter capital markets as long as the lack of that money prevented it from demonstrating "capability to truly balance its budget recurringly."

Goldin and Rohatyn both warned that refusal by the federal government to assist the city could result in bankruptcy. The comptroller noted that the city had met all the "milestones" imposed by the 1975 solution, but he said the city needed long-term help to become truly solvent.

"Without continued federal credit assistance it is not possible to put together a workable financing plan," Rohatyn said. "The risk of bankruptcy in that event is obvious-

ly of a very high order. . . . We have proposed a plan which avoids this risk at no cost to the federal government."

The two officials were supported by Bigel, who said that union pension systems could not afford the risk of buying more city bonds unless the bonds were guaranteed by the government. "Our veins are clogged [with city paper]," he said, adding that any pension trustee who agreed to buy city notes without a guarantee "ought to be prepared to go to jail."

The state pension system in early 1978 held no city bonds, and its trustee, Arthur Leavitt, said Feb. 22 he would not buy any without an ironclad federal guarantee.

Carter Administration Support

The Carter administration on March 2 came out in support of continued federal assistance to New York City, although it proposed less aid than the city had requested.

In testimony before the Economic Stabilization Subcommittee of the House Banking Committee, Treasury Secretary Blumenthal asked for standby authority to provide federal loan guarantees for up to $2 billion in city or MAC securities for as long as 15 years. The securities would be sold to city and state employee pension funds.

The secretary rejected New York's request for a continuation of the federal seasonal loan program, however.

As a condition to the aid program, Blumenthal said the guarantees would be secured by federal transfer payments to the city and by a New York State special reserve account or pledge of federal transfer payments. He also said he would insist that private lenders buy unguaranteed loans, that the city balance its budget by 1982 and that the state continue to monitor the city's finances.

Estimating the city's four-year capital needs to be $4.5 billion, Blumenthal said refusing federal aid wouldn't be worth the risk of bankruptcy.

"New York City in bankruptcy will prove far more expensive to this nation — both in expense and personal sacrifice — than any modest form of assistance," he said.

Legislative Action

House Passage of Aid Bill

House passage of legislation (HR 12426) allowing for federal loan guarantees for New York City by a vote of 247-155 on June 8 was in part the result of a series of interrelated developments in New York City and the New York State Legislature in Albany.

With Proxmire, Blumenthal and New York Gov. Hugh L. Carey all applying pressure, the city, its labor unions and the financial community put together several key elements of a new financial plan for preventing a city bankruptcy.

The federal loan guarantees were seen by city officials as the cornerstone of that plan. Under the bill approved by the House, the secretary of the treasury would be authorized to issue guarantees totaling $2 billion (including principal and interest) for up to 15 years on city bonds. The guaranteed bonds would be sold to city and state pension funds.

Other elements of the financial plan included:

● A pledge by banks, savings and loan institutions and insurance companies to buy $1 billion in unguaranteed long-term city bonds. That commitment has been made, subject to several conditions, including congressional approval of the guarantee bill.

● Passage by the New York State legislature of a bill expanding the borrowing authority of the state-created Municipal Assistance Corp. (MAC) to $8.8 billion from $5.8 billion. MAC has helped raise money for the city since the financial crisis of 1975. The legislature approved the bill May 26.

● Passage by the state legislature of a bill continuing the existence of the Emergency Financial Control Board, which has supervised city financial affairs. The extension, demanded by the financial institutions, Treasury Department and the House-passed bill, was approved by the state legislature along with the MAC expansion.

● Agreement on a contract involving the city and its 200,000-member coalition of municipal labor unions. After the direct intervention of Carey, an agreement was reached June 5.

None of those pieces of the financial plan were put together easily.

New York Mayor Edward I. Koch initially insisted on a labor contract that would cost the city only $610 million. In addition, he demanded that the Emergency Financial Control Board retain the power to veto labor contracts awarded by impasse panels or arbitrators, and he proposed that the panel lose many of its powers over the city's finances after seven years.

City labor unions demanded a larger contract and they strenuously objected to the veto power of the emergency fiscal board over contracts. The financial institutions, on the other hand, threatened to withdraw from the financial arrangement if the legislature weakened the control board.

The final compromises left no one entirely happy. The labor contract — which provided 4 per cent pay raises annually for two years — had a price tag of $757 million. The Emergency Financial Control Board lost its veto power over labor contracts, but the new law prevented arbitrators from granting wage increases unless they find that the city can pay for them. The law also authorized the control board to intervene in arbitration to argue against wage settlements it considers beyond the city's ability to pay.

HR 12426 had been reported by the House Banking, Finance and Urban Affairs Committee May 10 and the Ways and Means Committee May 22 (H Rept 95-1129).

Senate Hearings

Meanwhile, on June 6, the Senate Banking, Housing and Urban Affairs Committee finally opened long-delayed hearings on the issue. The hearings produced some additional encouraging signs for the city. Relaxing his opposition to continued aid a bit, committee chairman Proxmire said that he would keep an "open mind" on the matter even though he was still "leaning" against it.

Nonetheless, Proxmire questioned the financing arrangement on several grounds. He said the city could make more substantial spending reductions, called the banks' pledge to buy city bonds "pitifully inadequate," disputed whether city and state pension funds would be so "callous and indifferent" as to refuse to buy city bonds unless they were guaranteed, and — though agreeing that the city wage settlement was "modest" in view of inflation and other labor contracts — suggested that the "cruel" reality was that the city's workers would have to suffer for the city's insolvency.

The Senate Banking Committee chairman also complained that Koch had failed to win a demand that the municipal labor unions "give back" a variety of fringe benefits that have swollen labor costs, and he said that New York State government "hasn't done enough."

Proxmire also raised the possibility that, rather than provide federal loan guarantees, Congress might be wiser merely to continue the existing seasonal loan program. In support of that suggestion, he cited a letter from former Federal Reserve Board Chairman Arthur F. Burns. Burns warned that the city would face the real danger of going bankrupt without federal aid — a risk he said was too great to take because it would "seriously interrupt" essential services in the city, set off an exodus of people and business from the city that would inflict permanent economic damage, increase interest rates on all municipal bonds, weaken public confidence in the ability of government to handle financial matters, and diminish international confidence in the United States economy.

But Burns called the loan guarantee proposal "a radical departure from the principles of fiscal federalism." He said long-term federal involvement in local affairs could eventually result in city and state governments "withering away," and he warned that the guarantee program might prompt other cities to seek similar aid.

As an alternative, Burns recommended extending the seasonal loan program for three years at diminishing levels each year. Proxmire said the idea was worthy of careful consideration, especially since it would put more pressure on the city to control its finances.

City officials bluntly warned that an extension of the seasonal loan program wouldn't solve their problems.

"Without long-term financing, the city's physical plant — its infrastructure — will continue to deteriorate, economic development will be stifled and the city will stumble from crisis to crisis with no permanent solution in sight," Koch said.

Senate Action

In what its chairman called a "remarkable turnaround," the Senate Banking Committee on June 15 approved legislation (S 2892 — S Rept 95-952) to provide up to $1.5 billion in federal loan guarantees for New York City bonds.

The 12-3 vote was a major victory for New York aid supporters, who predicted that final congressional approval and a resulting rescue of the city from bankruptcy were virtually assured.

The apparent reversal was attributed to several factors, including some last-minute lobbying by President Carter and Vice President Mondale, the decision by several uncommitted senators — most notably Richard G. Lugar, R-Ind. — to support an aid package, and a number of restrictions the committee agreed to place on the aid bill.

Under the bill approved by the committee, the secretary of the treasury would have the authority to guarantee city bonds in the following amounts: $500 million in fiscal year 1979, $500 million in 1980, $250 million in 1981 and $250 million in 1982.

The final installment would be available to the city only if it balances its budget according to generally accepted accounting principles — something the city was committed to do anyway.

Senate-House Comparison. Significant differences between the Senate committee's bill and the legislation (HR 12426) previously approved by the House included:

● The $1.5 billion ceiling on the amount of guarantees. City officials and the Carter administration had requested a $2 billion ceiling, excluding interest. The House voted to include interest in the $2 billion figure. Since the Senate committee's bill excluded interest, the actual difference between it and the House bill was about $300 million.

● A provision limiting the guarantees to long-term bonds (those maturing after one year or more). The House bill would allow guarantees on short-term or long-term bonds.

● A limitation on the last $500 million in guarantee authority to 10-year bonds. The House bill would allow 15-year guarantees, while the Senate committee voted to allow guarantees up to 15 years on only the first $1 billion.

● A provision requiring the city to use at least 15 per cent of the proceeds from any public bond sales after June 30, 1982, to retire guaranteed bonds.

● A provision allowing either the House or the Senate to veto loan guarantees for New York City in either fiscal years 1980 or 1981.

● A provision requiring the state of New York or an agency of the state to set up a special fund equal to at least 5 per cent of the amount of the bonds guaranteed as "co-insurance" to be used to pay guaranteed bond-holders in the event of default.

City Reaction. City officials were generally pleased with the committee action, although some of the amendments caused them some concern. While they planned to use only $1 billion of the guarantee authority, they said they preferred the larger amount provided by the House bill.

They also noted that the shorter life of the last $500 million in guarantees would increase interest costs, and that the possible one-house veto would substantially increase the risks associated with buying guaranteed bonds.

Senate Passage. The Senate approved the New York City aid legislation June 29 by a 53-27 vote. The lawmakers rejected four amendments before passing the bill exactly as reported by the Senate Banking Committee.

Conference Action

The House-Senate conference committee hammered out an agreement on HR 12426 on July 13, after two previous meetings had failed to produce an accord. The conference report was filed July 18 (H Rept. 95-1369).

Besides differing on the amount of loans to be guaranteed (the House wanted $2 billion, including principal and interest; the Senate wanted $1.5 billion in principal only), conferees differed over the extent to which Congress should supervise the program.

Proxmire argued that extending federal guarantees to both seasonal and long-term borrowing would in effect "give the city more" than it got in the expired seasonal financing act. He also argued that private lending institutions in New York City should be called on to make more unguaranteed loans, and he noted that there would be "very little risk" to them in making short-term loans to cover the city's seasonal borrowing needs.

House members, on the other hand, warned that putting too many restrictions on the federal aid could scare away potential investors and defeat the goal of saving the city from bankruptcy.

"We are perilously close to passing a bill that will make sure not only that New York City doesn't make it, but that you and I will have egg on our faces," Rep. Stewart B. McKinney, R-Conn., warned Proxmire.

Congressional approval of the guarantee program reflected a belief that the city had made significant strides in putting its fiscal house in order, that the original seasonal

loan program was inadequate to solve the city's long-term problems, and that the guarantee program was preferable to taking the risk of allowing the economic and social disruption that might result from a New York City bankruptcy.

Still, supporters and critics of the measure were quick to assert that the new program would be the last time the federal government would come to the aid of New York City. In addition, arguing that the program caused an unfortunate federal involvement in local affairs, they said the bill would not serve as a precedent for other cities.

Partly to discourage other cities from seeking such help, Congress added to the program a number of conditions. They included requirements for annual audits of city books, a spacing out of the guarantee authority over four years coupled with a provision allowing either branch of Congress to veto guarantees in the second and third years, a provision allowing the guarantees only for bonds purchased by city and state employee pension funds, a requirement that the state of New York and private lending institutions participate in the city's financial plan, and a requirement that the state underwrite at least 5 per cent of the guaranteed bonds.

Even with those requirements, city officials hailed the bill, expressing confidence that it would enable New York City to regain its fiscal health.

Final Provisions

In its final form, HR 12426:

● Authorized the secretary of the treasury to issue federal loan guarantees totaling up to $1.65 billion for as long as 15 years on New York City bonds.

● Required the secretary to determine, as a precondition to issuing the guarantees, that the city cannot obtain enough credit from public credit markets.

● Required the secretary to determine that the city had a financial plan, involving commitments from New York State and private lenders, so that it could avoid bankruptcy if federal guarantees were provided.

● Limited the amount that could be guaranteed during fiscal year 1979 to $750 million. Of that total, guarantees up to $500 million could be extended to long-term city bonds (maturing in one year or more), and guarantees up to $325 million could be extended to seasonal loans (maturing after one year or less) to the city.

● Limited loan guarantees during fiscal year 1980 to $250 million, plus any unused or repaid amount from the sum authorized for fiscal year 1979. Only long-term bonds could be guaranteed during the year.

● Limited loan guarantees during fiscal year 1981 to $325 million, plus any unused or repaid amount from the sum authorized for fiscal years 1979 and 1980. Only long-term bonds could qualify.

● Limited loan guarantees during fiscal year 1982 to $325 million, plus any unused or repaid amount from the sum authorized for fiscal years 1979, 1980 and 1981. Only long-term bonds could qualify.

● Restricted federal loan guarantees only to bonds purchased and held by New York City and state pension funds.

● Provided that either the House or the Senate could unilaterally veto proposed guarantees during fiscal years 1980 and 1981.

● Terminated the secretary's authority to issue guarantees on June 30, 1982.

● Required the city to pay an annual guarantee fee equal to 0.5 per cent of the principal amount of the bonds guaranteed.

● Required the city to balance its operating expenditures and revenues during fiscal years 1979, 1980 and 1981.

● Required the city to have a budget balanced according to generally accepted accounting principles by fiscal year 1982.

● Required the city to attempt to sell short-term bonds to the public during fiscal years 1980, 1981 and 1982, and to attempt to sell long-term bonds to the public during fiscal years 1981 and 1982, unless the secretary finds such activity against the financial interests of the city.

● Required the city to submit to annual audits of its financial affairs by an independent audit committee.

● Required the city to establish a productivity council to develop ways of making city workers more productive.

● Required New York State to maintain at least its fiscal 1979 level of financial aid to New York City. ∎

Congress Reacts to California "Tax Revolt"

The approval June 6, 1978, by California voters of Proposition 13, a state constitutional amendment sharply reducing property taxes, rekindled a debate in Congress over federal spending and tax policies in 1978.

"The mood of Washington these days can be summed up in two words — Proposition 13," observed Senate Budget Committee Chairman Edmund S. Muskie, D-Maine, summarizing the way the California decision had become woven into the fabric of politics in Washington, denounced by some, and praised by many — although for very different reasons.

Few observers expected the California vote to lead to changes as dramatic in other states, or in Washington, as they were in California, where the voters slashed real estate taxes by almost 60 percent — about $7 billion — in one stroke. *(Provisions, p. 57)*

That was partly because the Proposition 13 movement had some characteristics peculiar to California. But it was also because lawmakers in Washington did not fully agree on what the national implications of the vote were.

In general, Proposition 13 was considered likely to reinforce a trend toward some restraint in spending. But beyond that, there was considerable disagreement over the best way to address the frustrations expressed in the 2-to-1 vote in support of the tax limitation initiative.

Some viewed the vote as an attack on the size of government itself. They insisted on substantial spending reductions, regardless of the effect on government services. But others predicting a backlash in California when voters there realized the extent to which Proposition 13 would reduce services, argued that the real message of the vote was that government must find ways to provide services more efficiently so that taxpayers would get more for their tax dollar.

Congress was even more divided over the federal tax implications of the Proposition 13 vote. Some have depicted it as a demand for lower federal taxes. But others believed it was mainly a reaction to inflation, which they argued could be worsened by large tax cuts that would swell the federal deficit.

Moreover, some viewed the vote as part of a broad-based tax revolt, while others saw it mainly as a reaction to California's unusually high property taxes. Behind that difference in interpretation lay a sharp disagreement among members of Congress on which federal taxes, if any, should be reduced.

"The reaction to Proposition 13 is in the eyes of the beholder," concluded John Shannon, assistant director of the Advisory Commission on Intergovernmental Relations (ACIR), an organization that monitors federal, state and local fiscal affairs.

Long-Term Trends

To the extent that Proposition 13 reflects a national reaction against rising government spending and taxes, there was some justification for it.

Federal spending has climbed steadily from about 18.7 percent of gross national product (GNP) in 1958 to an estimated 22.6 percent in 1978. Federal taxes have climbed as well. While they only surpassed 20 percent of GNP twice since 1958 — in 1969 and 1970 — they have been rising rapidly since 1976. In 1976, they comprised 18.4 percent of GNP, climbing to 19.4 percent in 1977 and to an estimated 19.6 percent in 1978.

State and local spending and taxes also have jumped significantly. Spending rose from 8.2 percent of GNP in 1959 (excluding federal aid) to 11.5 percent in 1974, although it dropped to an estimated 10.6 percent in 1977. State and local taxes, in the meantime, have risen from 7.25 percent of GNP in 1960 to 9.66 percent in 1976, according to the ACIR.

There were some signs that trend could be slowing. President Carter, for instance, pledged to bring federal expenditures down to about 21 percent of GNP. There also were signs of moderation on the state and local level, according to Shannon. He attributed the change to the fact that some of the pressures that rapidly increased expenditures there have eased somewhat. Education costs, for instance, were expected to decline as the school age population falls relative to the rest of the population.

A Harbinger?

The Proposition 13 vote has been depicted as the harbinger of tax limitation proposals in other states. *(Survey of state action, p. 57)*

To a certain extent, Shannon said, that could be true. But there were five major factors that contributed to the California vote that were unlikely to combine to produce so dramatic an outcome elsewhere, he said.

The first factor peculiar to California is that the state government there had accumulated a $5 billion surplus. That, according to Shannon, angered some voters who thought the money was being hoarded in Sacramento, and it also encouraged voters to support the property tax limitation scheme on the grounds that the state surplus could help cushion the impact.

Second, Shannon said, the Proposition 13 vote was prompted at least in part by the fact that California had an unusually high property tax burden, which had been rising at an exceptionally rapid rate. In 1943, the property tax in California was below the national average, consuming about 3.3 percent of residents' income. In 1976, however, it had climbed to 6.4 percent of income, a level 42 percent above the national average.

Third, the state and local tax burden in California was exceptionally high. Shannon estimated that it was about 20 percent above the national average.

Fourth, California had one of the easiest systems for initiative proposals in the country. In most states it would be much more difficult to enact constitutional amendments limiting taxes.

Finally, Shannon noted, residential property values had been climbing at very rapid rates in California. To

House Reaction to Taxpayer Revolt Pressures . . .

Just in case Carter administration officials missed the big news about the California taxpayer revolt, the House of Representatives relayed its version of the message to them in May 1978.

In a series of votes on appropriations bills, the House went on record in favor of forcing administration spending cuts in the fiscal 1979 budgets of dozens of federal programs. The tax revolt in California was one justification scalpel-wielding members gave for their support of the cuts.

Those votes let House members take credit for opposing big spending. But since the votes approved across-the-board cuts in the agencies' controllable spending, they left it up to the administration to answer the tough questions of exactly how the cuts would be made.

Thus House members avoided taking the heat from the numerous special interest groups that would be hurt when — and if — the administration must decide what to cut. By mid-1978, the Senate had not acted on the appropriations bills the House voted to cut.

"It's a chicken way to do things," said Edward W. Pattison, D-N.Y., an opponent of the sweeping cuts approved by the House. Pattison said the headlines about the California revolt created a "firestorm" in the House that showed its members were "much too responsive" to what was essentially a local issue.

Proposition 13

The California revolt involved the state's overwhelming vote June 6 in favor of Proposition 13, a plan to reduce the state's property tax rates. It also forced reductions in spending by the state government, but did not address federal taxes or how they are spent.

However, Proposition 13 quickly became the number one topic of conversation in Washington after its almost 2-to-1 passage on the West Coast. Many felt the vote had a symbolic message for all politicians — not just those in California. Members of the House, anxious not to appear unresponsive in an election year, immediately began responding to the "message" that had been aimed at California officials.

The House "response" — some called it Proposition 13 fever — concentrated on the annual appropriations bills for fiscal 1979, which set in law the amount of money federal agencies will get to fund each of their programs. In the week following the California vote, the House approved amendments to four appropriations bills calling for across-the-board cuts totaling about $803 million in spending for dozens of federal programs.

The bills and amounts cut by the across-the-board amendments were: Labor-Health, Education and Welfare ($380 million); State, Justice and Commerce ($172 million); public works ($206 million) and legislative appropriations ($45 million).

Several members said the House had shown signs of a developing anti-spending mood prior to Proposition 13. For instance, the Democratic leadership had to struggle in early May to narrowly prevent House adoption of several cuts in fiscal 1979 budget targets.

But many members agreed that the mood grew stronger after passage of Proposition 13. Most of the across-the-board cuts approved by the House were proposed by Clarence E. Miller, R-Ohio, who drew little support when he offered similar proposals in previous years.

One opponent of the cuts, Parren J. Mitchell, D-Md., attributed the mood to political fear. "The House has reacted almost blindly to Proposition 13," he said.

Just after the House passed the third of the four across-the-board cuts, Mitchell facetiously suggested some of his colleagues might need psychiatric care. "The situation in California has been a traumatic experience for many of us," he told the House. Mitchell prescribed "psychiatric services" for House members "to sort of cushion the psychological impact."

Meat Ax

Critics of Miller's across-the-board amendments call them the "meat ax approach" because they do not try to pick out specific programs that are the most wasteful or poorly run. "They penalize everyone for the sins of a few programs," said Bob Carr, D-Mich.

Carr described voting for across-the-board cuts as "what a politician does when he's chicken and doesn't want to go on record as opposing a particular cut."

Carr voted for some of the across-the-board cuts. But he described his action as a "last resort" attempt to reduce federal spending, after he had voted to cut specific programs he found wasteful. When those specific cuts were rejected by the House, those who wanted to register their "cost consciousness" were "left with no alternative" to the across-the-board cuts, Carr said.

One of the specific cuts Carr supported was an amendment offered by Robert W. Edgar, D-Pa., to kill funding for eight water projects in the public works bill. While Carr supported both Edgar's specific cut proposal and an across-the-board cut proposed for public works spending, more than a dozen of his colleagues opposed Edgar but supported the across-the-board cut.

make the resulting climb in taxes even more painful, the state had a better-than-average assessment system. "I just can't see all those things playing out in other states," he concluded.

Shannon did predict, however, that other states would enact limitations on spending and taxes. But he said a more common pattern would be to limit spending or tax growth to the rate of growth of the state economy — much as Tennessee has done. That would slow growth, but it wouldn't have the same sharp impact Proposition 13 has had.

Federal Reaction

Confirming Shannon's observations, both Democrats and Republicans claimed to be in step with Proposition 13.

Some liberals, such as Sen. George McGovern, D-S.D., expressed sympathy with the "frustrated" voters of California. But McGovern denounced a "degrading hedonism" implicit in the Proposition 13 vote, and he criticized politicians for becoming "instant economizers and flailing taxcutters" in response to the vote, rather than calling for "dynamic

...Leaves Tough Choices to the Administration

Avoiding specific cuts in favor of the across-the-board approach misleads the public, Pattison said. The 2 percent cut the House approved in the public works bill could force the administration to reduce fiscal 1979 spending on the eight water projects Edgar failed to kill and other items. But it would not save any money in the long run, Pattison said, because the House eventually would appropriate money to finish all projects in the bill.

Liberal Support

Several young, liberal Democrats who supported across-the-board cuts against the wishes of their party leaders echoed Carr's judgment that the amendments were a "last resort."

Phil Sharp, D-Ind., said congressional attempts to cut specific programs are usually unsuccessful because the special interest groups who benefit from them put pressure on members to keep up — or increase — the spending. "It's so hard for us to say 'no' . . . to individual programs," said Sharp, a consistent supporter of the across-the-board cuts.

Leon E. Panetta, D-Calif., a former director of HEW's Office of Civil Rights, said most federal agencies would sustain a 2 percent budget cut with minimal damage. Although he said cuts ideally should be made in specific programs after study by congressional committees, he defended his support of several floor amendments to cut across-the-board as "the only way you're going to get [spending] reductions."

Miller, chief sponsor of all but one of the across-the-board cuts approved by the House, agreed with his Democratic colleagues that scrutinizing individual programs for waste and inefficiency was the ideal way to cut spending.

But since Congress often funds federal programs for political reasons that have little to do with their merit or efficiency, Miller said he resorted to the across-the-board proposals. His amendments would not affect "fixed" programs, such as Social Security benefits established by law, but they would require federal agencies to come up with overall reductions in their flexible programs.

In the first 11 years he offered across-the-board cut amendments to appropriations bills, Miller succeeded only once. The amendments, which drew little support, were regarded as more symbolic than serious. "People never took Miller seriously in the past," said Carr.

But by mid-1978, Miller had succeeded in getting House approval of cuts in three bills, come close on several others, and lost a vote on the legislative appropriations bill

when the House decided it wanted a bigger cut than Miller had proposed.

Inflation Worries

Miller credited Proposition 13 with his success in 1978. But he agreed with others that the House had already begun to move in the direction of fiscal conservatism. He said the move — speeded up by what House members thought was the "message" of the California vote — had been prompted by increasing public unhappiness with high inflation and federal spending.

Miller also gained support in 1978 by scaling down his amendments. In previous years, his proposals called for 5 percent across-the-board cuts. In 1978, they all called for 2 percent cuts.

"It would be pretty hard to find any program, good or bad, that doesn't have at least 2 percent waste in it," said Carr, who acknowledged that he had been persuaded to vote for some of Miller's amendments in 1978 in part because they were scaled down.

After three successes, Miller's amendments began to lose. Miller credited the Democratic leadership with the defeat of four across-the-board cut proposals. Democratic leaders noticeably stepped up efforts to oppose Miller after the Republican's initial victories. For instance, when Miller appeared to have won on an amendment to cut the agriculture appropriations bill by 2 percent, the leadership went to work twisting arms until enough members had switched their votes to defeat Miller, 189-201.

Other factors both helped and hindered Miller. For instance, bad publicity about fraud and abuse in HEW programs increased sympathy for cutting that department's huge budget, several members said.

On the other hand, the House voted down a Miller amendment to cut the Housing and Urban Development Department appropriations bill partly because it also contained funding for veterans' programs, agreed some members. "That's a sacred cow in Congress," Sharp said.

Miller planned to offer his 2 percent across-the-board cut amendments to the remaining fiscal 1979 appropriations bills for foreign aid, defense and the District of Columbia. Some members were skeptical that any House-approved cuts would survive in the Senate, which is traditionally more sympathetic to many of the programs the House votes would affect.

But with California taxpayers still fresh in many minds, no one was willing to predict whether the Senate would uphold its traditions or succumb to the House's Proposition 13 fever.

government" unafraid to set important goals and to persist in their achievement.

"Today the fault for the heavy burden of unfair taxes rests not on liberal programs, but on needless war, a reckless arms race and an unjust tax system designed and continued by selfish special interests," McGovern said.

But for every liberal who argued that the answer to Proposition 13 was not to turn back on liberal programs, there was at least one conservative politician arguing just that.

Rep. Charles Thone, a Republican from Nebraska, related the outcry against property taxes to dissatisfaction with the welfare system. "The taxpayer mutiny now arising across America is most of all a revolt against the nation's welfare mess," he declared.

Referring to President Carter's welfare reform proposal, Thone added: "If the president wants to get in tune with the voters, he'd better withdraw that disaster and come back with a plan to make deep cuts both in the number of those on welfare and the billions it costs."

Limits to Government

One of the attitudes most criticized by activists such as McGovern was the belief, accentuated by the Proposition 13 vote, that government is limited in what it can do.

Muskie agreed that such a "negative" response was the predominant reaction to the California vote. "Fiscal conservatives cry gleefully that the battle lines have been drawn — that the public oracle has spoken, and free-spending politicians are on the run," Muskie said. "At the other end of the spectrum, some liberals are saying that the California vote has ominous overtones — that it signals a retreat from our long-standing promise to help those at the bottom of the economic ladder."

The Senate budget leader said the two interpretations were essentially the same, the only difference being that one side was "pleased," and the other "dismayed."

Muskie offered an alternative, "positive" interpretation. "People know government has a job to do, and they want it done well — with as little waste as possible, and with the maximum result," he said. "In effect, they told their elected leaders they want the fat in government eliminated before they agree to pay anymore."

The answer, Muskie said, is not to enact "willy-nilly cuts in spending across the board — cuts which erode not just the fat but the muscle of government as well." Instead, he argued, a complete re-examination of government programs was needed, one that would result in the ineffective programs being weeded out.

"So far [in mid-1978], neither Washington nor the public has come to grips with this sobering choice," Muskie concluded. "For that choice runs directly against the grain of a bad habit we've developed over the years — a habit of trying to please everybody, by spreading federal dollars around."

The Spending Debate

Looking at more immediate congressional issues, Senate Majority Leader Robert C. Byrd, D-W.Va., said the budget resolution setting spending targets for the fiscal year beginning in October 1978 proved that Congress was showing fiscal restraint.

The resolution, adopted before the Proposition 13 vote, called for federal outlays totaling $498.8 billion and revenues totaling $447.9 billion — enough to allow a $19.4 billion tax cut beginning Jan. 1, 1979. The $50.9 billion deficit envisioned in that 1979 fiscal year plan was almost $10 billion less than proposed by President Carter in January 1978.

That represented an increase of 10 percent over the estimated spending level for the fiscal year, as opposed to a 15 percent rise in fiscal 1978, 9.9 percent in 1977, 12.1 percent in 1976, 20.9 percent in 1975, 9.1 percent in 1974 and 6.5 percent in 1973.

The growth rate would have been even less, except that federal agencies were unable to spend all the money that Congress appropriated for fiscal year 1978. If spending had been up to the allowed level, the budget target for fiscal 1979 would be only a 7.9 percent increase.

"I think Congress has been ahead of Proposition 13," Byrd said. He interpreted the California vote as "not so much a protest against taxes as against paying more and getting less. The message they're sending is: 'We want greater efficiency. We want a dollar's worth of services for a dollar's worth of taxes.'"

Republicans disagreed. House Minority Leader John J. Rhodes, R-Ariz., criticized the Democratic-controlled Congress for rejecting a Republican amendment to the budget resolution that would have cut spending to $488.3 billion. The budget resolution, Rhodes said, was "the same old Democratic medicine — spend and spend, tax and tax."

A Federal Spending Limit?

Some proposals have been made, partly in response to the Proposition 13 vote, to place a clamp on the growth of federal spending. A variety of proposals were thrown in the 1978 legislative hopper, for instance, to require a balanced federal budget. Some were sent to the House Judiciary Committee because they would provide for a constitutional amendment requiring balanced budgets.

Despite efforts by supporters — most notably Bill Archer, R-Texas — to force hearings on the issue, the balanced budget proposals were given little chance of being enacted in 1978.

Besides the difficulty Congress would have in cutting spending or raising taxes enough to erase a federal deficit in the $50 billion range, the balanced budget proposals could have such a dramatic economic impact that they could cause a recession, many economists warn.

Finally, there was little consensus even among proponents of a balanced budget about the level of spending and taxing at which balance should be achieved.

In mid-1978, Rep. Philip M. Crane, R-Ill., introduced an alternative proposal (H J Res 985) to put a lid on federal spending. He would limit spending to 33.3 percent of the average national income of the previous three years. With national spending estimated in 1979 to be 34.5 percent of the national income, the Crane proposal would require a budget of about $482.4 billion — about $17 billion below the level tentatively approved by Congress in May 1978.

Short of those proposals, Congress was likely to consider more recommendations for across-the-board cuts in appropriations bills, much like four measures already approved by mid-1978 by the House.

Proponents argued that the across-the-board cuts reflected a desire by Congress to reduce the size of government. But others suggested that they demonstrated a lack of determination.

If Congress really had the will to reduce federal spending, they argued, it would specify where the cuts should be made, rather than leaving it to the administration to implement the cuts and take the political heat. They also suggested that across-the-board cuts were less likely to be permanent than cuts that resulted from actual policy changes ordered by Congress.

Still, the across-the-board cut method had some respected advocates in Congress. One such cut, proposed during consideration of the first fiscal 1979 budget resolution, fell only eight votes short of being approved.

But the across-the-board cutting approach was far from universally accepted, even among Republicans.

"I don't like across-the-board cuts," said Rep. Barber B. Conable Jr., R-N.Y. "They are not a very artistic way of exercising legislative discretion. They actually leave discretion to the president."

Conable also noted that across-the-board cuts fail to take into consideration the fact that some programs, such as entitlement programs, cannot be cut — a fact that means an across-the-board cut will actually result in larger cuts in controllable spending programs.

Efforts to Reform the Property Tax

The property tax is perhaps the least popular of all taxes. In a 1977 poll conducted by the Advisory Commission on Intergovernmental Relations 33 percent of the people questioned said their property taxes were unfair. Economists and taxpayers across the country agree that the system is badly in need of reform. Discontent over assessment practices and rising taxes has been the focus of political debate, not only in California, but in several other states as well. In such cities as Philadelphia property tax relief has emerged as a national "grassroots" issue.

Taxes on property — chiefly on real estate — are the principal sources of local revenues for such essential services as public schools and police protection. They accounted for 81 percent of the $67.5 billion that local governments throughout America collected from taxpayers in 1976, according to Census Bureau figures. Property taxes rose from a yearly average of $168 per person in 1970 to $242 in 1975, the bureau further reported. As a national average, the share of personal income taken by these taxes has also been increasing. The Conference Board, an independent economics research organization, estimated that in 1977 the major state and local taxes (income, sales and property) siphoned off 9 percent of Americans' income; federal taxes took about 14 percent.

Although protests against property taxes have become a familiar feature of the American scene, local governments have rarely been in a position to push for tax cuts. But since 1970, most states have passed laws enabling municipal jurisdictions to reduce residential taxes. And local budget surpluses — in some cases the result of increased federal revenue sharing — have made tax reductions inevitable. Urban experts said that New York City's widely publicized battle against bankruptcy averted attention from the fact that many municipal treasuries were fatter than they had been in years.

Lingering Inequities Despite 'Reforms'

Critics of property taxation argue that the spate of tax cuts and other "reform measures" have disguised existing tax inequities without correcting them. Rates and standards for assessing property vary from region to region, state to state and district to district. Taxes in the South and Midwest, for example, are generally lower than in the Northeast and West. In addition, there are often great differences between the taxes imposed on inner city residents and suburbanites. People living in Baltimore, Md., Newark, N.J., and Rochester, N.Y., pay taxes that run as much as 53 percent higher than those in nearby suburbs, while in other metropolitan areas such as San Francisco, New York and Washington, D.C., suburban taxes exceed those in the central city.

Rate differences frequently are cited as the most troublesome vagary of the existing system. But tax experts have identified a host of other property-tax problems: the regressive nature of the tax itself, the existence of too many exemptions, and the penalty it places on individuals who maintain and improve their property. Several remedies have been proposed. One is to establish tax-rate ceilings. Another — supported by the National

Association of Realtors — is to increase state sales taxes as an alternative to raising property levies. Other special-interest groups have argued that the burden could be lightened if certain services now paid for by local taxes were shifted to the states.

Yet "none of this tinkering and jiggering reaches to the heart of the trouble with property taxes," economist Guerney Breckenfeld has written in the spring 1978 *Journal of the Institute for Socioeconomic Studies.* "Most communities levy two or three times as much tax on structures as on the value of a site, by the convenient device of appraising the value of a structure at two or three times that of the land and then...applying the same tax rate to both. [The result] is a system that rewards land speculation and discourages the construction of new buildings and the proper maintenance of aging ones."

Approaches to Equalizing the Tax Burdens

Most economists agree that the rise in property taxes can be traced to the growth in local government spending. As the necessity to generate funds to pay for new programs has increased, inflation-induced gains in property values have provided a ready source of added tax revenue. The resulting jump in property taxes has been particularly hard on the elderly and other persons whose incomes have not kept pace with the rate of inflation. The U.S. Census Bureau reported in *Census of Governments* (1977) that between 1970 and 1975 the average cost of housing in the United States rose one and a half times faster than the owners' incomes.

Despite outcries from some angry taxpayers that property taxation should be abandoned, local governments are not likely to give up the practice. Under mounting pressure to reform the tax system, however, many jurisdictions have taken steps to make the property levy more progressive — more in line with the owner's ability to pay.

Some economic theorists view property taxes along with estate and gift taxes, as a levy on wealth. Yet because the local property tax is considered a deduction for federal income tax purposes, wealthy taxpayers often are able to escape its full impact. The homeowner taking the standard deduction does not have that advantage.

What has been viewed as a more promising type of tax relief is the "homestead exemption." Like the standard deduction for federal income tax, it exempts certain amounts of property from taxation. As of mid-1978, 39 states had enacted laws that exempt amounts ranging from $1,000 in Indiana to $20,000 in Hawaii. In Montana, qualified homeowners receive a 50 percent reduction on the assessed value of their property. In New Jersey those eligible for benefits received a credit on their tax bills.

Homestead exemptions are selectively applied. For this reason, most reformers generally regard so-called "circuit breaker" provisions as the best form of tax relief. First used in Wisconsin in 1964 and in effect in 23 states by 1978, circuit breakers guarantee that property taxes will not go beyond a fixed percentage of household income. This is done by (1) establishing a tax limit in relation to income, or (2) providing a tax rebate for each qualified taxpayer in a specific income group.

Tax Implications

The tax implications of Proposition 13 were even more obscure than the spending implications.

Probably the most enthusiastic of reactions to the California vote came from Sen. William V. Roth Jr., R-Del. He was the sponsor, along with Rep. Jack F. Kemp, R-N.Y., of a bill (S 1860, HR 8333) to reduce individual income tax rates to 45 percent from 48 percent, and to increase the floor for the maximum corporate rate to $100,000 from $50,000.

"The results from California prove beyond doubt that we are no longer on the verge of a taxpayers' revolt — we are in the midst of one," Roth said. "With California, an entire state has gone on record as recognizing taxpayers as an endangered species."

At least one liberal California legislator disagreed. Rep. Fortney H. "Pete" Stark, D-Calif., said the Proposition 13 vote resulted from a situation peculiar to California. "Very clearly, the vote in California signified a frustration by the voters with the governor and the legislature for failing to deal with the property tax problem," Stark said.

Roth and Kemp argued that their bill was needed to provide relief to beleaguered taxpayers — especially those in the middle income ranges. While some estimated that the bill would reduce federal revenues by as much as $80 billion, they also contended that it would encourage people to work harder, firms to invest more and the economy to grow more so that it would actually increase federal revenues.

Democrats were unimpressed with those claims. House Speaker Thomas P. O'Neill Jr., D-Mass., called the bill "a fraud," referring to Kemp as "a pretty boy with a lousy bill."

In the meantime, while Roth and Kemp argued for a larger tax reduction, there was considerable pressure from the business community for a smaller one in order to fight inflation. In response, President Carter scaled back his original request for a $25 billion tax cut effective Oct. 1 to $19.4 billion effective Jan. 1, 1979. Carter and the Democratic House leaders discussed a further reduction — to $15 billion — as a possible compromise with Ways and Means Committee members.

Negotiations over the size of the tax cut were inextricably bound up with the debate over tax reform. Carter hoped to be able to implement a larger tax cut by convincing Congress to pass revenue-raising reforms. But, by mid-1978, the reforms appeared all but dead. The House on Aug. 10, by a vote of 362-49, rejected the administration's bill and approved a $16.3 billion tax cut.

"Most people don't view tax reform as the president does, as the closing of loopholes, but as tax relief," Conable said.

Finally, in addition to the debate over the fiscal 1979 budget and tax policies, the Proposition 13 vote sparked renewed discussion about the process by which Congress sets fiscal policies. Some lawmakers, agreeing with Muskie's assertion that ways must be found to cut the "fat" but not the "muscle" out of government programs, argued that Congress needed to strengthen procedures by which it sets spending priorities and monitors the effectiveness of government programs.

To that end, Rep. Leon E. Panetta, D-Calif., proposed that Congress begin adopting biennial budgets. Under his plan (HR 9077), Congress would spend one year adopting the budget, and the next year it would work in "oversight."

On a somewhat more partisan level, Reps. Clair W. Burgener, R-Calif., and Marjorie S. Holt, R-Md., introduced legislation (HR 12345) that would require Congress to adopt overall spending and tax goals, or "aggregates," before approving totals for specific subsections.

Proponents of that approach argued that it would force Congress to consider overall economic policies, rather than just adding up spending totals to adopt an overall budget. Critics of the proposal claimed that it was an essentially political move designed to force lawmakers to take the politically embarrassing move of going on record voting for deficits that were inevitable in any case. ∎

States Vie to Curb Taxes, Spending

Call it a "taxpayers' revolt." Or the string of events "in the wake of Proposition 13." Whatever one labeled it, there was a growing tax-relief movement in the states which seemed to have gained impetus from California voters' approval June 6 of a state constitutional amendment that cut property taxes drastically.

Proposition 13, or the Jarvis-Gann initiative — named for its authors and chief proponents Howard Jarvis and Paul Gann — took effect July 1, 1978. Its provisions:

● Limited property tax collections by local governments to 1 percent of "full cash value" — 1975-76 assessments.

● Limited increases in assessments to 2 percent each year; allowed reassessments only when property is sold.

● Required a two-thirds vote of both houses of the legislature to levy any new taxes to increase revenue.

● Prohibited local governments from imposing any new property taxes, and required two-thirds voter approval for other new local taxes.

The effect was an estimated 57 percent decrease in property tax rates statewide, and a tax savings of between $5 and $7 billion for California residents. Governor Edmund G. Brown Jr., D, who opposed the proposition, agreed to work with the legislature to implement it.

Meanwhile, in other states many legislatures were considering or had approved measures to limit state spending, cut taxes, or shift the tax burden by creating new levies or increasing old ones.

Change on the federal level also could be brought about by the 1978 "revolt." By mid-year at least 22 states had called for a constitutional convention to adopt a constitutional amendment requiring a balanced federal budget.

Following is a summary of what was happening in the states in mid-1978. Those marked by an asterisk (*) have petitioned Congress to call a constitutional convention.

*Alabama: Governor's proposals for property tax relief and repeal of the state utility tax did not pass the legislature in the 1978 session. A special session might be called to consider a constitutional amendment putting a 20 percent lid on county tax increases. If passed, it would be put before voters in November 1978.

Alaska: Three tax-reduction petition drives were gathering support, and a state legislator predicted a "tax revolution." But there were not enough signatures for a vote in 1978 to amend statutes.

*Arizona: The legislature passed a constitutional amendment limiting tax revenue to 7 percent of personal income in the state. The proposal will be on the November ballot. Consideration was given to calling a special session to freeze property assessments. Two proposed amendments similar to Proposition 13 were pending.

Arkansas: A constitutional amendment sponsored by an initiative drive was expected on the November ballot. The proposal would eliminate sales taxes on food and drugs. The state legislature, which meets biennially, also might consider a comprehensive tax reform proposed by a citizens' advisory group when it convenes in January 1979.

California: The Jarvis-Gann initiative, Proposition 13, received overwhelming voter approval in June.

*Colorado: Two petition drives seek constitutional amendments. One that seemed near success proposes state

and local government spending limits equal to statewide cost-of-living increases. If qualified, the proposal would be on a November ballot. The other, which would limit property taxes, appeared unlikely to gather sufficient signatures. Colorado's legislature in 1977 voted a 7 percent hold on spending increases, and several tax relief proposals have been introduced.

Connecticut: A Connecticut taxpayers' association was working to influence the legislature to pass constitutional amendments that would provide for the initiative and referendum, create state and local spending ceilings, and prohibit passage of a broad-based personal income tax.

*Delaware: A bill to limit state spending to 98 percent of anticipated revenue passed the legislature. The governor has proposed an amendment to the state constitution to require a three-fifths vote of the legislature to raise any taxes.

*Florida: A proposal similar to the Jarvis-Gann amendment was being advanced by three state senators who hoped to put it to a November public vote. Plans were reportedly being made to circulate petitions for a limitation initiative to be placed on a 1979 ballot. Several groups were urging the legislature to vote tax relief in the 1978 session.

*Georgia: A spending limitation amendment was introduced in the legislature, and a local group was seeking representatives' support for the measure.

Hawaii: A state constitutional convention might consider a spending limitation amendment when it convened in 1978.

Idaho: A group seeking to limit property taxes to 1 percent of assessed value had by mid-1978 collected nearly enough signatures to place a tax cut initiative on the November ballot. The governor began planning for anticipated state revenue cutbacks.

Illinois: A spending limitation amendment was blocked by the state Senate. Supporters planned to reintroduce it. Residents of one county staged a massive property tax "strike" leading to a $60 million tax reduction. Other counties could follow suit. A measure that would rebate to taxpayers a percentage of annual income from property taxes passed the legislature, but the governor decided to veto it.

Indiana: Several bills providing property and sales tax relief, particularly for the elderly, were passed and signed into state law. Most of the legislation expands tax exemptions. One bill allows a larger tax base for financing schools.

Iowa: Tax reform measures introduced in the legislature died in committee. Supporters planned to reintroduce proposals.

*Kansas: A homestead property tax exemption measure and exemptions for agricultural equipment were enacted. Another new law allows rebates on sales tax to offset food tax burdens. The legislature on adjourning appointed an interim tax committee of legislators and representatives of citizens' groups and private interests to look into other proposals.

Kentucky: A gubernatorial candidate has commissioned research on tax and spending limitations.

*Louisiana: Legislators were said to be eyeing several tax reform proposals.

Maine: A referendum passed in December 1977 repealed uniform property taxes for education funding. A new law provides $20 million in tax relief.

*Maryland: A constitutional amendment (Maryland Resolution 13) to impose a ceiling on state spending was gathering signatures for consideration by the legislature.

Massachusetts: A constitutional amendment to limit state spending was passed by the 1978 legislature, but the 1979 session must concur to put the proposal on the 1979 ballot. Meanwhile, the legislature voted to freeze property taxes at 1977 levels, with only a 5 percent increase for inflation.

Michigan: A group supporting a constitutional state taxation lid filed 410,000 signatures to put the proposition on the ballot. Required are 266,000 valid ones. The plan would limit taxes to 8.3 percent of personal income. A vote was expected in 1978.

Minnesota: Spending limitation legislation was being drafted in 1978 for the next legislative session. Minnesota already limits property tax increases.

*Mississippi: Two tax relief measures passed the legislature in 1978. One removes the sales tax on utility payments, the other doubles the standard income tax exemption on homes.

Missouri: At least one local group (in Springfield) was sponsoring a petition drive aimed at encouraging state lawmakers to enact expenditure limitations. The legislature passed no major tax relief measures in its 1978 session.

Montana: A state senator's proposed referendum was gathering signatures for placement on the November ballot. The plan would shift property tax burdens to income tax and local governments facing significant losses would be reimbursed by the state. A new law provides increased exemptions on owner-occupied homes.

*Nebraska: A special session of the legislature in late June approved two bills to limit local government property tax increases and to allow spending lids imposed by local voters on themselves. The governor, who said he will let the bills become law without his signature, has urged voters to support an initiative petition drive to make spending limits constitutional.

*Nevada: Near qualifying for a November vote was an initiative styled after California's Jarvis-Gann proposal. It would limit tax assessments to purchase value. In the legislature, tax cut and tax shift measures were being discussed, but no legislative action was anticipated before 1979.

New Hampshire: The governor reportedly was seeking a referendum to limit property taxes and prohibit sales and income taxes.

New Jersey: The first state to enact a tax expenditure ceiling, New Jersey in 1976 shifted its tax burden by simultaneously instituting a statewide income tax. The law limits spending by linking increases to personal income growth.

*New Mexico: Cuts totaling $55 million in taxes were enacted in 1978. They took the form of a permanent reduction in state income tax, a sales tax decrease and expansion of low-income tax credits.

New York: A state senator, serving on a tax limitation task force, introduced a state constitutional amendment to

cap state spending at 8 percent of total statewide personal income.

North Carolina: Several tax relief measures were defeated in 1978.

*North Dakota: Petitions were being circulated to put to the public an initiative that would make a one-third cut in state income tax.

Ohio: Facing a 1977 court decision that put school financing into jeopardy, the state has been considering measures to shift the tax burden to personal and corporate income. At least two citizens' groups were pushing for initiatives — one to limit property taxes, the other to limit taxes generally.

Oklahoma: No proposals had been filed by mid-1978, but voters were said to be organizing tax reform efforts.

*Oregon: Supporters of an initiative similar to Proposition 13 enlisted the help of California's Paul Gann to get approval for limiting property taxes to 1.5 percent of market value.

*Pennsylvania: Two measures setting spending ceilings tied to the rate of inflation and personal income growth had been introduced in the legislature. One would amend statutes, the other the state constitution.

Rhode Island: A pressure group was said to be forming to move for a Jarvis-Gann type amendment, Rhode Island's "Proposition 14," to be enacted by the legislature.

*South Carolina: Pending in the legislature was a constitutional amendment to provide uniform taxation and assessments. A bill already signed into law gives constitutional tax relief to the elderly.

South Dakota: A bill to limit state spending to a percentage of personal income, prohibit decreases in state funding of local governments, and require a balanced budget failed by one vote in 1978 but plans were to reintroduce it next session.

*Tennessee: Many groups in other states have been patterning tax reform efforts after Tennessee's constitutional amendment linking state spending with growth in personal income. The measure was passed in March 1978.

*Texas: The governor was considering calling a special legislative session to consider a constitutional spending cap.

Utah: Groups have been circulating petitions to introduce a spending limitation proposal in the next legislative session. They hope for a 1980 ballot.

Vermont: Tax reform supporters in the state face a time-consuming process if they want to change the constitution. One requirement is that all towns hold meetings to decide on the amendment.

*Virginia: A group started by a businessman was trying to gather support for a proposed constitutional change limiting all state taxes to 6.34 percent of personal income.

Washington: A petition drive was under way to get the legislature to consider a spending limitation statute.

West Virginia: The legislature was considering an amendment to increase tax exemption categories. Another proposal would require a balanced state budget.

Wisconsin: A spending limitation amendment was blocked by the legislature in 1978.

*Wyoming: A committee in the legislature began hearings the end of June 1978 on proposals for limiting state taxes constitutionally. ∎

Community and
Human Development

CQ

Renewal of 10-Year Housing Goals in Doubt

Nearly 30 years ago, Congress established what has become an almost sacred national objective — a decent home for every American family.

The ideal is still strong.

But a principal symbol of the commitment to the ideal is about to die. Congress is likely to adjourn in 1978 without setting new goals for the number of housing units that must be built to meet the "decent home" objective.

The numerical goals, established for the first time a decade ago by President Lyndon Johnson, are due to expire in 1978.

But the Carter administration has not decided whether to propose updated targets for the coming years. And there is little interest in Congress about setting them, even though the original goals were never met and millions of Americans still live in substandard dwellings.

Neither on Capitol Hill nor in the White House is there any strong feeling that goals work. As a result, many expect Congress to let the 10th anniversary of the construction goals go by without doing anything to renew them or even pay them lip service.

Change in Attitude

Some analysts see the lack of interest as yet another example of the federal government withdrawing from its activism of the 1960s, when establishment of a program was considered all that was necessary to solve a particular social problem.

There is still some support for goals. The housing industry, many social activists and liberal politicians view them as a key aspect of federal housing policy, a way of emphasizing the importance of good housing, especially for the poor. Testifying in April 1978, James E. Kerr, director of the Durham (N.C.) Housing Authority, said new goals were essential so that the "place of housing in national priorities [will] not be obscured."

But others are not convinced. Numerical targets, set for long periods, represent a "way of making promises that cannot be kept," said Rep. Thomas L. Ashley, D-Ohio, chairman of the House Housing Subcommittee and one of the most knowledgeable members of Congress on housing issues. Ashley said he thinks the approach his subcommittee has taken — a year-by-year consideration of federal assistance programs — is the best way to proceed. This approach takes key factors into consideration — such as restraints on the federal budget — that were not uppermost in the minds of government leaders a decade ago.

Background

The 1978 attitude in Congress and the Carter administration was in striking contrast to the mood in 1968, when then-President Johnson proposed a massive housing program and, as part of that, called for 10-year construction goals.

The goal of a decent home for every American family actually predated Johnson's push. In passing the Housing Act of 1949, Congress had declared that the chief aim of a national housing policy should be a "decent home and suitable living environment for every American family." *(See box, p. 62, on U.S. housing programs since 1930s)*

What Johnson did was give some shape to that ideal by proposing specific numerical goals by which to measure progress toward meeting the nation's housing needs. During the coming 10 years, Johnson said in 1968, the nation needed to build 26 million homes and apartments. Within that target, Johnson added, the federal government should assist in constructing about 6 million housing units for the poor — roughly 600,000 a year. Pointing to the "great urban centers where millions live amid decaying buildings," Johnson urged congressional support for major public expenditures to replace "shameful sub-standard units of misery."

The housing goals, endorsed enthusiastically by Congress, became Title XVI of the 1968 Housing and Urban Development Act (PL 90-448). The statute said the decent-home goal should be "substantially achieved" within 10 years.

Results

As it turned out, actual construction fell somewhat short of the 26 million unit target. According to figures compiled by the Department of Housing and Urban Development (HUD) construction of new homes, rehabilitated units and mobile homes totalled 21.4 million during the 10-year period.

Production exceeded the goals in the first half of the decade, but fell well below them in the years following. The drop-off was attributed primarily to President Nixon's 1973 moratorium on federal housing programs and the economic recession of 1974-75. Actual production came within 80 percent of the overall target. But construction of federally subsidized housing was well below target — only 2.7 percent of the targeted 6 million units.

The Federal Government's Role in Housing...

The state of the nation's housing has been of vital concern to the federal government ever since the 1930s. Before that time, Congress had appropriated money to investigate city slums and had helped build housing for defense workers during World War I. But it was not until the Great Depression that the government began to assume a major role in the housing field, when it set out to stimulate and stabilize the economy through emergency housing and mortgage measures. Starting with passage of the Federal Home Loan Bank Act under President Hoover in 1932, the federal government steadily increased its housing activities.

In 1933, the first year of the New Deal, the Home Owners' Loan Corp. was organized to curb the rising trend of mortgage foreclosures, by granting long-term mortgage loans at low interest rates to those in urgent need of funds to protect their home investments. A year later the Federal Housing Administration (FHA) was established to encourage building and to increase the supply of mortgage funds by providing banks and other private lending institutions with government insurance against a loss on mortgage home loans. The FHA program was set up to encourage lenders, not buyers to invest in home mortgages. If home owners failed to make their payments, they were not bailed out. The guarantee was given to the lender. This arrangement enabled lenders to make virtually risk-free loans on new and used homes and on repair work that was covered by FHA guarantees. The lender was therefore willing to accept low down payments and long-term mortgages.

In an effort to increase the supply of mortgage funds, the Federal National Mortgage Association was chartered by the federal housing administrator on Feb. 10, 1938, as a subsidiary of the Reconstruction Finance Corporation. The FNMA, known as "Fannie Mae," bought mortgages to release more capital into the mortgage market, or sold its mortgages when money was plentiful. These transactions, in turn, tended to counter the prevailing economic situation in the mortgage market, thus providing stability. Fannie Mae became a private corporation in 1968 and two years later was authorized by the Emergency Home Finance Act to buy conventional mortgages.

Despite government assistance, housing production sagged during the depression-ridden 1930s and for the first half of the 1940s, when industry concentrated on wartime needs. This concentration drew millions of households into urban areas, creating a housing shortage. The end of World War II in 1945 brought the GI's home, and frequently into marriage, creating millions of new households in quest of a place to live. By now the housing shortage was acute.

Postwar Assistance to Overcome Shortages

In the postwar years, the extent and form of government assistance to housing was a matter of controversy and debate. Most programs, however, survived opposition and were gradually liberalized. Although the federal role in housing grew to considerable proportions, the number of federally assisted housing units amounted to less than one-fourth of all private non-farm housing units built from 1945 through 1965.

The Housing Act of 1949, in particular, significantly broadened the federal role in housing and set as a goal "a decent home and a suitable living environment for every American family." Private enterprise and state and local governments, in partnership with the federal government, were to take the lead whenever possible in meeting this goal. The act established a $1-billion program of federal urban renewal assistance to localities in clearing and redeveloping slums. It also revived and broadened the public housing program, authorized a housing census every 10 years and launched a program of economic and technical research in residential construction and finance.

In the years following the 1949 act, housing legislation was approved to meet new and specific needs. In 1950 the Veterans Administration was authorized to make direct home-purchase or repair loans to veterans living in small communities where private financing was not available. In the same year, a program of federal assistance in providing college housing was initiated. The Housing Act of 1954 carried urban renewal beyond slum clearance and fostered comprehensive federal and local cooperation to ensure sound community development.

During the Eisenhower administration, there were many conflicts in Congress between Democrats who favored a speedup of federal housing programs, particularly for low-income groups, and Republicans who favored slower advances or, in many cases, cutbacks. The Democrats clearly won out in 1961, during the Kennedy presidency, with a housing act that expanded all federal housing programs and extended federal activity into other areas. The 1964 Housing Act, called a "bare-bones" law by some, continued housing programs enacted in 1961, with a few minor changes.

Anthony Downs, who has written extensively on housing policy in the context of social history, observed in a 1977 article published in *Daedalus,* that by 1960 a balance between supply and demand for housing had been restored in most metropolitan areas "for households with reasonably good incomes." This situation prevailed until mid-decade, when the Vietnam War buildup began diverting the construction industry away from home building. And the urban riots of 1965-68 began focusing attention upon the continuing problem of low-income urban households, especially those in the racial ghettos.

Focus on the Urban Poor in the Late Sixties

The riots shifted federal housing policies toward the expansion of housing for America's urban poor, largely through a new set of subsidy programs. Congress enacted four major housing laws in 1965-68 during the Johnson presidency which, taken together, constituted the most far-reaching achievements in housing and urban development in decades.

The first two laws, both passed in 1965, authorized rent supplements to help poor people afford decent housing and established a Department of Housing and Urban Development, thus giving Cabinet-level status to the

...An Overview From the Depression to the 1970s

government's housing activities and bringing increased attention to federal efforts to solve urban problems. The third law, in 1966, established a model cities program intended to pump extra federal funds into needy cities. All three laws were highly controversial. Their central programs — rent supplements and model cities — were vigorously opposed by Republicans and conservative Democrats. Although this coalition was unable to prevent adoption of the programs, it succeeded fairly well in keeping funding at a low level.

The Housing and Urban Development Act of 1968 was the broadest of all. It contained 17 titles covering not only housing but also a variety of related activities including interstate land sales, mass transit and flood insurance. The basic part of the 1968 legislation was directed at home ownership and rental assistance. The homeownership plan (Section 235) provided a federal subsidy to lower interest rates on mortgages for low-income families. Generally, the program was limited to families with income of $3,000 to $6,500 annually, but exceptions were possible in high-cost areas and for very large families.

In 1976, eligibility under the homeownership plan was extended to families with incomes up to 95 percent of the median income for a particular area. Maximum limits on the amounts of mortgage loans eligible for subsidies under the program were also increased to between $25,000 and $33,000, depending on family size and geographical cost factors.

The 1968 act also established the Government National Mortgage Association (GNMA — "Ginny Mae") to subsidize the interest cost of mortgages on housing built under the various mortgage lenders or sometimes by the association itself, at interest rates below the prevailing yield in mortgage markets. Private mortgage lenders then sell these mortgages to GNMA at face value and it resells them to FNMA at a lower price that will bring the effective yield on the mortgages into line with current market yields. This arrangement, called the Tandem Plan, allows GNMA to limit its cash outlays to the difference between the price at which it buys the mortgages from private lenders and the price at which it sells them to FNMA.

Another aid to the housing credit market was the 1970 Emergency Home Finance Act, which, in addition to giving "Fannie Mae" the authority to buy conventional mortgages, also created the Federal Home Loan Mortgage Corp. FHLMC, under the direction of the Federal Home Loan Bank Board, has authority to buy, hold and sell mortgages within limits similar to those established for FHA and with authority to borrow funds and issue mortgage-backed obligations.

Attempts to Alleviate 1973-74 Credit Crunch

In 1973, the homebuilding industry entered its worst slump since World War II. Mortgage money dried up, under the impact of "tight-money" policies imposed by the Federal Reserve Board to fight inflation, and housing starts dipped close to 1970 levels. "The decline of housing starts in 1974 was a gruesome replay of a classic pattern,"

explained a 1975 study on home mortgage financing, prepared by the National Forest Products Association: "Inflation rises, the federal government tightens its monetary policies, credit in general becomes tight, interest rates skyrocket, savings are withdrawn to invest in high-paying short-term securities, mortgage money that is so dependent on savings dries up, home buyers and builders are unable to obtain mortgage money, new construction tumbles, orders for building materials decline, and all the industries dependent upon homebuilding nose dive into recession."

President Nixon had, early in 1973, declared a moratorium on major federal housing subsidy programs. Terming existing housing programs "failures," he said "our principal efforts should be directed toward determining whether a policy of direct cash assistance — with first priority for the elderly poor — can be put into practical operation." Consequently, the President requested authority to experiment more widely with the direct cash payment approach. The Nixon proposals met a chilly reception from the National Association of Home Builders and its allies in Congress. At the end of 1973, the federal housing program remained in limbo, with the moratorium on most subsidy programs still in effect and no new legislation to replace them.

The Housing and Community Development Act of 1974, the first major piece of housing legislation since 1968, included some but not all of Nixon's proposals. On FHA-guaranteed mortgages, the new law raised the maximum to $45,000 from $33,000, reduced the required cash down payment and gave HUD authority to set flexible interest rates. The new act also consolidated 10 urban aid programs into a single three-year $8.6 billion program of block grants for community development and established a new rental assistance program (Section 8) for low- and moderate-income families.

Congress approved the 1974 act in August, but by then it was becoming apparent that the action so far — both administrative and congressional — was having only modest effect on the housing market. President Ford, in office two months, asked Congress on Oct. 8 to pass emergency legislation to let GNMA buy conventional mortgages — those not insured by the federal government — as well as mortgages backed by the FHA and VA. The legislation was signed into law Oct. 18, making $3-billion available immediately for mortgage purchases.

By the spring of 1975 the nation's two-year economic recession had ended, according to the reckoning of government economists, and by that fall the housing industry had begun to move out of its slump. The number of new housing starts reached 1,987,100 in 1977, up from 1.5 million in 1976 and 1.1 million in 1975, although the recovery was uneven geographically.

Although mortgage credit was generally available in 1975 and 1976, interest rates remained high. According to figures from the Federal Home Loan Bank Board, the interest rates on mortgages averaged 9 percent in 1977 and had risen to almost 9.5 percent by June 1978. (See table, p. 64)

Focus of Debate

The difficulty in drawing conclusions from the target and production figures provides some insight into why policy makers in HUD and in Congress are uncertain whether new goals should be established.

Sen. William Proxmire, D-Wis., chairman of the Senate Banking Committee, cited the figures during an April speech on the Senate floor to conclude that the federal government had "failed miserably" in its commitment to provide decent housing for low-income families. "The record shows that only 45 percent of the housing goal for lower income families was actually achieved," Proxmire said.

But other statistics have led some to conclude that substantial progress has been made. Congressional Budget Office (CBO) data shows that the proportion of housing considered dilapidated declined from 9 percent to 4 percent between 1950 and 1970. During the same period, the CBO said, the proportion of housing that lacked adequate plumbing declined from 34 percent to about 5 percent. By 1976, the CBO added, the rate was down to only about 2.6 percent.

Citing HUD statistics, the CBO further reported that during the past three decades fewer poor families lived in unsatisfactory housing. In 1950, among the poorest 40 percent of all households, 57 percent were living in units that were dilapidated or lacked complete plumbing. By 1970 the percentage was down to 14 percent.

Finally, the CBO reported that between 1950 and 1976 the proportion of all households with more than one and one-half persons per room — one of the standards used to define overcrowding — declined from 6.2 percent to less than 1 percent. Even when a more stringent standard of no more than one person per room was applied, only 4.8 percent of all households were overcrowded, according to the CBO.

Complex Issue

"People have begun to realize that housing policy is far more complex than establishing production goals," said Morton J. Schussheim, senior housing specialist with the Congressional Research Service.

Schussheim, a former HUD official who as a consultant to the home builders helped draft the 1968 goals, said that in retrospect the 1968 goals represented a simplistic approach toward meeting the nation's housing needs. Other housing experts agreed. "The emphasis was on build, build, build — but there is more to housing than that," said one analyst.

New Views

Proxmire, a supporter of housing goals, introduced legislation in April 1978 (S 2855) to establish new production targets. But Proxmire agrees that setting new goals is complicated, and S 2855 implicitly recognizes that.

The legislation, although broadly worded, focuses attention on issues that received little attention when the first goals were established — such as the quality of housing and neighborhoods, equal opportunity and rising costs. Further, the legislation also recognized regional differences in housing markets, something that was not considered back in 1968.

The complexity of the issue was clearly evident during two days of hearings held by Proxmire shortly after he in-

Nationwide Average Interest Rates on Home Mortgages

Year		New Homes	Existing Homes
1968		6.97%	7.03%
1969		7.81	7.82
1970		8.45	8.36
1971		7.74	7.67
1972		7.60	7.51
1973		7.95	8.01
1974		8.92	9.01
1975		9.01	9.21
1976		8.99	9.11
1977		9.01	9.02
1978	April	9.30	9.35
	May	9.37	9.37
	June*	9.46	9.47

* Preliminary

SOURCE: Federal Home Loan Bank Board

troduced S 2855. None of the witnesses viewed housing goals in the simple context of production numbers. In fact, the National Association of Home Builders was reluctant to commit itself to numerical goals.

For example, Robert D. Reischauer, CBO assistant director for human resources and community development, argued against a single production policy by outlining the possible impact on rehabilitation of existing housing.

Pushing more construction of new homes, he said, can discourage maintaining still-sound homes and encourage the abandonment of housing that could be rehabilitated. This was especially possible, he said, if the new building took place in areas having high vacancies among existing, adequate housing. "No single policy or short-term policy target that relies on any one mechanism alone is likely to be the most efficient or effective approach for addressing all of the nation's housing objectives," Reischauer said.

Housing Costs a Concern

The cost of housing was also a major topic of discussion during the hearings. Studies, including one by HUD, have shown that rising housing costs are outpacing family income, thus, according to the federal agency, "effectively pricing countless families out of the housing market."

Responding to the concern over housing costs, Proxmire has proposed a new twist to the 1949 "decent home" goal. S 2855 includes a section calling upon the federal government and the private sector to provide enough housing to satisfy the goal of a decent home in a suitable neighborhood "at a price that every American can afford."

But, finding ways to do that is not easy. For example, within the Carter administration, there is considerable debate over whether more poor families could afford housing if federal housing programs were ended and the subsidies converted into basic transfer payments as part of the welfare system.

Some officials in the Office of Management and Budget (OMB) and the Department of Health, Education and Welfare favor "cashing out" rent subsidy programs as the least expensive approach. Not unexpectedly, HUD opposes

Higher Costs Pose Barrier to Good Housing

A decade ago, when the federal government adopted its first housing goals, the lack of adequate housing was considered the most pressing need.

Substandard units are still a problem. But increasingly federal officials are worried that even when good housing is available it might be out of reach of the people who most need it.

Reflecting the increased federal concern, the Department of Housing and Urban Development (HUD) and the General Accounting Office (GAO) completed studies of the cost problem in May 1978 and the Senate Budget Committee opened hearings on the same subject.

The study by HUD showed that between 1972 and 1976 housing costs increased dramatically, outpacing family income for the first time — in the process "effectively pricing countless families out of the housing market."

While median family income rose during that period at an annual rate of 7.05 percent, various housing costs posted even sharper increases:

● Residential construction costs grew at an annual rate of 8 percent.

● The cost of improved building lots rose almost 13 percent a year.

● The median sale price climbed at an average rate of 12.5 percent on a new single-family home and 9.3 percent on an existing home.

● Homeownership costs — property taxes, insurance, maintenance, repairs, fuel and utilities — increased at an average annual rate of 8.15 percent.

Not surprisingly, the increased costs of housing hit hardest at the poor.

The general rule of thumb in the housing industry is that a family should pay about one-quarter of its income for shelter.

Yet, testimony before the Senate Banking Committee in July 1978 showed that 68 percent of all renter households with incomes below $3,000 per year pay more than one-third of their incomes for housing.

"The problem of affordability is the most critical housing problem facing low-income people," said Cushing N. Dolbeare, a consultant who heads the Ad Hoc Low Income Housing Coalition.

The GAO study cited several factors in explaining the high costs, including government regulations, construction materials, labor, financing, property taxes and utilities.

GAO also attributed the increases in housing costs to the "changing nature" of new home buyers. More buyers, the GAO found, have substantial incomes, with both the male and female working. Such families can afford big down payments and larger monthly mortgage payments. The GAO also pointed out that many buyers already own homes, and the equity in the old home enabled them to buy higher priced new homes.

As a result, GAO said, the home building industry has to some extent catered to the needs of the wealthiest families, building larger homes with more amenities. But, the GAO indicated, first-time buyers with smaller incomes cannot afford such homes.

Recommendations

GAO and HUD both offered recommendations to hold the line on costs and, perhaps, even lower them.

The GAO said a builder could save between $1,400 and $7,000 on a house if he used less expensive materials. Smaller houses would also reduce costs, the GAO said.

HUD proposed streamlining federal regulations dealing with financing, land use and construction. And it said federal tax incentives could be used to encourage more housing investment by pension funds and life insurance companies. It also urged the removal of interest rate ceilings on loans insured by the Federal Housing Administration as a way of getting more mortgage money in the market. HUD proposed federally insured, 35-year, no-down-payment mortgage loans to credit-worthy borrowers, especially first-time home buyers.

Patricia Roberts Harris, the HUD secretary, is studying the recommendations.

Trends in Income, Prices and Housing Costs

Annual Percentage Increase

Median Family Income
'63 - '72 — 6.6%
'72 - '76 — 7.0%

Consumer Price Index (All Items)
'63 - '72 — 3.5%
'72 - '76 — 8.0%

Median Price of New, Single-Family Home
'63 - '72 — 4.9%
'72 - '76 — 12.5%

Median Price of Existing, Single-Family Home
'66 - '72 — 5.3%
'72 - '76 — 9.3%

Mortgage Payments for Median Priced New House
'63 - '72 — 6.7%
'72 - '76 — 15.9%

Operating Expenses for Median Priced House
'63 - '72 — 7.2%
'72 - '76 — 11.8%

Rents
'63 - '72 — 2.6%
'72 - '76 — 5.0%

SOURCE: Department of Housing and Urban Development

it. The department won an internal debate over the proposal in 1977, but the idea is still considered a live issue within the Carter administration.

Administration Position

HUD and OMB also have reportedly clashed over whether the Carter administration should propose new long-term construction goals. OMB is reportedly cold toward setting numerical targets, fearing anything that could stimulate inflation and increase federal spending.

HUD reportedly is more inclined toward numerical goals, but the agency's policy makers also have some reservations about them.

Patricia Roberts Harris, the HUD secretary, has been scheduled several times to testify on the issue. But each time her appearance was cancelled.

Harris' aides say she has been busy with more pressing issues, including a package of urban legislation proposed by Carter in March 1978. But, some aides said Harris has questions about fundamental aspects of housing policy, including the ways in which housing needs are measured. Publicly, Harris has given little hint of what she will do. Asked if HUD would propose new goals, she replied, "You'll just have to wait and see."

Proxmire, reacting to the administration's failure to testify and take a position, said, "I don't think they [HUD] have focused much attention on it."

Although he would like to see some goals legislation enacted in 1978, Proxmire said, "absent any action on the part of the administration I don't think we can get reasonable goals."

Goals Needed?

Some observers think the complexities of housing policy raise a basic question: Is there a need for housing production goals? Underlying that is another key question: Do goals really mean anything?

PRO: A Yardstick

Proxmire argues that goals serve several useful purposes.

"They focus our attention regularly on a subject that affects, in a very basic way, all Americans," he said. "They require us to think systematically about policies and programs to satisfy basic shelter needs."

Furthermore, Proxmire said, goals provide a way to test whether housing policies are accomplishing anything.

Some supporters argue that production goals enable the housing industry and other interest groups to prod the administration and Congress into providing increased funding for housing programs.

"It's a cycle," said one congressional source. "They get Congress to set goals they know they can't reach, and then they come back and say, 'we can't meet your goals without more money.'"

One analyst said it was in the best interest of the housing industry to push for goals. "The more pragmatic home builders realize that there is a buck to be made in subsidized housing," he said. "Therefore, anything that would increase the units of subsidized housing the government builds is good for business."

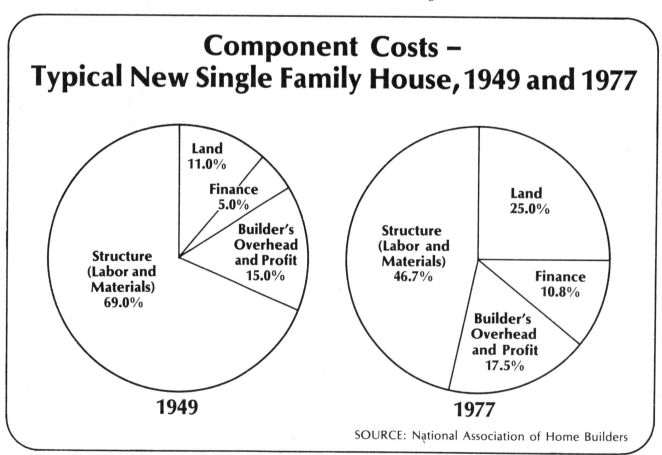

SOURCE: National Association of Home Builders

Some in HUD see another reason for goals — bureaucratic leverage. They argue that goals can be used to push OMB and the White House into supporting more federal spending for housing. These HUD officials acknowledge that goals are not binding, and that overall budgetary considerations shape the level of federal spending for housing. But, they nevertheless maintain that goals represent "one more argument in the battle," as one HUD policy analyst put it.

CON: No Effect

Some congressional housing specialists see goals as nothing more than an "intellectual exercise played by HUD bureaucrats and liberals," as one House housing aide said.

Administration and congressional housing sources agreed that failure to enact new goals this year would have little substantive impact.

"I don't think housing policy will change one iota if goals are not set for the next 10 years," said Anthony Valanzano, minority counsel to the Housing Subcommittee in the House. "We know what HUD will do next year. It will recommend about 400,000 units of assisted housing."

End of an Era?

Both sides believe the failure to enact new goals may have more symbolic meaning than anything else.

Schussheim, the CRS housing specialist, recalled the mood in 1968 when the goals were enacted. "We had a lot of trouble in the cities then," he said. "There was a feeling that the country, the Congress, the administration had neglected the cities, and had to make amends."

Urban blight and poor housing are still major domestic problems, but Schussheim and others say the commitment to alleviate those problems is lacking.

"That feeling [from 1968] has been muted. People are gun-shy today," Schussheim said.

HUD officials argue that the department, and the Carter administration, still have that commitment. But they say public housing is still recovering from the "bad name" it was given in the early 1970s, when disclosures of mismanagement and fraud drew extensive public attention.

Some HUD officials say the tales of scandal were overblown, but, they concede, the publicity created an especially poor image of federal housing programs, an image, they say, that is still quite prevalent.

Finally, those in and out of government note that inflation and excessive government spending are the major issues today, with a Democratic administration placed in the position of trying to confront what normally has been a Republican issue. As a result, traditional bread-and-butter Democratic issues, such as housing, have had to take a back-seat to fighting inflation.

One congressional housing aide, expressing a widely held view, said a decision to forego new housing goals underscores the fact that with tight budgets and high voter anxiety over taxes "the golden days of federal housing programs are over." ∎

UDAG Program Sparks Controversy

At the urging of the Carter administration, Congress in 1977 authorized $400 million annually during fiscal 1978, 1979, and 1980 for a new program, Urban Development Action Grant (UDAG), to spur urban revitalization efforts through joint public-private development projects to help out those cities with the most severe problems. The authorization was included in the Housing and Community Development Act of 1977 (HR 6655 — PL 95-128) extending the community block grant program — the nation's chief neighborhood revitalization effort — for three years, authorizing $12,450,000,000 to fund it. As part of his urban proposals, announced March 27, 1978, Carter requested an additional $275 million yearly for the UDAG program.

The law governing UDAG grants stipulated that 75 percent of the $400 million should be used for grants to cities with populations over 50,000, and the remaining 25 percent should be used for smaller cities and towns.

Eligible Projects

The law governing the grants specified that federal dollars could be used for commercial, industrial and residential projects that would help revitalize a community's economic base, provide jobs, especially for low- and moderate-income persons, or help reclaim deteriorated or aging neighborhoods.

A brochure published by HUD listed possible uses of action grants, including land clearance, site improvements, rehabilitation of housing and construction of public, commercial, industrial or residential structures. It suggested a number of financial arrangements, such as loan guarantees or second mortgages, for joint public-private development.

Underlying the whole program was the concept of "leveraging" — using public funds to stimulate private investment. Although there does not appear to be unanimous agreement on the point, many key HUD policy makers believe one important element in revitalizing cities is rebuilding downtown business districts and bringing the middle classes back to inner-city areas. Those who subscribe to this view see the action grant program as an integral tool in realizing their goals. In addition, the concept of "leveraging" fitted neatly in the cost-conscious Carter administration. *(Box, p. 70)*

Controversy Over Aid to Business

The Urban Development Action Grant has drawn strong supporters and opponents. In Kankakee, Ill., city officials received $85,500 in federal funds under UDAG to buy and prepare land for an aluminum plant. In Toledo, Ohio, the city received $12 million in federal funds for its downtown business district. In St. Louis, the federal government gave $10.5 million toward a $125 million shopping center, housing project and hotel complex.

All these grants were among the first round of UDAG projects in major cities announced April 6, 1978, by Housing and Urban Development Secretary Patricia Roberts Harris. The 50 first round grants totaled $150 million. *(Box, p. 71)*

Main Provisions of UDAG Program

Following are main provisions of the Urban Development Action Grant Program enacted by Congress in 1977:

● Authorized up to $400 million in each of the three fiscal years (1978-80) for urban development action grants for assisting severely distressed cities and urban counties.

● Established a program of urban development action grants to severely distressed communities to help alleviate physical and economic deterioration through neighborhood reclamation.

● Limited the grants to cities and urban counties that had demonstrated results in providing housing and equal employment opportunity for low- and moderate-income persons and members of minority groups.

● Required that action grant projects be developed to take advantage of unique opportunities to attract private investment, stimulate investment in restoration of deteriorated or abandoned housing stock or solve critical problems resulting from population outmigration or a stagnating or declining tax base.

● Required the secretary, in determining who received the grants, to include as the primary criterion the comparative degree of physical and economic distress among applicants. Such distress was measured by the differences in the extent of growth lag, poverty and adjusted age of housing, defined as proportion of pre-1940 housing in a community compared to the proportion of old housing stock in all metropolitan areas.

● Directed the secretary also to take into account, when awarding grants, impact of the proposed program on the problems of persons of low- and moderate-income and minorities, the extent of financial participation by public or private entities, extent of state assistance, extent to which the program provided an opportunity to meet local needs and the feasibility of accomplishing the program in a timely fashion within the grant amount available.

● Barred action grants designed to facilitate relocation of industrial or commercial plants from one area to another unless the relocation would not adversely affect the unemployment or economic base of the area giving up the project.

● Required citizen participation in the formulation of the action grant proposals.

● Set aside at least 25 percent of the funds available for action grants for cities under 50,000 population that were not central cities of a standard metropolitan statistical area.

Proponents of these grants believed that the investment of federal dollars would help spur needed revitalization of decaying cities across the country." This is going to be a lifesaver for our city," declared an official in Portsmouth, Va., shortly after the city received $2.9 million for a housing development.

But others were not so certain. The projects, funded under HUD's urban development action grant program, have drawn criticism on several counts from members of Congress, social activists and others.

Neighborhood groups, for example, contend that the projects are not sufficiently responsive to the needs of urban dwellers. "Sunbelt" spokesmen complain that the program focuses too much on the "Snowbelt" areas of the Northeast and Midwest.

The criticism has sparked a congressional debate over the $1.2 billion, three-year action grant program, raising the possibility of legislative changes in a major element of the Carter administration's effort to rebuild America's cities. President Carter proposed increasing action grant funding by $275 million per year, beginning in fiscal 1979, as part of his urban program.

In announcing the $150 million in first-round grants, Harris said the grants would go to projects backed up by $978.8 million in private financial commitments. According to estimates provided by HUD, the projects would create about 27,000 new jobs and save another 16,000.

"The urban development action grant program can now begin to fulfill its promise for the urban places in America where the economic base has eroded, neighborhoods have deteriorated, and the poor are in need of jobs," Harris said.

But critics quickly charged that there was an improper, unwise tilt in action grants toward commercial and in-dustrial ventures, at the expense of neighborhood residential projects.

Hotel Controversy

The use of federal dollars to help finance the construction of downtown hotel projects was especially controversial.

"HUD judges the revitalization of cities by the way the skylines look," declared Joseph F. Timilty, chairman of the National Commission on Neighborhoods. "They talk about people programs. I don't see parking projects or new hotels that just take business away from old hotels as net gains."

The National People's Action, a Chicago-based organization of neighborhoods from more than 100 cities, also attacked the hotel projects and accused HUD of being insensitive to the needs of urban dwellers.

Funding the projects, charged Gayle Cincotta, head of the organization, showed that HUD "is lining up with the mayors and big business and has no interest in low and moderate income people."

A check by Congressional Quarterly showed that seven projects, totaling $34.5 million in grant funds, directly involved the building of hotels, with the money being used for either construction loans, second mortgages or land purchase and site preparation. Another seven projects that received grant funds also included hotels, although the federal dollars were earmarked for other sections of the projects.

HUD Response

"The critics are wrong," Harris said at the April 6 announcement of the grants. "Hotels are the best employers of low and moderate income and unskilled people I can think of." Harris further charged that the criticisms were founded on "prejudice and lack of information on what hotel construction can do for a city."

Cities, she argued, "have a role as tourist centers and cultural centers, and there must be places to receive people coming to them...."

Harris rejected arguments that hotel work represented menial, dead-end jobs for the urban poor. "It is possible to start as a dishwasher and end up as a chef," she said, adding that chefs get good salaries.

Robert C. Embry Jr., assistant HUD secretary for community planning and development and a key architect of the action grant program, acknowledged that certain trade-offs were involved in financing hotels. In an interview, he conceded that hotels offer "no real advancement" for low or unskilled workers. But, he added, hotels generate much-needed dollars for inner-city economies. "It's not a matter of poor people working for the rich...it's people with money bringing dollars into [the city]," he said.

Question of Philosophy

To HUD officials, members of Congress and others, the debate over hotel construction symbolized a broader issue: how best to revitalize ailing cities, and what role the federal government should play in that enterprise.

To a large extent, the emphasis at the federal level during the 1960s and early 1970s has been on dealing with various social problems prevalent in urban areas — broken homes, poor schools, rampant crime and inadequate housing.

But some Carter administration policy makers believe that while focusing on those areas could ease short-term

---

'Leveraging' in Practice

The city of Detroit is using $1.2 million in urban development action grants to buy land for three inner-city industries. The firms in turn will use the land to expand their plants.

The city eventually will be paid for the land, although the companies will in all likelihood pay below market prices.

City officials and the Department of Housing and Urban Development (HUD) see a trade-off in providing the lower-cost land to the industries. By reducing land costs, proponents of the deal reason, they will keep the industries — and the jobs the companies provide — in the inner city.

City officials believe such trade-offs are necessary if Detroit is to be competitive with the surrounding suburbs, where land is cheaper and more readily available.

The $1.2 million in taxpayer funds will be used to buy about 12 acres of land. The three industries in turn have pledged to invest $4.6 million of their own money to expand their operations. Officials estimate that the planned expansions will create 120 new jobs, adding to the present 157 at the three plants.

HUD officials see the way Detroit is using the action grant funds as a perfect example of "leveraging" public money to stimulate private investment. For Detroit, each dollar of public money generated three dollars in private investment capital.

The First Round: $150 Million in Grants to 45 Cities

Here is how the Department of Housing and Urban Development allocated the first $150 million in urban development action grants:

Atlanta, Ga., $1.7 million for expansion of baking company plant.

Baltimore, Md., $10 million for second mortgage for hotel and pedestrian walkways to convention center.

Binghamton, N.Y., $1.09 million for industrial plant expansion.

Birmingham, Ala., $1.1 million for neighborhood project housing and commercial development.

Boston, Mass., two grants: $8 million for parking garage in retail-hotel complex; $2.4 million for upper income housing development.

Bridgeport, Conn., $696,000 for low income housing rehabilitation.

Buffalo, N.Y., $4 million for second position mortgage and interim construction financing to assist developer of hotel linked to city convention center.

Charleston, S.C., $4.1 million for hotel-convention center.

Cincinnati, Ohio, $6.77 million for industrial development project.

Cleveland, Ohio, $7.5 million for downtown business revitalization project.

Compton, Calif., $2.19 million to help establish nonprofit, manufactured housing corporation.

Detroit, Mich., $1.2 million for industrial expansion.

Evansville, Ind., $511,200 for neighborhood housing.

Gadsden, Ala., $1.3 million for downtown improvements, housing.

Greenville, S.C., $5.5 million for downtown hotel, convention center, parking garage, office building.

Hartford, Conn., two grants: $400,000 to help finance shopping mall; $250,000 for solar water heating manufacturing company.

Jersey City, N.J., $7 million for housing rehabilitation and construction of new housing for low and moderate income families.

Kankakee, Ill., $85,500 for land for aluminum plant.

Kansas City, Kan., $2.9 million for loan for hotel developer.

Lewiston, Maine, $2.4 million for downtown redevelopment.

Lima, Ohio, $175,000 for low income housing.

Los Angeles, Calif., $635,000 for commercial development.

Louisville, Ky., $2 million for loan for renovation of historic hotel, other commercial development.

Miami, Fla., $1 million for moderate income housing.

Newark, N.J., $1 million for housing program in which homeowners would receive rebates on home improvements.

New Britain, Conn., $375,000 to rehabilitate manufacturing plant.

Ogden, Utah, $2 million for shopping mall, parking and restoration of historic railroad station.

Paterson, N.J., $4.2 million for industrial expansion.

Pawtucket, R.I., $5.9 million for industrial, commercial and residential project using site of Narragansett Race Track.

Portsmouth, Va., $2.9 million for middle, upper income housing.

Poughkeepsie, N.Y., $1 million loan for hotel in the downtown area.

Reading, Pa., $4.8 million for storm sewer project.

Riverside, Calif., three grants: $700,000 for industrial project; $300,000 for citrus processing plant; $500,000 for commercial expansion.

St. Louis, Mo., $10.5 million for shopping, hotel, housing complex.

St. Paul, Minn., $4.8 million for shopping, hotel, office complex.

San Antonio, Texas, $6.5 million for hotel, retail center, parking garage and pedestrian walkway.

Schenectady, N.Y., two grants: $500,000 for downtown commercial project; $150,000 to help convert warehouse into housing units.

Scranton, Pa., $450,000 for nursing homes, physicians' building, apartment complex.

Seattle, Wash., $1.5 million for downtown retail office complex.

South Bend, Ind., $7.6 million for downtown office buildings, retail stores, hotel, parking, and ice rink.

Springfield, Mass., $1.01 million for commercial projects.

Tacoma, Wash., $1 million for rehabilitation of buildings for housing and retail purposes.

Toledo, Ohio, $12 million for downtown improvement project.

Utica, N.Y., $2.2 million for public pedestrian plaza and parking garage connected to hotel complex.

Wilmington, Del., $1.9 million for second mortgage on hotel project.

---

problems, the long-term solution may lie with basic economic development.

"You can have people with nice homes and a roof over their heads," said one administration official, "but without jobs who is going to pay the rent or feed the kids?"

Conversations with officials in HUD and in the White House suggest that there is no clear-cut agreement on the issue. Embry maintained that HUD still sees housing development as its major role. But the president's reorganization study is taking a close look at various economic development activities of HUD and other federal agencies, and may make some recommendations in 1979 which could serve to establish a clear-cut policy.

'Reasonable Balance'

Sen. William Proxmire, D-Wis., who wields considerable influence over HUD activities in his dual role as chairman of the Senate Banking, Housing and Urban Affairs Committee and chairman of the Senate Appropriations Subcommittee on HUD, has also joined in the debate.

Citing a mandate in the 1977 law to achieve a "reasonable balance" among commercial, industrial and residential projects, Proxmire wrote Harris in an April 14 letter that "it appears to me...that the first round allocation does not reflect the reasonable balance required by the law."

HUD's own analysis of the first $150 million awarded showed that 44 percent of the projects were commercial in nature, 32 percent industrial and 24 percent residential. Only $19 million was awarded for neighborhood projects, according to HUD.

Proxmire suggested in his letter to Harris that he thought "affirmative measures" would be needed to ensure that an increased proportion of money is spent in the future for neighborhood-residential projects.

Proxmire reportedly considered proposing an amendment to the fiscal 1979 HUD authorization bill (S 2637) to ensure that more neighborhood projects be funded, but decided against it. However, Sen. Edward W. Brooke, R-Mass., succeeded in adding an amendment to require HUD to assess the impact of a potential action grant project on a neighborhood before deciding whether to fund the project.

HUD officials say they are sensitive to neighborhood interests. Embry wrote a letter to mayors across the country urging the submission of neighborhood projects in future grant applications. HUD officials also point out that in the first round of grants of 116 applications only 14 could be classified as neighborhood projects.

But HUD is not willing to commit itself to any numerical balance. The law does not define "reasonable balance" and HUD officials have declined to define, in numerical terms, what the phrase means to them.

'We Would Like a Crutch'

The exchange lasted less than five minutes, but it brought out quite clearly two sharply different views of the urban development action grant (UDAG) program.

The sparring partners were Sen. Henry Bellmon, a two-term Republican from Oklahoma, and Patricia Roberts Harris, secretary of the Department of Housing and Urban Development (HUD).

Bellmon criticized the action grant program at an April 13 hearing of the Senate Appropriations subcommittee considering the HUD budget for fiscal 1979. The senator was concerned that Oklahoma City, the capital of his home state, did not qualify for action grants.

Harris explained that Oklahoma City, although it had some impoverished areas within its boundaries, did not qualify because its overall tax base was healthy. Outlining the action grant program, Harris said, "One of the major concerns is the rebuilding of the tax base of a community."

BELLMON: But what you are doing is punishing us...for being good guys.

HARRIS: Not at all.... We do not consider the UDAGs a reward. We consider the UDAG a crutch and a bandage.

BELLMON: Then we would like a crutch.

HARRIS: But I do not wish to have any health aid that I do not really need. I would prefer to be healthy.

BELLMON: But our needs are great.

HARRIS: But they are not as great as those of the distressed cities because you have a tax base that is a very healthy tax base.

Sen. William Proxmire, D-Wis., chairman of the subcommittee, sided with Harris, summing up what some advocates of the action grant program think is a major reason for much of the criticism.

"I think in the urban action grant program you are going to have this constant pressure to help everyone.... But unless we are very discriminating in how we spend our limited resources within a limited budget, we aren't going to provide the sort of assistance for the cities that are distressed.... You have to target. It is very painful to do it. It is a tough political problem. And it is one that is going to badger you and bother you and bother the Congress and the president, I think, for a long, long time."

Neighborhood activists have defined "reasonable balance" to mean an even distribution of money among the three main categories. But HUD officials reject that, and say they need the flexibility allowed under the current law in order to take advantage of any opportunity — commercial, industrial or neighborhood — as it comes along.

Furthermore, HUD officials say it can be difficult to categorize projects. How, Embry asked, would a business district housing project be categorized?

Regional Conflict

The debate over the action grants has not been limited to the kinds of projects that should be paid for by federal dollars. Reflecting the increasing regional orientation of Congress, the program has also come under scrutiny by the "Snowbelt" states of the Northeast and Midwest and the "Sunbelt" states of the South and West.

Some Sunbelt members of Congress have looked skeptically at the program. Sen. Henry Bellmon, R-Okla., tangled with HUD Secretary Harris at a Senate Appropriations subcommittee meeting over why major cities in his state were excluded. *(Bellmon-Harris exchange, this page)*

The Washington lobbyist for the Southern Growth Policies Board, David Peterson, reacted angrily to the first round of action grants. "So far it looks like the whole policy is oriented toward protecting investments in the Northeast," he said in an interview.

Peterson took issue with the formula used to determine eligibility, arguing that the indicators "correlate with the problems of the North" but do not take into account the problems experienced in southern and western cities.

The eligibility formula, which is designed to measure the degree of urban "distress," is based to a large extent on the rate of growth, or lack of growth, in such areas as per capita income, population and jobs. Sunbelt states have in recent years experienced higher levels of growth in all three areas than many Snowbelt states. But, Peterson argued, rate of growth is not a fair measure because the Sunbelt still ranks below the national average in the various categories.

Snowbelt spokesmen have been cautious in their comments on the action grant program. "We have to see the next few rounds of grants," said Tom Cochran, director of the Northeast-Midwest Research Institute, the research arm of the Snowbelt congressional bloc.

But, some congressional observers note, the eligibility requirements for action grants include key factors cited regularly by Snowbelt lobbyists as important indicators of urban distress, factors like the percentage of aged housing in a city and the lack of population growth. Those indicators have been found most in the Snowbelt, where cities were settled earlier and therefore have older housing stocks, and where many cities have been losing population in the last decade to Sunbelt areas.

HUD officials argue that the action grant program is not skewed to either region. They note that dozens of Sunbelt cities have qualified for grants.

HUD has declared about 300 cities with populations over 50,000 eligible for action grants. A little less than half of those can be considered Sunbelt cities.

Of the first 50 cities that received action grants, 17 were in the Sunbelt and the rest in the Snowbelt.

Another 1,800 small cities and towns have been declared eligible by HUD to apply for the smaller pot of money available for cities with populations under 50,000. The smaller cities are scattered across the country.

Legislative Outlook

Sunbelt members of Congress, who lost a 1977 battle over community development block grant formulas, concede that they do not have the votes to alter the action grant eligibility formula.

Meanwhile, Proxmire, Brooke and other congressional critics of the first-round grants intend to keep a close eye on the program in coming months, especially on the types of projects funded by HUD in the next few rounds of awards. No legislation on that issue was expected in 1978.

Whether Congress will increase the appropriation for the action grant program as requested by President Carter remained uncertain.

Carter called for additional funding of action grants to be tied to his proposal to set up a National Development Bank. But there is significant opposition to the bank proposal. Action on the bank has been postponed by the Senate Banking Committee until 1979.

Carter Disappoints Mass Transit Advocates

The Carter administration sent Congress legislation January 1978 proposing the establishment of a unified national surface transportation policy consolidating existing mass transit and highway programs. Called the Highway and Public Transportation Act of 1978 (HR 10578), the measure had been promised by the administration in response to demands for an increased commitment to urban mass transit. The bill, however, disappointed mass transit and highway program supporters. The president called for an increase of funding for transportation of only $472 million as part of his goal of a balanced budget by fiscal 1981.

The proposal to consolidate federal surface transportation programs resulted from a review of existing programs conducted in 1977 by a task force headed by Transportation Secretary Brock Adams. Adams said that the task force discovered "a crazy quilt" of aid programs. "We have different recipients for our highway and transit programs. Assistance for transportation planning is fragmented. Federal-local matching ratios are a hodgepodge of numbers.... In short, many of our programs are outdated, inflexible and arbitrary."

The administration's plan to combine planning and proposals for highway and mass transit programs marked a new departure. For years the competing modes of transportation were rarely studied together during the funding process. That encouraged piecemeal policy-making that did not weigh advantages — such as energy conservation — of one mode over another. For years highway and mass transit interests had fought each other to gain increased funding.

Matching Formula Altered

Differences in federal-state matching requirements for different types of programs had encouraged local authorities to design transportation schemes at least partly on the basis of the amount of federal money the project would bring in, rather than on the merits of the project.

Separate planning and funding programs for mass transit and highways impeded the development of a coordinated plan. And urban decay, pollution and the energy crisis were not recognized as serious transportation issues at the time the existing federal programs were formulated.

The Carter proposals attempted to redress these shortcomings by equalizing the government's share of funding for all forms of transportation; consolidating and simplifying a number of mass transit and highway planning and grant programs and requiring that federal, state and local authorities formulate transportation projects that consider land use plans, energy usage and social, economic and environmental needs.

Funding Levels Criticized

Funding levels in the administration's bill were not satisfactory to transit or highway interests. Members of both houses, as well as representatives of mass transit and

highway groups, insisted that substantially higher funding levels were vital to any transportation program.

The administration, though, proposed only modest increases in spending because of the priority given a balanced budget. Without a new revenue source, such as an increase in the federal gasoline tax or enactment of a crude oil equalization tax as proposed in fiscal 1979 energy legislation before a conference committee in August 1978, funding for transportation could not be significantly increased, administration officials concluded.

Congressional Response

Through mid-August 1978, Carter's mass transit and highway proposals had received an uneven response in Congress. The House Public Works Subcommittee on Surface Transportation rejected the plan to integrate highway and mass transit programs, and it recommended increased spending on both programs. The full House Public Works and Transportation Committee reported Aug. 11 a four-year, $66.5 billion combined highway-mass transit authorization bill.

In the Senate, three separate measures were reported May 15: a mass transit bill by the Senate Banking, Housing and Urban Affairs Committee; a highway bill by the Environment and Public Works Committee; and a highway safety bill by the Commerce, Science and Transportation Committee. A fourth bill, extending taxes feeding the Highway Trust Fund, was pending before the Finance Committee.

Background

The federal government has been wrestling with trust funds, appropriations, contract authority and various other mass transit funding proposals since the early 1960s.

Carter plan would combine all highway and mass transit programs into a single surface transportation policy.

Once primarily private businesses, bus and rail transit systems began serious ridership declines after World War II, paralleling the development of modern highways. *(Box on mass transit trends p. 78; table on declining passenger trips p. 80)*

The last year the industry as a whole showed a profit was 1962. About the same time, local governments began buying the troubled private transit systems in order to maintain the services for the public. By 1977, virtually every major bus, trolley and rail system was publicly owned.

Local governments, however, experienced the same financial problems that caused the shift from private ownership. Transit backers blamed the problems, at least partly, on the billions of dollars the federal government was giving transit's biggest rivals — highways. Attempts to abolish the Highway Trust Fund — financed by highway-user taxes including a 4-cents per gallon gasoline tax — or diverting some of it to mass transit met with minimum success.

But Congress did agree in 1964 to provide federal appropriations for capital costs — buying new buses and building or maintaining new transit systems. An attempt by Sen. Harrison A. Williams Jr., D-N.J., to set up a mass transit trust fund with automobile excise taxes failed in 1969.

The 1973 Arab oil boycott and the subsequent energy crisis forced the nation to again scrutinize the efficiency of its mass transportation systems and to look to mass transit as a way to cut down the economy's consumption of petroleum. Initially, in 1973 and 1974, concern with the energy crisis prompted congressional action to assist mass transit systems. In 1975 and 1976, however, Congress took no further action on mass transit legislation.

In the 1976 presidential campaign Carter indicated that the new Democratic administration would make mass transit one of its top priorities. But the administration offered no mass transit proposals in 1977. By the end of 1977, it was apparent that the administration was developing proposals which focused on developing an overall surface transportation policy (highway and mass transit) rather than a policy directed solely at improving urban mass transit systems.

1973 Action: Tapping the Highway Trust Fund

In a major mass transit breakthrough in 1973, mass transit supporters and urban lobbyists were able to push legislation through Congress authorizing limited use of the Highway Trust Fund for mass transit programs. The fund, established in 1956 to finance the Interstate Highway System and other federally aided highway programs, was fed from gasoline and other user taxes. It had been the exclusive preserve of the nation's highway lobby — truckers, manufacturers, contractors and other highway interests. During much of its existence the multibillion fund had been in surplus, and thus it had become an attractive target for money-starved mass transit operators.

The legislation permitting use of the Highway Trust Fund for mass transit programs was part of a three-year highway aid act (S 502 — PL 93-87) authorizing $6 billion for fiscal 1974, $6.85 billion for fiscal 1975 and $7 billion for fiscal 1976. Most of this money would come from the Highway Trust Fund and was earmarked for highway aid. For mass transit programs, the act authorized cities to tap the trust fund in fiscal 1975 for $200 million for bus transit and in fiscal 1976 for $800 million for bus or rail transportation.

1974: Mass Transit Subsidies

Continued concern with the energy crisis permeated debate over transportation policy in 1974 and provided impetus for congressional approval of a long-term urban mass transit subsidy program (S 386—PL 93-503) authorizing $11,854,000,000 billion over six years to help urban mass transit systems meet their increasing operating and capital expenses. The program, covering fiscal years 1975 through 1980, provided $7.8 billion for capital grants and $4 billion which could be used for either capital grants or operating expenses. This was the first time a federal program provided operating funds for mass transit.

1975 Senate Transit Bill

The Senate passed a bill (S 662) providing $500 million to operate mass transit projects in rural and semi-urban areas. The bill did not provide additional federal money to these areas, but simply would have allowed them to use any part of the $500 million made available to them under the 1974 act for capital grants. There was no House action in 1975 or 1976 on the bill.

1976: Highway Aid Bill

Constrained by election year considerations and the time limitations of a short session, Congress took no new initiatives in the transportation field in 1976 and undertook instead only legislation necessary to maintain existing programs. In action extending federal highway aid programs through fiscal 1978, Congress declined to tamper further with the Highway Trust Fund. The two-year, $17.6 billion highway authorization (HR 8235—PL 94-289) was described by sponsors as an interim measure to maintain existing programs while Congress re-evaluated the Highway Trust Fund.

1977: Carter Lowers Transit Priority

Presidential candidate Jimmy Carter raised the hopes of mass transit supporters in 1976 in an address to the Democratic Party Platform Committee. "Arresting this deterioration [of transportation systems] and completing needed work on new urban transit systems must become the nation's first transportation priority," Carter said.

Once in the White House, however, Carter's transportation policy proved a disappointment to mass transit advocates. Carter did not mention mass transit in his April 1977 energy message. While he stressed energy conservation in the message — a theme repeatedly used by transit supporters as a prime argument in favor of aid for mass transit, mass transit was not one of the solutions the president presented for saving gasoline. Asked at a press conference why his energy message had omitted mass transit, he responded: "I think that this is a separate item that will be handled under the Transportation Department."

Despite the administration's position, the Senate in June passed a bill (S 208) authorizing $4.75 billion over five years (fiscal 1978-82) for mass transit capital grants — used for building subways and replacing worn-out buses. The bill also created a new $295 million fund to help the nation's largest urban areas pay their spiraling bills for operating bus and subway systems. As initially proposed by Sen. Harrison A. Williams Jr., D-N.J., S 208 authorized $11.4 billion in capital grants over the five-year period. Williams claimed that since available mass transit funds were almost depleted, additional funding was necessary to begin new projects and assure that those already begun were fully financed.

Williams eventually agreed to a compromise that cut his original authorization by more than half after the Carter administration, in a surprise announcement, said it did not want to fund any new mass transit projects before fiscal 1980. Transportation Secretary Brock Adams said Feb. 25 that there were enough funds already authorized to keep transit projects moving through fiscal 1979. In the interim, the administration was working on its proposals for the future funding of mass transit and highway programs.

There was no House action in 1977 on S 208. The Surface Transportation Subcommittee of the House Public Works and Transportation Committee held extensive hearings on a bill (HR 8648) to fund both mass transit and highway programs.

Chairman James J. Howard, D-N.J., said he wanted to devise a balanced transportation plan under which all modes of transportation would be funded and administered in an interrelated manner. As part of the plan, Howard had hoped to set up a trust fund for mass transit financed by an increased federal tax on gasoline. That hope was dashed when the House not only refused to earmark gas taxes for mass transit but killed a gas tax increase altogether in August 1977.

1978 Congressional Action

House Subcommittee Rejects Carter Plan

The House Public Works Subcommittee on Surface Transportation rejected the Carter administration's proposal to streamline and integrate federal mass transit and highway programs, make them more adaptable to state and local needs and align them with other domestic goals sought by the administration such as a balanced budget, energy conservation and pollution control.

In a bill (HR 11733) cosponsored by 18 of the panel's 23 members, the Surface Transportation Subcommittee instead chose to:

● Require mass transit and highway projects to continue to compete for federal dollars.

● Place additional restrictions on state and local use of transit and highway funds.

● Ignore the administration's pleas to keep spending levels down.

● Drop a requirement that energy conservation and pollution control be considered in the design of mass transit and highway projects.

The subcommittee bill, drafted March 22, was studded with authorizations for "demonstration projects" and other provisions that, if enacted, could mean hundreds of millions of dollars in federal aid to public works projects located in the congressional districts of Public Works Committee members.

Discussing the subcommittee's bill March 22, Chairman Howard called it "undoubtedly the most significant piece of transportation legislation ever to come before [the House].... I am proud of this bill and look forward to bringing it to the floor."

However, Transportation Department officials, concerned over the funding levels in the subcommittee bill as well as other provisions, greeted the bill with alarm.

Transportation Funding Compared

(authorization levels in millions of dollars)

	FY '78 (actual)	FY '79 (Carter proposal)
Highway Programs		
Interstate highways	$ 3,341	$ 3,500
Interstate maintenance	175	175
Primary	1,514	1,500
Secondary	—	—
Urban	703	700
Rural	683	700*
Safety	500	500
Bridges	180	450
Miscellaneous	323	189
Highway, subtotal	$ 7,419	$ 7,714
Mass Transit Programs		
Discretionary	1,400	640
Formula	775	1,735
Interstate transfer	775	675
Commuter rail	45	—
Rural	—	86*
Planning	55	—
Miscellaneous	85	90
Mass Transit, subtotal	$3,135	$ 3,226
Total Authorizations	$10,554	$10,940

Rural highway and mass transit programs were consolidated under the administration plan. At least 10 per cent of the $786 million authorization was to be used for mass transit.

Once Thriving U.S. Urban Mass Transit Systems . . .

Urban mass transit has been in decline in the United States for so long that it is easy to forget that the industry once was dynamic, innovative and even profitable. The golden age of urban transit spanned the years from 1880 to 1920. The financial stability of many companies deteriorated during the Depression of the 1930s, and as revenues dropped, transit managers tried to lower costs by decreasing service and increasing fares — often simultaneously. More people turned to mass transit during World War II because of gasoline and tire rationing, but when automobiles again became more accessible after the war, ridership took another downturn. By the mid-1950s, the mass transit industry was in terrible shape. "So decrepit and deplorable was the state of mass transit and commuter railroad service and the quality of the equipment," wrote author George M. Smerk in *Urban Mass Transportation* (1974), "that it could truly be said that for people who could afford a choice, there was no suitable alternative to the use of the automobile in most U.S. cities." More than 190 transit companies went out of business in this country between 1954 and 1963.

Mass transportation of passengers in cities originated in the horse-drawn "omnibus" service established in Paris in 1819. Twelve years later, the first omnibus appeared in the United States. The vehicle operated in New York, on Broadway between Bond Street and the Battery, and charged about 12 cents a ride. The omnibus was soon to be outmoded by a new concept: a vehicle with flanged wheels that could be drawn along a track of iron rails set in the middle of the street. Two such vehicles of stagecoach design began service in 1832, on a track that ran for a mile and a half from Prince Street to Fourteenth Street along the Bowery. This New York and Harlem Railroad proved so popular that within a year the route was extended to four miles and additional cars were purchased. Surface transit in New York City was eventually supplemented by extensive subways and elevated railway lines.

People in other cities were slow to appreciate the advantages of street railway service. One short line was established in New Orleans in 1835. Then nothing happened until 1853, when a street railway was built in Brooklyn.

The first street railway in Massachusetts began operation between Boston and Cambridge in 1856. Two years later the idea spread to Philadelphia. Cincinnati, Baltimore and Chicago tried the experiment in 1859. From that time the progress of the industry was rapid. By 1890, there were approximately 105,000 horses and mules engaged in pulling 28,000 streetcars on some 5,700 miles of track in the United States.

Rise and Fall of the Electric Railway Industry

Meanwhile, the technology of urban transit continued to advance. San Francisco's cable-car system began service in 1873, and Richmond, Va., became the first city with an electric urban railway in 1888. Because of the great expense of installation and operation, the cable-car system never saw widespread use. But the spread of the electric railway was rapid. The U.S. Census of Street and Electric Railways for 1902 recorded nearly 22,000 miles of electrified track. Horse-drawn and cable lines had dwindled to only about 500 miles. New York and Washington employed underground current, while Cincinnati used a two-wire overhead system. Everywhere else the single overhead wire system was used in substantially the form that was originally developed in Richmond.

The greatest electric-railway expansion took place between 1902 and 1917. At the end of that period, the industry had about 80,000 passenger cars and 45,000 miles of track. But some of the problems that plague transit companies today were already beginning to appear. Fares were almost universally fixed at five cents, regardless of the length of ride, and extension of track into outlying areas made for marginally profitable lines. Furthermore, labor and material costs were rising steeply. In the early 1920s, increasing automobile ownership began to compete with public transit, and traffic congestion worsened. The street railway industry also was having difficulty replacing obsolete equipment. At the American Electric Railway Association's annual convention in 1926, it was noted that more than 28,000 electric railway cars over 20 years old were still in operation.

Public Works Committee Action

The subcommittee bill had provided for a four-year authorization totaling $65.9 billion. When the measure came before the full committee, the funding level was raised to $66.5 billion, despite Transportation Secretary Adams' earlier threat to recommend a veto of an authorization as high as the one the subcommittee had approved. The administration had proposed authorizations totaling about $45 billion for the four-year period 1979-1982.

(Companion legislation pending in the Senate would authorize program levels only a few billion dollars more than the administration-backed legislation for a comparable period. *See p. 80*)

HR 11733, as reported Aug. 11 (H Rept 95-1485), authorized about $16.8 billion for highway and mass transit programs in fiscal 1979. Included in this were about $12.2 billion for highway and highway safety programs in fiscal 1979, compared to $7.7 billion proposed by Carter. For

mass transit, the committee bill contained $4.6 billion for fiscal 1979, compared to a request for $3.2 billion.

Subsequently, however, the administration extracted a promise from subcommittee chairman Howard that he would offer floor amendments to reduce the authorizations to about $61 billion. He said he would accept cuts of $1 billion a year in highway programs and $400 million a year in mass transit authorizations.

Ways and Means Action

But before the measure could be reported to the House floor, it faced a formidable hurdle: the Ways and Means Committee. The committee traditionally acquiesced to the House Public Works Committee's recommendations concerning management of the Highway Trust Fund, which funds federal aid highway programs. Although Public Works shapes federal aid highway policy, Ways and Means has jurisdiction over the taxes that feed the trust fund.

. . . Have Declined Since The End of World War II

Another problem for transit companies was the appearance around 1914 of privately owned automobiles whose drivers solicited rides at five cents a head. Since these so-called "jitneys" were able to follow fairly flexible routes, jitney service fell somewhere between taxis and the fixed-route streetcars. A person looking for a ride could hail a jitney at a specified stop or anywhere along its route. In some cases, jitneys were driven by persons going to and from work, thus providing a variety of routes and schedules.

Largely as a result of political pressure from the street railways, jitneys were declared illegal and went out of business in most U.S. cities by the early 1920s. Many street railway companies saw the jitney as a forerunner of organized motorbus service and went into the bus business themselves. Between 1917 and 1937, electric railway trackage in the United States decreased from 45,000 to 25,000 miles and the number of electric railway passenger cars dropped from 80,000 to around 35,000.

Federal Assistance in the Field of Mass Transit

Federal support of urban mass transit in the United States has been fairly limited. The first major federal aid was provided for by Congress as part of the Housing Act of 1961, which authorized up to $25 million in grants for demonstration projects and $50 million in loans for transportation facilities. Most of the demonstration projects were small, such as $160,462 to test the use of low-fare miniature buses for shoppers in downtown Washington, D.C., and $10,000 to study the feasibility of monorail in Seattle. The aid program was expanded by the Urban Mass Transportation Act of 1964, and amendments of 1966. Also, mass transit aid was incorporated in the Housing and Urban Development Act of 1968.

Under the 1964 law and its extensions, cities that received grants were required to provide at least one-third of a project's net cost — that portion of the total cost which could not be financed from the transit system's revenues. Cities also had to show that a given project would conform to a unified public transportation system. Under an emergency grant program, however, federal funds were made available even if areawide transit planning was not complete. In these circumstances, the federal government paid only one-half the net cost of the project.

Until mid-1968, urban mass transportation programs were administered by the office of metropolitan development in the Department of Housing and Urban Development (HUD). A presidential reorganization plan during that year, however, transferred the programs to the Department of Transportation, where they were consolidated in the newly formed Urban Mass Transportation Administration (UMTA).

In 1969, President Nixon sent Congress his recommendations for greatly increasing mass transit funding to make "public transportation an attractive alternative to private car use." He proposed to set aside $10 billion in federal funds over a 12-year period to upgrade local mass transit. The bill that eventually passed Congress was in basic agreement with the president's original proposal. It provided for a 10-year, $12 billion program, with $3.1 billion authorized for the first five years. These funds would match local or state contributions on a 2-to-1 basis. The 1970 Urban Mass Transportation Act also allowed transit operators to make long-term commitments on new designs and equipment, a step intended to free them from the uncertainties of having to depend on year-to-year congressional appropriations.

In 1974, for the first time, Congress provided federal operating subsidies for mass transit systems under the National Mass Transportation Assistance Act of 1974. The bill authorized a total of $11.9 billion for urban mass transit over a six-year period with $7.8 billion earmarked for capital grants and $4 billion for operation grants. Under the act's formula, the federal government could pay up to 80 percent of the total costs for capital projects, but only as much as half the cost if the money was used to defray operating expenses. Enactment of the measure marked a victory for the U.S. Conference of Mayors, which had lobbied hard for the bill. "This marks the day when the automobile stops getting a monopoly of favored treatment from the federal government," said San Francisco Mayor Joseph Alioto, president of the organization.

However, in 1978 — the first year that authorizations for both highway and mass transit aid programs were combined in one bill (HR 11733) — Ways and Means would decide whether the Public Works bill was fiscally responsible.

While trust fund receipts were expected to range from between $7 billion and $8 billion annually during the four years, the bill would authorize trust fund expenditures of about $11 billion annually.

House Public Works Surface Transportation Subcommittee Chairman Howard earlier had said a two-cent increase in fuel taxes would be necessary to fund the legislation. Later, however, he said no new revenues would be needed.

His solution to the shortage of funds, the Ways and Means Committee and the Congressional Budget Office (CBO) concluded later, was to authorize highway projects out of the fund for four years, but to extend the Highway Trust Fund for six years. Trust fund revenues from the last two years would be used to cover costs incurred during the first four.

The mechanism Public Works was proposing caused the CBO to conclude in an April "draft analysis" that the practice constituted a "backdoor" tax. "The four-year program would be paid for by revenue anticipated over a six-year period," the draft stated, "apparently avoiding the need for immediate increase in highway taxes."

The legislation still might have made it through Ways and Means without a murmur had it not been for Ways and Means Oversight Subcommittee Chairman Sam Gibbons, D-Fla., and the full committee's ranking Republican, Barber B. Conable Jr., N.Y.

Ways and Means was scheduled to mark up the tax portions of HR 11733 on May 18. Public Works had completed markup of the authorizing portions of the bill May 12, but by May 17 that committee had transmitted to Ways and Means one copy of the legislation and nothing else.

Trend of Transit Passenger Trips, 1940-77

(in millions)

Year	Light Rail	Heavy Rail	Total Rail	Trolley Coach	Motor Bus	Total Passenger Trips
1940	5,943	2,382	8,325	534	4,239	13,098
1945	9,426	2,698	12,124	1,244	9,886	23,254
1950	3,904	2,264	6,168	1,658	9,420	17,246
1955	1,207	1,870	3,077	1,202	7,250	11,529
1960	463	1,850	2,313	657	6,425	9,395
1965	276	1,858	2,134	305	5,814	8,253
1970	235	1,881	2,116	182	5,034	7,332
1975	124	1,673	1,810	78	5,034	7,332
1976	112	1,632	1,759	75	5,084	6,972
1977 (Preliminary)	103	2,123*	2,251	70	5,247	7,081
					5,295	7,616

*1977 figures count a transfer from one subway line to another as two trips. Figures prior to 1977 counted transfers from one line to another as one trip.

SOURCE: American Public Transit Association

"They might have been able to slip it through if they'd at least sent over a copy of the report," commented a Ways and Means aide.

Because no report language accompanied the bill, Gibbons and Conable asked Ways and Means Chairman Al Ullman, D-Ore., to delay committee markup. They then asked the Transportation Department to draft an amendment that limited spending from the Highway Trust Fund to amounts equal to revenue projections for a given year.

The amendment provided that, when expenditures from the fund surpassed projected revenues, every project authorized would be funded on a prorated basis.

The amendment was supported by Transportation Secretary Brock Adams, Treasury Secretary W. Michael Blumenthal and Office of Management and Budget Director James T. McIntyre Jr. in a May 17 letter to Ullman.

"We hope that your committee will not follow the course of using tomorrow's revenues to pay for today's programs," the three wrote Ullman. "We hope you will work with your Ways and Means colleagues in generating support for our efforts to bring the program levels to an acceptable figure."

Five-Year Extension. While the bill was being considered by Ways and Means, Surface Transportation chairman Howard made his promise to offer amendments to reduce the authorization levels in HR 11733. The Public Works Committee then requested a five-year extension of the trust fund and the Ways and Means Committee approved by voice vote an amendment offered by Rep. James A. Burke, D-Mass., to extend the trust fund for five rather than six years.

The Ways and Means panel defeated two restrictive amendments and the Conable-Gibbons amendment was never introduced.

Senate Committee Action

Three Senate committees reported bills — S 3073, S 2541 and S 2441 — May 15 revising the nation's highway and mass transit programs. Mass transit authorizations were under the jurisdiction of the Banking, Housing and Urban Affairs Committee; highway authorizations were considered by the Environment and Public Works Committee and highway safety authorizations were considered by the Commerce, Science and Transportation Committee. A fourth bill (S 2440), extending taxes feeding the Highway Trust Fund, was pending before the Finance Committee.

Highway Bill. The Federal Aid Highway Act of 1978 (S 3073) was reported (S Rept 95-833) May 15 by the Senate Environment and Public Works Committee by a vote of 14-0.

The bill as reported proposed a number of changes in the structure and direction of federal aid highway programs. It also provided authorizations totaling $8.5 billion from the Highway Trust Fund for these programs for fiscal years 1979-80 and provided authorizations for the Interstate Highway System for fiscal years 1980-81.

As reported, S 3073 adopted a number of recommendations put forward by the Carter administration concerning funding levels, program consolidations and changes in program goals.

Highway authorization levels were kept in line with expected revenues from the trust fund, the committee stressed. To permit authorizations to "clearly exceed revenues over a comparable time period" could lead in the future to "drastically reduced" program levels or tax increases decided "in a crisis context." Either outcome would weaken the trust fund concept, the report concluded.

The statement was an apparent reference to HR 11733, which, as reported by the House Public Works Committee, authorized trust fund expenditures of about $11 billion annually for 1979-82, to be financed from trust fund receipts estimated at from $7 billion to $8 billion annually.

As reported, S 3073 authorized $3.5 billion annually for the Interstate Highway System for fiscal years 1980-81 and provided a number of incentives for accelerating completion of the system or dropping non-essential segments. The annual authorization for fiscal 1979 was $3.25 billion.

S 3073 authorized annually from the trust fund $1.5 billion for the federal-aid primary road system, $675 million for the secondary road system, $700 million for urban highways and $285 million for the highway safety improvement program.

The bill authorized an additional $485 million annually for fiscal years 1979 and 1980 for road aid projects requiring appropriations.

Authorizations for a number of other minor categorical grant programs were continued. One new categorical grant program created by the Federal Aid Highway Act of 1978 authorized $20 million annually for two years for the construction of bikeways.

Highway Safety Programs. S 2541 was one of two Senate bills providing funding for highway and motor vehicle safety programs, which are administered primarily by the National Highway Traffic Safety Administration (NHTSA).

The bill, reported (S Rept 95-870) May 15 by the Senate Commerce Committee, authorized funds for NHTSA activities under the Highway Safety Act of 1966 (PL 89-564). The other NHTSA authorization bill (S 2604) concerned programs provided for by the National Traffic and Motor Vehicle Safety Act of 1966 (PL 89-563) and the Motor Vehicle Information and Cost Savings Act of 1972 (PL 92-513).

Under the Highway Safety Act, NHTSA was authorized to award incentive grants and to develop mandatory safety standards to help states and localities develop their own safety programs for motor vehicles, drivers and highways.

As reported by the Commerce panel, S 2541:
● Authorized from the Highway Trust Fund $175 million for each of fiscal years 1979 and 1980, and $200 million for each of fiscal years 1981 and 1982, to carry out highway safety programs.
● Authorized $50 million annually from the Highway Trust Fund for fiscal years 1979 through 1982 for NHTSA highway safety research and development.
● Authorized from general Treasury funds $5 million for fiscal 1980, $10 million for fiscal 1981 and $15 million for fiscal 1982 for grants to states developing "innovative" approaches to highway safety. Under existing law, the grants were awarded as "incentives" to reduce highway fatalities.
● Continued the formula under existing law providing that the federal share of highway safety program funding be $70 of every $100 spent; the other $30 was provided by local funding.
● Provided a formula for apportioning the federal highway safety program funds to the states according to their population and miles of public roads.
● Set up mechanisms to improve enforcement of the 55-mile-per-hour speed limit.

High Funding in Transit Bill. As reported (S Rept 95-857) by the Senate Banking Committee May 15, the Federal Public Transportation Act of 1978 (S 2441) closely paralleled the Carter administration's recommendations to consolidate transportation programs. The bill was approved unanimously.

"The committee fully supports the president's stated objectives for a coordinated and rational national transportation policy," the committee stated in its report. "Of the challenges the United States faces on many fronts, the harsh realities of our energy extravagance and inefficiency are among the most serious.... But one essential ingredient in the total solution will be greater dependence and ever increasing reliance on public transportation to provide the mobility our population demands."

The major problem the committee found with the administration's proposals, the report explained, was "the inadequacy of the funding levels." Although mass transit authorizations for fiscal 1978 — not counting transfers from the Interstate account to fund substitute mass transit projects — totaled $2.4 billion, and the Carter administration recommended $2.6 billion for fiscal 1979, S 2441 as approved by the committee authorized $3.4 billion for fiscal 1979 federal mass transit aid, $3.7 billion for 1980, $3.8 billion for 1981 and $3.9 billion for 1982.

The committee also altered the administration's recommendations on restructuring existing formula and discretionary grant programs, and rejected altogether a recommendation to create a combined mass transit-highway aid program for small urban and rural areas.

The committee also adopted by a vote of 8-7 a controversial amendment offered by Edward W. Brooke, R-Mass., to authorize an additional $891 million over four years to subsidize up to 50 percent of a transit system's operating deficits, so long as the total federal operating subsidy did not exceed one-third of total operating costs. The provision would result in a marked increase in operating subsidies for Boston, New York and San Francisco. Secretary Brock Adams, in a May 1 letter to the committee, said the administration opposed the amendment.

Major Transit Provisions. S 2441 as reported:
● Authorized in federal aid to urban mass transportation $3.4 billion for fiscal 1979, $3.7 billion for 1980, $3.8 billion for 1981 and $3.9 billion for 1982.
● Narrowed the existing discretionary grant program to permit the transportation secretary to make loans and grants at his discretion, primarily for the construction of major new transit systems and extension of existing ones.

Included under the discretionary program were grants for construction costs of such systems; acquisition of equipment, facilities and real estate; the funding of new technology demonstration projects; grants or loans for urban development projects related to transportation, and for improvements in urban transportation facilities.
● Broadened the existing grant program in urban areas where federal transit aid was apportioned according to a fixed formula. The program continued to be the major source for funds to purchase equipment for public transit systems and to subsidize such systems' operating deficits, but was expanded to cover the costs of routine bus replacement, the modernization of bus facilities and equipment, the special transportation needs of the elderly and handicapped and commuter rail operation subsidies.

The formula by which the funds were allocated was altered to consider an area's population and population density, the age of its bus fleet, the number of miles the system served annually, and the size and capacity of existing mass transit services in the area. The formula also was altered to favor the largest urban areas.
● Created a new program within the Urban Mass Transportation Administration (UMTA) to provide capital and operating subsidies for the mass transit needs of small urban and rural areas.
● Directed the transportation secretary to discourage the purchase of transit materials and equipment from countries that offered those goods for sale at less than the cost of production or otherwise erected non-tariff trade barriers.
● Provided a mechanism for urban areas to reject metropolitan planning organizations designated for them by state governors. ∎

Carter, Congress and the Welfare System

True to his 1976 campaign promise, President Carter Aug. 6, 1977, set before Congress a plan to overhaul the nation's welfare system. But, a year later, passage of Carter's plan or any of the other comprehensive proposals put forward on Capitol Hill appeared unlikely in 1978. Instead, some members of Congress — feeling the pressures of an October adjournment date and having to face disgruntled taxpayers at the polls in November — began to look for compromises and scaled-down approaches to the welfare issue.

Carter had proposed replacing the existing welfare system with a program that he said would provide jobs for those who needed work, provide fairer and more uniform cash benefits, promote family stability and improve the self-respect of recipients.

The "Program for Better Jobs and Income" was to accomplish those goals by spending $3.1 billion to create 1.4 million public service jobs, provide a basic cash benefit to the needy, relieve the financial burden on every state by at least 10 percent the first year of the plan in fiscal 1981 and include benefits for the first time for the so-called working poor.

About 32 million persons were to receive benefits under Carter's proposed system, which would roll together the existing Aid to Families with Dependent Children (AFDC), Supplemental Security Income (SSI) and food stamp programs and replace them with the flat cash grant. About 30 million persons received aid under the existing programs.

Praise and Problems

The President's plan had not been without its congressional advocates. Rep. James C. Corman, D-Calif., described it as an "excellent blueprint" and said he hoped it would be kept "pretty much intact" as it made its way through Congress. Corman was chairman of the Welfare Reform Subcommittee which was specially created to consider Carter's welfare reform package.

Detractors, however, found a lot to criticize. Daniel Patrick Moynihan, D-N.Y., chairman of the Senate Finance Subcommittee on Public Assistance, called the bill spelling out the plan "grievously disappointing" and indicated that the climate for welfare reform might not be right.

Russell B. Long, D-La., chairman of the Senate Finance Committee, said the plan had "laudable objectives" but predicted the plan could cost two to four times as much as estimated. He suggested pilot-testing it "for a few years."

Rep. William (Bill) Clay, D-Mo., charged at initial House hearings that the plan "doesn't even begin to attack the problems of joblessness of the inner cities of this country.... This doesn't even scratch the surface."

Rep. L. A. (Skip) Bafalis, R-Fla., on the other hand, said the "American people should be indignant, outraged and thoroughly alarmed" at the plan, which will "require the printing of more artificial money.... The welfare state will have completely and fully taken over."

Supporters and detractors expressed reservations about some specific points, particularly the projected cost and the jobs section.

Costs. Noting that the administration's cost estimates had increased about $400,000 during the six weeks between when the plan was made public and when House hearings began, Bill Gradison, R-Ohio, told Health, Education and Welfare (HEW) Secretary Joseph A. Califano Jr. that the "sticker price is a lot higher than advertised."

The subcommittee's ranking Republican, Guy Vander Jagt, Mich., charged that the administration managed to keep the net additional federal cost to $2.8-billion by "grossly underestimating the cost of the new program and overestimating the cost of existing programs."

Jobs. Numerous concerns were aired over the jobs portion of the plan. While some subcommittee members complained that the proposal did not provide enough jobs, others questioned whether enough could be created.

Al Ullman, D-Ore., chairman of the House Ways and Means Committee, objected to the fact that large numbers of poor working people would be considered a part of the welfare population rather than the working population.

Other concerns about the jobs programs were:

● That public service employers might fire regular workers in order to hire cheaper, government-subsidized minimum-wage employees.

● That the government would be indirectly subsidizing employers who would have little incentive to raise their employees' salaries above the minimum wage.

● That the new public service jobs to be created would compete with public service jobs already in existence.

Congressional Action

Interest groups representing the nation's governors, state legislators, county officials and mayors lobbied aggressively for Carter's legislative package. The proposal was approved, with some slight changes, by the House Welfare Reform Subcommittee in February 1978.

When none of the panel's parent committees — Ways and Means, Education and Labor and Agriculture — took action on the bill, the administration and congressional advocates of welfare reform began to negotiate. In early June 1978 administration and House leaders reached agreement on the broad outlines of a welfare reform bill substantially scaled down from the President's original proposal.

But later that month, while staff aides were still attempting to work out actual draft legislation, House Speaker Thomas P. O'Neill Jr., D-Mass., pronounced the legislation dead for the 95th Congress. O'Neill said June 22 that the Senate leadership had informed him it was too late in the session for a major welfare reform bill to reach the Senate floor. Others said that, in the aftermath of the so-called "tax revolt" which led to approval of Proposition 13 in California, Congress was not interested in major new federal expenditures for welfare.

But another push for welfare legislation began the following week in the Senate. On June 28 Alan Cranston, D-Calif., and Moynihan announced a new welfare proposal which appeared to have the right ingredients: financial relief for state and local governments, a lower price tag than other proposals and the support of powerful Senate Finance Chairman Long. But congressional sources predicted that some trade-offs with advocates of more extensive changes in the welfare system might be necessary to win approval of the Cranston-Moynihan proposal. The proposal had not been introduced in the Senate as of mid-August.

Background

"Welfare reform" had about as many definitions as there were individuals and groups trying to redo the system. "Reform" can mean any number of things, ranging from broadening eligibility and increasing benefits to tightening requirements in order to keep people off the rolls.

The need for welfare programs depends largely on the success of employment, private savings and government social insurance programs in meeting basic income needs.

HEW classified seven government programs as "social insurance" programs—Social Security, Railroad Retirement, Workmen's Compensation, Black Lung, Unemployment Insurance, Veterans' Compensation and Medicare. Although not designed specifically for the poor, the programs redistributed among the population 2½ times as many dollars as welfare programs, according to HEW figures. By themselves they reduced the percentage of the U.S. population considered "poor" to 14 per cent, from 25 per cent. In fiscal 1977, benefits from the seven programs were expected to exceed $130-billion.

There were nine basic income assistance programs which HEW considered part of the welfare structure and which were the programs included in studies of welfare reform. With these programs, the percentage of poverty-level persons in the United States was reduced to less than 7 per cent of the population if in-kind transfers such as Medicaid and housing subsidies were counted as part of income. The nine programs cost federal, state and local governments about $50 billion a year. *(Box, next page)*

Starting with the development of general assistance in the nation's early years, the programs grew irregularly and were still increasing in number into the 1970s.

The 1930s saw the birth of veterans' pensions (1933), Aid to Families with Dependent Children (AFDC) (1935) and housing assistance (1937). In the ensuing 27 years there were changes in the programs—AFDC coverage was extended to needy parents in 1950 and to families with unemployed fathers (at states' option) in 1961—but no new ones were enacted until 1964. In 1964 and 1965 the two largest programs were created by Congress: food stamps and Medicaid. Two more programs were added in 1972: Basic Educational Opportunity Grants and Supplemental Security Income (SSI). Earned income tax credits were enacted in 1975.

The irregular growth of the programs led to wide disparities in benefit levels among states and to a cumbersome administrative structure. In the AFDC program, for example, annual benefit levels for a four-person family varied in June 1976 from $5,964 in Hawaii to $720 in Mississippi. At the same time, the federal share of those benefits equaled $2,982 in Hawaii compared to $600 in Mississippi.

Reform Attempts

The disparities and other shortcomings were responsible for numerous, unsuccessful attempts to bring about welfare reform.

Family Assistance Plan. In 1969, President Nixon sent to Congress his Family Assistance Plan (FAP), which was to be a substitute for AFDC. Momentum for reform had been building for years as the number of welfare recipients climbed and costs grew. Pressure was strong for the federal government to assume a much greater share of the welfare burden from hard-pressed state and local governments, for more uniform benefits and standards nationwide, and for providing some aid to the working poor.

Nixon's program, based essentially on recommendations of a task force headed by Richard P. Nathan of the Brookings Institution, called for a two-track system of federal payments and benefits to families of the unemployed and, for the first time, to families of the working poor.

The proposal passed the House in 1970 but foundered in the Senate.

A revised version of the plan was introduced in the 92nd Congress, again passed the House but was dropped by the Senate Finance Committee, which substituted a "workfare" program sponsored by Chairman Russell B. Long, D-La. Conferees failed to agree on the different proposals before the end of the session, and Nixon announced in early 1973 that he would not resubmit the plan to the 93rd Congress.

Griffiths Plan. Another approach to welfare reform was developed in 1974 by a subcommittee of the Joint Economic Committee chaired by former Rep. Martha W. Griffiths (D Mich. 1955-75). The combination cash allowance-tax rebate plan embodied the negative income tax concept which assured a minimum income to all eligible households based on family size. Support payments would decrease as earned income rose.

The grants would have replaced AFDC, food stamps, SSI and the existing personal exemption and standard deduction in the federal income tax. But the proposal was never acted upon.

Carter Promises

During the 1976 presidential campaign, Carter pledged "a complete overhaul of our welfare system," and the Democratic Party platform spelled out specific changes aimed at eliminating waste and inequities.

Calling the welfare system "an insult to those who pay the bill and those who honestly need help," Carter called for a program that would provide a fairly uniform standard of payments, with some cost-of-living adjustments, and strong work incentives.

He urged a two-track system which would separate the employable from the unemployable poor. Unemployed but able-bodied individuals—except mothers with preschool children—would be trained and offered a job which they would have to accept or be ineligible for benefits. Others on welfare—primarily the aged, blind, disabled and persons with dependent children—would receive a standard payment "adequate to meet the necessities of life," Carter told a meeting of the National Governors Conference in July 1976.

At that time Carter did not attach a price tag to his proposals, but said the federal government would assume a "substantial part" of the funding. States would continue to

Income Aid Programs: Basis for Welfare Reform Efforts

Nine existing income assistance programs were included by the Department of Health, Education and Welfare in its consideration of welfare reform. They were:

General Assistance

General assistance was a generic name for a wide variety of income maintenance programs financed and administered solely by state and local governments. In fiscal 1977, 900,000 recipients received about $1.2 billion in benefits. Most states had a work requirement for able-bodied recipients.

Veterans' Pensions

Veterans' pensions were available to persons permanently and totally disabled or over age 65 who had 90 days or more of active wartime duty or who were released because of a service-related disability. Benefits were based on income and family size. There was no work requirement. One million veterans and 1.7 million dependents received $3.1 billion in fiscal 1977 from the federal Treasury.

AFDC

Aid to Families with Dependent Children was a joint federal, state and local program administered by state and local governments, with the federal government paying 50 per cent of the administrative costs. The federal share of payments ranged from 50 to 83 per cent. Benefits were limited to families with children lacking parental support due to death, continued absence, physical or mental incapacity and, in some states, because the father was unemployed. Children had to be under 18, or 18 to 21 and in school. Benefit levels varied from state to state and by family size. Participants had to register for job training and could not refuse training or employment unless they were children under 16 or in school, aged, disabled, mothers with children under 6 or custodians for ill or incapacitated persons. The costs for benefits provided by the program were estimated at $10.2 billion in fiscal 1977 for an average of 11 million recipients per month. Of that amount, $6.4 billion was the federal share.

Housing Assistance

About 2.7 million individuals received some type of federal housing assistance through a number of programs including traditional public housing, subsidized rental housing, home ownership assistance and housing subsidies for the elderly. Total low-income housing subsidy payments reached $2.95 billion in fiscal 1977. About half of that was paid to local housing authorities in contributions to public housing programs.

Food Stamps

Under this Agriculture Department program, the federal government paid for 50 per cent of all administrative costs and 100 per cent of the benefits. Recipients bought food coupons worth more than the amount needed to pay for them. Under a 1977 amendment, the purchase requirement would be phased out by fiscal 1979. Eligibility was based on income and family size. There was a work requirement. Between 16 and 17 million persons per month received about $5.1 billion in benefits in fiscal 1977.

Medicaid

A joint federal-state program enacted in 1965 to consolidate and expand grants-in-aid to states for medical assistance to welfare recipients, the program was administered by state and local governments. The federal share of payments to medical care providers varied from 50 per cent to 83 per cent depending on state per capita income. Persons were eligible for the program as long as they were eligible for AFDC or Supplemental Security Income (SSI), but if they left public assistance they lost all benefits. Estimated fiscal 1977 Medicaid expenditures were $17.1 billion, of which $9.7 billion was the federal share. About 21.6 million persons received benefits.

Basic Educational Opportunity Grants

This scholarship program for low-income post-secondary students was totally federally funded and operated by the Office of Education in HEW. A student of any age could qualify if he was enrolled at least half-time in an accredited school. About 1.9 million persons received an estimated $1.8 million in grants in fiscal 1977.

Supplemental Security Income

SSI was a program for the aged, blind and disabled, funded by the federal government and the states and administered through the Social Security Administration. Payments were based on income and assets tests. About 42 per cent of all SSI recipients received a payment from their state in addition to a federal payment. In fiscal 1977, an estimated $6.1 billion was paid to about 4.2 million beneficiaries. Of that amount, $4.7 billion came from the federal Treasury and $1.4 billion from the states.

Earned Income Tax Credit

This program was operated by the Internal Revenue Service (IRS) under provisions of federal income tax law. The credit was equal to 10 per cent of earned income up to a maximum credit of $400 for individuals and couples maintaining a household that was the principal residence of their own or an adopted child who was under 19, 19 or over and in school or 19 or over and disabled. Households with adjusted gross incomes over $8,000 a year were not eligible. In fiscal 1977, the program provided about $1.3 billion in benefits to 6.3 million households.

assume some of the burden but local governments would not have to pay.

Carter also called for uniform national criteria for welfare benefits and the elimination of regulations that encourage fathers to desert their families.

Plan Developed

Six days after Carter's inauguration, HEW Secretary Califano announced the formation of a consulting group which he said would serve as the platform for "a great national debate on welfare reform." Headed by Henry Aaron, assistant HEW secretary for planning and evaluation, the group was composed of representatives of Cabinet agencies, congressional committees and state and local interest groups. It met in 10 weekly sessions to discuss the welfare question and alternative reform plans but did not make any formal recommendations.

The thoughts of this group were supplemented by those from more than 15,000 citizens around the country who provided written and oral comments at public meetings held in each of the 50 states. All the material was funneled to Califano who then made recommendations to Carter.

Outlining broad goals consistent with his campaign pledges, the President May 2 announced that he wanted to scrap the existing melange of welfare programs and replace it with a system that would provide a job for welfare recipients who could work and a "decent income" for those who could not.

Neither Carter in his statement nor Califano in May 4-5 appearances before House and Senate subcommittees provided details on how they would reach their stated goals. Those were not forthcoming until Aug. 6 when Carter outlined his welfare reform plan from the Plains, Ga., Agricultural Experiment Station.

The Plan

Carter's specific reform proposals generally adhered to his May 2 outline.

The major departure from his earlier pronouncement was the price of the program. He originally stipulated that the administration's welfare revisions would have "no higher initial cost than the present systems." That would have set a ceiling of more than $23-billion in 1978 dollars, which included the anticipated cost of AFDC, SSI, food stamps, the earned income tax credit and public service jobs included in the economic stimulus package, according to HEW Secretary Califano.

As Carter outlined his plan, it would cost $30.7-billion in 1978 dollars. But later estimates put the cost at $31.1-billion. The administration calculated that $28.3-billion of that amount would come from existing programs or savings and $2.8-billion would be additional cost. However, not included in the total was $3-billion in expanded earned income tax credits for middle-income persons who would not receive income supplements.

The "no higher initial cost" statement had drawn heavy fire from numerous quarters, especially from financially pressed state and local governments looking to Washington for relief. Carter pledged to reduce the financial burdens on those governments "as rapidly as federal resources permit," but they told him clearly that was not soon enough.

In his Aug. 6 statement, Carter said the decision to add more money came after careful consultation with state and local leaders. The additional funds would provide more than $2-billion in fiscal relief to the states, particularly those that had borne the heaviest burdens. As proposed, New York and California alone would receive more than $900-million of that money.

The administration said the $28.3-billion of existing funds would come from:

Aid to Families with Dependent Children (AFDC)	$ 6.4 billion
Supplemental Security Income (SSI)	5.7 billion
Food Stamps	5.5 billion
Earned Income Tax Credit	1.1 billion
Economic Stimulus Package Portion of Comprehensive Education and Training Act (CETA) jobs and the Work Incentive (WIN) Program	5.9 billion
Extended unemployment insurance (27-39 weeks)	.7 billion
Decreases in regular unemployment insurance (because more persons would be employed)	.3 billion
Increases in Social Security contributions (because more persons would be employed)	.7 billion
Savings within the HEW budget from efforts to prevent fraud and abuse	.4 billion
Decrease in required housing subsidies (as a result of the higher incomes of tenants)	.3 billion
Rebates to the poor of wellhead tax revenues (if passed by Congress)	1.3 billion
Total	$28.3 billion

The President itemized the cost of the proposed program as follows:

Employment and Training Programs	$ 8.8 billion
Cash Assistance	20.2 billion
Earned Income Tax Credit	1.5 billion
Emergency Assistance Block Grant	.6 billion
Total	$31.1 billion

All of the figures were in 1978 dollars, which meant that inflation would push the actual numbers up by the time the program went into effect.

Benefits

The administration's plan had two tiers. The upper one was for those not expected to work or for whom no job was available—the aged, blind and disabled, single parents with children under 7, single parents with children between 7 and 13 if a job and day care were not available and two-parent families with children if one parent was incapacitated. The lower tier was for those expected to work—two-parent families with children, single parents with their youngest child over 13, and single persons and childless couples unable to find full-time work.

The Carter proposal did away with AFDC, food stamps and SSI. Instead, eligible families would receive a flat cash payment depending on which tier they were in, the size of their family and their income.

Upper Tier. In the tier of those not working, a four-member family with no other income would get $4,200 a year in 1978 dollars. Aged, blind and disabled individuals would get $2,500 if they maintained their own household or $3,750 as a couple.

The $4,200 basic benefit for a family of four, about 65 per cent of the poverty level, would be higher than the federal share of AFDC and the bonus value of food stamps in all but seven states, according to HEW figures. The national basic benefit for aged, blind and disabled persons would be greater than existing federal SSI benefits plus the bonus value of food stamps.

Most persons in the upper tier—the aged, blind, disabled or persons caring for children under 7—would not be required to accept a job, but they could work if they wanted to.

Persons caring for a child aged 7 through 13 would be required to accept part-time employment during school hours. If an appropriate job were available but not accepted, that household's benefits would be reduced to the lower tier level.

For those not required to work, the national basic benefit would be reduced by 50 cents for each $1 of earned income in states which did not supplement payments. In states that did supplement, benefits would be reduced by up to 70 cents for each $1 earned.

For single parents with children between 7 and 13 benefits would be reduced by 50 cents for each $1 earned after the first $3,800 of earnings in states that did not supplement. In states that did supplement, the amount of earnings not counted could be slightly higher and benefits would be reduced by no more than 70 cents for each $1 earned.

Lower Tier. In the lower tier for those expected to work, the federal payment would be $2,300 for a four-person family with two parents or a single-parent family with no children under 14.

If the principal wage earner in the two-parent family or the single parent could not find a job after eight weeks of searching, the benefit would increase to $4,200, the amount available for the upper tier. As soon as a job was found, the family's benefit would go back to $2,300. If the job were refused, the family would stay at the lower tier level of $2,300.

Benefits for those in the lower tier would be reduced after the first $3,800 of earnings by 50 cents for each $1 earned in states that did not supplement. In states that did supplement, the reduction rate would be no more than 52 cents for each $1 earned and the amount of income not counted would vary.

HEW officials said the reason for disregarding the initial $3,800 of earnings was to provide immediate rewards to the family from working.

A four-person family would remain eligible for cash assistance until its earned income reached $8,400. The income ceiling for an aged, blind or disabled person would be $5,000 or $7,500 for a couple.

A healthy single person would receive cash assistance of $1,100 and a childless couple, $2,200, if no job were available.

Single persons and childless couples would be required to work. If they refused a job they would be ineligible for any cash assistance. When they accepted a job or training slot, their earnings at the minimum wage would make them ineligible for further assistance because their income would be too high. They were not eligible for assistance under any existing program.

For single persons and childless couples, benefits would be reduced by 50 cents for each $1 earned in states that did not supplement and by no more than 52 cents in states that did supplement. A single person would cease to be eligible for benefits at $2,200 of earnings.

Medicaid. One big unanswered question in the Carter proposal was how to handle program participants' medical expenses. Under existing law, AFDC and SSI recipients were automatically eligible for Medicaid; food stamp recipients were not. The nation's most expensive welfare program, Medicaid was expected to cost state and local governments about $17.2-billion in fiscal 1977 to handle 24.7 million persons, according to HEW figures. If Medicaid coverage were extended to all 32 million persons expected to participate in the Carter plan, the cost would rise far above the President's estimate.

The administration did not deal with the Medicaid problem in its proposal, anticipating enactment of a national health insurance plan, to be proposed during 1978, according to Michael Barth, deputy assistant HEW secretary for income security policy. However, representatives of state and local governments expressed concern that if welfare reform, slated to start in fiscal 1981, went into effect before national health insurance, they would be stuck with a huge Medicaid bill.

Barth said that "in the rare event" the new welfare program was enacted before national health insurance, it would be up to the states to decide who was eligible for Medicaid. All participants in the President's new program would not have automatic eligibility.

Jobs Program

The crux of the jobs program would be creation of up to 1.4 million jobs and training slots, 300,000 of them part-time, and placement of numerous participants in private sector jobs. The new jobs were intended to provide work for all low-income families with children, not just persons receiving welfare under the existing system. The Labor Department estimated that about 57 per cent of those participating in the jobs program would be the so-called working poor—persons receiving only food stamps or no income supplement at all under the existing system.

The Department predicted that about 2.5 million persons would occupy the 1.4 million slots annually as participants moved into more profitable private sector jobs. Of those, about 43 per cent would be AFDC recipients under the existing system, representing about 28 per cent of the AFDC caseload.

In 1981, the department said, the overall program would provide two-parent families with children a total minimum income of 20 per cent above the 1981 poverty line if a private sector job could be found or a total minimum income of 13 per cent above the 1981 poverty line if a public sector job were provided.

The public sector jobs and training slots would pay the federal minimum wage although the state minimum wage would apply if it were higher. States that supplemented the basic benefit would be required to do the same for the minimum wage. The amount added would have to be proportional to the benefit supplement up to 10 per cent.

The federal government also would pay an amount equal to 30 per cent of each worker's base wages to cover overhead.

Jobs, Jobs, Where Are the Jobs?

The Carter administration estimated that the 1.4 million jobs to be created under its welfare reform plan could be created in the following areas:

- Public Safety   150,000 jobs
- Recreation Facilities   200,000 jobs
- Recreation Programs   125,000 jobs
- Child Care   150,000 jobs
- Home Service for the Elderly   200,000 jobs
- Cultural Arts Activities   75,000 jobs
- Paraprofessionals in Schools   150,000 jobs
- School Facilities Improvement   100,000 jobs
- Environmental Monitoring   50,000 jobs
- Neighborhood Clean-Up   100,000 jobs
- Weatherization   50,000 jobs
- Other Categories   50,000 jobs

SOURCE: Department of Health,
Education and Welfare

All of the jobs would be created on the local level and would provide training for skills and work experiences useful in the private sector. Positions with flexible hours, including part-time jobs, would be included to accommodate the needs of single parents with young children. *(Job possibilities, box, this page)*

"The development of this jobs program is clearly a substantial undertaking requiring close cooperation of all levels of government," Carter said in his message to Congress. "I am confident it will succeed. Thousands of unmet needs for public goods and services exist in our country."

Providing subsidized jobs and training, job search and placement would be the responsibility of state and local officials who ran programs under the Comprehensive Employment and Training Act (CETA). *(CETA, p. 29)*

On the state level, the governor, in cooperation with CETA prime sponsors, would be responsible for developing a state plan setting numerical goals for private sector job placement, subsidized jobs and training.

Locally, a person would apply for a job at the local employment and training agency which would be responsible for placing the applicant in a job or training situation. The local agency would also provide five weeks of intensive job search assistance, would make arrangements with public agencies or nonprofit organizations to create subsidized work and training positions and would be responsible for placing all applicants, including those in public service jobs, in private employment as jobs developed.

Funding for the jobs program would be given directly to the local prime sponsor. The number of job slots authorized would be geared to the number of anticipated participants in that area. If state and local governments were unable to establish an adequate number of jobs, the Secretary of Labor could make direct arrangements with public and private nonprofit agencies to provide jobs and training.

To be eligible for the jobs program, a person would have to be the principal wage earner in a family, defined as having the highest earnings or having worked the most hours in the previous year.

Any applicant would have to be unemployed and have looked for a private job for at least five weeks before being placed in subsidized work or training. There would be no in-come or assets test for determining eligibility because such tests might arbitrarily exclude persons who needed and wanted work, the department said.

After a year in a subsidized job, the participant would have to spend another five weeks looking for a private sector job before being eligible again for a public sector job. All applicants would have to accept a private job paying at least the minimum wage if one were offered.

Work Incentives. By reducing benefits by about 50 per cent of earnings, disregarding the first $3,800 of earnings for most of those expected to work and expanding the earned income tax credit, the program would provide incentives to work, according to the administration.

"This new program will ensure that work will always be more profitable than welfare," Carter said, "and that a private or non-subsidized public job will always be more profitable than a special federally-funded public service job."

To make private jobs more profitable than public ones, the earned income tax credit would be expanded and would apply only to private sector earnings. Under existing law the program provided a cash credit or rebate of 10 per cent of all earnings up to $4,000 for a maximum credit of $400. The credit was phased down by $1 for each $10 of earnings on adjusted gross income over $4,000 and disappeared at $8,000 of adjusted gross income.

Under the proposed plan, the existing 10 per cent credit on earnings up to $4,000 would remain. There would be a 5 per cent credit on earnings between $4,000 and the point at which a family was no longer eligible for welfare benefits in a state with matching supplements, $9,100 for a family of four. The credit would be phased out above that point by $1 for every $10 of income up to $15,650. Paychecks would be adjusted to reflect the credit through the tax withholding process.

Unemployment Insurance. The proposed program would affect only the extended benefits program of the existing unemployment insurance system.

The extended program, which provided benefits from the 26th to the 39th weeks of unemployment, went into effect when the unemployment rate reached 4.5 per cent. Under the proposal the rate required to trigger the extended program would be raised to an unspecified level.

Persons on both tiers of the new program would continue to be eligible for unemployment benefits, but their cash assistance would be reduced 90 cents for every $1 in benefits collected.

Eligibility

The proposed system would do away with the differing, and often complicated, methods of applying for assistance under the existing AFDC, SSI and food stamp programs.

Filing Unit. If more than one "nuclear family"—a married couple or a parent with minor children—lived together, each unit could apply separately for benefits. A household consisting of a couple, their daughter and her one-year-old child, for example, would form two separate filing units. However, if the daughter did not have any dependents, she and her parents would be one unit.

Single persons who were not aged, blind or disabled could apply separately for benefits only if living by themselves or in a household in which they had no relatives.

Aged, blind and disabled persons would be treated as they were under the existing SSI program. They could apply separately whether living alone or in someone else's household. Their benefits would be reduced if they lived in another person's household and did not bear a pro rata share of the household's expenses.

Children living with relatives, such as grandparents or aunts and uncles, who were not legally responsible for them could file separately.

Students away at school would be considered part of the family unit and could not apply separately if they were claimed as dependents for federal income tax purposes. If they were not claimed as dependents, they could apply separately.

Income. The proposal would define income counted to determine eligibility as 50 per cent of wages from a job, 80 per cent of non-employment income (such as dividends, pensions or Social Security), and 100 per cent of income from other federal assistance programs based on means, such as veterans' pensions.

For single-parent families with children under 14, the cost of child care of up to $150 a month for each child, for a maximum of two children, would be deducted from family earnings before benefits were calculated.

Assets. Under the proposal, households could have assets of up to $5,000 and business assets up to a limit to be set by the Secretary.

Excluded from countable assets were the total value of a home occupied by the owner, the total value of household goods and personal effects, including vehicles plus tools and other items necessary for employment, and the total value of pre-paid burial contracts.

Accounting. In determining whether a person was eligible to participate, the proposal would measure the applicant's actual income over the preceding six months. The process would prevent families with relatively high but irregular incomes from receiving benefits. Under the existing system benefits were based on anticipated income for prospective periods which vary from program to program.

The administration said the six-month retrospective period would be more equitable because it would increase the likelihood that families with similar annual incomes would receive similar benefits. It also would avoid problems of overpayment which plagued the existing system.

Under the proposed system, for example, a family with no income but with previous annual earnings of $8,400, the proposed cut-off point for benefits, would be eligible for assistance immediately. The family of a school teacher with previous annual earnings of $12,000 would have to wait two months to receive benefits. An unemployed construction worker's family with $15,000 in previous annual earnings would have to wait three months.

However, states also would have available to them $600-million to be used to help those facing emergencies. These funds would be distributed to states on a formula basis.

Reporting. The proposed system would require more frequent reporting of income to authorities than under the existing system. Recipients with income from employment would have to report monthly. HEW estimated such a system would reduce overpayments by $800-million to $1-billion.

State Role

Under the administration's plan, every state would be assured that it would save at least 10 per cent of its existing welfare expenses in the first year of the program with "substantial increased fiscal relief thereafter," Carter said.

Welfare: An End to Housing Aid?

President Carter's decision to revamp the welfare system revived a controversy over the relationship between federal housing aid for the poor and welfare.

Paying for welfare, always an expensive proposition, prompted the reformers to comb the government looking for money that could be rolled into a welfare package. An inviting target proved to be the Section 8 rent subsidy program established by the 1974 Housing and Community Development Act. *(p. 9-A)*

In a July 1977 memo the Office of Management and Budget (OMB) suggested that poor people would be better off if the government ended the separate rental assistance program and redistributed the subsidies as welfare payments. In fiscal 1978, OMB said, the Department of Housing and Urban Development (HUD) would pay $4.9-billion to subsidize the rents of 2.7 million households. About 9.7 million households would be eligible for cash assistance under the proposed new welfare plan. The memo asserted that only one out of 13 households below the poverty line was currently receiving housing assistance.

In announcing its new plan, the administration put the OMB suggestion aside, but indicated the question would come up again when the fiscal 1979 budget was considered.

Officials did include some HUD money in the amount they expected to be available to pay for welfare, however. They predicted HUD would be able to reduce the amount it spent on housing subsidies by about $500-million because tenants would be better off under the new welfare program.

Sen. William Proxmire, D-Wis., chairman of the Senate Banking, Housing and Urban Affairs Committee, held a hearing in August in which a bevy of witnesses assailed any efforts to change the subsidized housing program. They argued that housing subsidies play an important role in revitalizing urban areas and that more poor persons would live in substandard housing if they did not exist.

Every state would be required to pay 10 per cent of the cost of the basic federal grant unless that amount was more than 90 per cent of what the state spent under the existing system for its share of AFDC, SSI, emergency assistance and general assistance. In that case the state would pay the 90 per cent figure.

That system would mean an immediate increase in payments for persons living in 12 states. However, the administration said many states would need to continue to supplement cash benefits if existing payment levels were to be maintained.

To help states bear the burden of supplementing payments, the federal government would take part in a matching system. In addition to paying for 90 per cent of the $4,200 that would be provided to an eligible family of four, the federal government would pay 75 per cent of the first $500 of a state supplement above that plus 25 per cent of any additional supplement up to the poverty line.

States that supplemented also would be required to add to the wages of persons in public service jobs in the same proportion, up to 10 per cent, that they supplemented the basic cash grant above $4,700.

Only supplements which used the same eligibility rules as the federal government would be eligible for matching. States also could adopt non-matching supplements which did not use the federal eligibility rules. One such supplement might continue payments to AFDC and SSI recipients who would lose their benefits because of the new eligibility standards.

The administration said it anticipated a five-year transition period for phasing in the new program. The AFDC caseload turned over by about one-third a year, so that period would be enough to protect the interests of recipients under the existing system, HEW officials said.

During the first three years, the states would be required to maintain a prescribed minimum percentage of the existing welfare expenditures. In the first year of the new program, each state would be required to spend at least 90 per cent of its existing expenditures in the AFDC and SSI programs, emergency assistance and general assistance. In the second year, states would be required to maintain 75 per cent of existing effort and in the third year, 65 per cent.

To avoid increased financial burdens for the states during the transition period, the administration said the federal government would make a "hold harmless" payment to the states for the expenditures that exceeded the required 10 per cent state payment, matching supplements up to existing benefit levels, grandfathering supplements for SSI beneficiaries and 75 per cent of the cost of grandfathering supplements for AFDC beneficiaries.

Administration. Benefit checks under the new system would not be distributed until three years after enactment of the program, the administration said.

Under the proposal, states would have the option to perform "intake functions," which meant all activities involving face-to-face contact with recipients, processing applications and determining eligibility. But the federal government would compute benefits and payments and so would make the final determination on eligibility.

A staff of 100,000 to 120,000 persons employed by the state and federal governments would be required to administer the program, compared to 143,000 state and federal employees administering the existing system, HEW said.

The federal government would pay 30 per cent above the basic wage for fringe benefits and administrative costs of the jobs program and would reimburse states for 90 per cent of the costs of administration of the work benefit and income support program. States with unusually good administrative performance would be reimbursed up to 110 per cent.

The total cost of administration was estimated at $2.2-billion in 1978 dollars compared to $2.7-billion under the existing system.

House Action

To expedite consideration of President Carter's welfare reform package, House Speaker Thomas P. O'Neill Jr., D-Mass., created a special subcommittee to handle the legislation. The 13-member House Ways and Means Subcommittee on Public Assistance, chaired by James C. Corman, D-Calif., was expanded to include the chairman of the full Ways and Means Committee plus the chairman and six members each of the Agriculture and Education and Labor committees, which had jurisdiction over the food stamp and jobs programs in the plan.

The so-called Welfare Reform Subcommittee held hearings in fall 1977 and then went to work marking up a bill.

Ullman Plan

While the subcommittee was plugging away at writing a welfare bill based on the President's plan, House Ways and Means Chairman Al Ullman, D-Ore., unveiled his own reform program, which he said was affordable and achievable in the 95th Congress. Ullman asserted that President Carter's welfare plan had no chance of passing in 1978.

Unlike the Carter program (HR 9030), which scrapped existing welfare programs in favor of a single cash payment, Ullman retained and revised those programs. The President proposed creating 1.4 million public service jobs for recipients unable to find work in the private sector. Ullman's proposal expanded the existing Work Incentive (WIN) program to provide about 500,000 public jobs, but he said his program did more than Carter's to encourage private sector employment.

"We don't have the money or the experience to open up a million new public jobs," Ullman said. "You don't solve the welfare problem with public jobs. You have to put them in private jobs. That is our main thrust."

If preliminary estimates were correct, the Ullman plan would cost considerably less than the administration program, primarily because of the difference in the public jobs to be produced and because states would receive less fiscal relief.

According to estimates by the Joint Committee on Taxation and the Ways and Means Committee staff, Ullman's program would cost between $7.5 billion and $9 billion more than existing programs. The Congressional Budget Office (CBO) put the additional cost to the federal government of the administration bill at $17.36 billion. Both estimates were for fiscal 1982.

Ullman said the high cost of the administration plan threatened general economic recovery. He also was critical of other aspects of the Carter program.

"The administration has fallen into an old trap," he said. "It is convinced we can make poor Americans happy and secure by giving them a guaranteed annual income based on family size and earnings. To accept that concept is to perpetuate the 'welfare syndrome.' I don't think there is the time or the climate in Congress to push through a massive all-or-nothing welfare program this year."

Ullman said his proposal could be put into effect one piece at a time. But he asserted it could be passed in its entirety in 1978 because it built on a structure familiar to members of Congress.

Ullman said he had not discussed the details of his proposal with Russell B. Long, D-La., chairman of the Senate Finance Committee and a key figure in the success or failure of any welfare program. But he added, "I have talked with the senator many times about welfare reform. My feeling is that we're on somewhat the same wavelength."

Health, Education and Welfare Secretary Joseph A. Califano Jr. said Jan. 25, 1978, prior to the introduction of the Ullman plan, that he would not support it.

The same day Corman predicted that Ullman would not be successful in getting the special House Welfare Reform Subcommittee to endorse his alternative welfare proposal.

"Ullman was not in the mainstream of the House [during debate on President Nixon's proposed Family Assistance Plan (FAP) in the early 1970s] and I think he is further from the mainstream now," said Corman, a member of Ways and Means. Ullman led the fight against a guaranteed annual income during the FAP debates.

Comparison with Carter Plan. Ullman's plan had a few characteristics in common with the Carter program. It established national eligibility standards for recipients, set national minimum benefit levels, made intact families eligible for assistance, made private sector jobs more attractive than those in the public sector, simplified administration, cut fraud and abuse and provided some fiscal relief to states.

But it differed in many more respects. Ullman's plan retained food stamps, Supplemental Security Income (SSI) for the aged, blind and disabled and Aid to Families with Dependent Children (AFDC). It provided a national minimum benefit — to be paid in cash and food stamps — but that benefit varied among states to reflect differences in median family income. Cash benefits would not vary by family size although food stamp benefits would. Some of the benefits paid to recipients with relatively high annual incomes would be recouped through the tax system.

Because cash benefits would not vary by family size, smaller families — particularly those with two or three members — would do better under the Ullman proposal than under the Carter plan. Four-member families would fare about the same, but families of five or more would do better under Carter, staff members said.

Ullman's plan also phased out cash assistance at a lower level than under the Carter plan. But expansion of the earned income tax credit would make up the difference if the recipient were in a private job. "They're getting the same amount of money but from an employer through the earned income tax credit instead of from the government," a staff member said. "It reduces stigma and saves going to the welfare office."

Ullman Plan Rejected. Less than a week after its unveiling, the Ullman plan went down to defeat at the hands of the Welfare Reform Subcommittee. By a 13-16 vote, the subcommittee rejected Ullman's proposal, and then went on to report its own bill.

Subcommittee Bill

A bill incorporating nearly all of the major points in President Carter's program was ordered reported Feb. 8, 1978, by the special House subcommittee. But there were few indications that the administration's success in pushing and preserving its program would continue. One immediate sign of trouble was the narrow margin — 13-16 — by which the subcommittee had turned down the Ullman proposal.

After turning down Ullman's substitute, the subcommittee voted 23-6 to report its own bill. All of the panel's nine Republicans voted in favor of the Ullman proposal, as did four Democrats. All but one of the six votes against reporting the subcommittee bill came from Republicans.

Before casting his opposing vote, Thomas S. Foley, D-Wash., chairman of the House Agriculture Committee, asserted that the subcommittee bill "cannot pass the Congress or the House in anything like its present form."

Several Republicans who voted in favor of the subcommittee bill indicated they were doing so in order to keep the welfare reform process moving, but said they had reservations about parts of the measure.

In urging defeat of the Ullman proposal, Corman noted that the major difference in the costs of the two plans was in the amount of money earmarked for jobs and for fiscal relief to the states.

"The higher expenditures in the subcommittee bill are justified on both counts," Corman said. "There is no way to get state relief without spending more money.... It costs more for people to work than merely to give them a welfare check. You're way ahead when you put people to work. It gives them dignity, self worth, and their work is of value to the community."

The subcommittee bill then went back to the panel's three parent committees — Ways and Means, Education and Labor and Agriculture.

Search for Compromise

Welfare reform went on the back burner for several months after the House subcommittee agreed on its version of the bill. And when the issue resurfaced in April 1978, it had a different focus. No longer were people concentrating on the "comprehensive" welfare measure proposed by Carter.

Instead, key legislators, their aides and officials in the Department of Health, Education and Welfare (HEW) had begun studying four different welfare measures, including the Carter proposal, looking for similarities and possible areas of compromise.

Besides the administration bill (HR 9030, S 2084), the other measures getting scrutiny included HR 10950 — the Carter plan as amended by the subcommittee; HR 10711, the Ullman plan and S 2777, sponsored by a bipartisan group of senators led by Howard H. Baker Jr., R-Tenn., the Senate minority leader; Abraham Ribicoff, D-Conn., a former HEW secretary; Henry Bellmon, R-Okla., and John C. Danforth, R-Mo. *(See box, next page)*

Baker-Bellmon Proposal

The Baker-Bellmon welfare measure took what its sponsors called an "incremental" approach to welfare reform, proposing limited changes in existing welfare programs without altering the basic structure of the overall system. It had been introduced in March 1978.

Some major players in the welfare debate, including Daniel Patrick Moynihan, D-N.Y., chairman of the Senate Finance Subcommittee on Public Assistance and chief sponsor of the Carter bill in the Senate, viewed the introduction of the Baker-Bellmon bill, regardless of its chances of passage, as an important step toward generating support for welfare reform in the 95th Congress.

They said the bill had stimulated some debate and rekindled interest in improving the welfare system. Moynihan, who had prodded the Carter administration on welfare reform, described the Baker-Bellmon proposal during an April hearing as a "very important option" to be considered if the Carter bill did not move.

One administration official who had lobbied for the Carter bill was more succinct. Welfare reform, he said, "was pretty much dead in the water" before Baker and the other senators introduced their bill.

Status of Carter Proposal

The Baker-Bellmon bill came at a time when high-ranking officials in the HEW bureaucracy and in the White

Administration, House Leaders Consider Four Bills...

In spring 1978 the Carter administration indicated its willingness to negotiate a compromise on welfare reform legislation. During discussions with House leaders, four measures were considered:

● President Carter's original proposal (HR 9030, S 2084).

● The Corman subcommittee bill (HR 10950), which was the administration proposal as amended by the special House Ways and Means subcommittee chaired by James C. Corman, D-Calif.

● The Ullman bill (HR 10711), sponsored by Al Ullman, D-Ore., chairman of the Ways and Means Committee.

● The Baker-Bellmon bill (S 2777), whose principal sponsors were Sens. Howard H. Baker Jr., R-Tenn., Senate minority leader; Henry Bellmon, R-Okla.; Abraham Ribicoff, D-Conn., and John C. Danforth, R-Mo.

After agreeing on the broad framework for a bill, staffers went to work on a draft measure. But before their work had been completed, the congressional leadership decided comprehensive welfare legislation could not be passed in the 95th Congress. *(Details, p. 94)*

Here was how the four measures dealt with some of the major issues in the debate over welfare reform:

Programs

The Carter and Corman bills would combine the existing Aid to Families with Dependent Children (AFDC), Supplemental Security Income (SSI), food stamp and general assistance programs into one single cash payment. Ullman and Baker-Bellmon would retain the existing separate programs.

Carter and Corman would transfer administration of all programs except emergency assistance to the federal government. Ullman and Baker-Bellmon would retain state control.

Coverage

Carter and Corman would extend welfare benefits to all needy persons, including single individuals and childless couples. Baker-Bellmon and Ullman would retain the prohibition against AFDC payments to single individuals and childless couples. All four bills made mandatory AFDC benefits to families with unemployed fathers, but Ullman limited the aid to 17 weeks in a year. (Under existing law, states decided whether to include

"intact" families in AFDC; 26 states did so. Existing law defined "unemployed father" as working less than 100 hours a month and having prior work experience.)

Benefits

All four proposals would establish national minimum benefits, with the Carter, Corman and Ullman proposals all setting a minimum benefit slightly higher than Baker-Bellmon. Carter, Corman and Ullman set a national minimum benefit of $4,200 for a single-parent family of four. Carter and Corman would pay cash, while Ullman would reach the minimum through a combination of cash ($2,550) and food stamps ($1,650).

Baker-Bellmon would allow states to continue to set benefit levels, but established targets at the following levels: 55 per cent of the poverty level in fiscal 1981, 60 per cent in 1982 and 65 per cent in 1985. In 1978, 55 per cent of the poverty level ($6,200 for a non-farm family of four) was about $3,400.

Tax Incentives

All four bills would expand the earned income tax credit, a tax break designed to increase the financial incentive for heads of low-income households to work. Under existing law, households with adjusted gross incomes over $8,000 a year were not eligible for the credit. Carter would set the maximum income ceiling at $15,650 for a family of four, Ullman at $15,000, Corman at $12,600, and Baker-Bellmon at $10,835. Each of the measures had different formulas and rates for computing tax credits on earned incomes below the maximum. All four included a "reverse withholding" provision under which credits would be payable to a family on monthly or other periodic basis during the year through the employer withholding system. All four would also prohibit tax credits on income earned from public jobs.

Job Credits, Vouchers

The Baker-Bellmon bill also contained two financial incentives for employers who hired welfare recipients and unemployed poor persons not on welfare. A job voucher program would allow employers to receive a subsidy of $1 an hour per employee for a year. Or, employers could receive tax credits of $1 an hour for one year for each eligible employee they hired. A ceiling of $100,000 in tax credits would be established. To qualify for either the

House were just about ready to throw in the towel on welfare reform for the 95th Congress.

A memorandum sent to President Carter on March 21, 1978 — the day before the Baker-Bellmon bill was introduced — acknowledged dim prospects for the administration's welfare proposal. The memo, a copy of which was obtained by the Associated Press, dealt with Carter's urban policy and was written by Stuart Eizenstat, the President's chief domestic policy adviser, and James T. McIntyre Jr., director of the Office of Management and Budget. Part of the President's urban package called for granting fiscal relief to states and cities for welfare during

fiscal 1979, rather than fiscal 1981, as proposed in the administration's welfare bill. HEW Secretary Califano had estimated that $976 million would be available for such aid, but McIntyre declined to endorse that figure, partly because, according to the memo "welfare reform [is] unlikely to pass."

That view was widely shared on Capitol Hill. Many sources, including senators and representatives, saw little prospect for passage of the Carter proposal.

The Carter proposal, as amended by the Corman subcommittee, would increase current welfare costs by about $20.22 billion, according to Congressional Budget Office es-

...In Attempt to Reach Welfare Reform Compromise

direct subsidy or the tax credit, an employer would have to hire AFDC recipients, persons unemployed for more than 26 weeks, youths who had searched for jobs for at least 90 days, or persons terminated from CETA public service jobs who had searched for work for at least 30 days.

The Ullman plan contained an expansion of the employer tax credit approved in the 1977 stimulus tax bill to provide an additional 10 per cent credit to employers who hire WIN (Work Incentive program) participants. Ullman would allow those employers to take a credit of 10 per cent on the first $6,000 of each employee's wages, up to $300,000 for all WIN employees, and 40 per cent thereafter.

Public Service Jobs

All four bills would establish public service jobs for low-income persons. Carter would establish the most — 1.4 million (including 300,000 part-time jobs), in a new section under the Comprehensive Employment and Training Act (CETA), with workers to be paid at the minimum wage. Corman had the same number of jobs, but would require workers to be paid prevailing wages. Carter and Corman would both abolish the WIN program.

Ullman would establish 500,000 public service jobs under the WIN program, at minimum wages. Baker-Bellmon would establish 375,000 public service jobs under CETA, at average CETA wages (about $7,800 a year, adjusted for regional and area differences). Baker-Bellmon and Ullman would give states control of the WIN program.

Work Requirements

All four measures included work requirements for able-bodied welfare recipients, with some exceptions, most notably mothers with young children. The bills differed on many details, including the cutoff age for single-parent families with children. Carter and Corman exempted from work requirements one adult member of a household that included a child under the age of 7. Baker-Bellmon and Ullman set the age cutoff at 6.

Baker-Bellmon also required AFDC recipients to participate in job-search programs, in addition to the existing requirements that they register for work through the WIN program. All four bills included penalties for failing to meet work requirements.

Fiscal Relief to States

Under existing law, the federal government paid 100 per cent of the cost of food stamps and SSI. The federal share of AFDC ranged from 50 to 78 per cent.

Carter and Corman would establish a 90 per cent federal contribution for single cash payments. Baker-Bellmon and Ullman would retain a 100 per cent federal payment for food stamps and SSI. Ullman set the state share of AFDC at 85 per cent of the 1977 cost of benefits; the federal government would then pay 100 per cent of all benefit costs beyond the fixed state share. Baker-Bellmon would increase the AFDC match to the 80-90 per cent range by fiscal 1982.

The following estimates were made for actual dollar amounts of fiscal aid to states under each of the plans: Carter, $3.4 billion; Corman, $2.2 billion; Ullman, $1.2 billion; Baker-Bellmon, $3 billion.

Costs

All four measures would increase the amount of money the federal government spent on welfare. Varying estimates were made of the Carter proposal, with the administration itself having revised its figures upward since the proposal was announced in August 1977. As of late April 1978, administration officials said the Carter bill would cost an additional $8.77 billion in 1982. The Congressional Budget Office (CBO) placed the price tag at $17.36 billion.

The Corman bill would cost about $20.22 billion more than existing programs, according to the CBO. Baker-Bellmon, according to preliminary CBO estimates, would cost about $9.33 billion more. Ullman's staff estimated the added cost of his proposal at between $4.75 billion and $9 billion.

The Senate Finance Committee, in an April 1978 compilation of data on welfare costs, estimated the federal government's costs for AFDC, SSI, food stamps and other social welfare programs (excluding Medicaid) at about $22.4 billion.

Altogether, the committee publication estimated total social welfare costs for federal, state and local governments at approximately $30 billion in 1978 (excluding Medicaid). As of October 1977, according to committee data, 10.8 million persons were receiving AFDC benefits; 4.2 million, SSI; and 15.9 million, food stamps. The recipients of general assistance totaled 800,000.

timates. The administration disputed that estimate, but the different cost figures only increased uncertainty over the Carter measure.

The cost of the administration proposal generated substantial opposition. Even in a non-election year, one congressional aide said, a program with such a large price tag would be received skeptically.

Secondly, while administration officials argued that fundamental changes were necessary, they conceded that Congress was not likely to accept them all at one time. "Congress likes to do things in bits and pieces," one official asserted.

Thirdly, key committee chairmen, like Ullman, Thomas S. Foley, D-Wash., of the House Agriculture Committee, and Russell B. Long, D-La., of the Senate Finance Committee, expressed opposition to major sections of the Carter plan. For example, Foley opposed "cashing out" food stamps and merging the program with other welfare benefits into one single cash payment. His committee had jurisdiction over the food stamp section of the bill, and few thought its members would buck him.

Long, whose committee shared jurisdiction over the measure in the Senate, repeatedly stated his opposition to providing cash benefits to single individuals and childless couples. "It's my judgment that you don't need any more people on welfare," Long declared.

Move Toward Compromise

Thus, administration officials conceded, "political realities" dictated that some compromises had to be made if a welfare reform measure was to be enacted in the 95th Congress.

Califano signaled the administration's readiness to talk during little-noticed testimony March 23, 1978. Appearing before the Senate Human Resources Committee to discuss welfare reform, Califano pointed to the Ullman and Baker-Bellmon bills, noted several similarities with the Carter plan, and declared, "In short, the introduction of the Ullman and Baker-Bellmon-Ribicoff proposals reflects an emerging consensus for significant reform upon which to build."

One adviser to the secretary said later that Califano's remarks were interpreted "correctly" on Capitol Hill to mean that the administration was ready to negotiate.

As a result, aides to Califano met with Ullman's aides, trying to work out differences between the administration bill and Ullman's proposal. And Califano met for about an hour on April 26 to discuss the Senate bill with Bellmon, Ribicoff and Danforth. (Baker was out of the country and unable to attend, according to an aide.)

Sources familiar with the meeting said no negotiating took place. Instead, they said, Califano indicated his desire to "work something out" in the House first.

The senators reportedly informed Califano that there was little support for the Carter bill in the Senate, and suggested that if the administration wanted a welfare measure this session, it had to be prepared to accept less sweeping changes, as embodied in the Baker-Bellmon or Ullman bills.

Areas of Agreement

HEW officials declined to provide details of the talks between Ullman's staff and Califano's aides. But Califano, in his March 23 testimony, outlined areas of possible agreement. He noted that all four welfare bills would do the following:

● Extend cash assistance coverage to two-parent families.

● Establish a national minimum benefit.

● Move in the direction of greater uniformity of rules and eligibility standards.

● Simplify administration.

● Provide public service jobs for poor families.

● Expand the earned income tax credit.

● Recognize the "importance" of cashing out food stamps for at least some recipients "as a step toward a consolidated cash system."

Participants in the discussions pointed out, however, that while there might be consensus on broad themes, there were numerous differences in the actual details. For example, each of the four bills set a different maximum income ceiling for qualifying for the earned income tax credit. *(Box, p. 92)*

If the areas cited by Califano did provide the basis for a possible compromise welfare bill, it meant that Carter was giving up, at least for the time being, two major elements of his plan: the merging of various existing welfare programs

into one single cash grant, and extending cash benefits to single individuals and childless couples.

Those were considered two of the most controversial portions of the Carter plan, and generated the most opposition. Extension of benefits to single individuals and childless couples was widely viewed as a major step toward a guaranteed minimum income, a step many in Congress did not want to take.

Compromise Agreement

The Carter administration and House leaders reportedly reached agreement in June on the broad outlines of a welfare reform bill substantially scaled down from the President's original proposal. The fundamentals of a compromise bill were worked out at a June 7 meeting in the offices of Ways and Means Chairman Ullman.

The compromise bill was expected to cost $9 billion to $12 billion more than existing welfare programs. It reportedly retained the present system of cash payments and food stamps, provided between $1.5 billion and $2.5 billion in fiscal relief for states, expanded the earned income tax credit, streamlined administration of the welfare system, provided for between 600,000 and 700,000 public service jobs, set a minimum national benefit standard for Aid to Families with Dependent Children (AFDC) of about $4,200 for a family of four (65 per cent of the official poverty level) and required states to provide AFDC benefits for so-called "intact" families where the husband lives at home.

Besides Ullman, those attending the meeting included Health, Education and Welfare Secretary Califano; Secretary of Labor F. Ray Marshall; Stuart Eizenstat, Carter's chief domestic adviser; Corman, chairman of the special House Ways and Means subcommittee that did the initial work on the Carter bill; Carl D. Perkins, chairman of the House Education and Labor Committee; Augustus F. Hawkins, D-Calif., chairman of the Education and Labor subcommittee that was to handle the jobs part of the welfare bill; Charles B. Rangel, N.Y., second-ranking Democrat on the Corman subcommittee, and Gov. Michael S. Dukakis, D-Mass. House Speaker Thomas P. O'Neill Jr., D-Mass., who had been skeptical that Congress would enact a welfare bill in 1978, nevertheless sent a staff member to the session.

Dukakis was representing the New Coalition, an organization composed of representatives of the nation's governors, state legislators, county officials and mayors.

But while staff aides were at work on draft legislation, O'Neill announced to a meeting of House Democratic whips June 22 that the Senate leadership had informed him that it was too late in the session for a major welfare bill to make it to the Senate floor.

Others said the Senate really wasn't in the mood to debate major increases in federal spending for welfare in light of Proposition 13.

Soundings by O'Neill and others in the House, including Corman, found a similar lack of interest.

The assessment by congressional leaders ended efforts to fashion a compromise welfare bill. Although negotiators had made some progress, cost was still a big problem when the discussions came to an end. The Corman bill had a price tag of $20.22 billion. Ullman had said Congress would not support anything costing more than $5 billion to $6 billion. Negotiators had come up with a bill costing about $14 billion, well above what Ullman was willing to support. *(Ullman's bill, p. 90)*

Cranston-Moynihan Proposal

Only a week after O'Neill pronounced welfare reform dead another drive was under way to steer a welfare bill through the 95th Congress.

At a press conference June 28, Alan Cranston, D-Calif., and Daniel Patrick Moynihan, D-N.Y., proposed what they called a "no frills" welfare plan which would cost $5 billion when fully effective in fiscal 1981. The initial cost for fiscal 1979 was estimated at $1 billion to $2 billion.

The proposal had three key sections: expanded tax credits for the working poor, tax credits for employers who hire welfare recipients, and fiscal relief for states and localities.

The fiscal relief may prove to be the most politically attractive aspect of the proposal. Increased federal funding of welfare would ease the financial burden on states and localities and could be cited by Congress as an example of how concerned its members are over state and local tax burdens. (The House Ways and Means Committee July 18 reported a bill to provide $400 million in fiscal relief to states in fiscal 1979 only.) *(Details, next page)*

"The infusion of additional federal funds that we are proposing will, in effect, cut in half the size of the welfare bill for states, cities and counties across the nation," Cranston said.

Many observers believed the passage of Proposition 13 in California, Cranston's home state, made fiscal relief — and the welfare measure itself — even more appealing. Cranston cited the property tax rollback approved by California voters as one of the reasons for developing the new welfare proposal. *(Proposition 13, p. 51)*

Details of Proposal

As announced in June, the Cranston-Moynihan proposal contained these main features:

● It would expand the so-called earned income tax credit for the working poor, a tax incentive first proposed by Long. The existing credit was 10 per cent of the first $4,000 of earnings and was gradually phased out, ending when earnings reach $8,000. The Cranston-Moynihan plan would allow a 10 per cent credit on the first $6,000 of earnings in fiscal 1979, on the first $6,500 of earnings in fiscal 1980, and on the first $7,000 of earnings in fiscal 1981. When fully effective that year, the tax credit would be phased out when earnings reached $14,000 per year. Cranston and Moynihan estimated that the expanded tax credit would cost $1.1 billion in fiscal 1979.

● It would expand an existing tax provision that gave a tax credit to an employer who hired a person who had been on welfare for at least 90 days. The existing credit was 20 per cent, and could be taken only on first-year wages up to a maximum credit of $1,000. The Cranston-Moynihan proposal would increase the tax credit to 50 per cent on first-year wages, up to a maximum credit of $3,000; allow a tax credit of one-third of the salary for the second year up to a maximum of $2,000, and allow a credit of 25 per cent of the salary for the third year, up to a maximum of $1,500. The sponsors said the tax credit would cost $1.5 billion.

● It would increase the federal government's share of welfare costs, and replace the existing system of the federal government matching state and local welfare payments with block grants, beginning in fiscal 1980. For the first year, the block grant would equal the share of federal welfare payments under existing law for the 12-month peri-od that ended June 30, 1978. The federal government would also pay one-half of the current state and local share during the same period.

The fiscal relief would cost the federal government about $2.2 billion in fiscal 1980, the sponsors said.

The block grant, which would represent a fundamental change in the way welfare funds are distributed to the states, would in effect amount to a ceiling on federal welfare costs, another idea favored by Long.

The Cranston-Moynihan plan would allow some exceptions, however. Each year the block grants would be adjusted to reflect changes in the cost of living. They could also be adjusted to reflect changes in a state's population and unemployment rate. The size of the grants would also increase if states where the minimum welfare benefit was below 65 per cent of the poverty line (below $4,200) raised their benefits.

Finally, under the Cranston-Moynihan proposal, when a state received its block grant it would be required to give the money first to any city or county which was paying part of the welfare costs. That provision was extremely attractive for New York and California. Counties in the two states, which have the largest Aid to Families with Dependent Children (AFDC) caseloads, shared in state welfare costs.

Moynihan estimated that financially pressed New York City would be relieved of some $300 million a year in welfare costs. In California, the state had assumed the county share of welfare, but only on a temporary basis, using money available from the state budget surplus. But with the property tax rollback mandated by Proposition 13, once the budget surplus was depleted the counties would be hard-pressed to meet their welfare bills. The Cranston-Moynihan proposal offered a solution to that potential problem.

"If our bill becomes law, the counties of California would be freed — permanently — from having to contribute to welfare. The new higher level of federal funding will more than compensate for all of the counties' normal share, plus part of the state share," Cranston said.

Reaction

The enormous financial impact the Cranston-Moynihan plan would have on California and New York — the two together would receive about one-third of the fiscal relief — led some cynics to see the measure primarily as a financial bail-out for the two states. But other observers pointed out that California and New York rightly deserved the money, since they had the highest welfare rolls.

Beyond that, however, the Cranston-Moynihan plan created some political problems for a host of people and interest groups that supported broader changes in the welfare system, including liberals like Corman and Rep. Charles B. Rangel, D-N.Y., the nation's governors and other state and local elected officials, and the Carter administration.

All saw the measure as too limited, focusing only on fiscal relief and tax incentives without making any structural changes in the welfare system itself.

"We'd like to get a bill that contains not only fiscal relief but brings about some structural reforms," said Henry Aaron, assistant secretary for planning in the Department of Health, Education and Welfare (HEW).

"We do not consider it welfare reform," said M. Kenneth Bowler, a staff aide on the House Ways and Means Subcommittee on Public Assistance.

But Bowler, Aaron and others recognized that fiscal relief had become one of the trump cards of welfare reform. It had been used as a carrot to line up support from groups such as the National Governors' Association and the National Association of Counties. But that support had been generated for a broader welfare package, including such changes as requiring all states to provide AFDC payments to so-called "intact" families where the father resides at home, and setting national minimum standards for AFDC benefits.

Some believed that pulling fiscal relief out from the package would reduce whatever support remained for a major overhaul of the welfare system.

Political Problem

The political equation was touchy. The governors' association supported broader changes than proposed by Cranston-Moynihan. But the lobby group was not about to say it would not take fiscal relief. "How can we say no thanks?" asked a staff member of the association.

Corman and Rangel faced a similar situation. Their states would be the principal beneficiaries if the Cranston-Moynihan plan was passed. But the measure did not contain welfare changes they considered essential.

Thus, while Corman did not consider the Cranston-Moynihan plan a welfare reform measure, he saw it as a "very constructive proposal," a "good interim step" for a broader welfare bill in 1979.

Several sources in HEW said they doubted that the president or his chief welfare advisers would take an official position on the proposal. While they regarded the Cranston-Moynihan plan as lacking, they did not want to place themselves in opposition to several legislators, especially Long, who would be crucial to any broader welfare changes in 1979 or later.

Some members indicated opposition to the Cranston-Moynihan plan. Ullman issued a statement after it was made public warning against "permanent sizable fiscal relief" without other changes in the welfare system.

Ways and Means Bill

Corman and Rangel had an alternative to the fiscal relief portion of the Cranston-Moynihan plan. The two House members were pushing HR 13335, which would provide $400 million in temporary fiscal relief to states for fiscal 1979 only.

The measure, which was reported by the House Ways and Means Committee July 18, would parcel the money out on the basis of AFDC caseloads, a state's revenue sharing allotment and its AFDC error rate.

Corman and Rangel saw the measure as a way to provide fiscal relief to states on a temporary basis until broader welfare changes were enacted by Congress.

Senate Compromise?

In the Senate, backers of the Baker-Bellmon bill were taking a look at the Cranston-Moynihan measure, comparing the provisions of each. An aide to Baker said he doubted that the Baker-Bellmon forces could support the new measure as proposed, but there was some talk of attempting to amend the Cranston-Moynihan plan to include some features considered essential by the Baker-Bellmon group, such as mandating AFDC coverage for intact families and setting national minimum levels for benefits.

Whether Long would support such amendments was unclear. But congressional sources said the situation was ripe for some political horse-trading. Missing from the Cranston-Moynihan proposal, for example, was another favorite concept of Long's, a requirement that welfare recipients perform some work in exchange for their AFDC benefits.

Some sources said they wouldn't be surprised if a so-called "workfare" provision was added to the bill, perhaps in exchange for some provisions favored by the Baker-Bellmon group.

The Cranston-Moynihan plan, made public in late June, had not been introduced in the Senate as of mid-August. ∎

Carter Proposes Increase in Education Aid

The nation's education community, which suffered budget cuts and veto threats during the Nixon and Ford years, looked expectantly in 1978 toward a more receptive administration under the leadership of Jimmy Carter.

Early in 1978, the president revealed his ideas about what the federal role in education should be and what sort of legislation would be necessary to carry it out.

The administration's first policy steps into the education arena came at a time when confidence in the nation's public schools was clearly waning. Parents were calling for stricter discipline in the classroom, the public was demanding an accounting for its education tax dollars and there was a clamor for ways to assure that students had mastered the most basic reading and writing skills before they were awarded a high school diploma.

Indications were that, from an educator's point of view, things would be better under Carter. The fiscal 1979 budget included a 14 percent increase in outlays for education, most of it earmarked for the disadvantaged, the handicapped and for needy college students.

In a message delivered to Congress Feb. 28, the president called for a big increase in funding for education, more federal aid to college students and creation of a Cabinet-level Department of Education.

The thrust of the package, Carter said, was to "reestablish education in the forefront of our domestic priorities." Overall, he called for $12.9 billion in appropriations for the education division of the Department of Health, Education and Welfare (HEW), a 24 percent increase over fiscal 1978 and a total increase of 46 percent and $4 billion in the last two fiscal years. For elementary and secondary education, Carter proposed a 15 percent jump, for a total of $6.9 billion. He said it was the largest increase since enactment of the Elementary and Secondary Education Act (ESEA) in 1965.

A 40 percent increase in student assistance programs for higher education was proposed as part of the effort to help moderate-income families who were hard pressed to meet rising tuition costs. The proposed fiscal 1979 funding level was $5.2 billion, up from $3.8 billion the previous year.

One vehicle for accomplishing some of what Carter had in mind was the Elementary and Secondary Education Act (ESEA) (PL 89-10), the major federal aid to education program, which was up for renewal in 1978.

In the past, reauthorization of ESEA has been the forum for some bloody legislative battles. Numerous amendments aimed at restricting school busing, for example, have been tacked onto the act, although observers did not expect the same squabbling in 1978.

In 1974, when the act was revised, members tangled over how to dole out funds for disadvantaged students. In 1978, there seemed to be a reluctance to reopen the formula fight, although there was disagreement over whether the focus should be shifted away from poor children and toward poor learners, regardless of income.

Other major programs in ESEA include impact aid for children of parents who live and/or work on federal property, funding to help districts carry out desegregation plans and bilingual education.

Background

Congress began considering some form of general federal educational aid to states and school districts in the late 1940s.

ESEA, which emerged in 1965, was the product of a long and bitter struggle to devise a method of providing aid that would not interfere with traditions requiring local control of schools.

Also at issue were the government's positions on school segregation and on church-related schools.

The segregation problem was largely resolved by the Civil Rights Act of 1964, which authorized the withholding of federal funds from institutions that practiced desegregation and federal court suits for desegregation of schools.

On the church-state issue, Congress ran into strong opposition to legislation considered in the late 1940s that would have allowed states to spend federal funds as they did their own tax revenue. In some states, that meant the money could go to private schools. Other legislation that specifically prohibited aid to private schools was opposed by the Catholic church.

ESEA was the compromise. It provided aid to disadvantaged children no matter which kind of school they attended.

Enactment of the law took only three months—largely because the old controversies were stilled by the new emphasis on aid to children, not schools, and because the Democratic Party had achieved huge majorities in Congress in the November 1964 elections. To make sure there was no hang-up in conference, the Senate accepted the bill exactly as the House passed it; it was almost identical to the measure submitted by the Johnson administration.

Title I: Heart of the Bill

The heart of the bill was Title I, which directed funds to school districts on the basis of the number of children from poor families. About 95 percent of the nation's counties were eligible for aid, but the bulk of the money was concentrated on inner cities and impoverished rural areas.

However, the unanimity over the need to have a general aid to education bill did not extend to the method to be used to dole out the money.

As passed, ESEA allocated funds to local school districts through state agencies using a formula that multiplied the number of school children from low-income families by one-half of the state's average expenditure per school child. Congress defined a low-income family as one earning less than $2,000 a year or on public assistance. The next year it raised the ceiling to $3,000 contingent on the availability of funds, but never put it into effect.

Opponents of the formula argued that it discriminated against poorer states and would be particularly hard on the

South, which spent less per student than did many northern communities. But the proponents, who prevailed, asserted that the formula recognized the extra cost of educating a child in a northern slum and gave credit for the effort some states already were making. They also said it would provide substantial increases in the school budgets of some southern states and would stimulate states to spend more money on education.

Congress also included in Title I a program of incentive grants to states that exceeded the national average for financing public education.

The formula came up again the next year when Congress enacted a provision permitting states to use the national average expenditure per school child instead of its own expenditure figure in determining Title I allotments. As a result, most southern states received a big increase.

There were a few changes in the formula in succeeding years, but there was not another full-fledged battle over it until 1974 when Congress adopted a different formula.

1974 Changes in Formula

The new formula, which was opposed by many urban members, cut back the number of welfare children who could be counted in computing the amount of aid a school district could receive. It had the effect of shifting the emphasis of compensatory education away from wealthier urban states toward the poorer and more rural ones.

Under the new formula, there were three types of children eligible to receive aid:

● Those aged 5 through 17 who came from families with incomes below the federal poverty level.

● Two-thirds of the children from families receiving payments under the Aid to Families with Dependent Children (AFDC) program that were in excess of the poverty level.

● Children not counted under the other two categories who lived in institutions for delinquent or neglected children and who were educated by the local school district.

To determine the payment rate, the total number of eligible children in a state was multiplied by 40 percent of the state average per-pupil expenditure. But if the state average was less than 80 percent of the national average per-pupil cost, the number of eligible children would be multiplied by 40 percent of 80 percent of the national average. If a state's average was more than 120 percent of the national average, the state would receive 40 percent of 120 percent of the national per-pupil average.

To cushion possible cutbacks resulting from the new formula, a "hold harmless" clause was included. It provided that no school district would get less than 85 percent of what it had received in the previous fiscal year.

In an effort to compensate for the shift of funds away from urban areas, members agreed to continue authorization of the special incentive grant program, which gave bonuses to states that exceeded the national average for financing public education.

However, in addition, Congress voted to phase out after fiscal 1975 another section of Title I that provided special grants to school districts with exceptionally high concentrations of disadvantaged children.

Effectiveness of Programs

Since 1974 there has been considerable discussion about the effectiveness of Title I programs and the method used to distribute the funds.

Title I was expected to serve about 5.6 million children in fiscal 1979, out of about nine million eligible. The fiscal 1978 appropriation was $2.7 billion. The Carter administration sought a $644 million increase for fiscal 1979. Fourteen thousand school districts were served. The average grant per student was about $400. Two-thirds of the students served were in grades 1-6.

Many of the questions about the program were answered by a National Institute of Education study mandated by the 1974 amendments. NIE determined that the program apparently was working. First-graders studied made average gains of 12 months in reading and 11 months in mathematics in the seven-month period between their testing in the fall and the spring. Third-graders gained eight months in reading and 12 months in math.

Another study, completed in 1976 for the U.S. Office of Education, also found that Title I programs had positive results. The study was conducted by the Educational Testing Service and RMC Research Corporation.

Researchers looked at several compensatory programs, not just Title I. They determined that the programs were retarding or preventing the relative decline in achievement among disadvantaged children that they said would almost certainly occur in the absence of such programs.

"Most of the unusually effective compensatory programs were Title I funded," the study found. The data suggested that "compensatory education programs carried out as part of the schooling process do offer promise in improving the educational deficits of disadvantaged students," the researchers concluded.

Distribution of Funds

NIE also looked at how Title I funds were distributed.

Researchers determined that two-thirds of the money went to major cities and rural areas and about one-quarter went to suburban areas.

But the actual amounts those areas received per child varied considerably. Suburban areas received 11 percent more and central cities 15 percent more than did nonmetropolitan areas. The nation's largest cities received 18 percent more per child than did rural areas.

The variation was caused by the formula factor that weighted allocations based on average state expenditures, so that per-pupil Title I expenditures were higher in predominantly urban and suburban states than in predominantly rural ones, the report said. South Carolina and Georgia, for example, received $163 per eligible child in 1977 compared to $244 per child in New York and $228 per child in Pennsylvania.

The differences showed up sharply when regional aspects of distribution were noted. The South, which had 45 percent of the eligible children, received almost 40 percent of the total allocation. But more than half of the states in the South received the minimum $163 per eligible child because of the low level of expenditure per pupil, compared to the $200 per eligible child received by almost all northeastern states. *(Regional distribution of funds, box, p. 100)*

The NIE study also determined that if AFDC-eligible children were not included in the formula that distribution of funds would have been considerably different. Those eligible under the AFDC portion of the formula were unevenly distributed around the country. About 75 percent of them lived in five states—New York, Michigan, California, Illinois and Pennsylvania. Those states contained only about a quarter of the children counted because they were from poverty families. Inclusion of the AFDC children had the effect of raising the allocations to the nation's largest cities by $36 million.

Overall, inclusion of the AFDC children resulted in a 20 percent gain in allocations ($29.4 million) for the large northeastern cities, a 12 percent gain ($13 million) for north-central cities, a 3 percent gain ($1.9 million) for western cities. Large southern cities lost $8.1 million, or 7.1 percent of what their allocations would have been without the AFDC counts, the study found.

1978 Legislative Proposals

Most of Carter's education proposal dealt with ESEA. The president said the measure should emphasize mastery of basic reading, writing and mathematics skills.

Under Title I of ESEA, Carter proposed providing special additional assistance to emphasize basic skills to districts with high concentrations of poor children. A district would be eligible for the aid — $400 million in fiscal 1979 — if 20 percent of its school children or 5,000 students were from poor familites. He predicted that about 3,500 school districts would be eligible and that assistance would be made available to about 900,000 more children than were being served under the existing Title I program. About 67 percent of the funds would go to city school systems and 33 percent to rural and suburban districts, Carter said.

Thomas M. O'Keefe, HEW deputy assistant secretary for planning and evaluation, said the new program was proposed because of the special problems and additional costs related to having large numbers of disadvantaged children in a group.

"We are convinced that education costs and needs do not increase in direct proportion to the number of kids. When a lot of disadvantaged kids get together, you have excessive costs," he said.

He noted that most of those children were concentrated in urban or rural areas. In urban centers, where tax bases often were declining, there also were particularly high expenses — caused by such things as deteriorating buildings and high salaries. In rural areas, costs were lower but so was the tax base, so the strain on school budgets was still high.

If for no other reason than that it would provide more education money to the states, the concentration factor proposal had the support of a number of education interest groups.

"It seems attractive because the needs of those districts with particularly high concentrations [of poor children] are higher," said Michael Resnick, director of legislative services for the National School Boards Association.

Spokesmen for the American Federation of Teachers (AFT) and the Council of the Great City Schools said they would favor a concentration provision. However, Gregory A. Humphrey, co-director of the AFT's department of legislation, said the new funds should be earmarked for instruction in basic skills, while Sam Husk, Council executive vice president, said it should be up to local school districts to decide how to spend the new money. The Council represented 28 cities with populations over 300,000.

Also proposed was a matching grant program to encourage states to create their own compensatory education programs. For every $2 a state spent on such a program the federal government would contribute $1, Carter said. Of-

ficials said that between nine and 12 states would qualify to receive funds under the program if it were enacted immediately.

Funding for Title I programs has never reached the authorized levels. Officials said the purpose of the matching grant program would be to encourage states to spend more money on compensatory education. If a state received matching funds, it would have to maintain current compensatory education efforts.

The School Board Association's Resnick said that group would support a matching program if it resulted in an expanded total amount of money spent on such programs. "Hopefully it won't be just a shift in state aid," he said.

Husk of the Great City Schools Council suggested that deteriorating big-city systems would be better served by a matching grant program aimed at revamping state school finance systems rather than by another compensatory program. "With a second categorical [program], you're really not addressing the basic problem—giving enough money to run a basic education program," he said.

Carter also proposed creation of a new Basic Skills and Educational Quality title in ESEA to encourage state and local demonstration projects to improve basic skills. The projects would include increased use of achievement testing and more parental involvement.

In addition, he proposed a new Special Projects title to consolidate programs dealing with educational quality and called for changes in the Adult Education Act to put more emphasis on competency in basic skills and on obtaining high school credentials.

To ensure that children in private schools benefited from federal programs, Carter proposed that:

● States be required to develop plans for enduring participation of private school students in all federal education programs.

● Economically disadvantaged children in private schools receive comparable Title I funds to those received by public school students with similar needs.

● If a school district failed to provide benefits to eligible private school students, the district would be bypassed and another agency would be designed to provide the services.

But Carter said he would not support a tax credit for private elementary and secondary school tuition. "There is grave doubt that such a tax credit program can meet constitutional requirements concerning separation of church and state," he said. He also noted that the federal government does not provide general education aid to public schools and said it would be unfair to do so for private schools. All federal programs except impact aid are earmarked for the disadvantaged, the handicapped or some other group.

Emergency School Aid

Approved by Congress in 1972 (Title VII of PL 92-318), the Emergency School Aid Act (ESAA) was designed to provide aid to school districts that were desegregating or had high concentrations of minority students.

It authorized $1 billion to provide financial aid to meet special expenses associated with desegregation, to encourage voluntary integration and to aid children in overcoming the educational disadvantages of minority group isolation. However, none of the funds could be used for the actual transportation of students.

The act stipulated that 5 percent of the total appropriated should go to grants for metropolitan area projects, such as establishing and maintaining integrated schools, developing a multi-district plan to reduce minority group isolation, or planning and constructing education parks. Four percent was earmarked for bilingual education programs, 3 percent for educational television, 6 percent for special programs and projects, 15 percent for pilot compensatory programs to overcome the adverse effects of minority group isolation by improving the academic achievement of minority group children, and 8 percent for grants to private groups or public agencies other than school boards.

The rest of the money was to be distributed among the states based on a formula. Each state was allocated a basic grant of $75,000 plus a sum based on the number of minority group children between the ages of 5 and 17 in each state compared to the national total of minority group children between those ages. Every state was guaranteed at least $100,000.

Individual school districts, provided they were not currently engaged in specified discriminatory acts, were eligible to compete for their state's funds by applying to the federal government. Districts which were eligible for funds were those that were carrying out desegregation plans voluntarily or under court or administrative order, or were taking other steps to reduce minority group isolation.

Regional Distribution Of Title I Funds

(Fiscal 1977)

Region	Eligible Children (millions)	Percent	Funds (millions)	Percent
Northeast	1.62	18.8	$378.9	22.9
North- Central	1.80	21.0	367.4	22.2
South	3.90	45.5	660.5	39.9
West	1.26	14.7	246.7	14.9

SOURCE: National Institute of Education

For fiscal 1979, the administration sought budget authority for the program of $290 million, a $14.5 million increase over the previous year. Of that amount, $103 million was for the national competition projects such as bilingual education, educational television, magnet schools, pairing and development of neutral site schools.

The remainder, $187 million, would be available to states under the formula. Funds could be used to meet specific educational needs incident to desegregation, for pilot projects to overcome the effects of segregation and for grants to non-profit organizations for conducting special programs supportive of desegregation efforts in local school districts.

Officials said most of the new funds requested would be used to assist local school districts that had adopted desegregation plans to be carried out in 1979-80 but who were too late to apply for aid under the regular funding cycle, and to help districts that had already adopted desegregation plans but that still needed assistance.

A report on the ESAA program released in January 1978 by the General Accounting Office (GAO) was critical of some of the methods used to dole out program funds and recommended both legislative and administrative changes. The GAO found that school districts had been allowed to use program funds for general education rather than to aid desegregation. The reasons, the study said, were that the Office of Education's regulations allowed funding of desegregation efforts completed years ago; there were inadequate criteria as to what constituted an eligible desegregation plan, and the funds were supporting activities not related to desegregation or in schools that were not affected by it.

"If the act is to be focused on desegregation aid rather than general aid to education," the GAO said, "the availability of ESAA funds should be limited to desegregation efforts which are ongoing, or to resolving those problems directly incident to the desegregation effort."

The study also found that the methods used for apportioning the funds often precluded money from going to the neediest districts. Districts with the largest numbers of minority children in a state sometimes were ineligible for ESAA funds because they did not have a desegregation plan or as a result of civil rights violations. In other instances, one or two large cities in a state could use the entire state apportionment, although there might be some deserving smaller districts.

One way to alleviate the problem, the GAO suggested, would be to conduct a national competition for the funds rather than having districts compete against others in their state.

In his Feb. 28, 1978, message to Congress, Carter proposed amendments to the ESAA to build more flexibility into the program and to encourage voluntary desegregation. He also recommended multi-year grants to reduce paperwork and to help local districts plan ahead.

Bilingual Education

Since establishment of the federal bilingual education program in 1967, there have been constant debates about its purpose and effectiveness.

It originally was designed to fund demonstration projects to help non-English-speaking children gain language skills so they could enter English-speaking classrooms. In fiscal 1978, the $135 million appropriated was expected to support 565 demonstration projects in 67 different languages serving approximately 255,000 of the estimated 3.6 million children eligible. The money also was expected to provide in-service training for about 38,000 teachers.

Many of the questions about the program (Title VII of ESEA) have dealt with whether it should continue to move children as quickly as possible into regular classrooms or whether it should be a more permanent program stressing bicultural education.

Backers of the transitional approach argue that the purpose of bilingual education is to move a child who has trouble speaking English into the mainstream of society as rapidly as possible. They consider the bilingual portion of the child's education temporary, to be used only until the child is caught up with English-speaking children. Transitional programs usually end by the time the child has finished third grade.

Proponents of the other approach say the purpose of the program is to educate children as bicultural-bilingual citizens. The two languages and cultures should be given equal importance in the classroom and both languages should be used equally as mediums of instruction. Ideally, the proponents of that approach say, the students should remain in the program throughout elementary school and perhaps through high school. The bicultural approach has its strongest supporters in the Hispanic community where in some areas bilingual classes have attracted wide community interest.

Preliminary findings of a study of the bilingual program for the Office of Education gave some insight into who was involved in the program and what it was accomplishing. Researchers found that 75 percent of the 5,300 students enrolled in Title VII classrooms examined in the study were of Hispanic origin. But less than one-third were of limited English-speaking ability. All of those studied were in grades two through six.

About 85 percent of the directors of the projects surveyed indicated that Spanish-dominant students remained in the bilingual project even after they were able to function in school in English. Only 5 percent of the project directors indicated that a student was transferred to an English-only classroom once he learned English well enough to function.

As for student achievement, the study found that Hispanic students, including those who spoke only Spanish, who were enrolled in Title VII programs performed better in mathematics computation than if there had been no program. However, results on English reading and vocabulary tests were mixed. Hispanic students in Title VII classes usually performed more poorly than other students. But the other students as a group spoke more English than the Title VII students, which researchers said could have accounted for the difference.

As for teachers of bilingual programs, the study determined that almost all of the teachers and most of the aides had been involved in in-service or district workshops in bilingual education and had taken courses in bilingual education. Two-thirds of the teachers and two-thirds of the aides had two or more years of teaching experience in bilingual education classrooms. About two-thirds of the teachers and almost all of the aides indicated that they spoke both English and Spanish in their homes.

However, a report by the General Accounting Office (GAO) in May 1976 found that only 27 percent of the 271 teachers involved in bilingual projects it surveyed had received any college training to teach in bilingual classrooms. Only 69 percent were bilingual themselves, the GAO said.

Administration Proposal

For fiscal 1979, the administration asked for $150 million for bilingual education, a $15 million increase. About $11 million of the increase would be used for research and evaluation of bilingual teaching and instructional techniques. An additional $4 million would be used to develop training programs at colleges and universities for project managers, administrators, paraprofessionals and other bilingual education personnel.

HEW officials said the administration wanted to continue the program's original emphasis on teaching English to those with limited skills in the language, rather than developing bicultural citizens.

In his education message, Carter suggested a number of changes in the bilingual education program which would, among other things, increase parental involvement, allow English-speaking children to take part, and emphasize the use of and training for bilingual teachers.

Carter also proposed limiting grants under the program to five years, with districts being required to show that children's educational progress was maintained after the phase-out of federal funds.

Impact Aid

Like all recent presidents, Carter proposed a cutback in impact aid, which compensates school districts for the effects of having tax-free federally owned property within their boundaries.

The Lanham Act of 1940 was the forerunner of the impact aid program, which was passed in 1950. Lanham authorized federal aid to local governments for construction, maintenance and operation of facilities, including schools. The aid was earmarked for communities with populations swollen by increased military personnel and defense workers.

Over the years three categories of students evolved for whom districts could receive impact aid. "A" students were defined as those whose parents lived and worked on federal property. "B" students were those whose parents either lived or worked on federal property but not both. "C" students were those who lived in federally subsidized housing.

In the 1974 education amendments, all C students were reclassified as A or B students depending on whether their parents worked for the federal government as well as lived in subsidized housing. In addition, the law stipulated that all funds paid in behalf of public housing students would be used for compensatory education programs and assured that no school district would receive less impact aid funding as a result of including public housing students in the program.

Administration Proposal

For fiscal 1979, the administration proposed $780 million in budget authority for impact aid, $51 million less than the 1978 request.

In his February education message, Carter also proposed:

● Eliminating payments for children whose parents work on federal property outside the county in which the school district is located.

• Holding fiscal 1979 and 1980 payments for "public housing" children at their 1978 levels and then phasing them out.

• Eliminating payments for districts with federal children equal to 3 percent of a district's non-federal enrollment, which was the national average.

• A "hold harmless" provision to enable districts to adjust to the changes. No district would receive less than 75 percent of its previous year's payments over the next three years.

Carter said the changes would save $76 million in fiscal 1979 and $336 million in fiscal 1982.

Senate, House Committee Actions

In marking up the ESEA extension bill, House and Senate education committees in April and May 1978 approved changes in the formula for distributing federal compensatory education funds that would result in at least a temporary bonus for a small number of heavily urbanized states.

In addition, both committees rejected Carter's proposal to cut back the impact aid program.

The Senate Human Resources Committee approved its bill (S 1753) May 9. The House Education and Labor Committee agreed to its ESEA extension bill (HR 15) April 5.

Title I Formula

An agreement between Human Resources Committee Chairman Harrison A. Williams Jr., D-N.J., ranking minority member Jacob K. Javits, R-N.Y., and Education Subcommittee Chairman Claiborne Pell, D-R.I., settled within the Senate committee the contentious issue of the formula for Title I funds.

The key element of the agreement reversed a change made by the 1974 law, which had shifted aid away from northern, urban states to southern, rural states. The 1974 law provided that only two-thirds of the children from families receiving Aid to Families with Dependent Children (AFDC) in excess of the poverty level would be counted in determining the level of Title I aid.

Southerners had complained then that fully counting the above-poverty AFDC children discriminated against poor states in favor of wealthier states that could afford to pay more to their AFDC families. The change made by the 1974 law shifted funds more in favor of the southern and rural states. *(See p. 98)*

The compromise reached by the Human Resources Committee retained the formula in existing law, except that all children aged 5-17 from AFDC families over the poverty level would be counted. This would result in a "short-run gain for a few states," according to Education Subcommittee counsel Jean Frohlicher. But additional benefits in the long run presumably would decline, since the number of AFDC families over the poverty level would decline as the poverty level itself increased with inflation.

Other elements of the agreement reached by the Senate committee expanded the proposed concentration program, which would provide extra money to areas where poor children numbered more than 5,000 or made up 20 percent of enrollment. The committee broadened the base of the program by allowing whole counties, rather than individual school districts, to qualify for the 5,000-student or 20 percent enrollment standard, thus including many rural districts with more than one school district.

The committee also set aside $400 million for the concentration program, and guaranteed small states at least one-quarter of 1 percent of the entire concentration funding.

The House ESEA extension bill established a formula for distribution of Title I funds that was similar to the Senate bill; however, funds to expand the program beyond existing levels would be distributed according to a survey that emphasized urban over rural poverty.

The Senate committee did not adopt this controversial House provision, which would allot new Title I money on the basis of the Census Bureau's 1976 Survey of Income and Education. Southerners in both House and Senate had expressed concern that the survey skewed the poverty count away from the South, where poverty is largely rural, in favor of the North, where poverty is heavily urban. Compared with the 1970 census, the survey counted more poor children in every Northeast and Great Lakes state except Rhode Island, and estimated lower numbers of poor in every southern and Great Plains state but Florida.

Impact Aid

The Senate committee voted down proposals by Pell to make modest cuts in the impact aid program. Impact aid is particularly important to school systems because it is the closest thing to general, unrestricted federal aid to education. Efforts by the last seven presidents to pare down the program have been frustrated by strong congressional support for the program, which provides benefits to schools in virtually every congressional district in the country.

Pell offered an amendment, supported by the administration, to eliminate payments for children of federal employees who work outside the county of residence. Noting that the change would save some $45 million a year, supporters argued that there was no need to give federal funds to counties that were not being directly affected by a parent's federal employment. The amendment was rejected 5-9.

The committee also rejected, by a 7-8 vote, a Pell motion to delete payments in the Education Subcommittee's version of the bill for children of employees of post office service centers on federally owned land. Javits, chief spokesman for the new payments, said only a small number of facilities for regional processing of mail are located on federal land.

The House committee not only declined to cut the impact aid program, but decided to expand it. Its bill would retain payments for out-of-county parents, and would return to law payments for children of federal employees who worked in another state, which had been taken out in 1974.

Private School Aid

The Senate committee rejected a proposal to provide new, unrestricted assistance to private schools. Pell described the proposal as an alternative to legislation granting tuition tax credits to parents of students in private elementary and secondary schools. Telling his colleagues they needed to show that they really did care about private education, Pell offered a new title to the bill to increase assistance to non-public schools for textbooks, health testing and other pupil-related services, and to provide all-purpose loans to private schools for maintenance and operation.

While the specific, pupil-related grants to private schools had clear precedent, Pell conceded that the constitutionality of general purpose loans to private schools had never been tested in the courts. Javits voiced strong doubts that the loan program would withstand the constitutional prohibition on aid to religion, because churches operate a large percentage of the nation's private elementary and secondary schools. Pell agreed to remove the loan program, leaving only the restricted grants.

Bilingual Education

Responding to criticisms by New York City teachers and others that Hispanic and other minority children were staying in federally funded bilingual classes long after they had gained command of English, the Human Resources Committee tightened the definition of students who were eligible for the program.

Concerns about the bilingual program were reinforced May 8 by the release of an Office of Education study which found that less than one-third of students in bilingual programs had serious problems with speaking English. The study also found that in 85 percent of the bilingual projects students were kept in the special classes even after they had the ability to function in school in English.

The Education Subcommittee had made students eligible for the programs if they were reading and speaking below their grade level. Arguing that such a standard would make half the students eligible for special classes, Javits convinced the committee to allow students to stay in only long enough to have had a sufficient opportunity to master English.

House Floor Action

A series of regional and fiscal compromises helped guide the ESEA five-year extension (HR 15) through the House July 13, where it passed by a vote of 350-20.

Before passing the bill, the House voted to cut up to $215 million from the committee-approved version of the impact aid program, bowing to the possibility of a veto and a changing attitude toward the long-popular program of aid to schools in areas affected by federal installations. The administration had wanted an even larger reduction.

Some regional vote-trading helped to block an attempt to shift funding for compensatory education aid in favor of southern and rural states, although many more states would have benefited from the change. The Education and Labor Committee had altered distribution of funds in favor of a few northern and urban states.

As passed by the House, HR 15 authorized more than $10 billion a year for a wide variety of aid programs for elementary and secondary schools. In general the bill avoided major changes in the 13-year-old education act.

Impact Aid

After prolonged negotiations, Education and Labor Committee Chairman Carl D. Perkins, D-Ky., offered an amendment designed to placate administration opposition to the impact aid provisions in the committee bill, without cutting too much from a program that benefits schools in almost every congressional district. At full funding of the program, the Perkins amendment would cut $215 million from impact aid provisions approved by the committee.

The administration had sought impact aid cuts which would have reduced spending for the program by over $300 million by 1982. The committee not only rejected these proposals, but restored some cuts made by the 1974 ESEA extension.

The Perkins amendment did not reduce the program below existing levels, but only cut some of the increases made by the committee. The amendment deleted provisions in the committee bill allowing payments for children whose federal employee parents worked in another state from the one in which they lived (the out-of-state B category), increasing payments for children whose parents worked for the federal government in another county (out-of-county B's), and guaranteeing full payment of the excess costs of educating handicapped children of military personnel and Indians.

Part A payments go for children whose parents live and work on federal property, while Part B goes for those who either work or live on such installations.

Perkins said the amendment was necessary "in order to make sure the bill is not vetoed by the administration." Budget Committee Chairman Robert N. Giaimo, D-Conn., supported the amendment, saying that the committee-approved provisions were "potential budget-breakers."

But Herbert E. Harris II, D-Va., who, along with other Washington, D.C.-area representatives, stood to lose most from the elimination of aid to out-of-state B's, said that the program should not be cut because of its relatively unrestricted, unbureaucratic nature. "It is the one education program that does not immerse itself in all sorts of red tape," but "gets money down to . . . the kids," he said.

The Perkins amendment was adopted by voice vote.

The House rejected, however, a further cut in the program proposed by Robert H. Michel, R-Ill. The Michel amendment would have restored existing law regarding payments for children living in subsidized public housing. The committee bill had eliminated restrictions on payments for public housing children, at an estimated cost of $110 million.

Opponents of the Michel amendment said it would endanger the delicate compromise put forward in the Perkins amendment. It was rejected by voice vote.

Title I Formula

The House July 12 rejected, on a 175-212 vote, a Mickey Edwards, R-Okla., amendment to restore to the bill existing language regarding Title I payments for children whose families received Aid to Families with Dependent Children (AFDC) payments in amounts above the official poverty line.

Under existing law, only two-thirds of such children in each state were counted for the purpose of determining state allocations under Title I. The committee had voted to restore full counting of all AFDC children.

Calling the committee change "patently unfair," Edwards argued that it would benefit a few states that made high welfare payments, at the expense of 37 states. He pointed out that three states, New York, Michigan and California, would get about three-quarters of the $24.6 million that would be redistributed under the committee version. "This bill as it now stands is largely another aid to New York bill," he said.

Opponents of the Edwards amendment argued that tampering with the Title I formula would undermine the careful regional compromises worked out in committee and on the floor. "We have a real well-rounded package here that we cannot unravel a thread at a time," said Michael T. Blouin, D-Iowa.

Albert H. Quie, R-Minn., observed after the vote that, by agreeing to support an earlier Blouin amendment, bill sponsors had picked up votes against the Edwards amendment from members whose states would have benefited from it. The Blouin amendment provided substantial increases in funding to small and rural states under a new concentration funds program created by the bill.

Concentration Funds

The Blouin amendment, passed by voice vote July 12, guaranteed small states at least one-quarter of 1 percent of the $400 million authorized for the new program distributing extra funds to schools with especially high concentrations of poor children.

Blouin said the amendment was "an eminently fair way to give equity to the states that were disadvantaged by the other parts of the [Title I] formula." He said the administration and most education organizations supported it. The larger states would give up about 1.5 percent of their concentration funds so that each small state could receive at least $1 million, Blouin said. Shirley Chisholm, D-N.Y., said the shift would result in a "disproportionate, fantastic rise in educational funds to the small states." Vermont, for example, would go from $5,000 to $1 million, and Wyoming from $2,000 to the minimum $1 million grant, Simon said.

The House rejected by voice vote, however, a move to further dilute the concentration program so that it would be available to almost every school district in the country.

The committee bill made school districts in counties with more than 5,000 poor children, or where poor children made up more than 20 percent of enrollment, eligible for the concentration program. John M. Ashbrook, R-Ohio, proposed an amendment that would have made counties eligible if the proportion of poor students equaled the average percentage of poor children in the 50 counties with the largest enrollments — a standard of about 2 percent poor enrollment.

Ashbrook argued that the 5,000-student or 20 percent criteria discriminated against small rural areas, even if they had pockets of poverty. He pointed out that large school districts, by sheer numbers, could qualify, even if their percentage of poor children was very low, while very poor rural areas could not.

Opponents of the amendment argued that it would undermine the whole purpose of the new program, which was to concentrate funds on the special problems of dense poverty areas. According to Perkins, the administration had said it would not seek funds for the program if the Ashbrook amendment was adopted, since it would change the focus of the program.

State Incentives

The House also rejected an amendment to provide more widespread participation in a new program offering matching grants for state compensatory education programs. Defeated by a 150-240 vote was a Quie amendment to allow school districts to apply for matching grants for their own compensatory programs, if there was no statewide program.

Community Schools

The House voted to prohibit federally funded community education programs, which involve using school facilities for non-school activities, from duplicating services already offered by other government agencies, unless the U.S. commissioner of education determined that the school and the other agency were collaborating.

Ashbrook Substitute

By a 79-290 vote the House rejected an Ashbrook substitute for the whole bill that would have radically revised the nature of federal elementary and secondary education aid programs.

The Ashbrook amendment would have substituted for the various categorical programs a single block grant to states, based on school enrollments. The same total amount of money would have been distributed, but in a single payment to each state, to use for education as it saw fit. The impact aid program alone would have retained its separate authorization.

Senate Floor Action

After rejecting a federal aid program for parochial schools and an amendment to limit school busing, the Senate Aug. 24 passed a bill authorizing about $55 billion for elementary and secondary education over the next five years. The vote was 86-7.

During two days of debate, the senators adopted 44 amendments to the bill (S 1753 — S Rept 95-856), including some major changes in the impact aid program. But they defeated attempts to make even more drastic cuts in impact aid and to delete a new program designed to improve basic skills, such as reading and writing. Opponents of the basic skills program argued that it impinged on local control of schools. The amendment to delete the program was rejected on a 30-62 vote.

A major difference between the House and Senate versions was in Title I, the heart of the bill, which provides funds for remedial help for poor children.

Both bills changed the fund distribution formula to count all of the children in a school district from welfare families receiving payments over the official poverty level. Existing law counted only two-thirds of those children. The change would have the effect of funneling more funds to big city school systems with high concentrations of welfare children.

But the House bill made another change — it included a new definition of poverty based on the controversial 1976 Survey of Income and Education instead of the 1970 census. The Senate bill kept the old system.

No Senate floor amendments were offered involving the Title I formula.

School Busing

The debate over busing involved an attempt by Delaware Sens. William V. Roth Jr., R, and Joe Biden, D, to attach to the bill the text of S 1651, which was reported by the Senate Judiciary Committee in 1977.

S 1651 was the first bill ever reported by a congressional committee that sought to restrict the courts' authority to order busing as a remedy in desegregation cases. All previous congressional action had sought to limit the authority of HEW to order busing.

The amendment would have barred any court from ordering busing without first determining that a "discriminatory purpose in education was a principal motivating factor" for the violation the busing was designed to correct.

It would have prevented the courts from ordering more extensive busing than "reasonably necessary" to restore the racial composition of "particular schools" to what it would have been had there been no discrimination.

The amendment would have affected any busing order that was not final or which had not taken effect by June 27, 1977. When the bill was considered by the Judiciary Committee in 1977 opponents predicted that 60 school districts would be affected. Among them was Wilmington, Del.

Roth said the amendment was intended to "establish guidelines that are consistent with the United States Constitution regarding the circumstances under which courts" could order busing. He argued that most people opposed busing, that it did not improve educational quality or better race relations and that it caused white flight from public schools.

Opponents of the amendment charged that it was unconstitutional and that it was an unfair encroachment by the legislative branch on the power of the judiciary. They also said the bill would interfere with the school desegregation process, which was working throughout the country.

Claiborne Pell, D-R.I., floor manager of the education bill, opposed the amendment, noting that it would prevent courts from ordering busing to correct discrimination caused by housing patterns.

S 1651 as reported by the Judiciary Committee was never brought to the floor because of a threatened filibuster. The same threat was made during debate on the amendment Aug. 23.

Edward W. Brooke, R-Mass., described the measure as "the most pernicious amendment" ever introduced on the subject and said he had drafted 95 amendments to it.

Pell eventually moved to table the Roth amendment, which killed it. The tabling motion narrowly passed, 49-47, after a plea from Majority Leader Robert C. Byrd, D-W.Va., who said he favored the substance of the amendment, but urged members to table it because of the Senate's tight schedule.

Biden told reporters later that the closeness of the vote signaled a "death knell" for the pro-busing position in the Senate. "This is not a harebrained amendment," he said.

Parochial Aid

The Senate bill included a provision, not in the House version, authorizing $500 million a year in fiscal 1979-83 for grants to private schools.

The grants could be used for secular textbooks, standardized tests, speech, hearing and psychological diagnostic services, guidance and counseling, secular instructional materials and equipment and transportation. In addition, the bill created an Office of Non-Public Education in the Office of Education.

Asserting that the section was a clear unconstitutional entanglement of church and state, Sen. Ernest F. Hollings, D-S.C., moved to strike it from the bill. His amendment was approved, 60-30.

Hollings said that 90 percent of the schools that would get the grants were parochial and that the $2.5 billion total

cost of the program would be better spent on public schools. He also asserted that it was "at least as unconstitutional" as tuition tax credits for non-public elementary and secondary school students, which the Senate had defeated Aug. 15.

Pell, defending the committee bill, said the panel had attempted to word the provision in a manner consistent with what it believed were the tests of constitutionality — that the programs have a secular purpose, that their principal effect be that they neither advance nor inhibit religion and that they not foster an excessive government entanglement with religion.

He noted that 9 percent of the nation's children are educated in non-public schools.

Impact Aid

The Senate adopted changes in the impact aid program, which is designed to compensate school districts for the effects of non-taxable federal property.

Carter, like every president since Eisenhower, has tried to cut the program, which received $770 million in fiscal 1978. One-fourth of the nation's school districts receive the aid for 2.5 million federally connected children. The money goes to all but three congressional districts. It is the only type of federal aid to local schools that is not earmarked for particular programs.

The program provides funds for "A" students, those whose parents live *and* work on federal property, and "B" students, those whose parents live *or* work on federal property.

The biggest assault on the program came from Sen. Thomas F. Eagleton, D-Mo., who offered an amendment to knock out all aid for "B" children. He said it would save $374 million a year. The amendment was defeated 20-66.

But some less sweeping changes were more successful.

The Senate adopted an amendment by Warren G. Magnuson, D-Wash., deleting a provision from the bill increasing mandatory payments for children living in public housing projects by $120 million. The amendment would give the Appropriations Committee, which Magnuson chairs, discretion in making the payments.

The amendment was adopted, 62-22, but not before producing some angry words from members from urban areas.

Describing his remarks as "brutally frank," Javits asserted that the committee bill increased aid for public housing students so that big cities "could get in on all this dough. . . .

"Now if we are knocked out we are being discriminated against and [it will be] necessary for us to go after the whole impact aid program. I promise, we will. The big cities of the country . . . will wake up and they will join me. They will knock it all out," Javits said.

Also adopted, 57-35, was an amendment by Henry Bellmon, R-Okla., which wiped out the tier system for making impact aid payments. The system was created in 1974. The effect of the amendment would be to give the Appropriations Committee discretion in determining how to fund the program. ∎

Appendix

CQ

Housing and Urban Affairs: 1973-76

Federal housing and urban aid policies underwent drastic changes between 1973 and 1976.

In those four years the Republican administration all but halted the traditional public housing program begun in 1937 and the housing subsidy programs for the poor enacted during the "Great Society" of the 1960s. A 1974 omnibus housing bill replaced both of them with a new, Republican-backed rental aid program. The concept of helping lower-income families to buy their own homes—promoted in the 1968 housing act—lost credibility under Presidents Nixon and Ford.

Under another Nixon administration proposal contained in the 1974 act, nearly a dozen categorical urban aid programs created in the 1950s and 1960s were merged into a single "block grant" program for community development. The new program offered funding to suburban areas and smaller communities, as well as to the big cities favored during the "urban crisis" years of the 1960s.

Nevertheless, the federal government took the precedent-setting step in 1975 of saving the nation's largest city—New York—from financial disaster. New York tottered on the brink of bankruptcy until Congress approved a three-year federal loan program for the city.

The 1974 act was the most important housing legislation enacted since 1968 and the only major housing bill passed during the 1973-76 period. Congress tried in 1975 to create new subsidy programs to prop up the sagging housing industry, which went through its worst construction slump since World War II. But President Ford vetoed the bill, and Congress settled for a less far-reaching mortgage aid program.

Battle over Subsidy Programs

On Jan. 5, 1973, the Nixon administration declared a moratorium on all new commitments for major subsidized housing projects. It then conducted an eight-month study and concluded that the suspended programs had been wasteful and unfair. It proposed to broaden an existing program under which public housing authorities leased units in privately owned dwellings for low-income families.

Congressional Democrats were unhappy with the suspension of the programs, especially as the nation headed into the housing production slowdown. But, as was often the case during the 93rd and 94th Congresses, HUD's critics lacked the votes to force the department to change its policies.

Federal efforts to improve housing for the nation's poor remained in limbo through 1973 and into 1974. Working under the threat of a presidential veto, Congress placed major emphasis in its 1974 housing bill on the leased-housing program promoted by the administration and it continued the suspended programs in name only. The new program provided subsidies to landlords covering the difference between a fair market rent for a leased unit in a privately owned building and a certain percentage of an eligible poor family's income.

Supporters of the leased housing program argued that it allowed lower-income families to find the housing they wanted instead of forcing them into massive and impersonal public housing "projects." They also contended that the leasing approach made more effective use of the nation's existing housing stock.

Congressional critics did not object to these principles as such, but rather to the proposed reliance on a single, untested program. The country still needed the suspended programs, they maintained, to assure production of enough new housing for lower-income families. Some House Democrats also complained that the new program ignored the needs of the very poor served traditionally under the public housing program.

Enactment in 1974 of the new rental aid program (Section 8) did not end congressional calls for revival of the suspended programs. In 1974 and 1975, Senate attempts to force HUD to reactivate the programs generally ran into House resistance.

In October 1975, however, HUD agreed to release $264.1-million in leftover money for one of the suspended programs—the homeownership subsidy program (Section 235) created under the 1968 housing act. But HUD officials made it clear that they did not want any new funding for the program. They continued to express doubts about whether the poor were equipped to handle the responsibilities of homeownership.

In 1976 the House agreed to go along with a Senate push for a limited revival of the public housing program. Congress required HUD to spend about one-eighth of its fiscal year 1977 housing funds on newly built public housing.

Public housing supporters pushed for revival of the program on grounds that the new rental subsidy program was helping only a fraction of the families Congress expected it to aid by early 1976. They also complained that

HUD was not putting enough Section 8 money into new construction.

In general, however, Congress came up with no bold new solutions to the problem of housing the nation's poor during the four-year period. It was forced to accommodate the Republican administration's views in the 1974 act and then decided to wait until 1977 (when, as it turned out, Democrat Jimmy Carter, a supporter of subsidy programs, would become President) to consider any major reworking of the 1974 act.

Private Housing Slump

The drop in federally supported housing production coincided with some terrible years for the private construction industry. Total housing starts stayed well below the annual goal of 2.6 million units a year set in the 1968 housing act.

Starts declined steadily from a record level of 2.4 million units in 1972 to 1.2 million units in 1975, the lowest

---

Proxmire and Ashley

The shape of housing legislation enacted during the 1973-76 period reflected the sometimes dissimilar views of the two men in Congress who had the most to say about housing matters—Sen. William Proxmire (D Wis.) and Rep. Thomas L. Ashley (D Ohio).

Proxmire, who became chairman of the Senate Banking, Housing and Urban Affairs Committee in 1975, clashed repeatedly with the Department of Housing and Urban Development (HUD). He fought for revival of housing subsidy programs suspended by the Nixon administration in 1973. He wanted much stronger emphasis on new construction of subsidized housing than did the administration. He pushed for a variety of new subsidy programs opposed by HUD. Senate-passed housing bills generally were unacceptable to HUD.

The department usually did not try to fight the Senate bills, however, because it counted on Ashley in the House to see things more the administration's way. Although he did not formally assume the position until 1976, Ashley was considered the *de facto* chairman of the Housing Subcommittee of the House Banking, Currency and Housing Committee for years before that.

Ashley's willingness to compromise with HUD was most critical during fights over the 1974 omnibus housing bill and a 1975 emergency housing aid bill. During these battles, Ashley formed an alliance with Garry Brown (Mich.), who among House Republicans took the leading role in housing matters.

Not surprisingly, House versions of housing bills tended to conform more closely to administration proposals. Ashley's approach earned him the enmity of some Democrats opposed to administration policies, but he argued that it was more important to get some legislation on the books than to engage in veto fights.

Ashley's attitude helped to guarantee that housing legislation enacted in 1973-76 accommodated administration views, while Proxmire's position kept HUD from getting its way completely. In conference with the Senate, Ashley's hand was strengthened by the general expectation that the House could not override a veto of housing legislation expanding federal activity.

---

building rate since 1946. A modest recovery in 1976 lifted starts to a 1.5 million level for the year.

The housing slump took its toll on jobs, an important issue for congressional Democrats. Unemployment in the construction industry went above 20 per cent in the spring of 1975 and the jobless rate still remained almost twice as high as the general unemployment level at the end of 1976.

Complicated, intertwined factors contributed to the production drop, which began in mid-1973. Under a tight monetary policy, the cost of borrowing (reflected by interest rates) climbed to record levels. Investors withdrew funds from savings and loan associations, the chief sources of mortgage credit, and put them into bonds paying higher interest than savings accounts. The resulting scarcity of mortgage financing caused a decline in new construction.

Even when mortgage money generally became available again in 1975, other developments braked a housing recovery. While they came down from 1974 levels of 10 per cent in many parts of the country, mortgage interest rates remained high. The effective interest rate on mortgage loans rose from about 7.5 per cent at the end of 1972 to about 9 per cent at the end of 1976, according to the Federal Home Loan Bank Board.

Inflation also priced new homes beyond the reach of many families. The average purchase price of a new home had climbed to about $50,000 by the end of 1976, compared with $37,900 at the end of 1972.

The problems of cost and high interest rates primarily affected middle-income homebuyers, especially young couples looking for their first homes.

Government Response

The Nixon administration addressed the mortgage credit problems in late 1973 by proposing to make it easier for potential home buyers to obtain mortgages guaranteed by the Federal Housing Administration (FHA). President Nixon called for increases in the size of mortgage loans eligible for FHA repayment guarantees and reduced cash down payment requirements under FHA programs. Congress approved the changes in the 1974 housing act, but FHA loan programs were not a major force in the mortgage market.

The Nixon administration also took steps to increase the amount of money available for mortgage loans. In general, it used the government's authority to buy mortgage loans from lending institutions in order to free more private funds for mortgage lending. HUD was authorized to buy up $9.9-billion in federally backed mortgage loans during the first half of 1974.

It became clear by the late summer of 1974 that these administrative steps would have only modest effects on the industry's problems. Congress and Ford, newly elevated to the presidency by Nixon's resignation, agreed on an emergency program in late 1974 that allowed HUD to buy up conventional loans—those not insured by the federal government—as well as FHA loans. (Conventional loans accounted for more than four-fifths of all mortgage lending.) The emergency program authorized an additional $7.75-billion in mortgage purchases.

Congress and the Ford administration clashed, however, in early 1975 over more aid for the housing industry. Congressional Democrats proposed to create three new subsidy programs aimed at middle-income homebuyers in an effort to stimulate construction. Ford vetoed this idea, and Congress was forced to settle for an extension of the 1974 emergency act with $10-billion in new mortgage

New Private Housing Starts

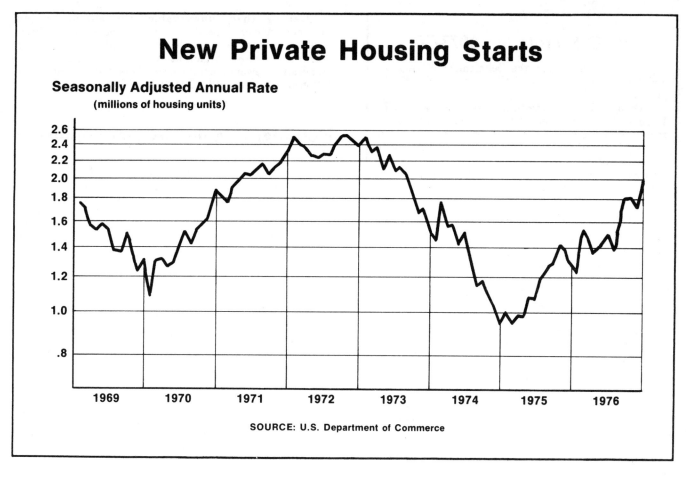

Seasonally Adjusted Annual Rate
(millions of housing units)

SOURCE: U.S. Department of Commerce

purchase authority. Legislation providing for a one-time tax credit for new housing purchases in 1975, however, was enacted over administration objections.

HUD used up the $5-billion in appropriations actually provided for the mortgage purchases in 1976, but, for the most part, the administration continued to maintain that general economic recovery was the most effective and non-inflationary way to pull the housing industry out of its slump.

HUD limited the mortgage purchases to loans on apartments in response to the industry's spotty recovery. While starts of new single-family homes returned close to normal levels in 1976, new construction of multifamily housing remained extremely sluggish during the first half of the year. It picked up later as the Section 8 rental aid program moved into the production stage two years after enactment.

While HUD provided these sporadic injections of new mortgage money, Congress attacked the construction industry's problems from another angle in 1976. Despite two presidential vetoes, it finally set up a new public works jobs program aimed at unemployment in the heavy construction industry.

Other Housing Legislation

Congress acted on two other pieces of housing legislation important to consumers—as well as the lending and real estate industries—during 1973-76.

Pressed to act by reports of high charges in many parts of the country, it passed a bill in 1974 requiring advance disclosure of real estate settlement costs associated with buy-

ing or selling a home. The disclosure period was designed to give homebuyers time to shop for settlement services, such as title insurance. An intensive lobbying campaign by lenders and other real estate groups in 1975, however, convinced Congress that it had gone too far. The advance disclosure requirement was repealed.

Congress was not swayed by lender protests against a 1975 bill requiring lending institutions to disclose how much mortgage money they made available in inner-city neighborhoods. The legislation was an effort to end the practice of "redlining," a blanket refusal to make loans in some parts of the city regardless of the financial position of the potential homebuyer. Neighborhood groups argued that the redlining contributed to urban decay.

Community Development, Urban Aid

Despite their clashes over housing policy, Congress and the Nixon administration generally saw eye-to-eye on the need to consolidate urban aid programs into a block grant system. The block grant proposal became a separate title in the 1974 housing act.

The basic theory behind the proposal—as well as behind other "special revenue-sharing" programs first suggested by Nixon in 1971—was that local officials were in a better position than the federal government to determine the best use for federal funds. Supporters also argued that the block grant system would deliver money more fairly than the categorical program did.

Nevertheless, debate over the proposal focused on what kind of community should benefit most under the "fair"

HUD Secretaries, 1973-76

Two Secretaries ran the Department of Housing and Urban Development (HUD) during the 1973-76 period.

On Jan. 31, 1973, the Senate confirmed **James T. Lynn** to the post. Lynn, a lawyer and former under secretary of the Commerce Department, participated actively in the negotiations that led to the development of the compromise 1974 housing bill. He left the HUD position in 1975 to become director of the Office of Management and Budget.

Lynn's successor was **Carla A. Hills,** the third woman in U.S. history to hold a Cabinet post. Hills, confirmed by the Senate by a 85-5 vote on March 5, 1975, had been assistant attorney general in charge of the Justice Department's Civil Division.

Some key senators and outside interest groups complained during the confirmation hearings about Hills' lack of experience in the housing area. But after a few months Hills had won respect for her administrative skill, determination to speed up HUD programs and ability to wring some concessions for the housing industry out of the White House.

---

allocation system. The resulting fund distribution formula hurt some of the larger cities that were the beneficiaries of federal aid programs written in the 1960s when the spotlight focused on the deteriorating condition of the nation's major population centers.

Hostility in Congress to the largest of those cities—New York—resulted in little initial legislative interest in helping that city cope with financial problems reaching crisis proportions in 1975. At first, the Ford administration also adamantly opposed federal help for New York.

Under heavy pressure to do so, Ford changed his mind in late November and agreed to support a federal loan program for the city. But the aid legislation passed by only a 10-vote margin in the House, even with presidential backing. House members from farm states and southern areas opposed "bailing out" a city that they felt had spent recklessly for years while their communities were making the sacrifices needed to keep them in fiscal health.

Although this sort of feeling was strong, Congress nevertheless approved the loan program in December 1975 and saved the city from bankruptcy.

Chronology of Action on Housing and Urban Affairs 1973

Congress began work on major new housing legislation after the Nixon administration cut off all new federal funding for housing programs for the poor early in the year.

Calling them unworkable, the administration suspended housing subsidy programs launched under President Johnson as well as the 36-year-old public housing program. Congress began hearings late in the year on proposals to rework federal housing laws, but took no major action in the housing field in 1973.

Housing, Community Development

Federal housing programs came to a halt in 1973 while the Nixon administration and Congress began to think about new ways to meet the nation's housing needs.

In January, the administration imposed a moratorium on all new commitments under existing federal housing subsidy programs for low-income families. While the suspension angered many of its members, Congress ultimately gave up efforts to force the Department of Housing and Urban Development (HUD) to revive the suspended programs. Legislation replacing them did not emerge until 1974. *(p. 9-A)*

The administration also proposed to end funding for categorical urban development programs, such as the model cities program. President Nixon wanted to combine these programs into a community development block grant system.

Congress took no action on the block grant proposal in 1973, deciding to consider it in conjunction with new housing legislation. It approved a minor housing bill extending authority for the categorical programs for one year and provided appropriations for them.

Housing Programs

Outgoing HUD Secretary George Romney announced the moratorium on Jan. 8, arguing that the time had come to review the "entire Rube Goldberg structure" of federal housing and urban development laws. The administration proposed to come up with new housing recommendations once it had studied alternatives.

The suspended programs included rental (Section 236) and homeownership (Section 235) subsidy programs enacted in 1968, a rent supplement program created in 1965 and the conventional public housing program launched in 1973.

Congressional Reaction. The moratorium angered many Democrats on Capitol Hill, especially since the Nixon administration had imposed it unilaterally without legislative approval or consultation.

Some Democrats charged that any problems plaguing housing programs were due to HUD's mismanagement, not to inherent faults in the subsidy programs. Investigations during the early 1970s charged HUD employees in many cities with defrauding the federal government in a variety of housing programs.

Congressional discontent was most apparent in the Senate, which voted July 20 to order HUD to end the moratorium. The order was included in a minor housing extension bill (H J Res 512) passed by the House May 21 (H Rept 93-206). The Senate Banking, Housing and Urban Affairs Committee added (S Rept 93-246) the moratorium provision to the bill.

"We still have serious housing conditions in this country...," said Sen. William Proxmire (D Wis.), who became chairman of the Banking panel in 1975. "It seems unconscionable that the administration, under any circumstances, would act without the consent of Congress...."

Three days after Senate action, a federal district judge found the moratorium illegal because "it is not within the discretion of the executive to refuse laws passed by Congress with which the executive presently disagrees." In August, however, the Supreme Court set aside the federal district court order to reinstate the suspended programs.

Acting before the Supreme Court did, House-Senate conferees accepted (H Rept 93-417) the Senate provision ordering HUD to resume the programs. Under the threat of a presidential veto, however, the House Sept. 5 recommitted the measure to conference by a 202-172 vote. The vote effectively killed the bill and ended congressional attempts to lift the housing moratorium.

Nixon Proposals. On Sept. 19, President Nixon sent his new housing plans to Congress.

He argued that the existing housing programs were inequitable, wasteful and discriminatory against the poor. They did not give poor families the right to decide where to live, he charged, and helped only an arbitrarily selected few of those eligible for aid.

While some public housing projects were impressive, Nixon added, "too many are monstrous, depressing places—run down, overcrowded, crime-ridden, falling apart.... All across America, the federal government has become the biggest slumlord in history."

As an alternative approach, Nixon proposed to broaden an experimental program giving the poor cash payments to use toward rent on units they selected themselves. Nixon, however, stopped short of endorsing the cash housing allowance plan as the best replacement for the suspended programs. And, as it turned out, the plan never moved out of the experimental stages during the Nixon and Ford administrations.

While keeping the other programs frozen, Nixon agreed to reactivate a program allowing HUD to lease units for low-income families from private owners. As revised by Congress in 1974, this housing program was the only one directed at the poor to receive any major new federal funding during 1973-76. *(1974 action, p. 9-A)*

Nixon proposed other changes that were designed to help the private housing market. He asked Congress to make larger loans eligible for federal insurance, to authorize flexible repayment plans for federally insured mortgages and to make it more attractive for private lenders to make mortgage loans.

Senate Democrats and the National Association of Home Builders remained critical of Nixon's proposals, especially since he planned to continue the housing moratorium on most existing programs. They argued that the cash housing allowance approach might not stimulate needed production of new housing for the poor.

One-Year Extension. Since it had to wait until September to receive the Nixon proposals, Congress did not complete action in 1973 on major housing legislation. On Oct. 1 it cleared legislation (H J Res 719—PL 93-117) extending most housing insurance and urban aid programs for one year.

H J Res 719 replaced the extension bill that the House killed Sept. 5. The House passed the second bill Sept. 17 without committee action. The Senate accepted the House version Oct. 1, also bypassing committee action.

Provisions. As signed into law, H J Res 719:

● Extended to Oct. 1, 1974, the Federal Housing Administration's (FHA) authority to insure mortgages under various programs.

● Authorized a $140-million increase in funding authorized for federal contributions toward the operational costs of local public housing programs.

● Extended HUD's authority to set flexible interest rates for mortgages insured by the FHA and the Veterans Administration to Oct. 1, 1974.

● Authorized fiscal 1974 funding of $664-million for urban renewal, $63-million for acquisition of recreational land in urban areas and $40-million for the development of neighborhood facilities.

● Extended the urban rehabilitation loan program (Section 312) through fiscal 1974.

● Extended the model cities programs through fiscal 1974.

● Authorized $110-million in fiscal 1974 for local and regional comprehensive planning grants (Section 701).

● Extended a variety of rural housing programs administered by the Farmers Home Administration to Oct. 1, 1974.

Community Development Proposal

Congress took no action in 1973 on Nixon's community development block grant proposal, called the "Better Communities Act." It was one of four block grant programs originally proposed by the administration in 1971.

As sent to Congress, the proposal had two major features. It provided automatic grants for community development purposes to larger cities and urban counties, basing assistance on population, poverty figures and the extent of housing overcrowding. It also guaranteed no major drop in funding for cities that had participated in categorical urban aid programs in the past.

Administration officials argued that the proposal offered local governments more flexibility, but some big cities worried that it would result eventually in lowered funding. Congressional sentiment favored enactment of the proposal, but key members wanted urban development activities coordinated with the housing needs of the poor.

As a result, Congress put off action until 1974, when it considered major housing legislation. The categorical urban aid programs were extended by H J Res 719.

Flood Insurance

Congress Dec. 20 cleared legislation (HR 8449—PL 93-234) designed to reduce disaster costs by forcing flood-prone areas to accept controversial restrictions on new construction.

A 1968 act had required flood-prone communities to accept these land-use restrictions as a condition of participating in the federal flood insurance program offering subsidized rates. In 1973 Congress effectively made the restrictions mandatory by cutting off federal construction aid and private mortgage money in communities that did not accept the land-use standards by 1975. Congress, however, delayed and then modified the requirement in 1976. *(1976 action, p. 30-A)*

Supporters of the land-use restrictions argued that federal taxpayers should not have to pay for property losses in communities that had followed unwise building practices on a flood plain. Opponents argued that the restrictions were too harsh, especially since their application would extend to communities that had only one chance of having a flood every 100 years.

Other key provisions of the bill doubled or more than doubled flood-damage coverage for homeowners and businesses under the national flood insurance program.

The administration generally supported the bill.

Legislative Action

The House passed HR 8449 on Sept. 5 after rejecting an effort to rid the bill of the land-use restrictions in flood-prone areas. The Banking and Currency Committee had reported (H Rept 93-359) the measure in June.

Senate passage followed Dec. 18 (S Rept 93-583).

Provisions

As signed into law, HR 8449 (PL 93-234):

● Increased total flood insurance coverage on single family dwellings to $35,000 from $12,500; on nonresidential buildings to $100,000 from $30,000; on residential contents to $10,000 from $5,000 and on non-residential contents to $100,000 from $5,000. Limits of coverage for Alaska, Hawaii, Guam and the Virgin Islands were set at $50,000 for single-family homes and $150,000 for multifamily units.

● Prohibited federal financial assistance for construction or acquisition purposes for projects in flood hazard areas designated by HUD and eligible for flood insurance unless the project was covered by such insurance for its full development cost, less land cost, or the new limit of coverage, whichever was less.

● Required HUD to identify flood-prone communities and notify them of their designation within six months. Upon notification, the community was required to apply for participation in the flood insurance program or prove that it was not flood-prone.

● Prohibited federal financial assistance for acquisition or construction in a community identified as flood-prone that was not participating in the flood insurance program by July 1, 1975.

● Directed federal offices supervising lending institutions to prohibit those institutions from making real estate or mobile home loans after July 1, 1975, in areas identified as having flood hazards unless the community participated in the flood insurance program.

● Allowed HUD to implement the national flood insurance program on an emergency basis until Dec. 31, 1975, while it completed determinations of flood-prone areas.

● Set a June 30, 1977, expiration date for HUD's authority to enter into new contracts to provide flood insurance.

1974

The housing industry served as the whipping boy for many of the nation's economic ills in 1974. It was caught by the "double whammy" effects of inflation, which forced up the cost of its product, and the tight monetary policy used to fight inflation, which dried up credit for the purchase of homes.

Besides taking steps in an omnibus housing bill to make more credit available, Congress late in the year passed

---

Housing Authorizations

As signed into law, S 3066 authorized the following amounts in new contract authority or new appropriations (the amounts do not include authorized ceilings on various kinds of payments for which open-ended sums were authorized):

Program	Total Authorization [1] *(in millions of dollars)*
Community development	$ 8,600.00
Housing assistance	1,225.00
Section 236 rental assistance	75.00
Housing for the elderly	800.00 [2]
Rural housing	112.25
Comprehensive planning	287.00
Urban homesteading	10.00
National Institute of Building Sciences	10.00
Total	**$11,119.25**

1 Total authorizations are used because not all individual authorizations are designated by specific fiscal year. Generally, authorized sums do not run beyond fiscal 1977.
2 Treasury borrowing authority.

Allocation of Housing Funds

While the measure did not earmark the $1.225-billion it provided in new contract authority for specific programs, HUD officials and chief sponsors of the bill had reached an informal agreement on allocation of the housing funds as follows:

● Expanded leased housing program (Section 8)—$1.014-billion.

● Commitments under traditional public housing programs—$50-million.

● Modernization of public housing projects—$40-million.

● Adjustments in existing contracts under the leased housing program—$11-million.

● Increase in contract authority for operating subsidies for public housing projects—$110-million.

---

an emergency mortgage aid proposal. The omnibus housing bill, the first important housing legislation approved in six years, also got federally subsidized housing programs going again after an 18-month moratorium. And it consolidated numerous urban aid programs into a single block grant program for community development.

The housing bill stressed a new rental subsidy program favored by the Republican administration, instead of other kinds of subsidy programs enacted during the Depression and the "Great Society" years.

Congress also passed consumer-oriented legislation designed to help homebuyers learn more about real estate settlement costs connected with purchasing a home. Under industry pressure, however, the bill was relaxed significantly in 1975.

Housing, Community Development

Charting an entirely new course for the nation's housing and urban aid programs, Congress gave its final approval Aug. 15 to the first major housing legislation (S 3066—PL 93-383) since 1968.

Key provisions of the bill created a new rental assistance program (Section 8) for low- and moderate-income families. The measure also consolidated 10 urban development programs into a single block grant system.

The new block grant program, first proposed by President Nixon in 1971, offered local governments $8.6-billion over three years for community development activities. Unlike general revenue-sharing funds, however, the money came with a few federal strings attached.

The Nixon administration heavily promoted the new rental aid program as a replacement for housing subsidy programs it suspended in early 1973. It argued that the suspended programs were ineffective and wasteful.

Congress, however, insisted on extending the existing homeownership (Section 235) and rental (Section 236) subsidy programs in the 1974 bill. But it did not provide any new appropriations for them before President Ford left office. Under legal and congressional pressure, the Department of Housing and Urban Development (HUD) finally agreed to revive the homeownership program in 1975, but only to use up money it already had available for Section 235 commitments. *(p. 20-A)*

The House and Senate fought over the 1974 bill in ways illustrating their general differences concerning housing issues during the 93rd and 94th Congresses. The Senate, a firm supporter of programs stimulating new housing construction, backed continued use of the Section 235 and Section 236 programs.

The House, on the other hand, generally was more willing to go along with HUD. With HUD Secretary James T. Lynn predicting a Nixon veto of the Senate version of S 3066, the House tailored its bill to win administration support. It continued the two suspended programs in name only, not providing any new funding for them.

The House and Senate also differed over the best way to distribute the new community development block grant funds. The Senate favored emphasis on aid for cities that had been actively involved in urban development projects in the past. The House agreed to divert funding from big cities active in the development area to suburban areas and smaller communities.

The House and Senate went to conference under pressure to act before the House began expected impeachment proceedings against President Nixon. If conferees did not reach agreement before then, the 93rd Congress was expected to adjourn without writing a housing bill. Under this pressure, the Senate essentially gave in to the basic framework of the House version.

Ironically, conferees reached agreement two days before Nixon announced his resignation Aug. 8, making unnecessary the impeachment proceedings that had fanned demands for speedy action.

Background

Congress had tried in 1972 to pass omnibus housing legislation simplifying housing programs and updating outmoded mortgage credit laws. The Senate passed an omnibus housing bill that year, but the House version died in the House Rules Committee at the end of the session.

In early 1973, the Nixon administration called a halt to new commitments for federal housing subsidy programs. It argued that they were wasteful and unfair because they gave poor people no choice of where to live. Later in the year, HUD reactivated a program under which public housing authorities leased units for low-income families from private owners. This program was the model for the one enacted in 1974. *(1973 action, p. 6-A)*

The administration liked the leasing approach for several reasons. It lessened government involvement in subsidized housing programs because ownership of the leased units remained in private hands. It gave lower-income families more choice about where to live instead of offering them a unit in a public housing "project." Furthermore, it reduced subsidy costs by making greater use of existing housing, which generally cost less to rent than newly built units.

In general, the administration argued that poor families needed money to pay for housing that was already available. It downplayed the need for new construction of subsidized units. To test this theory, HUD was experimenting in 1974 with a cash housing allowance program that Nixon in 1973 had proposed for expansion.

The Nixon administration had proposed the community development block grant program as one element of its general campaign to return more decision-making powers to state and local governments. It also contended that the block grant approach would distribute federal urban development dollars more fairly.

Senate Action

Committee. The Senate Banking, Housing and Urban Affairs Committee, reporting its version of S 3066 on Feb. 27 (S Rept 93-693), gave the Nixon administration only part of what it wanted.

Major sections of the bill reflected the administration's desire to consolidate federal housing insurance programs, expand the availability of home mortgage credit and return control of community development programs to the local level through the block grant approach. The committee also endorsed the proposed expansion of the leased housing program.

At the came time, the committee insisted on continuing the suspended Section 235 and Section 236 subsidy programs in revised form. It also imposed stiff federal control over the use of community development block grant funds.

The committee's decision to continue the Section 235 homeownership and Section 236 rental subsidy programs was widely expected. Virtually every housing and urban lobby group had pressed for an end to the moratorium on new commitments under the programs.

While agreeing that the government should encourage preservation of existing housing stock, the committee argued that the country still needed the two suspended "production" programs to increase the housing supply for the poor. "Evidence presented to the committee strongly supported the need for a high rate of construction and rehabilitation," the panel said in its report.

The committee approved $500-million in new authorizations for the two programs over a two-year period, as well as $365-million for traditional public housing. Comparable funding provided in the bill for the new leasing program was $880-million.

The committee proposal completely rewrote the administration's community development block grant legislation, called the "Better Communities Act."

Instead of basing allocation of funds on factors such as population, poverty and housing needs, the committee bill based grants on an average amount a community had received in previous years under 10 categorical urban aid

Urban Programs Covered by S 3066

The community development block grant program created by S 3066 consolidated the following categorical programs:

● Public facilities loans—loans to municipalities with populations under 50,000 for public works projects such as streets and gas distribution lines. The program was authorized by the 1955 Housing Amendments.

● Advance planning grants—advance funds to communities to plan public works and other projects, repaid at the time of construction. The program was authorized under the 1954 Housing Act.

● Open space land programs—grants to states and localities for acquisition of open land for recreational and other purposes. The program was authorized by the 1961 Housing Act.

● Basic water and sewer facilities—grants to local governments to finance construction of water and sewer facilities except waste treatment projects. The program was authorized under the 1965 Housing Act.

● Neighborhood facilities—grants to local public agencies for development of multipurpose neighborhood centers. The program was authorized under the 1965 Housing Act.

● Land acquisition—grants to local public agencies to help acquire land for future construction of facilities. The program was authorized under the 1965 Housing Act.

● Urban renewal—grants to local public agencies for slum clearance and rehabilitation of cleared areas. The program was authorized under the 1949 Housing Act.

● Code enforcement—grants to local public agencies for enforcement of local housing codes in order to reduce the need for slum clearance. The program was authorized under the 1949 Housing Act.

● Neighborhood development—grants to local public agencies to plan community development in urban renewal areas. The program was authorized under the 1949 Housing Act and expanded to cover non-renewal areas in 1965.

● Model cities—grants to selected cities to restructure the entire environment of neighborhoods chosen for demonstration projects. Funds could be used for education, antipoverty and other social programs as well as for housing and physical improvements. The program was authorized under the 1966 Demonstration Cities and Metropolitan Development Act.

programs. After two years, HUD could vary this amount by 20 per cent in either direction. The formula favored cities that had participated actively in urban renewal or model cities programs.

Rejecting the "no-strings-attached" approach of the administration proposal, the committee required communities to spend at least 80 per cent of their grant funds on programs directly benefiting low- and moderate-income families or helping deteriorating areas. The bill limited spending for public services to 20 per cent of the total grant and outlawed use of funds for a long list of construction projects.

The committee said it inserted the requirements to ensure that communities would use the money to help the poor, to eliminate blight and to undertake programs for which no other money was generally available.

Other major provisions of the 357-page bill increased the size of mortgages eligible for federal insurance by the Federal Housing Administration (FHA) and reduced cash down payment requirements for homes purchased with FHA-insured mortgages. As proposed by Nixon in 1973, the bill also gave HUD authority to experiment with FHA mortgage repayment schedules that would recognize a young couple's anticipated growth in income.

The bill also revised the homeownership and rental subsidy programs in ways designed to emphasize rehabilitation of existing units, to ensure in subsidized projects a greater mix of families with different income levels and to forestall mortgage default. Numerous other provisions tacked on to the omnibus measure dealt with subjects ranging from mobile homes to urban "homesteading."

Floor. The Senate passed the bill March 11 by a 76-11 vote. It made few substantive changes in the complex and lengthy bill. The only amendments of any note expanded eligibility for the revised Section 235 and Section 236 programs.

Both John Sparkman (D Ala.), chairman of the Banking Committee, and John G. Tower (Texas), top Republican on the panel, urged senators not to tamper with the basic structure of the committee version.

Tower himself was extremely opposed to the committee changes in the administration's community development proposal. But he decided to go along with the administration's decision to ignore the Senate bill. Rather than fight the Senate, HUD was working with a House subcommittee to ensure that the House version would be more to its liking.

"Since we were unable to resolve the [community development] issue successfully in committee," Tower said, "it does not seem fruitful to try to resolve it on the Senate floor." Tower and HUD objected to the Senate committee's restrictions on the use of community development funds.

House Action

Committee. The House Banking and Currency Committee reported (H Rept 93-1114) its housing bill on June 17.

The full committee's action sealed agreements made at the subcommittee level in an effort to make sure that President Nixon would sign some new housing legislation in 1974.

The key provisions of the committee bill expanded the new leasing program while curtailing the traditional public housing program and continuing the Section 235 and Section 236 programs in name only. The committee also rid the measure of the federal restrictions the Senate had placed on the use of community development funds.

While the House committee bill had the administration's general approval and the qualified support of mayors' groups, it displeased many key groups in the housing field, including the National Association of Home Builders and the National Association of Housing and Redevelopment Officials. Several groups, including the U.S. League of Women Voters, Americans for Democratic Action, National Tenants Organization and labor and civil rights groups, formed an informal coalition to try to expand the low-income housing provisions of the bill.

Sponsors of the bill were well aware that the compromises they had made with the administration would alienate supporters of strong public and subsidized housing programs and dissatisfy House members from big cities that would lose some federal urban development funds under the bill's community development allocation formula. But they insisted they had chosen the pragmatic approach, devising a bill the President could sign while guaranteeing development of some new subsidized housing and instituting a major new community development program.

"The committee bill is a bipartisan effort to break the deadlock over HUD's housing and community development programs so that the nation can resume its activities in these areas with broad political support," the Banking panel said.

As reported, the bill reserved more than $1-billion of the $1.2-billion authorized for housing for the new leased housing program. It provided no new funding for the Section 235 or Section 236 programs, but allowed HUD to fulfill commitments it had made under the two programs before they were suspended.

Despite its general willingness to go along with the administration's wishes, the committee branded the 1973 housing moratorium illegal. It also told HUD that it expected the department to revive the suspended programs if the leased housing approach did not meet needs.

The funding allocation formula was the most controversial part of the committee's community development block grant proposal. Unlike the Senate bill, it based grant amounts on population, poverty and housing needs—factors proposed by the administration.

Opponents of the formula argued that it eventually would cut community development funds in half for 80 to 100 big cities. The committee countered that overall increases in community development funding would work against any precipitous cutbacks.

The committee's community development plan differed from the Senate's in two other ways. It placed almost no requirements on the use of funds. But it did require communities to develop plans showing how they would meet the housing needs of the poor before they received block grants. Sponsors hoped that HUD would follow these proposed local plans when it awarded housing aid money.

Other provisions of the bill dealing with mortgage credit and other programs were similar to those in the Senate version.

Floor. The House passed the measure by a 351-25 vote on June 20. Sponsors were generally successful in guiding the committee bill through the House without change, but the House could not resist adopting an amendment reinstating a special housing program (Section 202) for the elderly.

Opponents complained that the measure would ignore public housing needs and force urban aid cutbacks on big cities.

Fight for Rental Aid Funds

The Senate moved to a fallback position once it lost its fight to include substantial new funding for a suspended rental subsidy program (Section 236) in the 1974 omnibus housing bill.

The Senate Appropriations Committee added to the fiscal 1975 housing appropriations bill (HR 15572—PL 93-414) language that made use of funds to run a new leased housing program, supported by the administration, contingent upon release of the Section 236 funds (S Rept 93-1091). The measure passed the Senate unchanged on Aug. 16. The House bill did not contain similar language.

House-Senate conferees (H Rept 93-1310) modified the provision so that it merely required the Department of Housing and Urban Development to release the funds, but not necessarily to commit them. HUD never spent any of the unused money for new commitments before President Ford left office.

The drive to revive the suspended program was led by William Proxmire (D Wis.), who chaired the Appropriations subcommittee responsible for HUD funding and who took over the chairmanship of the Banking, Housing and Urban Affairs Committee in 1975.

The bill was no compromise, argued Henry B. Gonzalez (D Texas). "It is a capitulation, it is a retreat, it is a surrender."

The bill's supporters agreed that it might not do everything that everyone wanted, but called it a good, practical measure that would be signed by the President.

An amendment to continue the Section 235 and Section 236 programs with $1-billion in new funding was rejected easily.

Conference, Final Action. House-Senate conferees reached agreement (H Rept 93-1279) Aug. 6 on a version erasing most major administration objections to the Senate bill.

On the controversial housing subsidies issue, conferees agreed to extend the Section 235 and Section 236 programs for two years, but authorized only $75-million in new funds for them. Most of the housing money went for the leased housing program favored by the administration. Conferees also dropped almost all Senate funding for the conventional public housing program.

In other actions, conferees also agreed to retain House provisions basing community development grant allocations on population, poverty and housing needs, rather than on previous funding levels under categorical urban aid programs. Senate provisions requiring communities to spend 80 per cent of their grants to help the poor or eliminate blight were changed to require them to give "maximum feasible priority" to such activities.

The special housing program for the elderly approved by the House also remained in the final version.

The Senate adopted the conference report by a unanimous vote Aug. 13. The House cleared the measure by a key vote of 377-21 (R 161-16; D 216-5) on Aug. 15. Most of the opponents were conservatives traditionally against increased federal spending for housing and urban aid programs.

Provisions in Brief

The 1974 Housing and Community Development Act (PL 93-383) made these major changes in federal housing and urban aid programs:

Leased Housing. The bill set up a new housing program allowing the Department of Housing and Urban Development (HUD) to lease units in existing, rehabilitated or newly constructed housing for eligible moderate- and low-income families. HUD was to make up the difference between the fair market rental of a unit and 15-25 per cent of a tenant's gross income. The program limited eligibility to families with income of up to 80 per cent of the median income in a particular region.

Other Subsidy Programs. The bill continued the traditional public housing program and homeownership (Section 235) and rental (Section 236) subsidy programs that were created in the 1960s and suspended in 1973. But it provided very little new money for these programs.

Housing for the Elderly. The bill revived a loan program for developers of housing for the elderly and handicapped (Section 202) that was phased out in 1969.

Community Development. The bill consolidated 10 categorical urban aid programs into a system automatically providing block grants to cities of at least 50,000. The amount of the grant was based on a three-part formula reflecting a community's population, poverty and housing needs. The bill provided for a six-year phase-in period if the shift to the formula reduced a city's previous funding under the categorical programs. While imposing few specific requirements for the use of funds, the bill generally instructed communities to give top priority to activities helping the poor and eliminating blight. They also had to prepare plans showing how they would meet the housing needs of the poor.

Mortgage Credit. The bill increased the size of a home mortgage for which the Federal Housing Administration would guarantee repayment. It also reduced the cash down payment needed to buy a home backed by a federally insured mortgage.

Housing Defects. The bill allowed owners of some federally insured housing to collect payments from the federal government for the repair of major life-threatening defects that should have been discovered by HUD inspectors.

Mobile Homes. The bill required HUD to establish standards for the safety and construction of mobile homes. Manufacturers were required to notify owners of major defects caused by their errors and to pay for their correction.

Sex Discrimination. The bill added sex discrimination to the kinds of discrimination banned in mortgage credit transactions by the 1968 Fair Housing Act.

Urban Homesteading. The legislation allowed HUD to make use of the "homesteading" principle used to settle the western frontier to help rehabilitate inner-city housing. The new program authorized HUD to sell federally owned properties at nominal cost to families who agreed to live there and make needed repairs.

Provisions

As signed into law, S 3066 (PL 93-383):

Title I—Community Development

● Consolidated 10 categorical urban development programs into a block grant community development program as of Jan. 1, 1975. *(Programs, p. 10-A)*

● Authorized $2.5-billion in fiscal 1975, $2.95-billion in fiscal 1976 and $2.95-billion in fiscal 1977 for the block grant program; authorized an additional $50-million in each of fiscal 1975-76 and $100-million in fiscal 1977 for transitional community development needs; authorized open-ended sums for the categorical programs until Jan. 1, 1975.

● Entitled to automatic block grants communities within standard metropolitan statistical areas (SMSAs) as defined by the Census Bureau which were 1) cities or twin cities with populations above 50,000 and 2) urban counties with populations (excluding cities) of at least 200,000 which were authorized by state law to carry out housing and community development programs.

● Based the amount of the block grant on a three-part formula reflecting the ratio of a particular community's population, extent of housing overcrowding and poverty (weighted twice) to the average figures for all similar communities.

● In fiscal 1975, guaranteed localities with automatic entitlements to the greater of 1) one-third of the formula amount or 2) the average annual ("hold harmless") amount it had received under categorical urban programs in fiscal 1968-72; in fiscal 1976, guaranteed such localities the greater of two-thirds of the formula grant or the hold harmless amount; in fiscal 1977, guaranteed such communities the greater of the full formula grant or the hold harmless amount.

● In fiscal 1978-80, phased down the hold harmless amount (if greater than the formula entitlement) by thirds to the formula level by fiscal 1980; required the HUD Secretary to report to Congress by March 31, 1977, any recommendations for changes in the allocation formula.

● Allocated any remaining funds 1) first, to meet the hold harmless requirements for small communities within SMSAs which had carried on either an urban renewal, model cities, housing code enforcement or neighborhood development program during fiscal 1968-72, but which were not entitled to automatic block grants and 2) second, to all SMSAs on the basis of the three-part formula; left allocation of specific grants to applicants within SMSAs under the second category up to the HUD Secretary's discretion.

● Allocated 80 per cent of block grant funds to SMSA areas and 20 per cent to rural, non-SMSA areas; allocated funds in rural areas 1) first, to communities qualifying for hold harmless treatment and 2) second, to states on the basis of the three-part formula for discretionary grants to rural applicants.

● Earmarked 2 per cent of appropriated funds for a discretionary fund for use by the HUD Secretary; limited use of such funds to projects under the new communities program, area-wide housing and urban development projects, innovative projects, emergency needs caused by disasters and special grants to correct any inequities in the basic formula distribution system; limited grants for emergency needs to 25 per cent of all grants in any one year.

● Required all communities applying for community development funds to submit an application 1) identifying community development needs, 2) formulating a program to meet needs, 3) outlining a housing assistance plan, 4) showing conformance with civil rights acts and 5) carrying assurances that citizens had an opportunity to participate in formulation of the application.

● Required the housing plan to 1) specify an annual goal for the number of housing units to be assisted, 2) determine assistance best suited to lower-income families, 3) indicate the size and type of housing projects needed, 4) indicate how many assisted units would be newly constructed, rehabilitated or adequate existing housing and 5) specify the general locations of proposed housing for lower-income families.

● In addition, required cities and urban counties entitled to automatic entitlements to outline a three-year plan of anticipated activities including programs designed to eliminate blight and provide improved community facilities and services.

● Specifically required communities seeking funds to certify to HUD that proposed programs would give maximum feasible priority to activities benefiting low- or moderate-income families or aiding the prevention or elimination of slums or urban blight.

● Authorized the Secretary to waive the application requirements for a community with population under 25,000 seeking a grant for a single development activity.

● Required the HUD Secretary to approve applications for communities with automatic entitlements within 75 days unless he determined that the applications were plainly inconsistent with or inappropriate for the community's needs or that they violated the act or other laws; provided automatic approval if the Secretary did not inform the applicant of specific reasons for disapproval within 75 days.

● Required the Secretary of HUD to evaluate performance reports on community development programs annually.

● Streamlined the provisions of the 1969 National Environmental Policy Act for community development.

● Allowed communities to use their grants for 1) general acquisition of land for public purposes, 2) construction or improvement of public works facilities, neighborhood facilities, senior centers, water and sewer facilities, parks and recreation facilities, flood and drainage facilities, street lights, parking facilities, solid waste disposal facilities and fire protection facilities, 3) housing code enforcement, 4) slum clearance and renewal 5) historic preservation, 6) relocation payments to individuals displaced by slum clearance, 7) planning and other activities; allowed use of grants to provide health, social, welfare, education or other community services if funds were not available under other federal programs.

● Authorized the Secretary to guarantee bonds and other obligations which communities receiving grants issued to finance the purchase of real property needed for development programs.

Title II—Assisted Housing

● Authorized $1.225-billion in fiscal 1974-75 in new contract authority for conventional public housing and a new rental leasing subsidy program (Section 8); earmarked $150-million of the new authority for the development of new public housing and $75-million for development of conventional public housing.

● Authorized the HUD Secretary to enter into up to 40-year contracts with private developers or public housing agencies who agreed to provide newly constructed, rehabilitated or adequate existing rental housing for moderate- and low-income families under the Section 8 program.

● Allowed the HUD Secretary to make rental assistance payments under the Section 8 program for up to 100 per cent of the units in any one project; allowed the Secretary, however, to give preference to applicants limiting assisted units to 20 per cent per project if the project were not designed for the elderly or handicapped or had more than 50 units.

● Limited each assistance payment to the difference between 15 and 25 per cent of a tenant's gross income and, generally, an amount no more than 10 per cent above the fair market rental as determined by HUD; for large low-income families or families with exceptional expenses, limited the tenant's share to 15 per cent of gross income.

● Provided for annual adjustments in the Section 8 assistance contracts to reflect increases in operating and maintenance costs, property tax and utility rates and fair market rental values.

● Limited eligibility for assistance under the Section 8 program to families with income up to 80 per cent of the median family income in a particular area; required that at least 30 per cent of the families assisted had income not exceeding 50 per cent of an area's median family income.

● Gave owners of existing housing participating in the Section 8 program the right to select tenants, and public housing agencies the sole right to evict those tenants.

● Barred Section 8 assistance payments to owners for units which had been unoccupied for more than 60 days.

● Increased the ceiling on operating subsidies to public housing agencies to $500-million in fiscal 1975 and $560-million in fiscal 1976.

● Required public housing tenants to pay a minimum rent equal to 5 per cent of their gross income or the amount of welfare assistance earmarked for rent; limited any required increases in rent to $5 every six months.

● Earmarked 20 per cent of all new public housing units for families with income below 50 per cent of the median income in an area.

● Extended the homeownership (Section 235) and rental assistance (Section 236) housing subsidy programs through fiscal 1976; authorized $75-million in new contract authority for the Section 236 program in fiscal 1975 and open-ended sums for the Section 235 program.

● Limited eligibility for assistance under the Section 235 and Section 236 programs to families with income up to 80 per cent of an area's median family income.

● Earmarked at least 20 per cent of the new Section 236 contracts for housing for the elderly or handicapped and at least 10 per cent for rehabilitation of existing housing.

● Generally, limited assistance payments under the Section 236 programs to the difference between 20 to 25 per cent of a tenant's income adjusted by various deductions and basic rents determined by HUD; authorized the Secretary to make additional payments for families occupying up to 20 per cent of the assisted units in any one project.

● Allocated at least 20 per cent, but no more than 25 per cent, of all housing assistance funds to rural areas; required the Secretary to allocate funds in conformance with local housing plans required under the community development program.

● In each of fiscal 1975-76, earmarked at least $15-million of the total housing authorization for the development of public housing for Indians.

● Authorized the Secretary to borrow up to $800-million from the Treasury for unsubsidized loans to developers of

Average Home-Buying Costs

*(Single-family homes, November 1976)**

Metropolitan Areas	Average Cost, New Homes	Effective Interest Rates	Average Cost, Old Homes	Effective Interest Rates
Atlanta	$55,700	9.17%	$46,100	9.26%
Baltimore	46,700	8.65	41,800	9.09
Boston	57,200	8.83	49,600	8.71
Chicago	56,000	8.87	50,300	8.98
Cleveland	60,600	8.85	46,700	8.98
Dallas	55,800	9.13	44,800	9.37
Denver	53,200	9.13	49,200	9.27
Detroit	49,300	8.98	39,800	9.24
Houston	54,500	9.38	42,600	9.46
Los Angeles	74,400	9.38	58,300	9.48
Miami	54,400	9.07	44,900	9.06
Minneapolis	59,100	9.09	48,900	8.87
New York	59,000	8.62	55,100	8.64
Philadelphia	45,800	8.85	40,400	9.19
St. Louis	48,200	9.01	34,500	9.07
San Francisco	71,400	9.29	59,500	9.37
Seattle	51,100	9.40	45,100	9.47
Washington, D.C.	58,200	9.11	66,500	9.21

*Preliminary figures

Source: Federal Home Loan Bank Board

housing for the elderly and handicapped; made those living in units developed under the loan program (Section 202) eligible for assistance under the Section 8 rental leasing program.

Title III—Mortgage Credit

● Extended regular Federal Housing Administration (FHA) mortgage insurance programs to June 30, 1977.

● Extended the HUD Secretary's authority to set flexible interest rates for FHA-backed mortgages to June 30, 1977.

● Increased the maximum FHA mortgage amount for a single-family home to $45,000 from $33,000; increased the maximum FHA home improvement loan to $10,000 from $5,000 for a single dwelling.

● Required cash down payments for homes backed by FHA mortgages of 3 per cent of the sale price up to $25,000, an additional 10 per cent on the price between $25,000 and $35,000 and an additional 20 per cent on the price above $35,000.

● Authorized the Secretary to provide FHA guarantees on mortgages which were co-insured by the lending institution until July 1, 1977.

● Extended FHA mortgage insurance to medical group-practice facilities for the practice of osteopathy or podiatry.

● Authorized the HUD Secretary to insure, on an experimental basis until June 30, 1976, mortgages with variable interest rates designed to reflect expected increases or decreases in a family's income.

● Authorized the Secretary to pay to correct or reimburse owners for the repair of major defects posing a threat to life or safety in housing insured by the federal government between Aug. 1, 1968, and Jan. 1, 1973; authorized similar compensation for defects in housing subsidized under the Section 235 homeownership program indefinitely.

Title IV—Comprehensive Planning

● Authorized $130-million in fiscal 1975 and $150-million in fiscal 1976 for grants to local and regional governments for planning activities; required governments applying for assistance to develop housing and land-use plans.

● Authorized $3.5-million in each of fiscal 1975-76 for training programs in urban management.

Title V—Rural Housing

● Authorized the Farmers Home Administration (FmHA) to refinance debts that were at least five years old.

● Increased the maximum FmHA rehabilitation loan to $5,000 from $3,500; increased total authority available for such loans to $80-million from $50-million in fiscal 1975-77.

● Increased total authority available for farm labor housing program grants to $80-million from $50-million in fiscal 1975-77.

● Authorized $1-million in each of fiscal 1975-77 for additional research on rural housing problems.

● Increased the annual authority for assistance to rural families developing their own ("self-help") housing to $10-million from $5-million in each of fiscal 1975-77.

● Expanded eligibility for FmHA assistance to rural communities with population of up to 20,000.

● Authorized rent supplements to low-income rural families; limited required rent for such families to 25 per cent of income; generally limited the supplement assistance to 20 per cent of the units in any one project.

● Authorized $10-million in each of fiscal 1975-76 for grants and loans for technical assistance for low-income rural housing development.

● Authorized the Agriculture Secretary to establish escrow accounts holding prepayment of property taxes and other expenses for FmHA borrowers.

● Authorized the Agriculture Secretary to make or insure loans for the purchase of condominiums in rural areas.

Title VI—Mobile Homes

● Required the HUD Secretary to establish standards for mobile home safety and construction and to conduct related research, demonstration and training programs.

● Required mobile home manufacturers to notify owners of defects and pay for correction of such defects if they posed an unreasonable risk of injury or death or were caused by a manufacturing error.

Title VII—Home Mortgage Assistance

● Increased to $55,000 from $45,000 the maximum mortgage loan a federally chartered savings and loan association could provide for a single-family home.

● Eased restrictions barring federal savings and loan associations from making total real estate-related loans equaling more than 20 per cent of their assets.

● Increased to $10,000 from $5,000 the maximum home improvement loan a federal savings and loan association could make.

● Removed restrictions barring federally chartered national banks from making total real estate-related loans exceeding 70 per cent of their total savings deposits.

● Increased lending authority for federal credit unions.

Title VIII—Miscellaneous

● Authorized the HUD Secretary to make grants to or guarantee obligations of state agencies carrying out urban renewal and housing development activities.

● Expanded HUD assistance under the new communities development program.

● Authorized the HUD Secretary to make annual payments of up to $40-million for an experimental program of cash housing allowances and authorized open-ended sums for the payments; required the Secretary to report to Congress on the experiment within 18 months of enactment.

● Barred sex discrimination in mortgage credit transactions.

● Established an independent National Institute of Building Sciences to propose nationally acceptable standards for local building codes and advise the housing industry on advanced construction techniques; authorized $5-million in each of fiscal 1975-76 for the institute.

● Authorized the HUD Secretary to transfer federally owned properties of one to four units to local public agencies for sale at nominal cost; required those participating in the "urban homesteading" program to live in the home for three years and make necessary repairs; authorized up to $5-million in each of fiscal 1975-76 for the program.

● Authorized HUD to provide counseling and other services for tenants aided under the Section 235 or Section 236 programs.

● Earmarked no more than $10-million of HUD research appropriations for study of the special housing needs of the elderly, handicapped, displaced individuals and large or broken families.

● Authorized HUD, in consultation with the National Science Foundation, to undertake solar heating and cooling demonstrations.

● Required the HUD Secretary and the Treasury Secretary to study the feasibility of financing rental assistance programs with direct federal loans instead of loans made by private lending institutions.

Emergency Mortgage Aid

Congress moved late in the year to help middle-income homebuyers frozen out of the housing market by scarce mortgage money and high interest rates.

Legislation (S 3979—PL 93-449) cleared Oct. 15 expanded the tight mortgage money supply by authorizing the federal government to buy up conventional mortgage loans—those not backed by the federal government—as well as government-insured loans. The purchases, in effect freed private funds for mortgage loans at interest rates slightly subsidized by the federal government.

President Ford had urged Congress to act quickly on the legislation to help the depressed housing industry.

The 1974 act envisioned a one-year emergency program, but Congress extended the legislation again in 1975 and 1976. *(pp. 19-A, 30-A)*

Background

The housing industry traditionally suffered severe setbacks during periods of tight monetary policy because, as Ford noted Oct. 8, "credit is the lifeblood of housing." The current credit squeeze, Ford said, had led to the "longest and most severe housing recession since the end of World War II."

The credit problems plaguing the housing industry were complicated, but interrelated. A key factor was the growing outflow of savings from savings and loan associations, which made about half of all mortgage loans.

During periods of high interest rates, investors tended to withdraw funds from savings institutions—barred by law from paying more than 6 per cent interest on most accounts—in order to put their money into higher interest investments such as Treasury notes. This outflow of savings, called disintermediation, reached a four and a half year high in August.

In addition, potential homeowners had to compete with other borrowers, including corporations, for scarce loan money. Even if they could find a source of credit, aspiring homeowners were being forced out of the housing market by high cash down payment requirements, higher housing prices caused by inflation and mortgage interest rates that had reached 9.5 to 10 per cent in many parts of the country.

FHA Mortgage Interest Rates

Listed below are maximum interest rates prescribed on mortgages insured by the Federal Housing Administration since it was created in 1934 through mid-1978.

Interest Rate	Period
5-1/2%	Nov. 27, 1934—June 23, 1935
5	June 24, 1935—July 31, 1939
4-1/2	Aug. 1, 1939—April 23, 1950
4-1/4	April 24, 1950—May 1, 1953
4-1/2	May 2, 1953—Dec. 2, 1956
5	Dec. 3, 1956—Aug. 4, 1957
5-1/4	Aug. 5, 1957—Sept. 22, 1959
5-3/4	Sept. 23, 1959—Feb. 1, 1961
5-1/2	Feb. 2, 1961—May 28, 1961
5-1/4	May 29, 1961—Feb. 6, 1966
5-1/2	Feb. 7, 1966—April 10, 1966
5-3/4	April 11, 1966—Oct. 2, 1966
6	Oct. 3, 1966—May 6, 1968
6-3/4	May 7, 1968—Jan. 23, 1969
7-1/2	Jan. 24, 1969—Jan. 4, 1970
8-1/2	Jan. 5, 1970—Dec. 1, 1970
8	Dec. 2, 1970—Jan. 12, 1971
7-1/2	Jan. 13, 1971—Feb. 17, 1971
7*	Feb. 18, 1971—June 30, 1973
7-3/4*	Aug. 10, 1973—Aug. 24, 1973
8-1/2	Aug. 25, 1973—Jan. 21, 1974
8-1/4	Jan. 22, 1974—April 14, 1974
8-1/2	April 15, 1974—May 12, 1974
8-3/4	May 13, 1974—July 7, 1974
9	July 8, 1974—Aug. 13, 1974
9-1/2	Aug. 14, 1974—Nov. 24, 1974
9	Nov. 25, 1974—Jan. 20, 1975
8-1/2	Jan. 21, 1975—March 2, 1975
8	March 3, 1975—April 27, 1975
8-1/2	April 28, 1975—Sept. 1, 1975
9	Sept. 2, 1975—Jan. 4, 1976
8-3/4 (Single Family)	Jan. 5, 1976—March 29, 1976
9 (Multifamily)	Jan. 5, 1976—March 29, 1976
8-1/2 (Single Family)	March 30, 1976—Oct. 17, 1976
9 (Multifamily)	March 30, 1976—Oct. 17, 1976
8 (Single Family)	Oct. 18, 1976—May 30, 1977
9 (Multifamily)	Oct. 18, 1976—June 27, 1978
8-1/2 (Single Family)	May 31, 1977—Feb. 27, 1978
8-3/4 (Single Family)	Feb. 28, 1978—May 22, 1978
9 (Single Family)	May 23, 1978—June 27, 1978
9-1/2 (Single, Multi-family)	June 28, 1978—

* FHA Authority lapsed June 30, 1973; renewed Aug. 10, 1973.

Source: Department of Housing and Urban Development

Builders also were plagued by tight monetary policies, which pushed up capital borrowing interest rates. At the same time, they faced the rising cost of labor and materials. Local sewer moratoriums and other efforts to control growth had depressed the housing industry in some parts of the country.

The effects of these problems were stark. Housing starts fell in August to their lowest level since early 1970. They totaled 1,126,000 at a seasonally adjusted annual rate, 45 per cent below the 1973 rate. The number of building permits issued—an indication of future housing starts—fell to a seven and a half year low that month.

Unemployment in the construction industry had reached about 12 per cent.

Builders, lenders and labor groups pressed President Ford to take additional steps to rescue the industry. Ford responded Oct. 8 by asking Congress to act on pending legislation allowing the Government National Mortgage Association ("Ginny Mae") to buy conventional mortgages at below-interest rates as well as mortgages insured by the Federal Housing Administration (FHA) or the Veterans Administration (VA). The President promised to make $3-billion available immediately for mortgage purchases, enough money to finance about 100,000 new homes.

The Nixon administration already had made a total of $9.9-billion available in 1974 under Ginny Mae's regular "tandem plan." The plan allowed the association to buy FHA-VA mortgages at below-market interest rates and resell them in the secondary market at market rates, with the Treasury covering losses from the interest subsidy. On May 10, the administration had made another $7-billion available for loan advances to savings and loan associations and commitments to buy mortgage loans.

But much of this money had not yet been committed. One problem was that most of it could not be used to purchase conventional loans, which dominated the mortgage market.

Senate Action

Acting on proposals suggested by Edward W. Brooke (R Mass.) and Alan Cranston (D Calif.), the Senate Banking, Housing and Urban Affairs Committee Oct. 3 reported (S Rept 93-1223) a version of the emergency bill that did not conform to Ford administration wishes in every respect.

When the bill reached the floor Oct. 10, however, Cranston and Brooke offered a substitute for the committee bill. The substitute was based on a proposal put forth Oct. 8 by President Ford in an economic address. The Senate passed the substitute by a 77-0 vote Oct. 10 after adopting a controversial amendment lowering the allowable interest rate on mortgages purchased.

As the administration proposed, the compromise allowed Ginny Mae to hold, at any one time, mortgages purchased under the program with a total value of up to $7.75-billion. Sponsors indicated that $3-billion would be made available immediately, as proposed by the President.

The substitute dropped provisions of the Banking Committee bill that would have required HUD to buy up mortgages on some existing homes; Ford wanted the program limited to newly constructed homes. The compromise allowed HUD to buy mortgages on existing homes at its discretion. The compromise limited the maximum mortgage eligible for purchase to $42,000—allowing families participating in the program to buy a house costing up to $52,500 if they paid a 20 per cent cash down payment.

As initially proposed, the substitute would have left it to HUD to set allowable interest rates on loans purchased by Ginny Mae. Sponsors said they did not want the rate to go above 9.5 per cent.

William Proxmire (D Wis.) complained that this rate was too high. "A rate of 9½ per cent is not going to give any relief to the middle-income homebuyer who has been forced out of the housing market because of tight money and high interest," he argued. "...There is no point in providing for a massive program to aid the mortgage market if the rate is beyond the ability of the average citizen."

Proxmire proposed an interest rate formula that set rates at around 8.2 per cent. Sponsors of the substitute feared that the change would provoke a veto, but the Senate adopted the amendment by a 48-27 vote.

House Action

The House passed the Senate version without change Oct. 15 in order to clear the legislation before it left on an election recess. Ford had asked Congress to finish up work on the measure before its departure.

House sponsors indicated that the administration could accept the Senate version with a suitable clarification of the Proxmire amendment during House debate. They maintained that the allowable interest rate might reach 8.9 per cent rather than the 8.2 per cent discussed during Senate debate.

Some House members grumbled about the bill's limited impact on urban housing needs, but sponsors argued that some help was better than none. "It can help a little," said Henry S. Reuss (D Wis.). "I do not think any of us want to oversell it."

Provisions

As signed into law, S 3979 (PL 93-449):

● Authorized the Government National Mortgage Association, at the direction of the Housing and Urban Development (HUD) Secretary, to buy and sell "conventional" mortgages on one- to four-family and government-insured mortgages on any size residence.

● Barred the association from buying mortgages on one- to four-family houses that were not the principal residence of the buyer.

● Limited the maximum loan amount for mortgages purchased by the association to $42,000; authorized a mortgage ceiling of $55,000 in Alaska, Hawaii and Guam; required a 20 per cent down payment on one- to four-family houses financed with mortgages purchased by the association.

● Limited the maximum interest rate on mortgages purchased by the association to the most recent monthly average yield on six- to 12-year Treasury bonds plus one-half of 1 per cent for administrative costs.

● Authorized the HUD Secretary to make a portion of association funds available for purchase of mortgages on existing housing.

● Limited the total outstanding value of mortgages purchased under the program and not yet resold to $7.75-billion at any one time; provided for the expiration of the program after one year.

Settlement Practices

Approving legislation it would undo a year later, Congress Dec. 11 cleared a bill (S 3164—PL 93-533) revising practices dealing with the settlement charges connected with buying or selling a home.

Key "reform" provisions of the bill required mortgage lenders to give homebuyers 12 days' advance notice of settlement charges—such as real estate commissions, title insurance and attorneys' fees—which could add thousands of dollars to the cost of buying a home. Sponsors maintained that advance disclosure would give homebuyers time to shop for settlement services.

Other major provisions of the bill imposed criminal penalties for kickbacks paid between those in the real estate industry for minor services. Title insurance companies, for instance, sometimes returned part of their fee to the lawyer who referred the client to them. The bill also limited the amount of property tax payments a bank could collect in advance from a homebuyer and hold in a non-interest-bearing escrow account. Some banks required homebuyers to pay these costs for as much as a year in advance.

Lenders and others in the real estate business decided after passage of the 1974 law that its requirements were too stringent. They led a successful lobby campaign to gut the measure in 1975. *(p. 24-A)*

In 1974, however, the real estate settlement lobby focused its efforts on winning repeal of the Department of Housing and Urban Development's (HUD) authority under a 1970 law to set standards for allowable settlement charges connected to purchase of homes backed by federally insured mortgages. HUD had never used this authority, but there was a lingering fear that it might some day.

The industry drive for repeal, backed by HUD, was unsuccessful. A House provision providing for repeal was dropped in conference. HUD, however, never used the authority before President Ford left office.

Background

The 1970 Emergency Home Finance Act authorized and directed HUD and the Veterans Administration (VA) to set standards governing allowable settlement charges for real estate transactions involving Federal Housing Administration (FHA) or VA mortgage loan guarantees.

In 1971 HUD and VA undertook a joint study of settlement charges throughout the country. The study found that the charges appeared unreasonably high in some areas, but not in all. Total settlement charges for FHA-VA mortgage transactions ranged from a low of $200 to a high of $5,000 across the country, the study found.

In response to the study and other evidence of high charges in some areas, the Senate included provisions in its 1972 housing bill that would have extended HUD's authority to set maximum charges for transactions involving conventional mortgages not backed by FHA or VA. The Housing Subcommittee of the House Banking and Currency Committee approved a similar provision in its version of the 1972 housing legislation.

But then on July 4, 1972, HUD proposed maximum charges for settlement costs in six metropolitan areas. Title insurance companies and other groups organized their opposition. "It was a mistake to publish the HUD regulations before the bill was out of the full committee," observed one congressional aide involved with the legislation.

Lobbying on Settlement Bill

Those supporting federal efforts to control settlement charges blamed their lack of success on fierce lobbying by real estate interests.

Consumer groups favoring settlement rate regulation were just overpowered, charged Sen. William Proxmire (D Wis.).

Proxmire traced the industry's strategy to the Washington law firm of Sharon, Pierson, Semmes, Crolius and Finley. The basic strategy, he said, was to sneak the repeal provision into a bill highlighting other reforms least opposed by the settlement industry.

The Sharon firm registered to lobby for 17 major title insurance companies on Aug. 4, 1972—after the HUD regulations were proposed, but before the House Banking Committee's action on the 1972 housing bill. Four other title companies also retained the firm as a lobbyist in September 1972 and January 1973.

While the law firm probably was influential, spokesmen for consumer organizations said they did not underrate the persuasive efforts of banks and attorneys who would be affected by rate regulation.

Those opposed to rate regulation downplayed the role of the Sharon firm. Title companies went to committee members as constituents with legitimate problems, one opponent said.

After the regulations were published, the full House Banking Committee voted to reverse the subcommittee's action and adopted an amendment to repeal HUD's maximum charge authority under the 1970 act.

However, the House Rules Committee killed the full committee bill and all housing legislation died at the end of the 92nd Congress.

In early 1973, James T. Lynn succeeded George Romney as HUD Secretary and the final regulations for maximum charges in the six metropolitan areas were not issued. Under the new regime, HUD officials contended that federal regulation was not a desirable or workable approach.

Senate Action

The Senate Banking, Housing and Urban Affairs Committee initially considered a compromise proposal in late 1973 that would have preserved the 1970 law, while barring HUD from using its maximum-charge authority for three years.

In May 1974, however, the committee rejected this approach, reporting (S Rept 93-866) a version of the bill containing some "reforms" but also repealing HUD's authority under the 1970 law. The principal "reforms" required advance disclosure of settlement charges and prohibited kickbacks in the settlement industry.

The committee majority argued that the disclosure approach would attack the real problems in the settlement industry on a targeted basis without applying federal rate regulation in a wholesale manner. If HUD found the law inadequate, the committee noted, it could ask for new regulatory powers later.

William Proxmire (D Wis.), however, argued flatly that the bill did not go far enough. "It is unrealistic to assume that consumeers will suddenly begin shopping for settlement services," he contended. The average person buys a home once or twice in a lifetime, Proxmire pointed out, and when he does, "he is a captive customer in the hands of the lender, the real estate agent or the attorney."

After three days of debate, the Senate passed the bill July 24 after voting 55-37 to knock the repeal provision out of the bill.

Bill Brock (R Tenn.), chief opponent of the 1970 law, argued that it took a "meat ax" approach toward regulation of the settlement industry. Besides, he added, why fight to keep a law that HUD had never used and had no plans to implement?

"Why is the senator from Tennessee, why is this whole group of people who benefit from settlement costs, so terribly anxious to knock [the 1970 provision] out?" Proxmire countered. "Why are they afraid of it, if it is not going to be implemented and not going to hurt them?"

Brock argued that it was unfair to "leave a sword of Damocles hanging over the head of the industry...," but the

---

Common Settlement Charges

Buyers and sellers of homes generally had to pay some of the following standard charges to "settle" the actual transfer of a property to a new owner:

Title search or examination fee: a fee paid for examination of the history of transfers of the property title to ensure that there are no outstanding claims to the property: paid by the buyer.*

Title insurance: insurance to protect the lending institution (which is financing the mortgage) or the new owner against the cost of outstanding claims to the property; paid by the buyer.*

Field survey: a survey to establish the exact boundaries of a property: paid by the buyer.

Loan origination fees: fees (generally up to 1 per cent of the mortgage loan principal) charged by a lending institution to "originate" a mortgage loan; paid by the buyer.

Other closing charges: charges including attorneys' fees for preparation of documents and other services, charges for appraisal of a property's value, credit report fees, pest inspection costs and other costs; generally paid by the buyer.

Realtor sales commission: sales commission (usually between 5 and 7 per cent of the property's sale price) to a real estate agent; paid by the seller.

Discount point payments: payments required by the lending institution to make up the difference between the going market mortgage interest rate and a lower maximum interest rate for a federally backed mortgage (each "point" equals 1 per cent of the sale price); generally paid by the seller, but passed on to the buyer through a higher sale price.

Statutory charges: charges required by law for recording of deeds or for state and local property transfer taxes; paid by the buyer.

Prepaid items: prepayment of charges for property taxes, fire or mortgage insurance, and mortgage interest costs between the closing date and the date of the first required mortgage payment (lending institutions usually hold these prepaid amounts in an "escrow" account not paying interest); paid by the buyer.

In the western half of the United States these charges and others sometimes were paid by the seller.

Senate decided to side with Proxmire. It then passed the bill by voice vote.

House Action

The House Banking and Currency Committee reported (H Rept 93-1177) a version of the bill July 3 that again repealed the 1970 law on settlement charges. Other provisions of the bill were similar to those in the Senate version.

The committee majority argued that it would be impossible or at least very costly to implement the 1970 law. It also maintained that there was no clear and convincing evidence that there was widespread abuse in settlement practices. Key Democratic members of the committee contended, however, that the bill protected those who "needlessly drain homebuyers and homesellers of hundreds of millions of dollars."

On Aug. 14, the House refused by a narrow 199-202 vote to reinstate HUD's authority under the 1970 law.

Leonor K. Sullivan (D Mo.) a key opponent of the repeal provision, argued that the "reform" provisions of the bill were meaningless if the 1970 law were repealed. Advance disclosure meant nothing if settlement costs were too high, she complained. "All we are doing with [the bill]...is to provide homebuyers and homeowners with the means to be well informed of the fact that they are being ripped off."

Conference, Final Action. In their report (H Rept 93-1526), House-Senate conferees recognized that HUD was not using its authority to set settlement charges under the 1970 act, but argued that keeping the law on the books was important in itself.

"...It is agreed that continuation of this standby authority is desirable for its deterrent effect" on settlement cost increases, conferees concluded. They also instructed HUD to use the law when it found abuses in particular real estate markets.

The Senate approved the conference version Dec. 9, and House approval followed two days later.

Provisions

As signed into law, S 3164 (PL 93-533):

● Required the HUD Secretary to prepare a standard form for banks to use to disclose settlement charges.

● Required the Secretary to prepare and distribute booklets describing common charges and, on a demonstration basis, describing the range of costs for specific settlement services in selected housing markets.

● Required mortgage lenders to provide the buyer and seller with an itemized disclosure of proposed settlement charges at the time of the mortgage loan commitment, but at least 12 days prior to settlement; allowed the buyer to waive the advance disclosure requirement; required lenders to pay buyers or sellers at least $500 if they failed to comply with the disclosure requirement, plus court and reasonable attorney fees if court action were involved.

● Barred lenders from making a loan commitment if the seller did not inform the buyer of the previous purchase price of a house bought within the last two years that was not used as a place of residence by the seller.

● Outlawed kickbacks between those in the settlement industry for services not actually performed; imposed maximum penalties of $10,000 and one-year's imprisonment for violation of the kickback prohibition.

● Barred sellers from requiring, as a direct or indirect condition of sale, buyers to obtain title insurance from any particular company.

● Barred lenders from collecting and holding in escrow more than one month's worth of advance property taxes and insurance premiums after settlement.

● Barred lenders from charging homebuyers for preparation of statements required under the Truth-in-Lending Act.

● Required the HUD Secretary to establish a demonstration program to develop model systems for the recording of land title information.

● Required the HUD Secretary to study settlement costs for at least three years and no more than five years in order to prepare a report including recommendations as to whether the federal government should regulate settlement charges or require lenders to pay part of settlement costs.

● Required continued compliance with state settlement laws that gave consumers more protection than the new federal act.

1975

A presidential veto frustrated congressional moves to create new subsidy programs to spur the stagnant construction industry. The housing industry had its worst production year in 1975 since World War II.

Congress early in the year developed a broad package of emergency aid for the industry, but it could not come up with the votes to override a veto by President Ford. Ford argued that the new subsidy programs would cost too much and prove ineffective.

After losing the veto fight, Congress settled for an extension of a mortgage aid program it approved in 1974. Earlier, it approved a tax credit for purchases of new housing in another attempt to stimulate construction.

Other important housing legislation cleared in 1975 was designed to prevent mortgage lenders from discriminating arbitrarily against older, inner-city neighborhoods. Congress, however, at the same time gave in to lender protests about a 1974 law attacking real estate settlement abuses and repealed its key provision.

In the area of urban affairs, Congress took the precedent-setting step of providing special federal aid for the nation's largest city. It approved federal loans to help New York avert a financial crisis threatening the city with bankruptcy.

Emergency Housing Aid

Congress settled for a compromise bill aimed at pulling the housing industry out of a severe slump after it lost a veto fight with President Ford over a broader aid measure.

The legislation (HR 5398—PL 94-50) allowed the Department of Housing and Urban Development (HUD) to buy up another $10-billion in mortgages carrying below-market interest rates. The purchases, originally authorized by a 1974 mortgage aid bill, freed private money for mortgage lending at lowered interest rates. By the time Ford left office, HUD had used up $5-billion of the new purchase authority. *(1974 bill, p. 15-A)*

Committee Name Change

The House gave greater visibility to the housing responsibilities of its Banking Committee in 1975. In the 94th Congress, the panel became the Banking, Currency and Housing Committee instead of the Banking and Currency Committee.

The House agreed to the change as part of a committee reorganization package approved in 1974.

A second major section of the bill allowed HUD to make loans of up to $250 a month for two years to jobless homeowners unable to meet mortgage payments. HUD never implemented the general loan program, but announced in June 1976 that it would help those holding federally insured mortgages.

Background

Congress initially passed a broader housing aid bill (HR 4485), vetoed by Ford on grounds that it would cost too much and prove ineffective. The first version of the bill would have created several new subsidy programs designed to stimulate housing sales. They would have offered middle-income homebuyers cash grants of $1,000 for housing down payments or temporary subsidies reducing mortgage interest rates to 6 per cent—about 3 per cent below market levels.

The first bill was one of several "emergency" economic measures enthusiastically promoted by the Democratic congressional leadership early in the year. The enthusiasm ebbed as it became clear that the heavy Democratic majorities in both houses did not make the 94th Congress "veto-proof."

The housing industry suffered a severe slump in 1974, due in large part to tight mortgage credit and high mortgage interest rates. Housing starts in 1974 fell to 1.3 million units down a third from 1973, and housing experts predicted no substantial improvement until at least mid-1975. Unemployment in the construction industry stood at 15 per cent in January 1975, almost twice the national rate.

While the mortgage credit crunch was easing by early 1975, the deepening recession and resulting cutbacks in consumer spending produced new problems for homeowners and for the housing industry.

A problem for many builders when consumers did without major purchases was the resulting inventory of unsold housing. The financial strain of paying off construction loans without the income from sold units had forced many builders into bankruptcy.

Rising unemployment also meant that many homeowners were having trouble meeting their monthly mortgage payments, the largest financial obligation of many unemployed individuals. Rep. Thomas L. Ashley (D Ohio) estimated that as many as 500,000 families could be facing loss of their homes by mid-1975 because of mortgage default.

Action on Vetoed Bill

House. The House passed two measures early in the year in an effort to spur home sales and help unemployed homeowners. In House-Senate conference, the measures were combined in the single bill that Ford later vetoed.

The first House bill (HR 4485), reported March 14 (H Rept 94-64) by the Banking, Currency and Housing Committee, offered middle-income homebuyers a choice of two new subsidy programs. One provided temporary subsidies lowering mortgage interest rates to 6 per cent while the other offered permanent subsidies cutting interest rates to 7 per cent.

The committee majority argued that it would take emergency federal aid to get the housing industry back on its feet. The Ford administration and most committee Republicans questioned the need for expensive new subsidy programs, contending that the industry was on the road to recovery. They also called it unfair to ask the taxpayers—many of whom could not afford to buy a home—to foot the bill for aid to middle-income families.

The House passed the bill March 21 after rejecting a Republican substitute sponsored by Garry Brown (R Mich.) by a 126-242 vote. The substitute, basically similar to the

measure eventually enacted, would have extended the 1974 mortgage aid legislation with additional funding.

The second House bill (HR 5398), reported (H Rept 94-124) by the Banking Committee April 7, provided for federal loans to jobless families about to lose their homes because of mortgage default. The House passed the bill with little dissent on April 14.

Supporters of the bill argued that it was important to act before the number of mortgage foreclosures reached serious levels. Republicans as well as Democrats found the bill fiscally responsible, primarily because those receiving loans eventually would have to repay the federal government.

HUD, however, questioned whether the actual foreclosure situation justified the new program. It also suggested that it would pose administrative problems.

Senate. The Senate Banking, Housing and Urban Affairs Committee also reported separate housing subsidy and homeowner loan bills, but the Senate combined them into a single measure (HR 4485) on the floor.

The committee's housing subsidy bill, reported (S Rept 94-86) April 18, was designed to deal with both current and future slumps in housing construction activity. A first part of the measure offered middle-income homebuyers the temporary 6 per cent interest subsidy or a $1,000 cash grant. The committee dropped the 7 per cent permanent interest subsidy approved by the House.

A second major section of the bill made the 1974 mortgage aid program permanent, an effort to "smooth out" the cyclical instability of the housing industry. The proposal, promoted by Committee Chairman William Proxmire (D Wis.), would have triggered the release of federal funds whenever housing starts fell below an annual rate of 1.6 million units.

The Senate passed HR 4485 April 24 amid Republican warnings of a presidential veto.

"The pending bill is...the number one put-our-people-back-to-work bill that the Congress will have an opportunity to act on," Proxmire insisted.

John G. Tower (Texas), ranking Republican on the Banking Committee, led the opposition to the measure, predicting that the new programs would not work and calling them unfair if they did.

"Pity the hardworking person who pays an 8-per-cent-plus interest rate," he said, "and the next week, when the trigger in this bill is released, his new neighbor can get a 6 per cent mortgage."

Republicans and Democrats also clashed over the addition of the loan program for jobless homeowners to the basic assistance bill. The Banking Committee reported (S Rept 94-78) this proposal April 17.

The Republicans generally supported the loan program, but objected to adding it to a bill that they expected the President to veto. The Senate version of HR 4485 also contained a number of other provisions revising the 1974 omnibus housing bill.

Conference, Final Action. House-Senate conferees generally accepted all the various subsidy programs in both versions, but threw out the Senate proposal to trigger federal mortgage aid whenever housing starts fell below certain levels. Following the Senate's lead, conferees also included the homeowners' loan program in the final version (H Rept 94-246).

The final version was sharply opposed by Democratic Rep. Ashley, considered the top housing expert in the

---

Homeownership Program

Bowing to congressional and legal pressure, HUD announced in October that it would release $264.1-million in funds available for a homeownership subsidy program (Section 235) for moderate-income families that had been suspended since early 1973. The General Accounting Office had gone to court to seek release of the unused funds under the anti-impoundment provisions of the 1974 budget reform act. *(1973 suspension, p. 6-A)*

The program, set to begin in revised form in January 1976, was expected to subsidize interest rates down to 5 per cent on about 250,000 homes. The maximum mortgage amount of housing eligible for subsidy was between $21,600 and $28,800 under existing law. Some housing experts complained that the program would not work in high-cost areas, but HUD Secretary Carla A. Hills predicted that it would stimulate the development of "no frills" housing.

The Ford administration made it clear, however, that it regarded the program as an economic shot in the arm for the housing industry rather than a permanent approach to the housing needs of lower-income families. Hills suggested in October that many poor families were not prepared to deal with the problems of homeownership, underscoring the administration's continued doubts about the appropriateness of federally subsidized homeownership programs for the poor.

The administration's decision to revive the program was widely connected to speculation that it was about to lose the impoundment case in court. Congress, however, also kept the pressure on the administration to reactivate the Section 235 program because of its dissatisfaction with the slow start of a new rental subsidy program (Section 8) it approved in 1974.

"To put it in a nutshell, the administration refuses to continue the tried and true housing programs and has been unable to properly start the new Section 8 housing assistance payments program," the Senate Appropriations Committee said July 24 in a typical criticism. "The result is less housing, more unemployment and an accentuation of the economic stagnation that has beset our country."

House. He called the conference bill "a turkey" that "will never see the light of day." He argued that the Senate-added provisions offering $1,000 cash grants and making other changes in housing laws gave the President ample reason for vetoing the bill.

Rep. Brown, a leading Republican House expert in the housing field, had no kinder words. He suggested that the housing subsidy part of the bill should be renamed "The Federal Handouts Act for 400,000 Lucky Homebuyers." But Congress cleared the bill June 11.

Veto, Override Attempt

Veto. President Ford vetoed HR 4485 on June 24. He maintained that the bill, "due to its cost, ineffectiveness and delayed stimulus, would damage the housing industry and damage the economy."

Specifically, the President contended that the new subsidy programs would cost too much, take HUD too long to implement and give some homebuyers "excessive" benefits at the expense of other taxpayers.

Instead, the President proposed legislation similar to a bill introduced by Ashley and Brown in a carefully orchestrated attempt to block a House override of the vetoed measure. *(Strategy, box, this page)*

The President's proposal would have authorized an additional $7.75-billion in federal mortgage purchases under the 1974 mortgage aid program; the Ashley-Brown bill was similar except it authorized $10-billion in new purchases. President Ford also offered to support a standby program of federal loans for jobless homeowners.

Override Attempt. Short 16 votes needed to reach the required two-thirds majority, the House June 25 sustained the veto by a key vote of 268-157 (R 19-122; D 249-35).

Smarting from failure to enact its party's anti-recessionary legislation over President Ford's vetoes, the Democratic leadership made an all-out effort to get every possible vote for an override. Housing and labor groups also lobbied heavily for an override.

But Ashley managed to win enough Democratic support for an alternative housing bill written to satisfy the White House. Thirty-five Democrats voted to sustain the veto.

During debate before the vote, partisan attacks all but overshadowed discussion of the merits of the bill.

"The President has designated Pennsylvania Avenue as a one-way street with veto barricades against the actions...of the overwhelming majority of the representatives of the United States," charged House Speaker Carl Albert (D Okla.).

Not so, countered Minority Leader John J. Rhodes (R Ariz.). "The President of the United States has done his very best to make Pennsylvania Avenue a two-way street."

Action on Second Bill

Chief sponsors of the vetoed bill sped the second compromise measure (HR 5398) through Congress after the House sustained the veto. While not satisfied with the approach taken in the Ashley-Brown bill, they felt it was important to get some legislation aiding the housing industry on the books as soon as possible.

Several hours after the House sustained the veto June 25, Proxmire proposed the new bill as a substitute for the House-passed legislation (HR 5398) providing federal mortgage loans for the jobless. The Senate had never acted on that numbered bill.

Democrats Thwart Override

Although House Democratic sponsors of the emergency housing bill knew all along that it would be an uphill fight to secure the votes needed to override the President's veto, a countermove by three Democrats opposed to the bill made their task more difficult. The two major groups lobbying for an override, the National Association of Home Builders and the AFL-CIO, also found that the dissidents' efforts hurt prospects of getting votes from southern Democrats.

Thomas L. Ashley (D Ohio), considered one of the leading housing experts in the House, orchestrated the countermove with Thomas M. Rees (D Calif.) and Robert G. Stephens Jr. (D Ga.). All three were members of the Banking, Currency and Housing Committee who voted against the conference version of the bill. Garry Brown (Mich.), ranking Republican on the Banking Committee's Housing Subcommittee, gathered Republican support, and both Ashley and Brown worked closely with the White House.

Essentially, their strategy was to line up support behind an alternative housing proposal that would be acceptable to the President. They needed time to develop the alternative and solidify support, and the President gave it to them.

After putting the alternative bill together in a day or two, Ashley said they concentrated initially on the 44 Democrats who voted against the conference version. Rees sought support from those from the western states, Stephens asked the southerners for their backing and Ashley contacted those from northern states.

Those working for an override were particularly concerned about Stephens because 26 of the 44 Democrats opposing the conference version were from the South. "Stephens was a big hurt," conceded an aide to William S. Moorhead (D Pa.), a key Banking Committee sponsor of the emergency bill.

Ashley promoted his countermove on grounds that it was more important to get a bill signed than to prove the Democrats could override a presidential veto after failing to do so three times earlier in 1975.

"When they [the Democrats] go home, they're going to find out people don't care a good goddam about intra-mural battles between the White House and Congress," Ashley argued. "...They care about getting from point A to point B and then from point B to point C."

Two days before the vote, the Ashley bill had more than 50 Democratic cosponsors. Those working for an override vote felt that the countermove disrupted efforts to pull the Democrats together to a uniform position. Majority Leader Thomas P. O'Neill Jr. (D Mass.) called Ashley the afternoon before the bill's introduction June 20, Ashley said, to ask him to hold up the bill until after the veto. "It goes in noon tomorrow," Ashley told O'Neill flatly in a reporter's presence.

On the eve of the vote, House Speaker Carl Albert (D Okla.) virtually conceded that the Democrats did not have the votes to override. The homebuilders at that point counted 254 firm votes for an override plus perhaps 10 more votes from undecided Democrats. It took 290 votes to override if every House member voted.

The Senate adopted the substitute by voice vote June 25 and passed the bill by a unanimous vote the following day. There was no formal committee action on the measure. The House agreed to the bill with two minor changes later June 26 and the Senate accepted the changes June 27, clearing the measure just before a July 4th congressional recess.

Provisions

As signed into law, HR 5398 (PL 94-50):

Mortgage Aid to Jobless

● Authorized HUD to make loans of up to $250 a month to help cover payment of mortgage loan principal, interest, taxes and mortgage or hazard insurance; limited eligibility for the loans to homeowners who had "incurred a substantial reduction in income as the result of involuntary unemployment or underemployment due to adverse economic conditions" and who were "financially unable to make the full mortgage payment."

● Authorized HUD to make loans to an individual homeowner for up to 12 months; allowed HUD to extend the loan period for an additional year if necessary; required those assisted to report any increase in income affecting their ability to meet mortgage payments.

● Barred HUD from approving loans unless 1) the lender had notified the homeowner of his intention to foreclose, 2) the lender had notified HUD in writing that foreclosure was probable (HUD could waive this requirement), 3) the homeowner had missed mortgage payments for at least three months, 4) the homeowner had a "reasonable prospect" of regaining the income needed to resume full payment of the mortgage and 5) the mortgaged property was the principal residence of the homeowner.

● Required homeowners to repay the amount of the loans under terms and conditions set by HUD at interest rates no higher than those on mortgages insured by the Federal Housing Administration; allowed HUD to defer any repayment until one year or longer after the date of the last loan payment; required HUD to obtain adequate security for repayment of loans, which could include liens (claims) on the mortgaged property.

● Authorized $500-million, without fiscal year limitation, for the program; barred HUD from making any new loan commitments after June 30, 1976. (The 1976 housing bill extended the program to 1977.)

● Under the same eligibility and repayment requirements, authorized HUD to insure mortgage lenders against losses if they provided similar loan assistance to jobless homeowners directly; stipulated that the HUD insurance would cover no more than 90 per cent of the loss on any individual loan.

● Allowed HUD to charge lenders premiums for the insurance of no more than 0.5 per cent of the outstanding principal of such loans.

● Limited the total value of insured loans to $1.5-billion; barred new commitments under the insurance program after June 30, 1976.

● Required HUD and federal agencies supervising financial institutions to take steps for one year after enactment to encourage lenders to forbear (hold off) in residential mortgage loan foreclosures; required the agencies to ask lenders to notify HUD, the supervisory agency and the homeowner at least 30 days before beginning foreclosure proceedings.

● Authorized the Federal Deposit Insurance Corporation to make loan advances to lenders participating in programs for jobless homeowners.

Mortgage Credit Assistance

● Extended a 1974 act (PL 93-449) authorizing HUD to buy up mortgage loans at below-market interest rates to July 1, 1976, from Oct. 18, 1975 (The 1976 housing bill extended the program to 1977.); gave HUD authority to purchase an additional $10-billion in mortgage loans under the 1974 program. (The 1974 act limited the total value of mortgage purchases to $7.75-billion.)

● Limited the maximum interest rate on mortgages eligible for purchase by HUD to 7.5 per cent.

● Made mortgages on multifamily residences and condominiums, as well as those on one- to four-family homes, eligible for purchase under the 1974 act.

Miscellaneous

● Extended an urban rehabilitation loan program (Section 312) through Aug. 22, 1976; authorized $100-million for the program in fiscal 1976.

● Extended to Jan. 1, 1976, from July 1, 1975, the effective date of provisions of a 1973 flood insurance act (PL 93-234) barring lenders from making mortgage loans on existing housing in areas that had not adopted HUD land use standards for flood-prone areas.

Housing Tax Credit

Trying one other gimmick designed to stimulate the housing industry, Congress included a tax credit for purchases of newly built homes in an emergency tax cut bill (HR 2166—PL 94-12) cleared March 26.

The tax bill provision, tacked on the measure in the Senate, allowed a homebuyer to take a tax credit (up to a $2,000 limit) equal to 5 per cent of the purchase price of a newly built home that was finished or under construction when the bill was cleared. The credit was available only through the end of 1975, and Senate moves in December to extend the provision were unsuccessful.

Studies later suggested that the credit had little effect on housing sales because most of those receiving the credit would have purchased new homes anyway. The tax credit generally was aimed at reducing the unsold inventory of new homes.

'Redlining' Disclosure

Congress Dec. 18 gave final approval to legislation (S 1281—PL 94-200) giving city residents new tools to discourage mortgage lenders from discriminating arbitrarily against their neighborhoods. The bill responded to charges that lenders were "redlining" certain city neighborhoods by refusing to make mortgage loans there regardless of the credit-worthiness of the potential borrower.

As cleared, the bill required mortgage lenders in metropolitan areas to disclose the amount of mortgage money they lent within each city tract area used by the Census Bureau for statistical purposes. If census tract disclosure were not feasible, then lenders could disclose their information by postal zip code areas, which generally were larger and less apt to conform to neighborhood boundaries.

The theory behind the bill was that many city residents would not deposit their savings in institutions found to curtail mortgage lending in their neighborhoods. Supporters of the legislation argued that redlining was one significant cause of urban decay.

Lenders denied that redlining existed. They and Republican opponents of the bill contended that the measure would increase paperwork and mortgage lending costs, place undue emphasis on lending activity as a cause of urban decline and create irresponsible pressure to make unsound loans. They also pointed out that the disclosed information would be misleading without a corresponding indication of mortgage loan demand from city neighborhoods.

Congress narrowly rejected attempts to water down the measure. Republican-backed amendments to turn the bill into a three-year demonstration study in selected cities failed by one vote in the Senate and two votes in the House.

The Ford administration questioned whether mortgage lending disclosure was necessary, but did not actively oppose the bill.

As cleared, the bill also contained unrelated provisions extending the authority of federal bank regulatory agencies to set ceilings on interest paid on savings accounts by banks and savings and loan associations.

Background

In a literal sense, "redlining" referred to drawing a red line on a city map around neighborhoods where lenders would not make mortgage loans.

While they did not contend that lenders actually used such maps, leaders of urban community groups argued that their statistical studies of mortgage lending by neighborhood showed discrimination against some parts of their cities. They attributed redlining to lenders' inability to judge the health of many older, inner-city neighborhoods — vibrant neighborhoods that might not have the surface sparkle of a new suburban subdivision. The community leaders stressed that redlining was not racial discrimination because it affected white ethnic neighborhoods as well as black ones.

Lenders contended that studies claiming redlining often were incomplete or misleading, especially if they did not measure mortgage loan demand by neighborhood. They also maintained that they were merely exercising good business judgment and protecting depositors' assets by refusing to make loans in a neighborhood on the decline.

Senate Action

The Senate passed the bill Sept. 4 after rejecting, 40-41, a substitute that would have required a three-year demonstration survey of mortgage lending practices in 27 cities instead of disclosure in all urban areas.

Jake Garn (R Utah), sponsor of the substitute, conceded that redlining was a problem in some cities, but saw no reason to impose disclosure requirements on all urban lenders until the approach had been studied. "There is no need to solve a problem with a 105-millimeter howitzer when a flyswatter will do," he said.

He also maintained that the measure was a first step toward telling lenders where to make credit available.

William Proxmire (D Wis.), chairman of the Banking, Housing and Urban Affairs Committee, contended (S Rept 94-187) that the substitute would gut the measure. He said that the disclosure approach would not force lenders to make loans in any neighborhoods if they considered them risky.

He also pointed out that his committee already narrowed the bill by limiting the disclosure requirement to urban areas. "I do hope that we will not go so far as to gut the bill by subtracting 93 per cent of it and leaving a pitiful little 7 per cent...to limp into the House...," Proxmire said.

House Action

The House passed a similar redlining bill on Oct. 31. The Banking, Currency and Housing Committee reported

The Death of a Neighborhood

Urban community groups contended that redlining by mortgage lenders was a major cause of neighborhood deterioration. But lenders maintained that the groups were confusing cause with effect and ignoring a host of other factors that contributed to neighborhood decay.

According to the Milwaukee Alliance of Concerned Citizens, however, the lenders play a key role as a neighborhood goes through six stages of deterioration:

Phase 1: The neighborhood is healthy and its housing in good condition. Conventional (non-government subsidized or insured) mortgage money and home improvement loans are available from many sources.

Phase 2: The "pace-setter" lenders in the city and neighborhood still make conventional loans in the neighborhood, but have a clear preference for mortgages made in the suburbs or other parts of the city.

Phase 3: Seeing some risk of neighborhood deterioration, some local savings institutions and the pace setters begin to set stricter terms for mortgages in the neighborhood such as higher down payments, higher interest rates or shorter-term loans. Eventually, these lenders will not make any mortgage or home improvement loans and the quality of housing begins to decline. The prophecy of deterioration is self-fulfilled. Conventional mortgage money still may be available from some lenders in the city, but many potential buyers are steered to more "desirable" areas.

Phase 4: All lenders regard conventional loans in the neighborhood as too risky. Only loans insured by the Federal Housing Administration (FHA) are available and property values begin to decline. Buyers with FHA loans cannot meet the repair or mortgage expenses for homes of poor quality that should not have been approved by the FHA. Mortgage default increases and the resulting turnover in home ownership offers lenders and realtors more profit because of the federal loan guarantees. More families are forced to move out of the neighborhood.

Phase 5: The neighborhood has deteriorated. Institutions holding FHA mortgages have no incentive to get owners to improve their property because of the federal guarantees. Property and fire insurance is not available. More buildings are abandoned and crime increases.

Phase 6: Urban renewal begins. The neighborhood is torn down and conventional money is again available to developers of large-scale projects. The cycle begins again.

(H Rept 94-561) it Oct. 10, arguing that disclosure would give everyone a chance to plan ways to save a neighborhood before it was too late.

The House rejected an amendment to kill the redlining provisions of the measure by a 152-191 vote. A second amendment to limit disclosure to lenders in 20 cities during a three-year study failed by a narrow 165-167 vote.

House-Senate conferees resolved (H Rept 94-553) minor differences between the two versions.

Provisions

As signed into law, the redlining provisions of S 1281 (PL 94-200):

● Required lending institutions within standard metropolitan statistical areas to disclose the number and total dollar amount of mortgage bans they made each fiscal year within tract areas used by the Census Bureau for statistical purposes; required disclosure by zip code area if the Federal Reserve Board determined that disclosure by census tract was not feasible.

● Applied the disclosure requirements to loans made beginning in fiscal 1976.

● Required lenders also to disclose the number and amount of mortgage loans they made that were federally insured or used to purchase property that the buyer did not intend to use as a residence; required lenders to disclose the number and amount of home improvement loans they made in each urban area.

● Required lenders to keep the disclosed information available for inspection and copying for at least five years at an institution's home office and at least one branch office (if it had branch offices).

● Required state-chartered institutions to comply with similar state disclosure laws instead of federal law if the state requirements were stricter than or not inconsistent with federal law.

● Required the Federal Home Loan Bank Board to develop ways to facilitate disclosure by census tract areas.

● Required the Federal Reserve Board to conduct a three-year study of whether the disclosure requirements should apply to lending institutions outside metropolitan areas.

● Exempted lending institutions with total assets of $10-million or less from the disclosure requirements.

● Set an effective date of June 30, 1976, for the requirements.

● Terminated authority to require disclosure four years after the effective date.

● Stipulated that the bill should not encourage unsound lending practices or the allocation of credit.

Settlement Practices

Under heavy pressure from the banking and real estate industries, Congress backed away from the idea that homebuyers had a right to find out what real estate settlement charges they must pay well before they complete the sales transaction.

In 1974 Congress approved a bill (PL 93-533) requiring lenders to tell homebuyers at least 12 days before closing a sale what the settlement charges would be. The theory behind the requirement was that it would give homebuyers time to shop for settlement services. Common settlement charges, such as title insurance premiums, real estate com-missions and lawyers' fees, could add thousands of dollars to the cost of buying a house. *(1974 bill, p. 17-A)*

The real estate settlement bill (S 2327—PL 94-205) cleared in 1975 repealed the 12-day advance disclosure requirement. The final version, however, required lenders to give homebuyers an estimated range of charges when they applied for a mortgage loan. Homebuyers also could find out one day before settlement the actual amount of the charges that had been set by then.

Other provisions of the bill killed requirements of the 1974 law designed to disclose excessive profits by real estate speculators and streamlined the paperwork involved in preparing a list of charges for use at settlement.

Lenders had led a persuasive lobbying campaign against the requirements of the 1974 bill. They argued that the law created unnecessary paperwork, increased lending costs and caused moving delays.

Opponents of the bill claimed that it would make it impossible for consumers to shop for the least expensive settlement services, the purpose of the original 12-day advance disclosure requirement. "This bill is an out-and-out real estate industry triumph over the homebuying public," complained Rep. Leonor K. Sullivan (D Mo.).

Debate Over Repeal

Bankers and mortgage lenders argued that the 12-day disclosure period was not serving its intended purpose. Instead, argued a savings and loan association representative, the required paperwork and disclosure period were adding $35 to the cost of making a mortgage loan and delaying settlement for almost 12 additional days.

Lenders also maintained that homebuyers were not using the disclosure period to shop for settlement services. "People just don't shop," argued Lee Holmes of the U.S. League of Savings Associations. "They don't shop for home mortgage money like they do for a car loan."

Consumer groups opposed repeal of the disclosure requirement. "A mere three months after the legislation's enactment, serious thought is being given to an abandonment of the most meaningful provision of the legislation," complained Kathleen F. O'Reilly of the Consumer Federation of America.

"The Consumer Federation of America is stunned and outraged at this development, particularly in light of the transparently self-serving arguments advanced by the settlement industry opposition," O'Reilly said.

Lenders would have preferred an outright repeal of the law or its most troublesome provisions. But it was generally recognized that William Proxmire (D Wis.), chairman of the Senate Banking, Housing and Urban Affairs Committee, would not go that far, so lenders were ready for a compromise.

Legislative Action

Legislation suspending the disclosure provision of the 1974 act for one year slipped through the Senate Oct. 9 after it was reported (S Rept 94-410) Oct. 6 by Proxmire's committee. The suspension bill was designed to give the committee longer to come up with a permanent compromise.

The House, however, favored repeal of the 12-day disclosure requirement. Its version, passed Nov. 17 (H Rept 94-667), simply stipulated that settlement charges should be disclosed "at or before" settlement. The measure also required lenders to give homebuyers a booklet when they applied for a loan describing likely settlement charges. Information in the booklet would help homebuyers shop for settlement services if they wanted to, sponsors of the bill maintained.

Sullivan was one of the few House members to oppose repeal of the disclosure requirement.

"It took five years of hard work and some bitter battles...to enact a law last year to protect homebuyers against predatory abuses, unconscionable overcharges and flagrant 'featherbedding' practices in the transfer of residential real estate," she complained. "It is now taking only five months of real estate industry lobbying pressure to convert that law into a hollow shell which would permit elements of the industry to resume doing many of the very things which made the original law necessary."

The Senate Dec. 8 refused to go along with complete repeal of the advance disclosure requirement. It wanted homebuyers to get at least one business day to look over charges before they had to be paid.

House-Senate conferees (H Rept 94-769) resolved the stalemate by giving homebuyers the right to find out actual charges that had been set by the day before settlement, but did not require lenders to make any special effort to gather charge information by that time. The compromise also did not require lenders to disclose any information in advance unless the homebuyer requested it.

Congress cleared the compromise Dec. 19.

Provisions

As signed into law, S 2327 (PL 94-205):
● Allowed regional variations in the items included on a standard form setting forth settlement charges.
● Required lenders to give homebuyers a booklet describing common settlement charges and good faith estimates of the range of charges likely to be paid when they applied in writing for a mortgage loan.
● Repealed provisions of a 1974 law (PL 93-533) requiring lenders to disclose exact settlement costs at least 12 days before actual settlement; instead, required the person conducting the settlement to make available for a homebuyer's inspection whatever exact charge information he had on hand one business day before settlement.
● Repealed provisions of the 1974 law barring lenders from making a loan commitment if the seller did not inform the buyer of the previous purchase price of a house bought within the last two years that was not used as a place of residence by the seller.
● Clarified that provisions of the 1974 law prohibiting kickbacks between those in the real estate industry did not apply to cooperative brokerage and referral arrangements of real estate agents.
● Modified provisions of the 1974 law barring lenders from collecting and holding in escrow more than one months' worth of advance property taxes and insurance premiums to allow two months' worth of escrow payments.

Mobile Homes, Flood Insurance

Congress Dec. 16 sent the President legislation (S 848—PL 94-173) making minor year-end changes in various housing and federal flood insurance laws.

The housing provisions increased limits on the size of federally insured loans for mobile homes and apartments. Supporters of the changes argued that inflation made the existing loan limits out of date.

A second part of the bill allowed the Department of Housing and Urban Development to continue to implement the national flood insurance program on an emergency basis through 1976. Under a 1973 flood insurance law, the emergency program was supposed to expire Dec. 31, 1975. But because HUD had not completed studies required before moving to the regular program, Congress agreed to extend the emergency insurance program. The 1976 housing bill extended the program again. *(1973 bill, p. 7-A; 1976 bill, p. 30-A)*

The Senate routinely approved the measure Sept. 10 (S Rept 94-341). The House cleared the bill Dec. 16 by accepting the Senate version without change and without formal committee consideration.

Provisions

As signed into law, S 848 (PL 94-173):
● Increased the limits on mobile home loans insured by the Federal Housing Administration (FHA) to $12,500 from $10,000 for regular homes and to $20,000 from $15,000 for double-width homes.
● Authorized HUD to increase basic mortgage limits for FHA-insured, multifamily housing projects by up to 75 per cent instead of 45 per cent in high-cost areas.
● Extended authority to implement a national flood insurance program on an emergency basis to Dec. 31, 1976.

Variable Rate Mortgages

Unhappy with some of the proposal's possible effects on consumers, Congress blocked a regulatory plan to alter the kind of mortgage loans available to homebuyers.

Congressional action prevented the Federal Home Loan Bank Board from implementing proposed regulations that would have allowed federally chartered savings and loan associations to make mortgage loans bearing interest rates that would rise and fall with the market over the term of the loan. Savings and loans made nearly half of all residential mortgage loans.

Although Congress did not complete action on the legislation, both houses passed measures signaling their intent to stop the proposal. The bank board then withdrew the proposed plan.

Background

The variable rate mortgage controversy began Feb. 14, when the bank board proposed regulations allowing lenders to offer future homebuyers mortgage loans carrying interest rates that would go up or down with the market. A homebuyer's monthly mortgage repayment could fluctuate under these "variable rate mortgages." By contrast, most mortgages in the United States carried fixed interest rates allowing uniform monthly repayments over the typical 30-year term of the loan.

The bank board had proposed regulations to allow variable rate mortgages before, but never put them into effect because of the opposition they aroused. Without the regulatory changes, federal savings and loan associations were barred from offering variable rate mortgages. State-chartered institutions could offer them if state law permitted.

The regulations issued Feb. 14 would have allowed federal institutions to offer variables subject to conditions the bank board hoped would protect the consumer. The interest rate could not increase by more than 2.5 per cent over the entire life of the loan or by more than 0.5 per cent in any six-month period. The rate need not decrease by more than 0.5 per cent in any six-month period either. Lenders would be required to pass on decreases, but increases would be discretionary. Lenders also would have to give homebuyers 45 days' advance notice of any proposed increase.

Supporters of the variable rate concept argued that it would help assure a steady supply of mortgage money. They essentially maintained that the variable rate mortgage brought a lender's return on mortgage loans more in line with interest rates that must be paid out on savings deposits.

Opponents contended that variable rate mortgages would confuse consumers and offer them no cost advantages because the long-term trend in interest rates was up, not down. Allowing interest to vary, they said, only guaranteed homebuyers higher costs.

Legislative Action

The House passed a bill (HR 6209) May 8 that simply blocked implementation of the proposed regulations. The Banking, Currency and Housing Committee reported (H Rept 94-183) the bill April 30.

"The variable rate mortgage is analogous to the fuel adjustment charges so many of us are familiar with," argued Rep. Fernand J. St Germain (D R.I.). "The costs keep going up and we cannot anticipate when, if ever, the price will come down. The same has been more than true with interest rates."

Before passing the bill, the House rejected a substitute that would have allowed federal institutions to offer variable rate mortgages during a two-year experimental period in states where state-chartered lenders could make such loans.

The Senate June 16 passed a resolution (S Con Res 45) expressing its belief that the Federal Home Loan Bank Board should not allow the regulations to take effect without congressional approval. The Senate Banking, Housing and Urban Affairs Committee reported (S Rept 94-170) the measure June 3.

The bank board had withdrawn the proposed regulations before Senate action, but the Senate wanted the congressional position on the issue clearly stated.

Condominium Regulation

Senate and House committees held hearings in 1975 and 1976 on proposals to regulate condominiums, but the 94th Congress never acted on comdominium legislation.

The Senate and House Banking Committees investigated condominiums in response to reports that some buyers confronted shoddy construction, problems gaining control of their condominium projects and unexpectedly high maintenance and other costs.

A 1975 HUD study documented tremendous growth in condominium housing in the past five years, highlighting the fact that condominiums met the needs of many families who could not afford traditional single-family homes. In a condominium project, the buyer owned his own unit and shared an interest in additional facilities, such as swimming pools, that no one buyer could afford on his own.

As of April 1, the study found, there were 1.25 million condominium units in the United States, 15 times as many

as there were in 1970. In 1973 and 1974, condominiums also accounted for 25 per cent of all for-sale housing starts. In all, the study reported, 4 million persons lived in condominiums in 1975.

The study also pointed out that most condominium development had occurred in the South and West. Almost half of all units were located in Florida, California and New York.

Although HUD reported that 95 per cent of the condominium owners it surveyed said they were satisfied or very satisfied with their units, the study also underlined many of the problems associated with condominiums. They inclued:

● Poor quality of construction.

● Loss of buyer deposits on their units when a developer went bankrupt before construction was completed.

● Underestimated maintenance costs paid by owners in addition to mortgage debts, a practice known as "lowballing."

● Additional "rental" payments to developers who retained long-term (sometimes 99-year) leases on key recreational facilities. These leases, which were used almost exclusively in Florida, allowed developers to recover their investment in facilities quickly. The payments often increased automatically with changes in the cost of living.

● Lengthy periods of time before a developer transferred control of a project to a homeowners' association.

● Limited homeowner control because a developer had entered into long-term contracts for services or project management.

● Tenant displacement when existing buildings were converted to condominiums, and resulting strains on other available middle- or low-income housing.

Some members of the House and Senate proposed to deal with the problems through new legislation. HUD Secretary Carla A. Hills, however, recommended development of national regulatory standards. Others wanted all regulation left to the states. The 94th Congress decided not to pursue the matter further.

Aid to New York City

While many of its members opposed the move, Congress agreed late in the year to lend financially ailing New York City the cash it needed to avoid going bankrupt.

Legislation (HR 10481—PL 94-143) cleared Dec. 6 allowed the Treasury Secretary to make federal loans of up to $2.3-billion a year through mid-1978 to help the city meet its seasonal cash needs. The city was required to repay the loans and interest of about 8 per cent by June 30 of each year. A fiscal 1976 supplemental appropriations bill (HR 10647—PL 94-157) cleared Dec. 15 funded the loan program.

Enactment of the legislation ended, at least temporarily, a harrowing string of money crises for the nation's largest city. New York had faced financial default for many months, but used a variety of rescue measures to stave it off. By December, however, the city had run out of ways to pay its bills except by getting some form of aid from the federal government.

Background

The New York aid issue provoked one of the most heated battles of the legislative year. Supporters argued that the federal government could not let the nation's largest city and financial capital collapse. Opponents objected vehemently to the precedent of "bailing out" a city that had mismanaged its financial affairs for years.

Prospects for federal aid were remote when city officials first petitioned Ford for his help in May. Throughout the summer, Congress showed no interest in the issue and Ford administration officials remained adamantly opposed to federal aid.

Although the President remained opposed, key members of Congress began to push for federal help in September and October as events started to wear down traditional congressional hostility toward New York. The city tottered dramatically on the edge of default on Oct. 17, but managed once again to scrape up the cash to continue operating through November.

The Senate and House banking committees accelerated their work on aid legislation after the near-default and eventually both committees developed legislation that would have allowed the federal government to guarantee bonds issued to help the city meet its expenses. In the meantime, however, Ford had vowed Oct. 29 to veto any bill designed to "bail out" New York before a default.

Sponsors of the committee bills held up floor action on the guarantee legislation in the hope that Ford would reconsider his position. They admitted that they did not have the votes to override a veto of the legislation they had written. There was some question as to whether they even had sufficient votes to pass the legislation.

After the state had taken several new steps to raise the city's taxes and reduce its immediate spending needs, Ford agreed to support federal loans to help New York meet its seasonal cash needs on Nov. 26. Ford argued that New York had bailed itself out by approving those steps and insisted that his hard-line stance on the aid issue had prodded the city into approving them.

Faced with an impending default deadline, supporters of aid to New York then threw out the guarantee proposals the banking committees had spent several weeks preparing and rushed the President's plan through Congress in five days. They recognized that Ford's proposal was the only one that stood a chance of becoming law before a default.

Despite the President's position, many members of Congress, particularly from southern and farm states, remained opposed to aid to New York. They argued that their constituents would not stand for any use of their tax dollars to help a city that had been living beyond its means for more than a decade.

But the fact that a number of Republicans supported the legislation indicated that political sentiment on the issue had shifted dramatically in seven months. During this period, New York City's financial problems were widely publicized, with some economic experts predicting that a New York default would have a serious impact on the national economy and financial markets. The inevitable pressure for some kind of federal action pushed the issue to the top of the congressional agenda.

Factors in Plight. New York's financial problems had complex roots. In some ways, the city's predicament symbolized the difficulties of many large, older central cities, particularly in the northeastern and north central states.

First of all, those most dependent on specialized city services—the poor, the elderly, minorities and the uneducated—comprised a growing proportion of the city's population as more prosperous city residents moved to the suburbs. Between 1950 and 1970, the percentage of the city's families with income below the nation's median level rose to 49 per cent from 36 per cent.

The city's spending requirements outstripped growth in its tax base. Businesses left the city to relocate in the suburbs or other parts of the country. The number of jobs available in the city declined. The stagnant condition of the tax base led to increases in city tax levels. The tax increases had the circular effect of steering new businesses or families away from the city, again hurting potential tax receipts.

New York's remaining residents—many of them poor—needed special social services. The city also was required by state law to bear a welfare burden not shared by other large cities. New York's welfare-related expenses came to about $1-billion in 1975—far more than any other big city.

New York also had a tradition of providing services not offered by other cities, including a free city university, a network of municipal hospitals and an extensive mass transportation system.

Analysts also blamed questionable accounting procedures and gimmicky fiscal management for camouflaging the city's financial troubles for many years.

New York: One Year Later

In 1976, one year after Congress voted to give the city federal loan aid, New York's financial future—while still uncertain—looked a lot brighter than it did during the panicky days of 1975.

The city impressed some of its former critics with its belt-tightening resolve. By the end of 1976, the city had cut its staff of city workers by more than 15 per cent, sharply curtailed services ranging fron police protection to garbage collection and begun to overhaul its accounting system. It resisted pressure to lift a freeze on municipal wages when it renegotiated contracts with city workers on July 1.

The federal loan program worked fairly smoothly. The city repaid all federal loan aid received in fiscal 1976 on time by July 1.

Nevertheless, there were two major problems on the city's financial horizon at the end of 1976. In November the state's highest court ruled that a moratorium imposed in 1975 on repayment of some of the city's short-term debt was unconstitutional. The city needed to come up with a plan to repay nearly $1-billion in notes. The court said, however, that the repayment plan should not seriously disrupt the city's financial balance.

New York also needed to find another $500-million in savings by July 1, 1977, to meet a requirement to bring its budget into balance by that time.

New York officials tended to think that the city would need some new form of federal aid to cope with all its problems. They were heartened by the election of Jimmy Carter as President, counting on Carter to make good on a promise to help the city. Aides suggested that Carter was thinking less about providing direct aid for New York and more about making broader program changes—such as expanding jobs programs or cutting local welfare costs—that would aid New York and other cities.

Many of the city's problems were unique. But San Francisco Mayor Joseph Alioto (D) warned in July that "the seeds of New York are in every American city."

Short-term factors brought the financial troubles to a peak in 1975. The city lost investor confidence and, by March 1975, was unable to borrow any money it needed in the municipal bond market. The recession dampened sales tax and income tax receipts while boosting required spending for welfare and other services. But the key reason that the financial crisis developed in 1975, instead of some other time, was that the city no longer could borrow cash from any source.

City and State Action. During the summer, hostility to New Yorkers "living high off the hog" was the dominant attitude of both Congress and the Ford administration toward requests for federal aid for New York. Administration officials and most members of Congress tended to dismiss New York's plight as the price it had to pay for years of living beyond its means.

City and state officials continued their trips to Washington with hats in hand. But they took a number of steps during the summer to keep New York from defaulting on its financial obligations.

In June the state created a Municipal Assistance Corp., dubbed "Big Mac," to sell long-term bonds backed by the state in order to pay off the city's short-term debt. The city, among other steps, froze municipal wages, increased transit fares, deferred capital spending and laid off workers.

Big Mac sold enough bonds to keep the city afloat for awhile, but in September its bond market also dried up as investors became increasingly leery about the city's financial condition. On Sept. 9 the state approved a new rescue plan providing financing for New York City through November and putting a state-controlled board of overseers virtually in charge of the city's fiscal management.

Committees Begin Work. The city won some important converts in Congress in September, but committees did not really begin to move on legislation providing federal aid until the city nearly went under.

The city remained on the brink of default Oct. 17 until, two hours before the deadline, the city's teachers' union finally agreed to make the investments providing the cash the city needed to pay off debts falling due that day and to meet payrolls.

Until Albert Shanker, head of the United Federation of Teachers, agreed to use $150-million from the teachers' pension fund to buy New York bonds, default was virtually certain. During this period, President Ford sent city officials word that the federal government would not come to New York's assistance, reaffirming his previous stance when it came to an actual showdown.

The actions taken Oct. 17 helped keep the city afloat until early December.

Hoping to provide federal aid before that deadline, the House and Senate Banking Committees prepared legislation that would have allowed the federal government to guarantee repayment of New York City bonds.

The Senate Banking, Housing and Urban Affairs Committee reported a bill (S 2615—S Rept 94-443) Nov. 4 providing $11.5-billion in bond guarantees through mid-1979 if the city balanced its budget by fiscal 1978 and met other conditions. The House Banking, Currency and Housing Committee reported legislation (HR 10481-H Rept 94-632) on Nov. 6 that also provided several kinds of federal bond guarantees if the city and state met certain conditions.

New York's supporters on both committees argued that a default by the city would be intolerable. They said it would make it hard for other cities and states to market their bonds, disrupt banking activity and hurt international money markets. They also contended that it would cost less—and be more humane—to prevent a default than to pick up the cost of maintaining services after the city went bankrupt. Clearly, the supporters added, the federal government was not going to allow New York residents to go without essential services.

Committee opponents of aid argued that the proposed legislation would lead to massive federal involvement in the city's financial affairs and expose the federal government to major financial risks. They also insisted that the evidence did not support the bald assertion that a New York default would dry up the entire municipal bond market.

Ford Veto Promise. The committees readied the federal guarantee legislation despite a promise by President Ford to veto a New York aid bill.

"I can tell you—and tell you now—that I am prepared to veto any bill that has as its purpose a federal bail-out of New York City to prevent a default," Ford announced Oct. 29.

The President argued that the bond guarantee proposals would just postpone the day New York had to learn to live within its own resources. Ford also objected to the "terrible precedent" the proposals would set for other cities seeking special federal aid.

The President's position made default seem inevitable for a time because key Democrats in both houses conceded that it would be next to impossible to override a veto. An early head count in the House raised questions about whether the city's supporters could find the votes to pass a bill at all. Sponsors of the House Banking Committee measure held up floor action twice in the hope that Ford would change his mind.

Ford Reversal. On Nov. 26, Ford did. He asked Congress to approve legislation offering the city federal loans on a seasonal basis.

Because New York State had taken stringent steps Nov. 25 to meet the city's financial needs, Ford argued, federal aid no longer amounted to a New York "bail-out." Asked why he did not arrive at this position earlier, Ford contended that it was his original hard-line stance that had convinced the state legislature Nov. 25 to raise New York taxes and reduce future spending in an effort to get a handle on the city's money problems.

Mindful of the potential political fall-out among conservative Republicans opposed to New York aid, Ford also stressed that his loan proposal would pose no financial risk for the government. Federal loans would have to be repaid before other debts, he noted.

House Action

Congress moved quickly to approve the President's plan. The work of the two Banking Committees went out the window.

The House passed HR 10481 by a key vote of 213-203 (R 38-100; D 175-103) on Dec. 2 after substituting the President's proposal for the Banking Committee bill.

The close vote reflected the continuing resistance to aid for New York City despite the President's change of heart. Opposition remained strong among Republicans and House members from southern and rural states. Aid opponents interviewed by Congressional Quarterly said they could not justify use of their constituents' tax dollars to "bail out" a city that had seriously bungled its financial affairs.

Republican supporters of the plan contended that the plan was no "bail-out."

"It is a stretch-out plan aimed at giving the city and New York State time to make necessary adjustments in spending and revenue-raising and to balance its budget," argued House Minority Leader John J. Rhodes (R Ariz.). The city was required to balance its budget by 1978 under state law.

Senate Action

The Senate cleared the bill in the early morning hours of Dec. 6 by accepting the House version without change. Final passage came at the end of a marathon session during which opponents waged a last-ditch battle against the bill.

The Senate began debate on the legislation Dec. 3. Opponents James B. Allen (D Ala.), Jesse A. Helms (R N.C.) and Harry F. Byrd Jr. (Ind Va.) promptly launched a filibuster against the measure. They objected to rewarding New York for financial misconduct. They also predicted that New York would be back asking for more money in no time.

On Dec. 5 the Senate invoked cloture by a 70-27 vote and shut off the filibuster. But Allen used a variety of parliamentary tactics to delay the final vote for another 13 hours. He sought roll call votes on procedural matters and repeatedly asked for quorum calls. The delay raised some senatorial tempers.

Finally, Allen agreed to let the Democratic leadership schedule a vote after midnight, and the Senate passed the measure, 57-30. After losing the fight over the authorization measure, Allen decided not to filibuster the bill containing the actual appropriations for the loan program when it reached the Senate floor later in December.

Provisions

As signed into law, HR 10481 (PL 94-103):

● Authorized the Treasury Secretary to make loans to New York City or a financial agent authorized by the state to administer the city's financial affairs; limited the total value of loans outstanding at any one time to $2.3-billion.

● Required the city or its financial agent to repay the loans made in any fiscal year by the last day of the city's fiscal year (June 30) at an interest rate 1 per cent higher than the prevailing Treasury borrowing rate.

● Barred the Secretary from making loans unless he determined that there was a reasonable prospect of repayment; authorized the Secretary to set terms and conditions for the loan that he deemed appropriate to assure repayment.

● Authorized the Secretary, to the extent allowed in appropriation acts, to withhold other federal funds due the city to offset the amount of any unrepaid loans.

● Barred the Secretary from making loans unless all prior loans had been repaid on time.

● Authorized the General Accounting Office to audit the state's and city's financial records.

● Ended authority to make loans to the city on June 30, 1978.

Municipal Bankruptcy

Just in case federal aid did not prevent a New York default, the House and Senate passed legislation (HR 10624—PL 94-260) late in 1975, making it easier for cities such as New York to use municipal bankruptcy proceedings to adjust repayment of their debts.

President Ford had asked Congress to provide this standby protection. The bill would "spread a safety net under New York City's financial high-wire act," noted House Minority Leader John J. Rhodes (R Ariz.). Final action came early in 1976. *(p. 33-A)*

Both versions allowed any city to file for bankruptcy without the approval of its creditors and permitted the city to continue the borrowing needed to maintain essential services. While a city developed a debt adjustment plan under court supervision, creditors could not sue to collect payment.

Both versions also eased provisions of existing law that required creditors holding two-thirds of a city's debts to approve an adjusted payment plan. Only creditors holding two-thirds of the debt who actually voted on the plan would have to approve; the Senate version also required approval by a numerical majority of creditors.

The Senate bill contained two other major provisions not included in the House version. The first, proposed by the Ford administration, required a bankrupt city to satisfy the court that it would balance its budget within a reasonable period of time. The second struck down state laws that barred investment in the securities of a municipality that had been in default.

Background

Congress added municipal bankruptcy provisions to federal bankruptcy laws in 1934 to help a number of small cities and towns with financial problems during the Depression. The Supreme Court decided in 1936 that these provisions interfered unconstitutionally with state powers, so Congress rewrote the municipal section of the bankruptcy act in 1937. This section had not been updated since 1946.

The requirements of the 1946 bankruptcy law made it next to impossible for cities such as New York to file. Under chapter IX of the Federal Bankruptcy Act, a city in default could halt legal actions and claims of creditors by filing a "debt readjustment" plan showing how it would pay off its obligations over an extended period. But the filing of the plan must have the prior assent of a majority of all creditors, including bondholders (in New York's case, thousands). And to be implemented, the terms of the plan must be approved by two-thirds of all creditors.

In practice, New York could not file under the bankruptcy law, since it would be impossible to even identify, much less obtain approval from, a majority of all creditors.

Legislative Action

The House passed its version of the bill on Dec. 9.

The only real dispute over the bill, fought in the Judiciary Committee (H Rept 94-686) and on the House floor, centered on whether the changes in municipal bankruptcy laws should apply to all communities or just to very large cities.

Republicans favored limiting the changes to very large cities. By making it easier for any city to go into bankruptcy, they maintained, the bill would make it more expensive for cities of any size to borrow money because investors would have more reason to fear losses.

Committee Democrats rejected the idea that cities would be eager to go into bankruptcy once the law was revised. They also said that establishing two types of municipal bankruptcy proceedings would be unfair and chaotic. "I suggest that one chapter [of the law] for municipal bankruptcy is enough," commented Don Edwards (D Calif.), floor manager of the bill.

The Senate, passing its version (S Rept 94-458) of the bill Dec. 10, also sidestepped an attempt to limit the provisions of the bill to very large cities.

1976

Congressional Democrats heaped election-year criticism on the Republican administration's housing record, but they decided to wait until 1977 to consider new ways to meet the nation's housing needs.

In line with that strategy, Congress passed a "mini" housing bill that merely extended housing and related programs into 1977. The legislation, however, did mandate a limited return to the traditional public housing program—discarded by the administration in early 1973—and also expanded a housing program for the elderly.

Housing Extension

Unhappy with the Ford administration's heavy reliance on a new rental subsidy program created in 1974, Congress revived the traditional public housing program. The program, suspended by the Nixon administration in 1973, was the oldest of all federal housing subsidy programs. *(New rental program, p. 9-A; history of public housing, p. 31-A)*

Congress stated its policy objectives in an "off-year" housing authorization bill (S 3295—PL 94-375) extending many housing and related programs for one year, through fiscal 1977. It followed up by providing $85-million in contract authority to support newly built public housing in the fiscal 1977 appropriations measure (HR 14233—PL 94-378) for the Department of Housing and Urban Development (HUD).

Background

The administration objected to the public housing revival, calling it an expensive and discredited way to provide shelter for the poor. Republicans warned repeatedly that the authorization bill might be vetoed. But congressional Democrats argued that the new rental subsidy program (Section 8) had done little to relieve the need for new housing during its first two years of operation.

Despite his opposition to the public housing revival, President Ford agreed to sign the authorization bill in exchange for a reduction in proposed public housing funding provided in the appropriations measure.

Other important features of the authorization bill provided a major increase in funding for a housing program for the elderly (Section 202) and directed HUD to pay more attention to local desires for newly constructed housing under the Section 8 program. HUD's critics contended that the department was placing too much emphasis on Section 8 subsidies for existing housing, a cheaper subsidy approach.

The authorization bill also provided help for owners of defect-ridden housing backed by federally insured mortgages and eased a ban on mortgage-lending in some flood-prone areas. Various other programs, including a mortgage aid program started in 1974, were extended through fiscal 1977.

While reviving the old public housing program, the authorization bill generally made no major changes in the operation of federally subsidized housing or community development programs, reworked substantially in 1974. The bill continued to channel most new housing money to the Section 8 program created by the 1974 omnibus housing bill. The Section 8 program had the administration's firm support.

Senate Action

The Senate Banking, Housing and Urban Affairs Committee reported (S Rept 94-749) the bill April 12.

The committee had several complaints about HUD's handling of its subsidized housing efforts. It took the department to task for slow implementation of the Section 8 program, its refusal to revive other subsidy programs to take up the resulting slack in housing production and its emphasis on existing housing under the Section 8 program.

"Even in the coming year, with new housing starts estimated at 1.4 million to 1.6 million new housing started—one million below our needs and goals—the administration persists with a puny, half-starved, midget, assisted housing construction program," complained Committee Chairman William Proxmire (D Wis.).

The committee expressed its displeasure by earmarking $465-million of the $850-million in new contract authority for housing programs provided in the bill for new construction. It instructed HUD to use $200-million for construction under the conventional public housing program, chopping funding available for subsidies on existing housing under Section 8 to $171-million.

HUD Secretary Carla A. Hills warned April 24 that she would recommend a presidential veto of the Senate committee bill. She argued that the Section 8 program could deliver housing more quickly than public housing. Hills also contended that HUD could subsidize two units of existing housing under Section 8 for each unit of newly constructed public housing.

The Senate passed the bill April 27 after refusing to rework the measure to avoid a veto. A motion to return the bill to committee for administration-backed alterations failed, 23-57.

Supporters of the measure argued that until Section 8 proved itself, HUD needed to take other steps to meet the housing needs of the poor. They conceded that the public housing program had some flaws, but pointed out that it had produced more than 1 million units of housing while Section 8 had produced only a few thousand.

"If we did not have conventional public housing, I hate to think where the low-income people would be living in this country," said Edward W. Brooke (R Mass.). "They might literally be living in the streets."

The Senate made no major changes in the committee bill, but added provisions of another housing measure (HR 9852) to it. The Senate passed HR 9852 on Jan. 23, but the House had shown no interest in going to conference on the bill.

Key provisions of HR 9852 relaxed a ban on mortgage lending in flood-prone areas that had not adopted HUD land-use standards.

Public Housing: A Controversial Past

The 1976 housing extension bill (PL 94-375) revived the government-owned public housing program, the oldest federal approach to housing the nation's poor. The program had a controversial past.

The Beginning

Public housing programs got a modest start during the Great Depression of the 1930s. The New Deal administration viewed the programs as an effective way to create jobs, clean up slums and provide better housing for the poor. Congress formally endorsed a public housing program in the 1937 housing act.

After World War II, President Truman called for a larger federal role in the housing field as the country faced a shortage of decent housing for veterans as well as the poor. The proposed expansion of public housing programs met with vigorous opposition from the homebuilders, real estate industry, lenders and other private business groups. Opponents called the public housing scheme socialistic.

After four years of debate, Congress approved a major expansion of public housing programs in the landmark 1949 housing act that set the national goal of a decent home for every American family. The 1949 act authorized subsidies for 810,000 units of public housing over a six-year period.

The goal of the 1949 act was not realized. Public housing opponents continued their attack in the early 1950s and succeeded in limiting appropriations for the program.

The largest annual appropriation in 1951-56 provided funding for 50,000 units of public housing, compared with the annual goal of 135,000 units under the 1949 act.

The battle against public housing also was fought at the local level. "Do you want to pay somebody else's rent?" was the slogan used by a number of public housing opponents.

Problems Arise

The traditional opposition to public housing faded by the late 1950s, but some of its supporters became disturbed by defects that were appearing in the public housing approach. "No doubt any program on the scale of public housing would have its problems...," wrote Leonard Freedman in *Public Housing: The Politics of Poverty* in 1969. "Still the deficiencies of public housing went far beyond any normal degree of malfunctioning."

Experts saw many of the problems as built-in defects. Public housing projects sheltered the chronically poor. The most ambitious and stable families left the projects when they could, leaving behind those firmly caught in the cycle of poverty. As a result, some public housing projects became institutionalized slums. Crime and juvenile delinquency became commonplace.

Site restrictions were another problem. Faced with local resistance to building projects in the suburbs, local public housing authorities were forced to locate them in older, dilapidated areas.

And cost restrictions contributed to the depressing character of many projects. Wanting to use land to the fullest, public housing authorities constructed high-rise buildings that were spartan and unadorned. The projects were clearly separate from the rest of the community.

Other approaches were tried during the 1960s in an effort to improve public housing. Changes included "scatter-site" location of public housing throughout a city, a move to construction of low-rise buildings and use of building design blending with a neighborhood.

The federal government also developed alternatives to the conventional public housing program, which paid for public construction of new buildings. The 1965 housing act allowed local public housing authorities to lease units in privately owned existing buildings and to make them available to families eligible for public housing.

In 1967 HUD developed another approach, called the "Turnkey" method. Under the Turnkey program, private developers built housing and then sold it to local housing authorities. Rehabilitation and modernization of public housing projects also became an alternative to new construction.

Suspension

Deciding that it still worked poorly, the Nixon administration suspended the conventional public housing program in early 1973. While a 1973 HUD review noted that public housing programs had improved the quality of housing available to the poor. President Nixon officially condemned this approach to the problem in a 1973 housing message.

"I have seen a number of our public housing projects. Some of them are impressive, but too many are monstrous, depressing places—run down, overcrowded, crime-ridden, falling apart," Nixon said. "The residents of these projects are often strangers to one another—with little sense of belonging."

As others did, Nixon cited the Pruitt-Igoe project in St. Louis as an example of public housing's failure. Considered one of the best public housing projects in the country when it was built in the mid-1950s, Pruitt-Igoe had deteriorated so much by 1973 that a decision to demolish it met with little opposition.

The administration's objections focused not only on the quality of public housing. It also argued that the program was inequitable and left the poor no choice in the type or location of their homes. HUD also called reliance on new construction costly and wasteful of existing housing stock.

Another concern was cost. When the program was suspended, there were 1.2 million units of public housing. Under the original public housing program, the federal government subsidized the capital costs of building a project under contracts with local housing authorities running for up to 40 years. HUD's budget estimated that these continuing obligations would cost $1.2-billion in fiscal 1977.

Under later amendments to the program, the federal government also was required to pay operating subsidies to public housing projects. The cost of operating subsidies increased after Congress moved in 1969 to limit rent paid by public housing tenants to 25 per cent of their income. Operating subsidies, amounting to $31-million in fiscal 1970, were to reach an estimated $576-million in fiscal 1977.

House Action

The House Banking, Currency and Housing Committee also voted to tighten congressional control over the operation of federal housing subsidy programs. Its housing bill, reported (H Rept 94-1091) May 6, reserved nearly $400-million in new contract authority for new construction and $140-million for new public housing construction or acquisition of existing projects by public housing authorities. HUD preferred the latter approach to new construction of public housing units.

Committee Republicans strongly opposed these funding "set-asides." Once the bill reached the floor, Housing Subcommittee Chairman Thomas L. Ashley (D Ohio) tacitly agreed to cooperate with them. Before passing the measure May 26, the House dumped the set-aside provisions.

Essentially, the move to rid the House bill of earmarked funding was a tactical one. House committee sponsors wanted to be in the best bargaining position, once the legislation went to conference, to tone down the set-aside provisions in the Senate bill in order to avoid a veto.

Conference Action

Over Republican objections, conferees (H Rept 94-1304) voted to devote $140-million of total contract authority of $850-million for conventional public housing. They wanted $100-million of it spent on construction of new public housing.

This amount was not acceptable to HUD officials, who had suggested informally that the department could live with $75-million for new public housing. But HUD and Congress resolved the stalemate by agreeing to lower actual appropriations for new public housing to $85-million.

Conferees also compromised on the issue of how much money HUD should spend on new construction. Rather than earmark specific amounts for new construction, they decided to instruct HUD to follow local requests for Section 8 subsidies on newly built vs. existing housing.

Provisions

As signed into law, S 3295 (PL 94-375):

● Authorized new contract authority of $850-million in fiscal 1977 for subsidized housing programs.

● Within the total authority, set aside at least $60-million for modernization of existing public housing; reserved at least $140-million for new public housing programs, of which at least $100-million was earmarked for new construction or substantial rehabilitation.

● Set aside another $17-million for the construction of public housing for Indians.

● Stipulated that, to the maximum extent practicable, HUD should allocate funding under the Section 8 rental subsidy program for newly built versus existing housing in accordance with housing assistance plans submitted by local communities under the community development block grant program.

● Made single persons who were not elderly or handicapped eligible for public housing under certain conditions.

● Authorized HUD to continue to pay off mortgage loans on Section 8 housing for up to one year even if the housing contained vacant units.

● Stipulated that the value of assistance received under subsidized housing programs should not count toward income for the purpose of determining eligibility for or benefit levels under the Supplemental Security Income program for the elderly poor.

● Extended a homeownership subsidy program (Section 235) through fiscal 1977; extended eligibility for the program to families with income up to 95 per cent of the median income for a particular area.

● Increased the maximum limits on the amounts of mortgage loans for housing eligible for Section 235 subsidies to between $25,000 and $33,000, depending on family size and geographical cost factors, from existing limits of between $21,600 and $28,800.

● Authorized HUD to extend assistance under the Section 235 program for the purchase of double-width mobile homes; limited mobile home assistance to 20 per cent of all units assisted under the Section 235 program after Jan. 1, 1976.

● Extended another rental subsidy program (Section 236), suspended by the executive branch since 1973, through fiscal 1977.

● Extended HUD's experimental authority to insure mortgages at variable interest rates through fiscal 1977.

● Increased the general limits on mortgages for multifamily housing insured by the federal government by 50 per cent for efficiencies and 20 per cent for all other types of units; reduced the percentage by which limits in high-cost areas could exceed the general limits to 50 per cent from 75 per cent.

● Authorized HUD to pay for the correction of defects creating a serious danger to the life and safety of owners of federally insured housing in declining urban areas purchased after Jan. 1, 1973, but before enactment; gave these owners up to one year after enactment to apply for assistance; limited reimbursement to defects that existed when the federal government insured the home and that should have been disclosed by inspection.

● Required HUD to report to Congress by March 1, 1977, with recommendations for an effective program to protect buyers of federally insured housing against serious hidden defects in their homes.

● Authorized up to $500-million to cover losses by the general federal housing insurance fund.

● Increased the Treasury borrowing limit for a housing program for the elderly and handicapped (Section 202) from $800-million to $1.48-billion immediately, $2.39-billion in fiscal 1978 and $3.3-billion in fiscal 1979; required approval under appropriations acts for borrowing above $800-million; revised the interest rate on funds borrowed by developers of housing for the elderly and handicapped, in a way lowering the effective rate to about 7.5 per cent.

● Authorized $100-million in fiscal 1977 for an urban rehabilitation loan program (Section 312).

● Extended an unemployed homeowners mortgage loan program and an emergency federal mortgage purchase program through fiscal 1977; limited the sales price of housing assisted under the mortgage purchase program to $48,000 in general, $52,000 in high-cost areas and $65,000 in Alaska, Hawaii and Guam.

● Exempted from a ban on mortgage lending in flood-prone areas that had not adopted HUD land use standards loans 1) used to purchase a residential dwelling occupied before March 1, 1976, 2) of up to $5,000 to improve existing residences, 3) to finance purchase of a building occupied by a small business before Jan. 1, 1976, and 4) to finance improvements for agricultural purposes on a farm.

● Extended authority to implement the national flood insurance program on an emergency basis through fiscal 1977.

● Authorized $100-million in fiscal 1977 for studies of potentially flood-prone areas.

● Allocated $200-million in fiscal 1977 under the community development block grant program for grants to governments within metropolitan areas not entitled to assistance by formula; stipulated that no more than 50 per cent of this funding could go to governments entitled to "hold-harmless" assistance, but not to formula grants.

● If HUD ran out of money to provide formula and hold-harmless community development block grants to communities within metropolitan areas, required HUD to make proportionate reductions in grants to all of these communities.

● Authorized $100-million in fiscal 1977 for a state and local comprehensive planning program (Section 701).

● Extended a planning program for new communities through fiscal 1977.

● Authorized $5-million in each of fiscal 1977-78 for an urban homesteading program.

● Authorized $65-million in fiscal 1977 for HUD research.

● Authorized $5-million in each of fiscal 1977-78 for the National Institutes of Building Sciences.

● Providing for a gradual phase-out of Farmers Home Administration housing assistance in rural areas that were becoming more urban.

● Required HUD to study the need for counseling purchasers of federally insured, unsubsidized housing in at least three cities.

Municipal Bankruptcy

While something of a footnote to the federal aid program voted for financially ailing New York City in 1975, legislation (HR 10624—PL 94-260) cleared by Congress March 25 made the first changes in municipal bankruptcy laws in 30 years.

Key provisions of the bill eased outdated requirements that made it virtually impossible for a financially strapped city to use bankruptcy proceedings to set priorities and a timetable for repayment of its debts. President Ford had asked Congress to act on similar legislation in 1975 in case New York City needed to use bankruptcy proceedings. The House and Senate passed different versions of the bill in 1975. *(Background, 1975 action, p. 29-A)*

Conference Action

House-Senate conferees resolved the few differences between the two versions (H Rept 94-938).

Both versions repealed laws requiring a city to have the approval of a majority of its creditors before it could file for bankruptcy—a key impediment to use of the existing municipal bankruptcy laws. Both bills also allowed the city to continue borrowing while it drew up a debt adjustment plan.

Conferees' key decision governed creditor approval of the debt adjustment plan. They followed Senate provisions requiring approval by a numerical majority of creditors as well as those holding two-thirds of the amount of creditor claims.

Other Senate provisions requiring a bankrupt city to balance its budget eventually and striking down state laws

barring investment in bonds issued by a city that had been in bankruptcy were dropped.

Provisions

As signed into law, HR 10624 (PL 94-260):

● Authorized any political subdivision or public agency of a state to file a petition for adjustment of its debts with a bankruptcy court if it was insolvent or unable to meet its debts and if it was generally authorized to file by the state.

● Repealed provisions of existing law that required a municipality to obtain the approval of a majority of its creditors before filing a petition, but required a municipality to satisfy one of three other conditions if it did not win majority approval: 1) to try in good faith, but fail to win such approval, 2) to find negotiation with creditors impractical or 3) to find that certain creditors were likely to try to collect payment at the expense of others in anticipation of bankruptcy action.

● Provided for an automatic stay (delay) of all proceedings to collect payments from a municipality once it had filed a petition.

● Required a municipality to file a list of known creditors with the court and to notify creditors of the proceeding.

● Authorized the court to permit the municipality to continue borrowing through the issuance of certificates of indebtedness; barred the court from interfering with the political or governmental powers of the municipality.

● Required the court to designate classes of creditors with substantially similar claims.

● Required a municipality to file a plan for adjustment of its debts at a time set by the court; barred the plan from taking effect unless it was approved by creditors in each class holding at least two-thirds of the amount of claims held by all creditors in that class who actually voted on the plan; also required approval by a numerical majority of the creditors voting in each class; eliminated the approval requirements for classes of creditors whose claims would be paid in full under the plan.

● Required the court to confirm an approved plan if it was fair, equitable and feasible and did not discriminate unfairly against any creditor.

Related New York Bill

Congress March 4 gave final approval to legislation (HR 11700—PL 94-236) allowing five New York City employees' pension plans to purchase $2.5-billion in city bonds through mid-1978 without losing tax advantages. The pension plans agreed to buy the bonds in November 1975 to help the city avoid bankruptcy.

The Senate cleared the bill March 4 by giving its approval to the House version, passed March 1 (H Rept 94-851). The Senate acted without formal committee action.

Under existing law, the pension plans stood to lose tax advantages because the city bond purchase agreement violated a requirement that pension plans be run exclusively with their beneficiaries' interests in mind.

Veterans' Housing

Congress June 16 cleared legislation (S 2529—PL 94-324) increasing the size of loans available to veterans under federal housing programs. The key provision of the bill increased the loan ceiling under the Veterans Administration's direct home loan program to $33,000 from

$21,000. Sponsors argued that the increase was needed to keep pace with inflation, but the VA opposed the measure on budgetary grounds.

Other provisions of the measure made permanent another VA home loan program. Under that program, the VA guaranteed repayment of mortgage loans made by private lenders instead of lending the money directly.

The Senate passed the bill May 13 (S Rept 94-806) and the White House followed suit May 18 (H Rept 94-1129). A compromise final version was developed without a formal House-Senate conference.

Taxable Municipal Bonds

The House Ways and Means Committee April 7 endorsed the idea of giving state and local governments the option of issuing taxable bonds, but the bill (HR 12774) went no farther in the 94th Congress.

Under existing law, investors paid no federal taxes on interest paid on bonds issued by state and local governments—making such bonds attractive investments. City governments were willing to trade some of that attractiveness to induce the federal government to subsidize municipal bond interest rates, a move reducing their borrowing costs. HR 12774 would have provided a 35 per cent interest subsidy.

The House committee divided closely on the measure, reporting it by a 20-16 vote (H Rept 94-1016). Supporters argued that making state and local bonds taxable would eliminate "windfall" tax advantages they offered the wealthy. Opponents called the proposal "a stab in the dark" attempt to bolster financially shaky city governments. They also suggested that the proposed change would disrupt U.S. capital markets. Competition from the high-yielding municipal bonds, they said, "would have dire effects on the capacity of the American business community to raise necessary funds...."

Congress previously had considered such legislation as part of the 1969 tax bill. ∎

Housing and Urban Affairs: 1977

President Carter's first major policy initiative in 1977 having an impact on housing and urban affairs was a two-year, $31.6 billion package of tax cuts and job creation programs aimed at stimulating a sagging economy.

Cities benefited from the economic stimulus program, which included money for public service jobs, public works projects and countercyclical aid targeted to hardship cities. Nevertheless, the urban employment picture remained bleak, especially for minority teen-agers.

Under pressure from black leaders, Carter in late summer stepped up plans for development of a national urban policy. The program, focusing on the creation of jobs through incentives to business, was announced in March 1978. *(Carter's urban policy, p. 11)*

In major 1977 legislative action, Carter proposed and Congress enacted a $12.5 billion urban aid bill directed primarily at assisting cities of the Northeast and industrial Midwest. The bill also included a one-year extension of major government housing programs.

In other legislative action Congress cleared a supplemental housing act authorization, and the Senate passed a bill to create a Neighborhood Reinvestment Corporation.

Housing, Community Development

Congress completed action Oct. 4 on a $12.5-billion urban aid authorization that channeled new funds to the aging cities of the Northeast and industrial Midwest.

The bill, the Housing and Community Development Act of 1977 (HR 6655—PL 95-128) extended the community development block grant program—the nation's chief neighborhood revitalization effort—for three years, through fiscal 1980, and authorized $12,450,000,000 to fund it. That figure included $400-million to be spent annually on a new program of urban development action grants proposed by the Carter administration to help out those cities with the most severe problems. *(Urban Development Action Grants, p. 69)*

As requested by the administration, the bill also provided a one-year extension, through fiscal 1978, of major federal housing programs. Included was a $1,159,995,000 authorization for fiscal 1978 designed to finance about 317,-000 new, rehabilitated and existing units under the Section 8 rent subsidy program and 56,000 units of conventional public housing.

The bill also increased insurable mortgage limits and decreased downpayment requirements for Federal Housing Administration (FHA) programs, a move designed to encourage and aid lower-income persons in homeownership.

Although passed by the House May 11 and by the Senate June 7, the bill was tied up in conference committee for nearly three months because of a dispute over the formula to be used to distribute the community development block grant funds.

As cleared by Congress, the bill provided for allocation of funds under either a new formula that took into account age of housing, poverty and population growth lag—factors that would work to the advantage of older cities in the Northeast and Midwest—or the existing formula, which tended to favor cities of the western and southern regions that had growing populations. The community would receive the higher amount.

In signing the bill Oct. 12, President Carter said it would provide "a giant step forward" in improving urban living conditions. But he criticized a provision easing restrictions on loans to property owners in flood-prone areas, which he said would weaken the federal flood insurance program.

BACKGROUND

Created by the Housing and Community Development Act of 1974 (PL 93-383), the block grant program lumped 10 old categorical urban development programs into a single grant distributed to cities and counties according to a needs formula based on population, overcrowded housing and the extent of poverty. The money had to be spent on programs that would give maximum benefit to low- or moderate-income families or aid in the prevention or elimination of slums or urban blight.

The funds could be used for such projects as land acquisition, housing code enforcement, historic preservation, slum clearance and renewal, and construction or improvement of facilities for neighborhoods, senior citizens, parking, street lighting, solid waste disposal and recreation. The law required that in their applications communities seeking the funds identify community development needs and their program for meeting them, outline a housing assistance program, show conformance with civil rights acts and assure that citizens would participate in putting together the application.

Congress authorized $8.6-billion for the program over three years. Eligible communities were cities or twin cities with populations above 50,000 and urban counties with populations, excluding cities, of at least 200,000 which were authorized by state law to carry out housing and community development programs. Eighty per cent of the funds were to go to standard metropolitan statistical areas (SMSAs) and 20 per cent to rural, non-SMSA areas.

In addition, in fiscal 1975-77 localities were guaranteed to receive at least the average annual ("hold harmless") amount they had received in fiscal 1968-72 under the old categorical grant programs. In fiscal 1975 they were entitled to one-third of the formula amount or the hold harmless amount. In fiscal 1976 they could receive two-thirds of the formula grant or the hold harmless amount, and in fiscal 1977 they were entitled to either the full formula or hold harmless amount. But the law specified that in fiscal 1978-80, the hold harmless amount would be phased down by thirds to the formula level.

Formula Revision

The existing formula—based on population, amount of housing overcrowding and poverty, weighted twice—tended to favor cities of the western and southern regions of the country, studies had shown. Critics of it noted that those cities often were not so needy as their aging counterparts in the Northeast and Midwest which were losing population.

If the formula were not changed funds would, in effect, flow from the older cities, as their hold harmless entitlements were phased down, to newer communities. Among the cities that would lose money under the existing formula if there were no hold harmless provision were Boston, Charlotte, Detroit, Cincinnati, Cleveland, Philadelphia, Milwaukee, Atlanta, Minneapolis, St. Louis, Kansas City and Newark. Among those that would gain were Dallas, Memphis and Houston.

In some cases, the differences would be staggering. In fiscal 1977, Washington, D.C., was entitled to a hold harmless amount of $40.9-million. Under the formula it would receive only $15.8-million. The funding to Philadelphia would go from $60.8-million under hold harmless to $30.1-million if only the formula were used, according to figures supplied by HUD. On the other hand, Dallas' fiscal 1976 payment was $13.3-million under the formula, but would have been only $2.6-million under hold harmless. In Memphis, the formula amount was $13.3-million compared to $6-million under hold harmless.

ADMINISTRATION PROPOSALS

Secretary of Housing and Urban Development Patricia Roberts Harris proposed a dual formula approach to improve the equity of the block grant program. "It targets greater funds to those needy cities we especially want to reach while not taking away from a city's current formula allocation," she said.

A city would receive the larger of amounts computed under the existing formula or under a new formula proposed by Harris.

The new formula would use age of housing weighted 50 per cent, poverty weighted 30 per cent and growth lag weighted 20 per cent. Age of housing referred to the number of existing units built in 1939 or earlier. Harris defined growth lag as the extent to which a city's population growth rate between 1960 and 1973 fell short of the average population growth rate of all metropolitan cities during the same period.

Urban Development Action Grants

Harris proposed earmarking $400-million of the block grant funds over each of the next three fiscal years (1978-80) for urban community development action grants. As proposed, the program would enable cities to react quickly to take advantage of specific investment opportunities and market conditions as they arose, she said. A special thrust of the program would be to stimulate new and increased private investment. *(Urban Development Action Grants, p. 69)*

The grants would make it possible, Harris said, for severely distressed cities to alleviate physical and economic deterioration through:

• Specific economic development activities in areas of population outmigration and stagnating or declining tax base.

• Reclamation projects in neighborhoods that exhibit excessive housing abandonment or deterioration.

Harris said the grants would be restricted to cities that had successfully provided housing for low- and moderate-income persons. Other eligibility measurements would be the condition of the applicant's housing stock, tax base, median income levels, jobs lost and unemployment exceeding the national average.

Rental Subsidies, Public Housing

With the goal of providing 400,000 units of housing for low-income persons in fiscal 1978, Harris proposed additional annual contract authority of just over $1.2-billion. Her proposal contemplated 344,000 new, rehabilitated and existing units under the Section 8 rental subsidy program, including 20,000 units to be provided under the auspices of state housing finance agencies. The remainder of the 400,-000 units would be conventional public housing.

The Harris proposal also called for $35-million for public housing modernization aimed primarily at assisting local housing authorities in capital improvements projects to save energy and correct local health and safety code violations.

The Secretary also asked for $665-million for public housing operating subsidies. About $13-million of that would go for exceptionally high utility costs incurred during the current winter.

Harris asked for an additional $378-million in contract authority for Section 8 for fiscal 1977 so that 400,000 units of assisted housing also would be available that year. *(Fiscal 1977 housing authorization, p. 44-A)*

The Section 8 program, created in its existing form by the Housing and Community Development Act of 1974 (PL 93-383), provided for government subsidies of the rent of low-income persons. Eligibility was limited to families with income of up to 80 per cent of the median family income of a particular area. The law also required that at least 30 per cent of the families have income not exceeding 50 per cent of an area's median family income.

The HUD Secretary was authorized to enter into up to 40-year contracts with public housing agencies or 20-year contracts with private developers who agreed to provide newly constructed, rehabilitated or adequate existing rental housing for participants in the program. The Secretary could make rental assistance payments for up to 100 per cent of the units in any one project, but was allowed to give preference to applicants limiting assisted units to 20 per cent per project if the project were not designed for the elderly or had more than 50 units.

Participating families were required to contribute not less than 15 per cent nor more than 25 per cent of their total income to rent, which was not to exceed by more than 10 per cent the fair market rent as established by HUD. The government made up the difference between the family's required rental share and the actual rental price.

The 40-year-old government-owned public housing program, suspended by the Nixon administration in 1973 but revived by Congress in 1976, was designed to create decent housing for the poor. Under the latest revisions, adopted in the 1974 housing act, tenants were required to pay a minimum rent equal to 5 per cent of their gross income or the amount of their welfare assistance payment earmarked for rent. Required increases in rent were limited to $5 every six months.

Twenty per cent of all new public housing units was earmarked for families with income below 50 per cent of the median income in an area. Public housing agencies were required to establish 1) tenant selection criteria to assure an income mix in the projects, 2) procedures for prompt rent payments and evictions for nonpayment, 3) effective tenant-management relationships to assure tenant safety and adequate project maintenance and 4) viable homeownership opportunities.

Homeownership Aid

Harris sought to increase the maximum limits on amounts of mortgage loans eligible for subsidies under the Section 235 homeownership program for low-income families. She proposed raising the limits from $25,000 to $31,000 and from $29,000 to $36,000 in high cost areas. The maximum provided for families of five or more persons would go from $29,000 to $36,000 and from $33,000 to $42,000 in high cost areas. The existing limits were adopted in 1976. *(1976 Almanac p. 343)*

The Section 235 program authorized HUD to subsidize the interest on home mortgages down to 5 per cent from the market rate, which normally is substantially higher. In 1976, eligibility was extended to families with income up to 95 per cent of the median income for a particular area. Previously, the income limit was 80 per cent of median area income.

Designed to enable low-income families to own a home, the program originally subsidized mortgages down to 1 per cent. However, in some areas it failed miserably, with HUD winding up as the owner of abandoned, dilapidated properties.

Mortgage Insurance

Harris sought to raise from $45,000 to $60,000 the maximum insurable mortgage amounts on several programs covering single-family units and to lower the downpayment requirements for mortgage amounts in excess of $25,000. The programs affected would be Section 203 (basic home mortgage insurance), Section 222 (mortgage insurance for servicemen) and Section 234 (mortgage insurance for condominiums).

Existing mortgage limits under the affected Federal Housing Administration (FHA) programs were unrealistic, Harris said. She noted that while the FHA maximum mortgage amount had increased 50 per cent (to $45,000) since 1966, the median price of a new home had increased about 68 per cent (to $47,000) between 1966 and 1976.

The proposed change in the downpayment requirements "is considered necessary to afford many middle-income families the opportunity to purchase their own homes," she said.

Comprehensive Planning

The Secretary proposed a revision of the Section 701 planning grant program which would authorize $62.5-million for it, provide increased funding for metropolitan and non-metropolitan area-wide planning organizations, continue direct funding for states and provide assistance to small communities through programs administered by the states. She said large cities and urban counties would not receive funding under the program because the community development block grants would meet the need.

The 1974 Housing and Community Development Act required grant recipients to use the money for land use and housing planning activities.

HOUSE ACTION

Committee

The House Banking, Finance and Urban Affairs Committee reported HR 6655 (H Rept 95-236) May 2. The bill emerged generally as the administration wanted it.

The committee endorsed the dual formula concept proposed by the administration, noting that the new formula would account for the physical aspects of community development need, which it said the existing formula failed to do.

The "age of housing" factor, which studies had shown was "by far the best indicator of physical blight and development need," also correlated highly with problems of neighborhood or community maintenance, with high tax effort and with a weakened local tax base, the report said.

That factor, coupled with "growth lag" in the new formula, "insures that those metropolitan cities with the most severe physical, social and fiscal problems receive adequate assistance," the committee said.

The committee noted HUD's failure in recent years to translate housing proposed under Section 8 to actual occupied units, and expressed concern about the increasing costs of Section 8 construction.

The committee said it anticipated 57 per cent of Section 8 units would be new construction or substantial rehabilitation and 43 per cent existing housing.

Floor

The House passed the bill by a 369-20 vote May 11 after three days of debate and the adoption of numerous floor amendments.

Controversy centered on an amendment to remove from the bill the second of two formulas that communities could use to establish the size of their allotment under the block grant program. Proponents argued that the second formula favored the older cities of the East and Midwest at the expense of the so-called Sun Belt area of the West and South.

Dual Formula. The regional dispute developed over an amendment by Mark W. Hannaford and Jerry M. Patterson, both California Democrats, which sought to strike the new block grant formula from the bill. It was defeated 149-261, with the vote breaking down largely along sectional lines. *(Regional split, box, p. 38-A)*

Hannaford charged that the new formula created "great distortions" and that the taxpayers of the South and West were, in effect, being taxed to support the revitalization of cities such as Newark and Detroit.

According to figures supplied by HUD, 240 of the 537 existing entitlement communities would gain through the use of the dual formula. Of those, 103 were in the Northeast, 86 in the North Central states, 31 in the South and 20 in the West. *(Effect on cities, box, p. 40-A)*

Small Cities. Another major floor fight developed over an amendment by Charles E. Grassley, R-Iowa, to earmark 25 per cent of the funds available for urban development action grants for cities under 50,000 population which were not

---

Regional Split

The vote on the Hannaford amendment to scrap the new community development block grant formula broke down on regional, not philosophical, lines.

The East and Midwest overwhelmingly opposed it.

In the East—the New England states, New York, New Jersey, Delaware, Maryland, West Virginia and Pennsylvania—the vote was 1-110 against the amendment.

In the Midwest—Illinois, Indiana, Michigan, Ohio, Wisconsin, Iowa, Kansas, Minnesota, Missouri and Nebraska—the vote was 7-105.

But in the southern and western states with newer, growing cities, there was a different outlook.

The combined vote of delegations in Florida, Georgia, Alabama, Arkansas, Louisiana, Mississippi, Oklahoma, Texas, New Mexico, Arizona, California, Virginia, North Carolina, South Carolina, Tennessee and Kentucky was 132-28 in favor of the amendment.

---

central cities in a standard metropolitan statistical area (SMSA).

Proponents argued that smaller cities were not equipped to compete against larger cities because they did not have the same technical expertise available to them.

The amendment was adopted 279-129.

Flood Insurance Program. A seventh title was added to the bill by an amendment by Gene Taylor, R-Mo., as amended by Richard H. Ichord, D-Mo. Their amendment removed the prohibition on federally insured private lending institutions from making loans to property owners in HUD-designated flood-prone areas which were not participants in the federal flood insurance program. The amendment required the institution to notify the recipient that he would not be eligible for federal disaster relief and that the federal government could not bail out individuals who undertook development in flood-prone areas without adequate flood-proofing measures.

Ichord called the flood insurance program "one of the worst examples of coercive and inequitable federal land use controls ever devised" because of the stringent regulations imposed on those who did not enroll.

Ashley opposed the amendment, arguing that a voluntary program without lending prohibitions would not accomplish the purpose of the flood insurance program—to reduce federal disaster relief costs.

The amendment was adopted 220-169.

SENATE ACTION

Committee

The Senate Banking, Housing and Urban Affairs Committee reported its version of the bill May 16 (S 1523—S Rept 95-175). The Senate version targeted substantially more aid to aging cities than the House-passed bill.

To pay for the increased grants to older cities, the Senate committee bill would take funds from the proposed $400-million Carter administration plan for urban development action grants which would provide one-time payments to cities to cure severe urban ills.

The Senate bill also included a provision to require financial institutions to meet the credit needs of the areas in which they were chartered.

Block Grants. The Senate committee bill included the two formulas which were part of the House bill—the one in existing law and the one proposed by Secretary Harris — plus a third formula proposed by Sen. Harrison A. Williams Jr., D-N.J.

The Williams formula, cosponsored in committee by ranking Republican Edward W. Brooke (Mass.), used the same factors in the same proportions as the Harris formula. But in addition to counting the amount of pre-1940 housing, it measured the proportion of pre-1940 housing in the community compared to the proportion of old housing stock in all metropolitan areas.

The national average was about 38 per cent pre-1940 housing, according to an aide to Williams. A city would not benefit from the "impaction" adjustment in the Williams formula unless it had a higher than average concentration of older housing. Among the cities that would benefit were some of those considered among the most needy by HUD, such as Newark, Boston, St. Louis and Cleveland.

However, cities considered the least needy by HUD would not lose funds under the Senate committee bill. Communities like Houston, Oklahoma City, Nashville, Albuquerque, Omaha, San Diego and Phoenix would get the same grants using any of the three formulas in fiscal 1980.

The committee endorsed the second formula proposed by Harris, saying that age of housing is the "best single indicator" of physical development need and is strongly related to a weakening tax base, a high rate of tax effort and other factors that reflect urban distress. That factor coupled with growth lag "generally ensures that metropolitan cities with the most severe physical, social and fiscal problems will receive funding that is more in accordance with their needs" than would be provided through the existing law formula, the report said.

But the committee added that the Harris formula "did not sufficiently take into account the adverse effects of heavy concentrations of older residential structures." The impaction adjustment in the Williams formula would "target scarce community development funds more directly to cities and urban counties where urban decay and neighborhood deterioration are most advanced," the report said.

To pay for the Williams formula the committee bill provided that funds would be taken from the action grant program and would be phased in over three years. In fiscal 1978, phased in at 50 per cent, the Senate bill formula would take about $125-million from the action grant program. At a 75 per cent phase-in in fiscal 1979, it would take $200-million and at 100 per cent in 1980 it would take $275-million of the $400-million authorized for action grants, Williams' aide said.

The committee bill provided that the basic dual formula would be funded first if the amount appropriated did not cover all programs authorized. Supplemental payments would then be made according to the adjusted age of housing formula. The action grant program would be funded only if additional appropriated funds remained.

Application Requirements. In addition to the existing law requirements for applications for block grant funds, the committee bill specified that communities include a housing preservation plan. The plan would have to identify deteriorated housing stock or stock in danger of deterioration and would have to include a proposal for preserving or rehabilitating it.

The bill required that housing rehabilitation subsidies benefit primarily persons of low and moderate income and that guidelines be included to ensure that a "reasonable proportion of rehabilitated units" be set aside for tenants displaced from the immediate neighborhood through rehabilitation efforts.

The House bill did not include a housing preservation plan requirement for applications but said communities had to include a program to improve conditions for low- and moderate-income persons living or expected to live in the community and to foster neighborhood development to induce higher-income persons to stay in or return to the area.

Housing Rehabilitation. Like the House bill, the Senate bill authorized an appropriation of $60-million for fiscal 1978 for Section 312 rehabilitation loans. However, the Senate bill increased residential loan limits to $27,000. Existing law set the limit at $12,000, which could be increased to $17,400 at the discretion of the HUD Secretary in high cost areas.

Housing Programs. Generally, the House and Senate committee bills reauthorized the same housing and mortgage insurance programs and made similar broad changes in them with a lot of minor differences.

The Senate measure authorized $1,239,620,000 in new contract authority, about $7.5-million more than the House bill, to pay for about 400,000 additional units under the Section 8 rent subsidy and conventional public housing programs. The Senate total was higher because the amount earmarked for public housing modernization, $42.5-million, was $7.5-million higher than the amount in the House bill.

The committee bill set aside at least $120-million of Section 8 funds, enough to assist 30,000 units, for aiding residents of low-income housing projects permanently financed by loans under the Section 202 housing for the elderly and handicapped program.

The Senate bill also authorized $708.1-million for public housing operating subsidies, $43.1-million more than was included in the House bill.

Community Reinvestment: Redlining. The Senate committee bill included a section, not in the House bill, designed to encourage federally regulated financial institutions to meet local credit needs. It was aimed at combating "redlining," a practice by some lending institutions of designating areas, usually in inner cities, as bad risks and refusing to make loans there. *(Previous legislation, p. 22-A)*

Floor

The Senate passed HR 6655 by a 79-7 vote June 7 after two days of debate.

Prior to passage, the Senate substituted the text of its own version of the bill (S 1523) for that of the House-passed measure.

Regional Dispute. Unlike the House, the Senate did not get into a major dispute over the formulas to be used to distribute community development block grant funds to big cities. However, questions about the regional aspects of the distribution system, which tended to favor the older cities of the East and industrial Midwest, were raised. *(Comparison of urban aid levels, p. 40-A)*

The regional impact of the new distribution system under S 1523 as reported figured in debate on an amendment, offered by Jim Sasser, D-Tenn., that would have changed the method for distributing block grant funds to cities with populations under 50,000. The House and Senate bills both gave small cities a choice of two formulas similar to those available to big cities. One formula, carried over from existing law, allotted funds based on population, housing

overcrowding and poverty, counted twice. The alternate formula included age of housing counted 2½ times, poverty counted 1½ times and population counted once. The second formula used population instead of growth lag, as in the big cities' formula, because growth lag statistics were not available for small cities.

Sasser's amendment, which failed 43-45, would have eliminated the alternate formula for small cities and would have created a task force to study small city problems.

Thomas J. McIntyre, D-N.H., sponsor of the dual formula for small cities in the Senate Banking, Housing and Urban Affairs Committee, acknowledged that using age of housing as a factor in determining the size of grants would shift the flow of funds.

"I make no bones about the fact that we are attempting to change this formula from the Sun Belt areas of new populations and new cities and turn around to where it should be going now, back to areas that were the first parts of this country," McIntyre said.

The regional rift showed itself again in debate on an amendment by John G. Tower, R-Texas, to permit the Department of Housing and Urban Development (HUD) to make action grants to distressed areas of any city. The bill specified that the grants, designed to attract private investment to cure specific urban ills, had to go to "severely distressed cities and urban counties."

The amendment was rejected, 36-53.

"This bill strongly discriminates against those cities and counties that will not be termed 'distressed,' but in fact have areas within their borders that are just as needy as any other community," Tower said.

However, Edward W. Brooke, R-Mass., argued that the special needs of distressed areas in prosperous cities would be taken care of with regular block grant funds.

Redlining. The Senate defeated by a 31-40 vote an amendment by Robert Morgan, D-N.C., that would have cut the section of the bill designed to combat redlining.

Morgan said the provision would lead eventually to credit allocation—forcing a financial institution to make unsound loans in a specific location in order to meet its quota of loans for a given locality.

William Proxmire, D-Wis., who sponsored the anti-redlining provision, said the section was included "to reaffirm that banks and thrift institutions are indeed chartered to serve the convenience and needs of their communities...and needs does not just mean drive-in teller windows and Christmas Club accounts. It means loans."

Budget Control. Edmund S. Muskie, D-Maine, chairman of the Budget Committee, was successful in deleting from the bill a provision that would have changed the method used to calculate budget authority for housing assistance programs. Muskie's amendment to remove the section was adopted 70-18.

Under the existing system, new budget authority — legal authority to enter into obligations which result in immediate or future outlays—was calculated by multiplying the total amount of new contract authority by the maximum term of the contract authorized.

The $1.16-billion in new contract authority contained in the bill for assisted housing programs, for example, represented a commitment of nearly $34-billion over future years. Without the Muskie amendment, the only portion of that figure that would have shown up as budget authority in the fiscal 1978 budget would be about $54-million, the amount that actually would be spent in fiscal 1978 on those

Urban Aid Levels Compared

The table below shows how much selected cities would receive in fiscal 1980 in community development block grants under existing law and the House- and Senate-passed versions of the Housing and Community Development Act of 1977 (HR 6655). The cities shown are those with populations over 250,000 considered to be the 15 most needy and the 15 least needy by the Department of Housing and Urban Development.

The block grant program, established in 1974, was the nation's major urban aid effort and was aimed primarily at neighborhood revitalization. The House and Senate bills took into account physical deterioration, aged housing stock and population losses in determining grants, a boon for older cities in the East and industrial Midwest. However, the Senate version emphasized the per cent of pre-1940 housing in a city and would give more funds than the House bill to cities with above average concentrations of old buildings. The final version followed the House approach.

Fiscal 1980

Most Needy	Existing Law	House Bill	Senate Bill
		(In thousands of dollars)	
Newark	$11,646	$16,249	$17,866
St. Louis	17,321	37,524	41,512
New Orleans	20,062	23,080	23,080
Baltimore	21,618	32,497	33,626
New York City	179,563	255,687	284,616
Cleveland	16,613	40,199	44,662
Boston	13,746	26,928	33,928
Buffalo	8,738	24,947	31,884
Washington	18,967	23,277	23,277
Jersey City	5,714	10,708	13,775
San Francisco	14,641	29,119	34,090
Birmingham	8,574	12,308	12,308
Chicago	73,415	132,881	148,177
Detroit	30,745	65,733	67,457
Oakland	8,082	12,536	12,536
Least Needy			
Dallas	17,318	17,318	17,318
Austin	5,786	5,786	5,786
Houston	26,934	26,934	26,934
Oklahoma City	7,332	7,332	7,332
Nashville-Davidson	8,618	8,618	8,618
Fort Worth	8,159	8,076	8,076
Omaha	6,095	6,095	6,095
Albuquerque	5,073	5,073	5,073
San Diego	12,255	12,255	12,255
Wichita	4,706	4,992	4,992
Tulsa	5,709	5,709	5,709
Indianapolis	12,459	12,459	12,459
Tucson	5,872	5,872	5,872
Phoenix	11,412	11,412	11,412
San Jose	7,232	7,232	7,232

SOURCE: Department of Housing and Urban Development

contracts; fiscal 1978 budget authority also would include about $3-billion for payments on contracts from prior years.

Muskie said that the bill as proposed would "rip major loopholes in the federal budget" by hiding the future year costs of housing programs and removing them from congressional control. It also would establish "a dangerous precedent that could lead other special interest groups to develop new ways to disguise the budgetary impact of programs under their jurisdiction," he said.

Proxmire said the change was designed to seek equal, not preferred treatment, for housing programs, which he asserted were the only federal assistance programs budgeted in 1978 for costs that might be incurred in the year 2071.

Flood Insurance. An amendment by Thomas F. Eagleton, D-Mo., identical to one adopted on the House floor, changed existing law to permit federally insured lending institutions to make loans to property owners in HUD-designated flood-prone areas which were not participants in the federal flood insurance program.

The amendment, which was adopted 49-36, also required notification of the recipient that he or she would not be eligible for federal disaster relief and that the federal government could not bail out individuals who undertook development in flood-prone areas without adequate flood-proofing measures.

CONFERENCE ACTION

The conference report on the bill (H Rept 95-634) was not filed until Sept. 26.

The conference committee first met June 28 and held six sessions before recessing in a deadlock July 18.

Early sessions were devoted to working out differences in less controversial items in the bills—and in lengthy debates over the distribution formulas.

The major spokesmen for the Senate plan were Harrison A. Williams Jr., D-N.J., and Edward W. Brooke, R-Mass., who cosponsored the third formula in the Senate Banking Committee and who represented states that would benefit from it.

They argued that impaction was merely a refinement of the new formula and would more precisely measure urban decay, a factor the block grant program was designed to combat.

House conferees, led by Thomas L. Ashley, D-Ohio, chairman of the House Banking Subcommittee on Housing, accused the senators of "plundering" the action grant fund.

During the negotiations the senators offered two compromises. One would have funded impaction at 66 per cent during each of the three years instead of using the 50 per cent, 75 per cent and 100 per cent phase-in approach in the Senate bill. The second compromise would have funded impaction at 55 per cent each year. Both proposals were rejected by the House conferees.

More than two months passed before the conferees met again. Two stopgap extensions (PL 95-60, PL 95-90) were needed to keep some programs from expiring.

In the interim, pressure to reach an agreement increased. There was heavy lobbying from builders, lenders and others interested in the housing programs (set to expire Sept. 30) being held up by the block grant controversy. Meanwhile, parties in the formula fray—including the administration, which favored the House position—were trying to pick off their opposition.

After several weeks of maneuvering in early September, Ashley proposed a compromise. His proposal eliminated the Senate formula but said that in distributing action grants the HUD Secretary had to "take into consideration" the factors in the Senate formula—impaction, poverty and growth lag—in determining the economic and physical distress of cities. The Senate conferees accepted the compromise with the proviso that the Secretary "must include" impaction, growth lag and poverty as the "primary criterion" in determining a city's distress.

Williams said he was "extremely pleased" with the compromise which "fully endorses and preserves the concept of impaction as a principal means of defining urban distress."

As part of the compromise, the House conferees accepted a Senate anti-redlining provision requiring financial supervisory agencies to take a lending institution's record of meeting the credit needs of its entire community, including low- and moderate-income neighborhoods, into account when deciding whether it could open a new branch.

Final Action

Final approval of the measure came four days after the end of the fiscal year, Sept. 30, which was the expiration date for most of the programs reauthorized in the bill.

Senators took time out of a Saturday, Oct. 1, filibustering session to adopt the conference report. The vote was 54-19.

The House approved the conference report Oct. 4 on a 384-26 vote.

PROVISIONS

As signed into law, the Housing and Community Development Act of 1977 (HR 6655—PL 95-128):

Title I—Community Development Amendments

● Provided that "hold harmless" grants guaranteed under the 1974 Housing and Community Development Act (PL 93-383) would phase down against the higher of amounts computed under the existing or the new formulas.

● **Authorizations.** Authorized the Housing and Urban Development (HUD) Secretary to make block grants to Indian tribes.

● Authorized up to $3.5-billion for community development block grants in fiscal 1978, $3.65-billion in fiscal 1979 and $3.8-billion in fiscal 1980. Of that amount, the act set aside $350-million, $265-million and $250-million for fiscal years 1978, 1979 and 1980 respectively for discretionary balances available to communities not eligible for funding under the formulas.

● Authorized $100-million during each of the three years for financial settlement and, to the extent feasible, the completion of projects and programs assisted under the old urban renewal programs consolidated by the block grants.

● Authorized up to $400-million in each of the three years for urban development action grants for assisting severely distressed cities and urban counties.

● Specified that if appropriations did not cover the full authorization, the block grants would be funded first, the financial settlement of old projects second and the action grants third.

● **Application Requirements.** Required communities to include in their applications for block grants a summary of housing as well as community development needs. The act also required communities to set out a program to improve conditions for low- and moderate-income persons living or expected to live in the community, to foster neighborhood development in order to induce higher-income persons to remain in or return to the community and to insure full opportunity for participation by the handicapped.

● Required Housing Assistance Plans to include an identification of housing stock in deteriorated condition, adequate provision that low- and moderate-income families would have available to them the preponderance of subsidized rehabilitated housing, and provisions to give tenants displaced as a result of housing rehabilitation reasonable opportunity to relocate in their immediate neighborhood.

● Required communities to prepare and follow a written citizen participation plan which provided citizens an opportunity to participate in the development of the block grant application.

● Permitted the HUD Secretary to waive some application requirements for small communities where the application did not involve a comprehensive community development program.

● Authorized the HUD Secretary to allow states to participate in the selection process for funding discretionary grants to localities within the state.

● Authorized the HUD Secretary to make a lump sum payment of a community's grant allotment to allow the community to establish a revolving loan fund at a private financial institution to finance rehabilitation activities. The rehabilitation activities had to begin within 45 days of the HUD payment.

● **Eligible Activities.** Added as activities eligible for assistance, when carried out by public or private nonprofit entities or by minority enterprise small business investment companies, 1) property acquisition, 2) acquisition, construction, reconstruction, rehabilitation or installation of public facilities and commercial buildings, 3) planning and 4) assistance to local development corporations.

● Allowed block grant recipients to provide financial assistance to private entities to acquire for rehabilitation and to rehabilitate privately owned properties.

● Made minority business enterprises eligible for funding under the act.

● Barred the use of grant funds for local services, such as fire and police, if those services were financed by local revenues the preceding year.

● **Allocation of Funds.** Provided for the allocation of funds to metropolitan cities and urban counties according to the formula under existing law or a new formula. The community would receive the higher amount. The existing formula was based on population, housing overcrowding and poverty counted twice. The new formula was based on age of housing, counted 2½ times; poverty, counted 1½ times; and growth lag, counted once. "Age of housing" was defined as the number of existing housing units built in 1939 or before, according to census data. "Growth lag" was defined as the extent to which the community's population had failed to grow at the average rate for all metropolitan cities since 1960.

● Provided that "hold harmless" grants guaranteed under the 1974 Housing and Community Development Act (PL 93-383) would phase down against the higher of amounts computed under the existing or the new formulas. *(p. 9-A)*

● Established a dual formula system for distributing metropolitan and nonmetropolitan discretionary balances for smaller communities on a state-by-state basis. The system would use the existing formula for metropolitan cities and urban counties or a second formula which counted age of housing 2½ times, poverty 1½ times and population once.

● Authorized the HUD Secretary to make funding commitments to smaller communities for up to three years. The Secretary was required to give special consideration to communities presently carrying out community development programs and receiving hold harmless grants before making new commitments.

● **Reporting Requirements.** Required the Secretary to report to Congress by Sept. 30, 1978, on the adequacy, effectiveness and equity of the formula for distributing grant funds.

● Required HUD to study and report within one year on the developmental needs of small cities and to present legislative recommendations including alternative fund distribution formulas.

● **Discretionary Funds.** Extended the Secretary's discretionary fund through fiscal 1980 and increased the percentage of total formula funds to be set aside for the fund to 3 per cent from 2 per cent.

● Reduced to 15 per cent from 25 per cent the percentage of amounts set aside in the discretionary fund each year which could be used for grants to meet community development needs caused by disasters.

● **Loan Guarantees.** Authorized the Secretary to guarantee notes or other obligations issued by units of local government or public agencies for financing acquisition or rehabilitation of property provided the recipient's total outstanding obligation guaranteed was not more than three times the amount of the recipient's block grant. The total amount of obligations guaranteed could not exceed the amount appropriated for the block grant program.

● **Urban Development Action Grants.** Established a program of urban development action grants to severely distressed communities to help alleviate physical and economic deterioration through neighborhood reclamation.

● Limited the grants to cities and urban counties that had demonstrated results in providing housing and equal employment opportunity for low- and moderate-income persons and members of minority groups.

● Required that action grant projects be developed to take advantage of unique opportunities to attract private investment, stimulate investment in restoration of deteriorated or abandoned housing stock or solve critical problems resulting from population outmigration or a stagnating or declining tax base.

● Required the Secretary, in determining who received the grants, to include as the primary criterion the comparative degree of physical and economic distress among applicants. Such distress was measured by the differences in the extent of growth lag, poverty and adjusted age of housing, defined as proportion of pre-1940 housing in a community compared to the proportion of old housing stock in all metropolitan areas.

● Directed the Secretary also to take into account, when awarding grants, impact of the proposed program on the problems of persons of low and moderate income and minorities, the extent of financial participation by public or private entities, extent of state assistance, extent to which the program provided an opportunity to meet local needs and the feasibility of accomplishing the program in a timely fashion within the grant amount available.

● Barred action grants designed to facilitate relocation of industrial or commercial plants from one area to another unless the relocation would not adversely affect the unemployment or economic base of the area giving up the project.

● Required citizen participation in the formulation of the action grant proposals.

● Set aside at least 25 per cent of the funds available for action grants for cities under 50,000 population that were not central cities of a standard metropolitan statistical area.

● **Rehabilitation Loans.** Extended the Section 312 rehabilitation loan program for two years through fiscal 1979 and authorized $60-million for fiscal 1978.

● Increased the maximum Section 312 loan amount for residences to $27,000 per dwelling unit.

● **Planning.** Authorized $75-million for fiscal 1978 for Section 701 planning grants.

Title II—Housing Authorizations

● **Contract Authority.** Authorized $1,159,995,000 of additional annual contract authority for fiscal 1978. The authorization was expected to assist about 157,000 new and rehabilitated units under the Section 8 rent subsidy program, about 160,000 existing Section 8 units and about 56,000 units of public housing.

● Required that not less than $197,139,200 of the additional authority be made available for low-income housing projects permanently financed by loans from state housing finance or state development agencies.

● Required that not less than $120-million of the additional authority be made available for low-income housing projects for the elderly and handicapped permanently financed by loans under Section 202.

● Required that not less than $42.5-million of the additional authority be made available for modernization of low-income housing projects.

● Directed the Secretary to prohibit high-rise elevator projects for families with children unless there was no practical alternative.

● Authorized an additional $685-million for operating subsidies for public housing projects.

● **Urban Homesteading.** Increased to $15-million from $5-million the authorization for fiscal 1978 for the urban homesteading demonstration program.

● **Research.** Authorized $60-million for fiscal 1978 for study, research and demonstrations at HUD.

● **Section 236 Operating Subsidies.** Authorized the Secretary to make additional monthly assistance payments to project owners for the amount their utility costs and property taxes exceeded the initial operating expense level. Owners accepting such payments would have to lower rents in the project.

Title III—FHA Mortgage Insurance

● **Program Extensions.** Extended basic HUD-Federal Housing Administration (FHA) mortgage insurance and loan programs for one year, through Sept. 30, 1978.

● Extended through Sept. 30, 1978, the authority of the HUD Secretary to make special planning assistance grants to private and public new community developers.

● **Insurable Amounts.** Increased the maximum insurable mortgage amounts under Section 203 (b)(2) (basic home mortgage insurance) and Section 220 (d)(3) (rehabilitation and neighborhood conservation housing insurance) to $60,000 from $45,000 for single-family units, to $65,000 from $48,750 for two- and three-family units and to $75,000 from $56,000 for four-family units.

● Increased maximum insurable mortgage amounts for Section 221 (d) (2) (housing for moderate-income and displaced families) to $31,000 from $25,000 for single-family units, to $35,000 from $28,000 for two-family units, to $48,-600 from $38,800 for three-family units, and to $59,400 from $47,520 for four-family units; set new limits of $36,000, $45,000, $57,600 and $68,400 respectively in high cost areas.

● Increased maximum insurable amounts under Section 222 (mortgage insurance for servicemen) and Section 234 (mortgage insurance for condominiums) to $60,000 from $45,000 for single-family units.

● Increased the maximum insurable amount under Section 235 (homeownership for lower-income families) to $32,-000 from $25,000 (and to $38,000 from $29,000 for homes for five or more persons); in high cost areas the limits were raised to $38,000 from $29,000 (and to $44,000 from $33,000 for families of five or more).

● Limited to 40 per cent the number of units in a subdivision that could be insured under Section 235 except in the case of rehabilitated units or except in urban areas where the units were part of an overall redevelopment plan.

● **Downpayment Requirements.** Decreased downpayment requirements under Section 203, Section 220, Section 222 and Section 234 by authorizing the insurance of mortgages up to 97 per cent of the first $25,000 of appraised value plus 95 per cent of appraised value in excess of the first $25,000.

● **Mobile Homes, Home Improvements.** Increased the loan ceiling for National Housing Act Title I mobile home loans to $16,000 from $12,500 and to $24,000 from $20,000 for mobile homes composed of two or more modules.

● Increased the ceiling for Title I property improvement loans to $15,000 from $10,000.

● Increased the term of maturity for Title I home improvement loans to 15 years and 32 days from 12 years and 32 days. The maturity term was increased to 23 years and 32 days from 15 years and 32 days in the case of a loan for a mobile home composed of two or more modules. For a loan to finance the purchase of a mobile home and an undeveloped lot for the home the loan maturity period was increased to 23 years and 32 days from 20 years and 32 days.

● Authorized the Secretary to increase up to 40 per cent the mobile home Title I home loan ceilings in Alaska, Guam and Hawaii.

● **Land Claims.** Authorized the Secretary to insure under Section 203(b) mortgages in communities where widespread foreclosures or distress sales were likely to result from temporarily adverse economic conditions due to Indian land claims provided that 50 or more individual homeowners were defendants in land claims litigation prior to Dec. 31, 1976.

● **Graduated Payment Mortgages.** Limited principal obligation of mortgages insured under Section 245 to 97 per cent of the appraised value of the property unless the mortgagor was a veteran or the mortgage was to be insured under Section 203.

● Repealed a provision of existing law limiting to 1 per cent the number of graduated payment mortgages and loans that could be insured by FHA in any fiscal year.

Title IV—Savings and Loan Lending Powers

● Authorized federal savings and loan associations to make line of credit construction loans up to 5 per cent of assets, rather than 3 per cent.

● Increased to $60,000 from $55,000 the limitation on real estate loans for single-family dwellings and provided that only the excess over $60,000 would count against the 20 per cent of assets limit.

● Increased to $15,000 from $10,000 the limit on property improvement loans.

● Authorized federal savings and loans to make loans for farm purposes as part of the 5 per cent of assets category allowed for nonconforming loans under existing law.

● **GNMA.** Authorized the Secretary, to the extent feasible and consistent with stabilizing housing production, to direct the Government National Mortgage Association (GNMA) to exercise its mortgage purchase authority to promote homeownership opportunities for moderate-income families.

● Authorized the Secretary to require GNMA to use part of its mortgage purchase authority to buy mortgages executed to finance rehabilitation or acquisition of housing in older or declining neighborhoods.

● Authorized GNMA to buy a mortgage involving an original principal obligation of not to exceed $49,000 per dwelling unit for Section 8 properties located in high cost areas. Under existing law, Section 8 housing was subject to a $42,000 limit applicable to all units outside Alaska, Hawaii or Guam.

● Authorized GNMA to buy a mortgage involving a principal residence with a sales price of up to $55,000 for Section 8 properties in high cost areas. Under existing law the limit was $52,000.

● Limited GNMA purchase and commitments under Section 313 of the National Housing Act to $7.5-billion during fiscal 1978.

● Extended until Oct. 1, 1978, the authority of GNMA to buy mortgages under the Emergency Home Purchase Assistance Act of 1974.

Title V—Rural Housing

● Extended through Sept. 30, 1978, the Farmers Home Administration (FmHA) programs for low-income repair loans and grants and domestic farm labor grants.

● Authorized an additional $25-million for each of those programs, bringing the total authorization for each to $105-million for fiscal 1978.

● Extended through Sept. 30, 1978, the authority of the Secretary of Agriculture to carry out rural housing research.

● Extended through Sept. 30, 1978, the authority of the Agriculture Secretary to insure rural rental housing loans, to make and insure Section 502 single-family housing loans for low- and moderate-income families and to make mutual and self-help housing loans and grants.

● Authorized up to $10-million for fiscal 1978 for the self-help housing loan program.

● Waived a Section 502 requirement that home loans contain the agreement that the borrower refinance the loan through private credit sources.

● Barred transfer of funds between the guaranteed loan and insured loan programs.

● Required that loans guaranteed under Section 517 be made only to borrowers with above average incomes.

● Authorized expenditures, after Oct. 1, 1977, to 1) correct defects, 2) pay owner's claims arising from defects or 3) acquire title to a property where a newly constructed unit purchased with financial assistance from FmHA was found by the Secretary to have structural defects. Decisions of the Secretary would not be subject to judicial review.

● Authorized the agriculture secretary to make farm labor housing loans and grants in Puerto Rico and the Virgin Islands.

● Made clear that Section 515 rental housing loans could be used to finance the development of congregate housing for the elderly or handicapped.

● Required that at least 60 per cent of FmHA loans made under Section 502 (single family) and Section 515 (rental) programs benefit persons of low income.

● Eliminated the preferential treatment accorded land grant colleges in security research contracts from FmHA and provided for establishment of a research capacity within FmHA.

● Directed the Secretary to make rental assistance payments authorized in connection with Section 514 (farm labor housing) and Section 515 (rental housing) projects in rural areas.

● Allowed local, county and state governments to levy property taxes on property taken over by FmHA through default.

Title VI—National Urban Policy

● Amended the Urban Growth and New Community Development Act of 1970 to require development of a national urban policy and a biennial report on that policy by the President to Congress.

Title VII—Flood Insurance

● Extended through Sept. 30, 1978, the authority of HUD to enter into new contracts for flood insurance under the national flood insurance program, and extended for the same period the emergency flood insurance program.

● Authorized up to $108-million for fiscal 1978 for flood insurance studies and surveys.

● Repealed a provision of existing law that prohibited federally insured private lending institutions from making loans to property-owners in HUD-designated flood-prone areas that did not participate in the federal flood insurance program.

● Required the lending institutions to notify loan recipients that they would not be eligible for federal disaster relief and that the federal government would not bail out individuals who undertook development in flood-prone areas without adequate flood-proofing measures.

● Increased the ceiling of optional flood insurance coverage, at nonsubsidized actuarial rates, on residential structures from $35,000 for single-family and $100,000 for multiple unit dwellings to $150,000 and increased content coverage to $50,000 from $10,000.

● Increased optional structure and content coverage at non-subsidized actuarial rates for small business properties to $250,000 (plus $200,000 for each small business occupant). Coverage would be allocated among occupants according to rules prescribed by the Secretary and total coverage for the structure itself could not exceed $250,000.

● Retained the authority of the HUD Secretary to buy property covered by flood insurance where the insured property was damaged substantially beyond repair by a flood.

● Gave the Secretary additional authority to buy damaged property if the property 1) had incurred signifi-

cant flood damage at least three times during five years and each time the average cost of repair was equal to or more than the value of the structure at the time of the flood, or 2) had been damaged as a result of a single incident and existing law precluded its repair or permitted its repair only at significantly increased cost.

● Authorized the HUD Secretary to make 2 per cent loans to owners of single-family dwellings in the most severe flood areas so they could elevate their homes. The loans would be authorized in cases where the property had suffered damage and the Secretary deemed its repair necessary to meet elevation standards. The act authorized $4.5-million to implement the provision.

● Directed the Secretary to reimburse individuals and communities for the expenses of surveying or engineering in connection with appeals of the Secretary's determination of flood-prone communities. The act authorized up to $250,000 for appeals of flood elevation levels and $250,000 for appeals of flood-prone community designation.

Title VIII—Community Reinvestment

● Directed federal financial supervisory agencies, in examining financial institutions, to assess a lending institution's record in meeting the credit needs of "its entire community including low- and moderate-income neighborhoods," consistent with safe and sound operations, and to take that record into account in evaluating the institution's application for a deposit facility (branch).

Title IX—Miscellaneous

● **Indian and Alaska Native Programs.** Created in HUD a special assistant for Indian and Alaska native programs responsible for coordinating all housing and community development programs related to those groups.

● Required the HUD Secretary to submit to Congress by Dec. 1 of each year a report describing the actions of the special assistant, estimating the cost of his activities for the coming years, outlining the conditions of Indian and Alaska native housing and making legislative recommendations.

● **Mobile Homes.** Exempted from coverage under the National Mobile Home Construction and Safety Standards Act of 1974 structures certified by the manufacturer to be designed only for installation on a site-built permanent foundation and manufactured to comply with a nationally recognized or equivalent local model building code, with a state or local modular building code equivalent to site-built housing or with FHA minimum property standards.

● **Counseling.** Extended HUD's authority to provide homeownership counseling services to owners of single-family units. Existing law limited such counseling to persons insured under the Section 235 program.

● **Prototype Costs.** Directed the Secretary to prepare and publish annually, beginning in calendar year 1979, prototype housing costs for one- to four-family dwelling units for each housing market area in the United States.

1977 Housing Authorization

Congress completed action April 28 on the Supplemental Housing Authorization Act of 1977 (HR 3843—PL 95-24).

Final action came when the House approved the conference report (H Rept 95-221) on the measure by a 355-47 vote. The Senate approved the report April 26 by voice vote.

HR 3843 authorized additional contract authority of $378-million for fiscal 1977 for housing assistance payments for low-income persons and included a provision to establish a national commission to study neighborhood revitalization.

The bill also authorized the Department of Housing and Urban Development (HUD) to contract with private developers to make Section 8 rental housing assistance payments for 30 years. Existing law set the limit at 20 years. The change was requested by the Carter administration.

The additional contract authority for Section 8, the subsidized leased housing program, would enable HUD to provide assistance payments for 400,000 dwelling units. Available funds would have subsidized about 236,000 units.

The bill also increased authorizations for public housing operating subsidies by $19.6-million to pay for high fuel bills caused by the cold weather, increased the authorization for the urban homesteading program by $10-million, extended the federal crime and riot insurance programs and increased the authorization to cover losses incurred by the Federal Housing Administration's (FHA) general insurance fund.

Legislative History

The major differences between the House and Senate versions involved the neighborhood commission and the authorization to cover losses from the FHA general insurance fund.

On March 10, the House struck the neighborhood commission from the bill on a 243-166 vote. The House measure (H Rept 95-42) also imposed a ceiling of $1,341,000,000 to cover insurance fund losses. The existing ceiling was $500-million.

The Senate version of the bill (S 1070—S Rept 95-61), passed April 4, included the neighborhood commission provision and set the FHA insurance fund ceiling at $1-billion.

The conference committee adopted the neighborhood commission language of the Senate bill, but went with the House version of the measure on the FHA insurance fund ceiling.

Provisions

As signed into law, HR 3843 (PL 95-24):

● Authorized an additional $378-million in contract authority for housing assistance payments to support low-income persons in conventional public housing and Section 8 leased housing, bringing the total authorization for fiscal 1977 to $1,228,050,000.

● Authorized an additional $19.6-million for public housing operating subsidies, to $595.6-million from $576-million, to cover unexpectedly high utility costs.

● Extended to 30 from 20 years the Section 8 contract term for new or rehabilitated units financed conventionally or under HUD's coinsurance program.

● Increased the authorization to cover losses from the FHA general insurance fund to $1,341,000,000 from $500-million.

● Extended the HUD crime insurance and riot reinsurance programs from April 30, 1977, to Sept. 30, 1978, and extended from April 30, 1978, to Sept. 30, 1981, HUD's authority to continue riot reinsurance and crime insurance coverage for policies existing at the time the program might be terminated.

● Increased the fiscal 1977 authorization for the urban homesteading program to $15-million from $5-million.

● Established a National Commission on Neighborhoods to assess existing policies, laws and programs that have an impact on neighborhoods and suggest improvements. The commission had a $1-million budget and one year in which to report.

● Amend the National Housing Act to make eligible limited dividend sponsors under Section 221.

Neighborhood Preservation

A bill to create a Neighborhood Reinvestment Corporation to sponsor local programs for preserving neighborhoods was approved by the Senate in 1977, but the House did not act on it.

The measure (S 1724), which authorized $65-million to carry out the corporation's activities in fiscal 1979-81, was passed by voice vote Sept. 9.

The bill would convert the *ad hoc* Urban Reinvestment Task Force into a public corporation. The task force was made up of the Secretary of Housing and Urban Development (HUD), the chairman of the Federal Home Loan Bank Board (FHLBB), the chairman of the Federal Deposit Insurance Corporation, the Comptroller of the Currency and a governor of the Federal Reserve Board.

It sponsored neighborhood preservation projects in more than 30 cities, and the legislation would permit expansion of the program to about 500 neighborhoods by 1981. The new corporation, to be chaired by the FHLBB chairman, would be composed of all of the members of the task force plus the National Credit Union Administrator.

The Senate Banking, Housing and Urban Affairs Committee, which reported (S Rept 95-410) the bill Aug. 18, described the characteristics of a task force program as:

● A group of residents interested in preserving their neighborhood.

● A local government willing to improve the neighborhood by making public service improvements and conducting a housing inspection program.

● A group of financial institutions that agree to reinvest in the neighborhood by making normal market rate loans to homeowners meeting normal credit standards and which will make tax deductible contributions to support the operating cost of the program.

● A high risk revolving loan fund to make loans at flexible rates and terms to residents not meeting commercial credit standards.

● A private, non-profit corporation to run the program, composed of community residents, representatives of financial institutions and a three-member staff. ▮

Selected Bibliography on Urban Policy

Books and Reports

Aaron, Henry J. *Shelter and Subsidies: Who Benefits from Housing Policies?* Washington, D.C.: Brookings Institution, 1972.

_____. *Who Pays the Property Tax?: A New View.* Washington, D.C.: Brookings Institution, 1975.

_____. *Why Is Welfare So Hard to Reform?* Washington, D.C.: Brookings Institution, 1973.

Adams, Arvil V., and Mangum, Garth L. *The Lingering Crisis of Youth Unemployment.* Kalamazoo, Mich.: W. E. Upjohn Institute for Employment Research, 1978.

Anderson, Martin. *Welfare: The Political Economy of Welfare Reform in the United States.* Stanford, Calif.: Hoover Institution Press, 1978.

Berke, Joel S., et al. *Federal Aid to Education: Who Benefits? Who Governs?* Lexington, Mass.: Lexington Books, 1972.

Berry, Brian J. L., and Gallard, Quentin. *The Changing Shape of Metropolitan America: Commuting Patterns, Urban Fields, and Decentralization Processes, 1960-1970.* Cambridge, Mass.: Ballinger, 1977.

Breneman, David W., and Finn, Chester E. Jr., eds. *Public Policy and Private Higher Education.* Washington, D.C.: Brookings Institution, 1978.

Burns, Eveline M. *Social Welfare in the 1980s and Beyond.* Berkeley: University of California, Institute of Governmental Studies, 1977.

Campbell, Colin D., ed. *Income Redistribution.* Washington, D.C.: American Enterprise Institute for Public Policy Research, 1977.

Carroll, Stephan. *The Consequences of School Finance Reform.* Santa Monica, Calif.: The Rand Corporation, 1978.

Chiswick, Barry R., and O'Neill, June A., eds. *Human Resources and Income Distribution: Issues and Policies.* New York: W. W. Norton, 1977.

The City in Transition: Prospects and Policies for New York: The Final Report of the Temporary Commission on City Finance. New York: Arno Press, 1978.

Committee for Economic Development. *Developing Jobs for the Hard to Employ.* New York: 1978.

_____. *Financing the Nation's Housing Needs.* New York: 1973.

_____. *Training and Jobs for the Urban Poor.* New York: 1970.

_____. *Welfare Reform and Its Financing.* New York: 1976.

_____. Research and Policy Committee. *An Approach to Federal Urban Policy: A Statement on National Policy.* New York: 1977.

Donovan, James G. *The Politics of Poverty.* Indianapolis: Bobbs-Merrill, 1976.

Downs, Anthony. "Urban Policy." In *Setting National Priorities: The 1979 Budget,* pp. 161-192. Edited by Joseph A. Pechman. Washington, D.C.: Brookings Institution, 1978.

_____. *Who Are the Urban Poor?* New York: Committee for Economic Development, 1970.

Editorial Research Reports. *Jobs for Americans.* Washington, D.C.: Congressional Quarterly Inc., 1978.

Garms, Walter L., et al. *School Finance: The Economics and Politics of Public Education.* Englewood Cliffs, N.J.: Prentice-Hall, 1978.

Gelfand, Mark I. *A Nation of Cities: The Federal Government and Urban America, 1933-1965.* New York: Oxford University Press, 1975.

Goldstein, Benjamin, ed. *Neighborhoods in the Urban Economy: The Dynamics of Decline.* Lexington, Mass.: Lexington Books, 1978.

Gorham, William, and Glazer, Nathan, eds. *The Urban Predicament.* Washington, D.C.: Urban Institute, 1976.

Grönbjerg, Kirsten A. *Mass Society and the Extension of Welfare, 1960-1970.* Chicago: The University of Chicago Press, 1977.

Harloe, Michael. *Captive Cities: Studies in the Political Economy of Cities and Regions.* New York: Wiley, 1977.

Harrison, Bennett. *Public Employment and Urban Poverty.* Washington, D.C.: Urban Institute, 1971.

_____. *Urban Economic Development: Suburbanization, Minority Opportunity, and the Condition of the Central City.* Washington, D.C.: Urban Institute, 1974.

Haveman, Robert H., ed. *A Decade of Federal Antipoverty Programs: Achievements, Failures and Lessons.* New York: Academic Press, 1977.

Hilton, George W. *Federal Transit Subsidies: The Urban Mass Transportation Assistance Program.* Washington, D.C.: American Enterprise Institute for Public Policy Research, 1974.

Hobbs, Charles D. *The Welfare Industry.* Washington, D.C.: Heritage Foundation, 1978.

Hoffman, Wayne L. *Work Incentives and Implicit Tax Rates in the Carter Welfare Reform Plan, with a Comparison to Current Policy.* Washington, D.C.: Urban Institute, 1977.

Holt, Charles C., et al. *Unemployment-Inflation Dilemma: A Manpower Solution.* Washington, D.C.: Urban Institute, 1970.

Jones, Benjamin. *Tax Increment Financing of Community Redevelopment.* Lexington, Kentucky: The Council of State Governments, 1977.

Lambert, Richard D., ed. *Planning for Full Employment.* Philadelphia: American Academy of Political and Social Science, 1977.

Lawrence, William J., and Leeds, Stephen. *An Inventory of Federal Income Transfer Programs.* White Plains, N.Y.: Institute for Socioeconomic Studies, 1977.

Lecht, Leonard A., ed. *Employment and Unemployment: Priorities for the Next Five Years.* New York: Conference Board, Report no. 718, 1977.

Leven, Charles L., et al. *Neighborhood Change: Lessons in the Dynamics of Urban Decay.* New York: Praeger, 1976.

Mangum, Garth L. *Employability, Employment, and Income: A Reassessment of Manpower Policy.* Salt Lake City, Utah: Olympus Publishing Co., 1976.

Mermelstein, David, and Alcaly, Roger. *The Fiscal Crisis of American Cities: Essays on the Political Economy of Urban America with Special Reference to New York City.* New York: Random House, 1977.

Moynihan, Daniel P., ed. *Toward a National Urban Policy.* New York: Basic Books, 1970.

Newfield, Jack, and Du Brul, Paul. *The Abuse of Power: The Permanent Government and the Fall of New York.* New York: Macmillan, 1977.

Ostow, Miriam and Dutka, Anna B. *Work and Welfare in New York City.* Baltimore: Johns Hopkins University Press, 1975.

Ott, Attiat F. *New York City's Financial Crisis: Can the Trend be Reversed?* Washington, D.C.: American Enterprise Institute for Public Policy Research, 1977.

Owen, Wilfred. *Transportation for the Cities: The Role of Federal Policy.* Washington, D.C.: Brookings Institution, 1976.

Palmer, John L., ed. *Creating Jobs: Public Employment Programs and Wage Subsidies.* Washington, D.C.: Brookings Institution, 1978.

_____. "Employment and Income Security." In *Setting National Priorities: The 1979 Budget,* pp. 61-90. Edited by Joseph A. Pechman. Washington, D.C.: Brookings Institution, 1978.

_____. *Inflation, Unemployment and Poverty.* Lexington, Mass.: Lexington Books, 1973.

Peterson, George E. *Federal Tax Policy and the Shaping of Urban Development.* Washington, D.C.: Urban Institute, 1977.

_____. *Property Taxes, Housing and the Cities.* Lexington, Mass.: Lexington Books, 1973.

Phillips, Kenneth E. *Urban Underemployment and the Spatial Separation of Jobs and Residence.* Santa Monica, Calif.: The Rand Corporation, 1977.

Reische, Diana L., comp. *Problems of Mass Transportation.* New York: H. W. Wilson, 1970.

Reuss, Henry S. *To Save Our Cities: What Needs to Be Done.* Washington, D.C.: Public Affairs Press, 1977.

Seidel, Stephen R. *Government Regulation and Housing Cost.* New Brunswick, N.J.: Center for Urban Policy Research, 1977.

Sheppard, Harold L., ed. *The Political Economy of Public Service Employment.* Lexington, Mass.: Lexington Books, 1972.

Stanback, Thomas M., and Knight, Richard V. *Suburbanization and the City.* Montclair, N.J.: Allanheld, Osmun & Co., 1978.

Storey, James R., et al. *The Better Jobs and Income Plan: A Guide to President Carter's Welfare Reform Proposal and Major Issues.* Washington, D.C.: Urban Institute, 1978.

Trend, M. G. *Direct Cash Assistance for Low Income Housing: A Social Experiment.* Boulder, Colo.: Westview Press, 1978.

Twentieth Century Fund. Task Force on Employment Problems of Black Youth. *The Job Crisis for Black Youth.* New York: Praeger, 1971.

Vaughan, Roger J. *Public Works as a Countercyclical Device: A Review of the Issues.* Santa Monica, Calif.: The Rand Corporation, 1976.

————, and Barro, Stephen M. *The Urban Impacts of Federal Policies.* 4 vols. Santa Monica, Calif.: The Rand Corporation, 1977.

Vicent, Phillip E. *School Finance Reforms and Big City Fiscal Problems.* Cambridge, Mass.: United States Committee on Taxation, Resources and Economic Development Conference, 1977.

Welfeld, Irving H. *America's Housing Problem: An Approach to Its Solution.* Washington, D.C.: American Enterprise Institute for Public Policy Research, 1973.

Articles

Adams, Brock. "Welfare, Poverty, and Jobs: A Practical Approach." *Challenge,* September/October 1976, pp. 6-12.

Albin, Peter S., and Stein, Bruno. "The Impact of Unemployment on Welfare Expenditures." *Industrial and Labor Relations Review,* October 1977, pp. 31-44.

Bell, Carolyn S. "The Carter Bill: Is It Welfare Reform?" *The Journal of the Institute for Socioeconomic Studies,* Summer 1978, pp. 9-19.

Boorstein, Edward. "The Crisis of the Cities." *Political Affairs,* January 1978, p. 613.

Cherlin, A. "No Long Delay Needed: Guaranteed Income and the Carter Program." *New Republic,* 17 December 1977, pp. 13-15.

Clayton, James L. "The Fiscal Limits of the Warfare-Welfare State: Defense and Welfare Spending in the United States Since 1900." *Western Political Quarterly,* September 1976, pp. 364-383.

Coleman, James S. "Can We Revitalize Our Cities?" *Challenge,* November/December 1977, pp. 23-34.

"Congress and the Welfare Reform Controversy." *Congressional Digest,* May 1978.

Cose, Ellis. "Can America's Cities Survive?" *Focus,* November/December 1977, pp. 4-5.

Craft, James A. "Federal Influence in Manpower Programming: An Analysis of Recent Initiatives." *Labor Law Journal,* March 1978, pp. 168-177.

Dausch, James F. "Using Title VII for Urban Redevelopment." *Urban Land,* December 1977, pp. 11-15.

Doolittle, Frederick. "The Mirage of Welfare Reform." *Public Interest,* Spring 1977, pp. 62-87.

Downs, Anthony. "Public Policy and the Rising Cost of Housing." *Real Estate Review,* Spring 1978, pp. 27-38.

Durst, Seymour B. "If the Cities Go Down, So Goes the Nation: An Urban Analysis and Prescription for Housing Revival." *The Journal of the Institute for Socioeconomic Studies,* Autumn 1977, pp. 25-32.

Elazar, Daniel J. "Restructuring Federal Housing Programs: Who Stands to Gain?" *Publius,* Spring 1976, pp. 75-94.

Frieden, Bernard J., and Kaplan, Marshall. "Urban Aid Comes Full Cycle: Community Development and the Model Cities Legacy." *Civil Rights Digest,* Spring 1977, pp. 12-23.

Guzzardi, Walter Jr. "How to Deal With the 'New Unemployment.'" *Fortune,* October 1976, pp. 132-135.

Havemann, Joel, and Stanfield, Rochelle. "Housing as Part of Welfare." *National Journal,* 30 July 1977, pp. 1190-1192.

Havighurst, Robert J. "Educational Policy for the Large Cities." *Social Problems,* December 1976, pp. 271-281.

Holland, Robert C. "Jobs for the Hard to Employ." *The Journal of the Institute for Socioeconomic Studies,* Summer 1978, pp. 48-53.

Keith, John P., and Thomas, Joseph M. "The Impact of the Carter Welfare Reform Proposal on the New York Region: A Preliminary Assessment." *The Journal of the Institute for Socioeconomic Studies,* Autumn 1977, pp. 65-76.

Kingman, Woodward. "The Challenge at HUD: Getting Housing Programs to Work." *The Journal of the Institute for Socioeconomic Studies,* Spring 1977, pp. 39-49.

Leahy, William H. "An Economic Perspective of Public Employment Programs." *Social Economy,* October 1976, pp. 180-200.

Leavitt, Helen. "In Search of an Urban Policy." *New Leader,* 30 January 1978, pp. 10-12.

————. "Shifting Gears in Urban Transportation." *New Leader,* 13 March 1978, pp. 12-13.

Liner, Charles D. "Property Tax Relief Through a Circuit-Breaker System." *Popular Government,* Fall 1977, pp. 28-31.

Long, Norton E. "A Marshall Plan for Cities?" *Public Interest,* Winter 1977, pp. 48-58.

McGraw, Marvin A. "The Impact of Proposition 13 on the Poor." *Focus,* June/July 1978, pp. 1a-4a.

McLure, Charles E. "The 'New View' of the Property Tax." *National Tax Journal,* March 1977, pp. 69-76.

McNamara, William. "The Tax Credit Debate." *Change,* March 1978, pp. 44-45; 60.

Marshall, F. Ray. "Employment Policies that Deal With Structural Unemployment." *Monthly Labor Review,* May 1978, pp. 30-32.

Munnell, Alicia H. "Federalizing Welfare: The Fiscal Impact of the Supplemental Security Income Program." *New England Economic Review,* September/October 1977, pp. 3-28.

Nathan, Richard P., and Dommel, Paul R. "Understanding the Urban Predicament." *The Brookings Bulletin,* vol. 14, nos. 1 & 2, 1977.

Neufield, John. "Taxrate Referenda and the Property Taxpayers' Revolt." *National Tax Journal,* December 1977, pp. 441-456.

Perlman, Laura. "Replacing Welfare with Work." *Worklife,* November 1977, pp. 2-8.

Peterson, K. A. "Allocating Federal Funds Through Local Unemployment Rates." *Monthly Labor Review,* October 1977, pp. 45-46.

Polinsky, A. Mitchell, and Rubinfield, Daniel L. "The Long-Run Effects of a Residential Property Tax and Local Public Services." *Journal of Urban Economics,* April 1978, pp. 241-262.

Rein, Martin, and Rainwater, Lee. "How Large Is the Welfare Class?" *Challenge,* September/October 1977, pp. 20-23.

Rogg, Nathaniel H. "Urban Housing Rehabilitation in the United States." *Urban Land,* January 1978, pp. 10-18.

Rufolo, Anthony M. "Housing Decay: Cause or Symptom of Urban Decline?" *Federal Reserve Philadelphia,* March/April 1978, pp. 13-21.

Schorr, Alvin L. "Welfare Reform and Social Insurance," *Challenge,* November/December 1977, pp. 14-22.

Seater, John J. "Coping with Unemployment." *Federal Reserve Philadelphia,* January/February 1977, pp. 3-12.

Shefter, Martin. "New York City's Fiscal Crisis: The Politics of Inflation and Retrenchment." *Public Interest,* Summer 1977, pp. 98-127.

Singer, James W. "Administration Adjusts Its Aim at Job Training Targets." *National Journal,* 30 April 1977, pp. 680-683.

————. "The Welfare Package: 1.4 Million Jobs, 1.4 Million Questions." *National Journal,* 12 November 1977, pp. 1764-1768.

Sommers, Albert T. "Inflation, Unemployment and Stabilization Policy." *Conference Board Record*, September 1976, pp. 52-64.

Stanfield, Rochelle L. "The Carter Urban Strategy: Principles In Search of a Policy." *National Journal*, 25 February 1978, pp. 304-308.

Steffens, Dorothy R. "Employment by Mandate: The Promise of Humphrey-Hawkins." *The Nation*, 21 January 1978, pp. 50-52.

Stein, Rona B. "New York City's Economy: A Perspective On Its Problems." *Federal Reserve New York*, Summer 1977, pp. 49-59.

Sundquist, James L. "Needed: A National Growth Policy," *Brookings Bulletin*, vol. 14, no. 4, 1978, pp. 1-5.

Thomas, William V. "Saving America's Cities." *Editorial Research Reports*, 18 November 1977, pp. 871-888.

Tyler, Gus. "The Other Economy: America's Working Poor." *New Leader*, 8 May 1978, pp. 3-35.

Weidenbaum, Murray. "Government Regulation and the Cost of Housing." *Urban Land*, February 1978, pp. 4-6.

Weil, Frank A. "The Property Tax: A Billion Dollar Problem." *Empire State Report*, January 1977, pp. 29-30.

West, E. G. "Tuition Tax Credit Proposals: An Economic Analysis of the 1978 Packwood/Moynihan Bill." *Policy Review*, Winter 1978, pp. 55-60.

"Work and the Welfare State: An Interview with Sar A. Levitan," *Challenge*, July/August 1977, pp. 29-33.

Zald, Mayer N. "Demographics, Politics, and the Future of the Welfare State," *Social Service Review*, March 1977, pp. 110-124.

Government Publications

The Budget of the United States Government, 1979. Washington, D.C.: Government Printing Office, 1978.

The President's Urban and Regional Policy Group. *Cities and People in Distress.* Washington, D.C.: U.S. Department of Housing and Urban Development, 1977.

_____. *A New Partnership to Conserve America's Communities: A National Urban Policy.* Washington, D.C.: U.S. Department of Housing and Urban Development, 1978.

"Selected Federal Programs." *Special Analyses, Budget of the United States Government*, Part 3. Washington, D.C.: Government Printing Office, 1978.

U.S. Congress. Congressional Budget Office. *Administration's Welfare Reform Proposal: An Analysis of the Program for Better Jobs and Income, April 1978.* Washington, D.C.: Government Printing Office, 1978.

_____. *Barriers to Urban Economic Development, May 1978.* Washington, D.C.: Government Printing Office, 1978.

_____. *Employment Subsidies and Employment Tax Credits.* Washington, D.C.: Government Printing Office, 1977.

_____. *Federal Aid to Postsecondary Students: Tax Allowances and Alternative Subsidies, January 1978.* Washington, D.C.: Government Printing Office, 1978.

_____. *Incomes Policies in the United States: Historical Review and Some Issues, May 1977.* Washington, D.C.: Government Printing Office, 1977.

_____. *Poverty Status of Families Under Alternative Definitions of Income.* Washington, D.C.: Government Printing Office, 1977.

_____. *Real Estate Tax Shelter Subsidies and Direct Subsidy Alternatives, May 1977.* Washington, D.C.: Government Printing Office, 1977.

_____. *Transportation Finance: Choices in a Period of Change, March 1978.* Washington, D.C.: Government Printing Office, 1978.

_____. *Urban Mass Transportation: Options for Federal Assistance, February 1977.* Washington, D.C.: Government Printing Office, 1977.

_____. *Youth Unemployment: The Outlook and Some Policy Strategies, April 1978.* Washington, D.C.: Government Printing Office, 1978.

U.S. Congress. House Committee on Banking, Currency and Housing. *The Rebirth of the American City: Hearings, September 20-October 1, 1976.* Washington, D.C.: Government Printing Office, 1976.

U.S. Congress. House Committee on Banking, Finance and Urban Affairs. *Impact of the Federal Budget on Cities: Hearings, March 29, 1977.* Washington, D.C.: Government Printing Office, 1978.

_____. Subcommittee on the City. *How Cities Can Grow Old Gracefully.* Washington, D.C.: Government Printing Office, 1977.

_____. Subcommittee on the City. *Toward A National Urban Policy, April 1977.* Washington, D.C.: Government Printing Office, 1977.

_____. Subcommittee on Economic Stabilization. *National Domestic Development Bank Act: Hearings, Oct. 4-Nov. 1, 1977.* Washington, D.C.: Government Printing Office, 1977.

_____. Subcommittee on Housing and Community Development. *Housing and Community Development Act of 1977: Hearings, February 24-March 1, 1977*, 3 vols. Washington, D.C.: Government Printing Office, 1977.

U.S. Congress. House Committee on Education and Labor. Subcommittee on Employment Opportunities. *The Full Employment and Balanced Growth Act of 1977: Hearings, February 8-10, 1977.* Washington, D.C.: Government Printing Office, 1977.

U.S. Congress. Joint Economic Committee. *Current Fiscal Condition of Cities: A Survey of 67 of the 75 Largest Cities, July 28, 1977.* Washington, D.C.: Government Printing Office, 1977.

_____. *Program for Better Jobs and Income: Analysis of Costs and Distributional Effects, February 3, 1978.* Washington, D.C.: Government Printing Office, 1978.

_____. *Work, Welfare and the Program for Better Jobs and Income: A Study.* Washington, D.C.: Government Printing Office, 1977.

_____. *Youth and Minority Unemployment: A Study.* Washington, D.C.: Government Printing Office, 1977.

U.S. Congress. Senate Committee on Banking, Housing and Urban Affairs. *Budget Context of the Emerging Urban Policy, February 23, 1978.* Washington, D.C.: Government Printing Office, 1978.

_____. *Housing and Community Development Authorization Legislation for Fiscal Year 1978: Hearings, April 18-22, 1977.* Washington, D.C.: Government Printing Office, 1977.

_____. *Report on the New York City Loan Program, February 10, 1978.* Washington, D.C.: Government Printing Office, 1978.

_____. *Welfare Reform and Housing Programs: Hearings, August 8; September 8, 9, 1977.* Washington, D.C.: Government Printing Office, 1978.

U.S. Congress. Senate Committee on Human Resources. *Desegregation and the Cities: The Trends and Policy Choices, February 1977.* Washington, D.C.: Government Printing Office, 1977.

U.S. Department of Commerce. Bureau of the Census. *Characteristics of the Population Below the Poverty Level: 1976.* Current Population Reports, Consumer Income, Series P-60. Washington, D.C.: Government Printing Office, 1978.

_____. *Money Income and Poverty Status of Families and Persons in the United States: 1977.* Current Population Reports, Consumer Income, Series P-60. Washington, D.C.: Government Printing Office, 1978.

U.S. Department of Labor. *Employment and Training Report of the President.* Washington, D.C.: Government Printing Office, 1978.

U.S. General Accounting Office. *Assessment of New York City's Performance and Prospects Under Its Three Year Emergency Financial Plan.* Washington, D.C.: 1977.

_____. *Information on the Buildup In Public Service Jobs, March 6, 1978.* Washington, D.C.: 1978.

_____. *The Long-Term Fiscal Outlook for New York City: Report to the Congress, April 4, 1977.* Washington, D.C.: 1977.

_____. *More Benefits to Jobless Can Be Attained In Public Service Employment, April 7, 1977.* Washington, D.C.: 1977.

Index